Introduction to

Serials Management

**FOUNDATIONS IN LIBRARY AND
INFORMATION SCIENCE, VOLUME 11**

Editor: Robert D. Stueart, *Dean, Graduate School of Library and
Information Science, Simmons College*

Foundations in
LIBRARY AND INFORMATION SCIENCE

A Series of Monographs, Texts and Treatises

Series Editor: **Robert D. Stueart**
Dean Graduate School of Library and Information Science
Simmons College, Boston

"Librarians and library school faculty members are becoming accustomed to finding the volumes of this series among the most useful studies of their subjects."
— JOURNAL OF ACADEMIC LIBRARIANSHIP

To David and Betsy

Introduction to
Serials Management.

by MARCIA TUTTLE
Head, Periodicals and
Serials Department
University of North Carolina
at Chapel Hill Library

with chapters by LUKE SWINDLER
Social Science Bibliographer
University of North Carolina
at Chapel Hill Library

NANCY I. WHITE
Head, Serials Cataloging
University of North Carolina
at Chapel Hill Library

 JAI PRESS INC.

Greenwich, Connecticut   *London, England*

Library of Congress Cataloging in Publication Data

Tuttle, Marcia.
  Introduction to serials management.

  (Foundations in library and information science;
v. 11)
  Bibliography: p.
  Includes index.
  1. Acquisition of serial publications.   2. Collection
development (Libraries)   I. Swindler, Luke.   II. White,
Nancy I.   III. Title.   IV. Title: Serial management.
V. Series
Z692.S5T87   1982   025.2'832   81-81658
ISBN 0-89232-107-5

Copyright © 1983 JAI PRESS INC.
36 Sherwood Place
Greenwich, Connecticut 06836

JAI PRESS INC.
3 Henrietta Street
London WC2E 8LU
England

ISBN Number 0-89232-107-5
Library of Congress Catalog Card Number 81 81658
Manufactured in the United States of America

CONTENTS

List of Figures

List of Tables

Chapter 3

Preface

The idea for this book on serials management originated in the mid-1970s in the Library School Education Committee of the Serials Section, Resources and Technical Services Division, American Library Association. Each committee member was to write one chapter. The purpose of the book then, as now, was to provide a textbook for library school courses on serials management as an encouragement to library science faculty and administrators to include a serials course in the curriculum. The committee, in fact, had been created in response to practicing serials librarians who felt that their professional education had not prepared them for their responsibilities in the field of serials work. The primary audience for *Introduction to Serials Management*, then, is library school students and librarians who are new to serials work. But the authors hope that other librarians concerned about or involved with serials librarianship may learn or, at least, identify with the experiences illustrated in these pages.

The chapters in this book have been arranged in an orderly progression of serial functions, beginning with collection development: the selection, evaluation and related management issues of the serial collection. The next concern is acquisition: ordering, receiving, and paying for serials and sending them for further processing. Serial cataloging follows, with its discussion of the present code, *AACR* 2. Chapter 5 concerns the preservation of serials with emphasis on the traditional means of binding and microforms. Then serial public service covers topics ranging from circulation and periodical indexes through online reference services and the selective dissemination of information. The final chapter concerns resource sharing among libraries and the national and international developments that facilitate the cooperative use of serials.

There is an unavoidable academic library bias in this book since the authors are academic librarians, and libraries in academic institutions

xv

are those most likely to have serials departments and staff members working exclusively with serials and serial related service. However, each author has made an effort to remember that librarians other than those in academic libraries work with serials.

A number of recent works on serials librarianship are available for readers who want to study serial management or some aspect of it in more depth. No one has yet surpassed Andrew Osborn in presenting the full range of the topic, and his third edition of *Serial Publications* was published in 1980. Clara D. Brown, with the assistance of Lynn S. Smith, published the second edition of her work, entitled *Serials: Past, Present and Future*, in 1980. Brown's first edition was limited to acquisitions, but the second, although still heavy on acquisitions, is somewhat expanded in scope. *A Practical Approach to Serials Cataloging*, by Lynn S. Smith, gives thorough coverage to the serials cataloging function up to the eve of the implementation of *AACR 2*, and there is in addition significant discussion of serial management in general. Bill Katz and Peter Gellatly published *Guide to Magazine and Serial Agents* several years ago. The content of their book is much broader than the title indicates, and this work is also recommended reading for librarians interested in serial management.

Several collections of articles, some based on conferences, have appeared within the past few months. William Gray Potter and Arlene Farber Sirkin edited *Serials Automation for Acquisition and Inventory Control*, papers from an ALA/Library and Information Technology Association institute held in 1980. Nancy Jean Melin coordinated *Microform Review*'s First Annual Serials Conference, entitled "Serials Management in an Automated Age," and has edited its proceedings for 1982 publication. Pierian Press is launching a new series of collected articles, Current Issues in Serials Management, with Nancy Melin as series editor. The first volume, edited by Melin, is *The Serials Collection: Organization and Administration*. Volume 2, edited by Dianne Ellsworth, is *Union Lists: Issues and Answers*. Additional books on serials and serials management are in the final stages of preparation. This trend is entirely appropriate, for serials librarianship is changing rapidly as a result of the developments in computer technology. This serials librarian is grateful for each publication and the information and contribution to the management of serials it brings. This is an exciting time to be a serials librarian!

The final section of *Introduction to Serials Management* is an annotated bibliography of books, journals and articles useful to the serials librarian. The bibliography is divided into sources valuable in day-to-day work— Working Tools—and those that support the serials librarian's research— Research Tools. Within each category entries are classified according to the chapters of this book. An author/title index to the Annotated Bibliography permits the location of a specific work. Most of the Working Tools will be part of a research library reference collection, if they are not housed in the serials unit. The Research Tools are generally recent books and articles, published in English, and to be found in a library science collection. The bibliography is not evaluative, and inclusion of a work does not indicate endorsement. The authors believe that readers of this book will welcome as extensive a collection as possible of opportunities for further reading.

Marcia Tuttle
University of North Carolina at
Chapel Hill
February 1982

Acknowledgements

Thanks to the following persons for their assistance during the writing of this book:

In Chapel Hill: Susan Atkins, Robert Broadus, Donna Cornick, Patricia Buck Dominguez, Roberta Engleman, Robert France, Sharon Gleim, James Govan, Joe Hewitt, October Ivins, Mary Kingsbury, Lois Lineberger, Tucker Respess, Mary Robison, Peter Schledorn, Alfred Sharlip, Diane Strauss, and everybody who asked and listened. *Elsewhere*: John James, University of Washington at Seattle; Kathleen Moretto, Yale University; Lynn S. Smith, University of California—Riverside; and Lee and Mae Tuttle, Lake Junaluska, N.C., master proofreaders.

Special thanks go to Luke Swindler, who wrote the chapter entitled "Developing the Serial Collection," to Nancy I. White, who wrote the chapter entitled "Cataloging the Serial Collection," and to Nancy Jean Melin, who generously supplied advance copies of three recently published works so they could be included in the Annotated Bibliography.

The biggest "Thank you" of all goes to David C. Taylor, Undergraduate Librarian at the University of North Carolina at Chapel Hill, who gave up many lunch hours and much personal time to read, listen to, and advise about several chapters. It is not an overstatement to record that without the friendship and patience of David Taylor this book would not have been completed.

Introduction

Increasing interest in serials activities in libraries provides a ready audience for a text on serials management, and Marcia Tuttle assembled a wide range of material to provide such a book. In the dynamic field of serials, it is not easy to grasp the major movements and trends, but they are presented here in seven chapters. This introduction provides a brief overview of the chapters in this book with some comments on how this text provides essential background for the management of serials.

This is followed by discussion of some of the current developments in serials management. Most of these are fully covered by the text of this book, and all are part of the challenge which the management of serials provides.

Many of these developments are not really new, but these activities need reexamination and redefinition for those new to the profession and to rekindle interest and understanding in those already working with serials. Perhaps the most easily recognized trend is really the organization of serials work. New departments are being created and older ones are disappearing in an effort to integrate activities. Both are happening at about the same rate, but little has been done to measure effects or to determine which direction is administratively superior. Perhaps no general answer can be given because, despite some overarching similarities in serials work among libraries, local conditions are still local, and general rules are difficult to define.

Other management considerations for serials include: public service, the appearance of new titles, costs, the literature of serials librarianship, new guidelines, and cooperative activities. Each of these is discussed as a major management consideration and with the idea that reference should be made to the chapters in Tuttle for fuller discussion and analysis. First, an overview of Tuttle's book.

Tuttle offers seven chapters on serials work and a general statement about these chapters and their arrangement will place them into focus. The book first presents some history and some definitions to establish a framework for what follows.

An immediate way this book differs from others is the recognition of collection development as a necessary activity, and Chapter 2 is devoted to this topic. Very little is available in the literature on collection development for serials, but this is now changing. Aside from accurate identification, Swindler points to the need for on-going selection and evaluation in an organized program. A value of this chapter is the point that collection development is both done first and is an active program both before a library acquires and processes serials and after they become a part of the collections. Managers above the serials departmental level should take note of this and build development activities into library budgets and staffs.

Many activities in the acquisition of serials differ greatly from what happens with monographs. Tuttle points out some of these differences in her third chapter and offers numerous suggestions about their treatment. The actual activities are discussed without attempting to provide universal truths or an approach found in operational manuals. The discussion can easily be related to the chapter's bibliography and parallel sections found in the book's bibliography. In this way, Tuttle offers a basic text and an excellent guide to further details without repeating them.

The cataloging of serials frequently presents problems to both new and experienced librarians. The rules in the past were confusing if only because an attempt was made, often artificially, to differentiate serials. Within the rules in AACR 2 a new attempt is made to treat serials the same way as other materials are handled. Still, there are differences many of which relate to the nature of serials to change. These aspects of serials treatment are succinctly covered in White's fourth chapter.

Preservation is as important for serials as for other materials. Here, the obvious topics of binding and microforms are examined. But so also is the endemic problem of security. Restricted access and exit controls are explored as is the availability of photocopy. For this chapter an important supplement is the material in the general bibliography.

And this preservation activity is directly related to public service, the topic of Chapter 6. Suggestions on public records, availability, reference service, indexes, and bibliographic verification—all from the user viewpoint—are touched on. Librarians frequently forget that all librarians have one common goal, service to library patrons. No dichotomy should exist between public and technical service staffs, and this sixth chapter suggests ways to ease these differences.

Perhaps no technique will be more useful in providing uniform control of and access to serials than automation. Union lists, the activities of CONSER, international standards, the services of bibliographic utilities, and other types of resource sharing are all discussed. Some of these ways to service serials are only starting and will change dramatically in the 1980s. The information in this chapter is necessary background for a comprehension of the current state of the art and for managers to understand what will be taking place rapidly as the 1980s continue.

The last section of Tuttle's work is a bibliography which is about one-third of the whole work. Tuttle annotates 649 working and research tools which relate to current activities as well as interpretation and history. Both parts have a similar subject-oriented sub-arrangement reflecting standard activities such as collection development, cataloging, and public service. The strength of this listing makes it the basic bibliography for serials works through 1982. The volume of material on serials activities is clear evidence of the current awareness of serials and is a vivid statement of the quality of scholarship available from serials librarians.

An important trend is the development of public service for serials. Barbara Pinzelik is one who clearly identifies some of the problems[8]. From the viewpoint of serials management, one of her conclusions holds that "At each attempt at control, another possibility of error is introduced" (p.94). This perceptive comment, and article, suggests both some things which are desirable and some barriers which arise in convenient, rational serials control. Public service for serials is more fully discussed in Tuttle's Chapter 6.

Despite difficult financial situations in most of society, publishers continue to produce new serials. Many of these new titles are of some importance, and many will be wanted in libraries of all types. How will decision makers manage? The issues in this area involve: identifying serial publishers and why they issue so many new titles, the ways in which books and serials differ, guidelines on what to collect, and determinations of which titles are most used. These and other management challenges are examined by David Taylor in his new book [12]. These management problems are also covered by Swindler and Tuttle in Chapters 2 and 3.

Costs of serials are a major management consideration, and among the factors are: postal rates are now about twelve times what they were in the early 1960s; the cost of advertising and seeking renewals has risen at least equally; the cost of advertising per reader is far higher than the cost per viewer of television; dealers and jobbers now make service charges rather than giving discounts; and importantly, if not decisively, prices are rising. Each year *Library Journal* publishes a survey of these prices, an article which is required reading for managers. The 1982 survey by

Norman Brown [4] reports the "average 1982 subscription price of an American journal is $44.80. This is a 14.5 percent increase from the 1981 average price..." As additional cost factors, Brown points out that most scholarly journals, issued by commercial publishers, increase in price each year; most of these titles are available to libraries only at institutional rates; and many more publishers are establishing institutional prices. The important factor here is that these rates range up to 100 percent above the subscription rate for individuals.

Another cost factor of considerable management importance is that online systems generally cost more to maintain than manual systems do; they take more time; and they are otherwise less efficient than manual systems, especially in providing positive public services.

The literature of serials work is rapidly growing and improving. Two books, both published in 1982, are examples. The book edited by Melin [7] discusses the organization of a collection of serials. The fourteen essays discuss many aspects of serials management and often look at both the present and what the future holds. The book edited by Gellatly [5] is specifically aimed at the management of serials automation problems. Here, two dozen articles and bibliographies provide a summary of and direction for these problems. Both books are essential for managers and set the tone of future developments for serials management activities.

An important trend in any management area is the existence and strength of this serial literature. Many professional serials contain some information on serials, but these appearances are sporadic in most journals. Since the disappearance of *Serial Slants* [9] two journals started in the mid-1970s fill a need for professional serials devoted to serials. *The Serials Librarian* [10] calls itself "The International Quarterly of Serials Management," and that ambitious phrase describes the journal well. This journal publishes articles in a wide range of management problems and also issues monographs which deal with the management of serials, such as the Gellatly book. These offer additional opportunities for serials experts to share their abilities in the control of serial publications. The success of *The Serials Librarian* clearly demonstrates the trends of development in serials management and also that experts in serials are essential to large libraries.

Another example of the special serial in this field is *Serials Review* [11]. This journal has greatly increased in value as a management tool. Not only are reviews and recommendations carried, but each issue tends to carry at least one long review article, for example, on little magazines or the titles from a single state. In 1982, this journal also carries a section called "Collection Management Resources." Many management problems are covered here, for example, serials administration, union lists, automation, cataloging, and issues on the control of serials at the international level.

From the trend of both these journals to publish articles of multi- and international interest as well as from the growth of international standards, a management trend becomes quite clear: the interest in serials is growing internationally, and the tendency to develop methods and systems which will work on the international level is obvious.

The development of new guidelines for various aspects of serials work is an answer to a need and a recognition that serial publications have special characteristics which require special controls. Perhaps the basic international document is *Guidelines for ISDS* [6]. While internal changes have been made, and other understandings have been accepted, a new edition of this document is slow to appear. This critical need may be met by the mid-1980s.

Meanwhile, other guidelines for various aspects of bibliographic control are becoming available. The *American National Standard for Serial Holdings Statements at the Summary Level* [1] was a long time in development, but is now a welcome document which can be used to forge national understandings and agreements used in shared programs. Another ANSI standard for holdings statements at the detailed level is being prepared.

An international effort in guideline development is one which had its start in IFLA: Jean Whiffin's *Guidelines for Union Catalogues of Serials* [14]. The first draft of this was issued in June 1981 and was distributed for comment in mid-1982. At this writing, two possibilities exist for publication: the full document will be issued outside the IFLA publishing program, and an abbreviated version, similar to the *Guidelines for ISDS* in detail, will be issued by IFLA. Both documents are needed to establish consistency in the bibliographic descriptions of serials in catalogs, both manual and online.

A fourth example of the guidelines trend is Marjorie Bloss' *Guidelines for Union Lists of Serials* [3]. The union list is not a new concept, but in the 1980s it has suddenly experienced new importance and growth, especially in the light of cooperation and machine-assisted systems.

Another standard which has received mixed reviews to date is the new edition of the *Anglo-American Cataloguing Rules* (AACR 2) [2]. These rules attempt to provide uniform rules for description which can be applied in a multi-national setting, and they provide rules for choice and form of headings and added entries which can be uniformly applied to all formats of material, serials being considered as a publishing condition and not as an expression of format. It is ironic but necessary that while emphasis on serials is growing, these rules tend to suppress the differences.

At the same time the fact that serials really do present special problems can be seen in the "rule interpretations" now being offered by the Library of Congress for certain cases in AACR 2. Only three of these will make the point that the control of serials does present bibliographic situations which differ for serials. One of these is the addition of a new category to Rule 21.1B2, namely category "f" for cartographic items, some of which are serials. Another interpretation is to create situations in which uniform titles are to be used to differentiate non-distinctive titles which are the same.

The third interpretation is for the cataloging of microforms. AACR 2 holds that one catalogs what one has in hand and not what a title may have been. For microformats this means that catalog records describe the microform and reflect the original in a note, unless the production is an original microform. The Library of Congress' rule interpretation changes this to cataloging the original, a return to a practice of the past. This interpretation is bound to have many effects on the control of serial publications. It remains to be seen if these will result in better service for library users or not. The controversy on these aspects of the application of standards expressed in AACR 2 will be slow to change to consensus.

Cooperation as a management concern includes the four active bibliographic utilities in North America which are: Online Computer Library Center (OCLC), Research Libraries Information Network (RLIN), University of Toronto Library Automation Systems (UTLAS), and Washington Library Network (WLN).

OCLC, Inc. has both strengths and weaknesses which need to be carefully investigated before participation. While it is the largest library data base and also has the only online serial check-in system currently available from a utility, neither the utility nor the serials subsystem is operationally perfect. RLIN, UTLAS, and WLN do not have systems for serials check-in, although they are under discussion. From news reports alone, all the networks are undergoing change, have apparent functional and financial problems. and differ from one another in their qualities of bibliographic standards. None of these utilities is *the* national network. The United States has a long way to travel before that goal can be achieved.

The ideas and desire for national, if not international, cooperation in a single network, or a network of nodes, is surely present. This seems to be a trend, and at least the altruistic talk at conferences and in the literature indicates a desire for this trend to take shape.

While networks develop and grow, other changes are also taking place. As this is being written in September 1982, news that MIDLNET is folding its operations is reported. This can be taken as some evidence that network development is not always forward, but rather is still experimental and not always successful. Managers, take note.

Still another automation and cooperation area for managers to study is the growth of computer-based systems to control the ordering of serial back issues. The Universal Serials and Book Exchange (USBE) provides some back issues through the Bibliographic Retrieval Services (BRS). F.W. Faxon has another system, LINX, which offers online check-in capability and access to other Faxon files, as well as automatic claiming. The LINX system is especially valuable for the many management reports which it provides. The California Library Authority for Systems and Services (CLASS) offers Checkmate, a microcomputer system for serials control including check-in, claiming, financial control, and other functions. This form of serials work is rapidly developing and will see many changes during the 1980s.

Among new developments in the 1980s for serials is the growth of techniques for document delivery by electronic means. The major work in this area is currently European, with some in Great Britain. A summary of some of these programs, ADONIS, ARTEMIS, AND DIANE, for example, is included in Benita Weber's "The Year's Work in Serials: 1981"[13]. An alert manager of serials work will study these developments and the possible appearance of these projects, or similar ones, in the United States. Will they be incorporated in operational facilities? Will new networks arise which will provide these systems? Are these projects capable of answering the needs of American libraries? These and many other questions are among the serials automation challenges of the 1980s.

These are a few of the major aspects of serials management needing consideration in libraries of all sizes and types. It is hard to say which is paramount; each has importance; and all are, to some degree, interdependent. Each of these management factors, as well as many others, is discussed in the chapters of Marcia Tuttle's book. The manager who studies them will have a solid foundation for understanding how serials are a part of library activity and why their management is an important library administration challenge for the 1980s.

Neal L. Edgar
Associate Curator
Special Collections
Kent State University Library

BIBLIOGRAPHY

1. *American National Standard for Serial Holdings Statements at the Summary Level.* New York: American National Standards Institute, 1980. (ANSI Z39.42-1980).
2. *Anglo-American Cataloguing Rules.* Second edition. Chicago: American Library Association, 1978.
3. Bloss, Marjorie E., at al. *Guidelines for Union Lists of Serials.* Chicago: American Library Association, 1982. (Prepared by American Library Association, Resources and Technical Services Division, Serials Section, Ad Hoc Committee on Union Lists of Serials).

4. Brown, Norman B. and Jane Phillips. "Price Indexes for 1982: U.S. Periodicals and Serials Services." *Library Journal* 107 (August 1982): 1379-1382.

5. Gellatly, Peter, ed. *The Management of Serials Automation: Current Technology & Strategies for Future Planning.* New York: The Haworth Press, 1982.

6. International Centre for the Registration of Serial Publications. *Guidelines for ISDS.* Paris: United Nations Educational, Scientific and Cultural Organization, 1973.

7. Melin, Nancy Jean, ed. *The Serials Collection: Organization and Administration.* Ann Arbor, MI: Pierian Press, 1982.

8. Pinzelik, Barbara. "The Serials Maze: Providing Public Service for a Large Serials Collection," *The Journal of Academic Librarianship* 8 (May 1982): 89-94.

9. *Serial Slants.* Chicago: American Library Association, 1950-1956.

10. *The Serials Librarian.* New York: Haworth Press, 1976- . ISSN 0361-526X.

11. *Serials Review.* Ann Arbor, MI: Pierian Press, 1975- . ISSN 0098-7913.

12. Taylor, David C. *Managing the Serials Explosion: the Issues for Publishers and Libraries.* White Plains, NY: Knowledge Industry Publications, 1982.

13. Weber, Benita M. "The Year's Work in Serials: 1981." *Library Resources and Technical Services* 26 (July/September 1982): 277-293.

14. Whiffin, Jean. *Guidelines for Union Catalogues of Serials.* Victoria, BC, 1981. (Preliminary edition prepared for the IFIA Section on Serial Publications).

Chapter 1

The Serial: Its Definition and Place in the Library

What is a serial? To set the scene, here is what one serials librarian says:

> Almost all books are published by sophisticated, experienced, well financed professionals who understand their self-interest in as well as their customers' need for bibliographic consistency. Problems abound, but the standard is well-defined and usually adhered to. On the other hand, any knucklehead with a typewriter and access to an offset press can publish a serial.[1]

To most librarians and library school students the word *serial* evokes a definite positive or negative response; few responses are neutral. The nature of one's feelings towards serials librarianship is influenced by experience, by personality characteristics, and by hearsay. Serials work is full of problems because the serial itself is a problem. It is the problems, though, that make working with serial publications challenging and rewarding. While one resolves a series of disguised title changes or manages to reinstate a subscription to an English professor's favorite little magazine, patrons are bringing apparently meaningless citations to be explained and located, another subscription has stopped coming, or a periodical suddenly appears in a variety of formats unsuitable for binding. The work is not seasonal, it does not end, and it is never dull.

Librarians cannot agree on a definition of the term *serial*. Further, the placing of a continuing serial order involves the library in a long-term commitment. The acquisition of a monograph is a one-time transaction: the book is selected, searched and verified, ordered, received, paid, cataloged and sent to the bookstacks. On the other hand, a subscription to a journal or a standing order for a nonperiodical serial is a transaction that continues until someone acts to stop it. The purchase of a serial commits funds (and the total amount of serial acquisition funds may be

1

the major part of a library's materials budget), including any surcharges as well as future price increases. Although the subscription cost is the most visible financial commitment the library makes, there are other considerations. Staff must be employed to process incoming serials, space is required to house them, and funds are needed to bind them or purchase microform replacements. Trained staff members must be available to provide service to patrons seeking access to the contents of serials.

Serials are problems because, being unending (in theory), they are almost certain to change. The price changes, the title changes, the publisher changes, the frequency changes, the scope of the journal changes, serials merge or split, publication is suspended for varying lengths of time, and so on. Clara Brown lists eighteen such things that can happen to serial titles,[2] and her list is probably not exhaustive. Figure 1.1 is almost a stereotype of the concept of title change, but it is an authentic example.

The lack of standardization and standards for serials has promoted a wide range of ways publishers design and identify serials and of forms and descriptive terms used by librarians. Serial numbering is a fertile area for confusion and frustration, for some publishers name issues for the seasons, skip the number for an issue or volume not published, combine issues, or use two numbering systems. The use of a season to identify one issue of a quarterly journal is not always ambiguous: Summer 1957, for instance, is acceptable, but what is Winter 1978? Does it appear before Spring 1978, or after Fall 1978 and before Spring 1979? What if the title is published in New Zealand? Sometimes producing a combined issue is an effective means for editors and publishers to get a slow journal back on schedule, but there are acceptable and unacceptable ways to combine. Issues 1 and 2 or any other consecutive numbers within one volume may be combined without problem, but the following letter from one publisher created visions of a nightmare for librarians who received it:

Dear Subscriber:

In October we will publish a special double issue, combining our *spring/summer* and *fall/winter* issues: this will be *volume 14, no. 2/volume 15, no. 1.*

These two issues will be bound together, and for this reason, we cannot mail one without the other. Your subscription will lapse after 14, no. 2, the first half of this double issue. We are therefore requesting that you renew early so that we may keep you on our mailing list for the double issue.

A year's renewal at this time will cover the second half of this double issue, 15, no. 1, and the next single issue, 15, no. 2 (which we expect to publish early in 1978).

Thank you in advance for your attention.

Sincerely,

PERSPECTIVES OF NEW MUSIC

P.S. If you do not wish to renew at this time, we will send you our next single issue, vol. 15, no. 2, instead of 14, no. 2.[3]

Figure 1.1: Saturday Review Title Changes

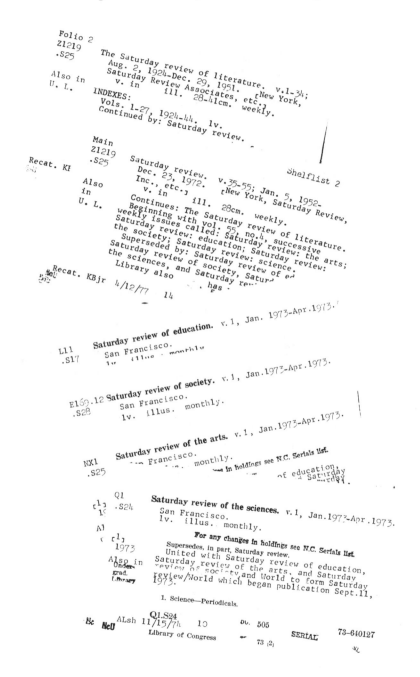

Folio 2
Z1219
.S25   The Saturday review of literature. v.1-34;
Aug. 2, 1924-Dec. 29, 1951. ₍New York,
Saturday Review Associates, etc.₎
Also in   v. in   ill.   28-41cm.   weekly.
U. L.   INDEXES:
Vols. 1-27, 1924-44.   1v.
Continued by: Saturday review.

Main
Z1219
.S25   Saturday review.   Shelflist 2
Dec. 23, 1972.   v.35-55; Jan. 5, 1952-
Inc., etc.₎   ₍New York, Saturday Review,
Also   v. in   ill.   28cm.   weekly.
in   Continues: The Saturday review of literature.
U. L.   Beginning with vol. 55, successive
weekly issues called: Saturday review: the arts;
Saturday review: education; Saturday review:
the society; Saturday review: science.
Superseded by: Saturday review of ed
Saturday review of society, Satur⌐
the sciences, and Saturday re·
Library also   has ⌐.

Recat. KF

Recat. KBjr   4/12/77   14

Saturday review of education.   v.1, Jan. 1973-Apr.1973.
L11
.S17   San Francisco.
1v.   illus.   monthly

Saturday review of society.   v.1, Jan.1973-Apr.1973.
E169.12
.S28   San Francisco.
1v.   illus.   monthly.

Saturday review of the arts.   v.1, Jan.1973-Apr.1973.
NX1
.S25   ⸺ Francisco.
⸺.   monthly.
⸺ in holdings see N.C. Serials list.
⸺ of education;
⸺ Saturday
⸺rday.

Q1
₍1₎ .S24   Saturday review of the sciences.   v.1, Jan.1973-Apr.1973.
1₍   San Francisco.
1v.   illus.   monthly.
A₎
₍ ₍1₎
1973   For any changes in holdings see N.C. Serials list.
Supersedes, in part, Saturday review.
Also in   United with Saturday review of education,
Under-   Saturday review of the arts, and Saturday
grad.   review of society, and World to form Saturday
Library   review/World which began publication Sept.11,
1973.

1. Science—Periodicals.

Q1.S24
NcU   ALsh 11/15/74   10   DU. 505
Library of Congress   73 ₍2₎   SERIAL   73-640127

Figure 1.1: Saturday Review Title Changes *(Continued)*

Under-
grad.
Library
World. v. 1-2, July 4, 1972-Aug.28, 1973.
New York, World Magazine, inc.

2v. illus. 28 cm. biweekly.

"A review of ideas, the arts and the human condition."
1-2 United with Saturday review of education,
1972/73 Saturday review of the arts, Saturday review
of the sciences, and Saturday review of society
Also in to form Saturday Review/World, which began
Main publication Sept.11, 1973.
AP2
.W74824 For any changes in holdings see N.C. Serials list.
[1]-2
1972/73
AP2.W74824 051 SERIAL 72-624664
Repl.WKsh 6/12/74 6
NcU Library of Congress 72 [2] 9REC

AP2 **Saturday review/world.** v. 1-2, no.7; Sept. 11, 1973-
.S273 Dec. 14, 1974. New York, Saturday Review/
World, Inc.
1-2, no.7 v. illus. 28 cm. biweekly.
1973-74 Formed by the union of Saturday review of education, Saturday
review of society, Saturday review of the arts, Saturday review of
Also in the sciences, and World.
U. L. Running title. : SR/world.
1-2, no.7 Continued by: Saturday review.
1973-74 For any changes in holdings see N.C. Serials list.
I. Title: SR/world.
AP2.S273 051 73-645517
ISSN 0091-620-X MARC-S
Recat. CKjm 2/24/76 8
NcU Library of Congress 74 [2] SERIAL St

AP2
.S273 **Saturday review.** v.2, no.8-
Jan. 11, 1975-
2, no.8- New York, Saturday Review/World, Inc.
1975- v. ill. 28cm. biweekly.
For any changes in holdings see N.C. Serials list
Also in Continues: Saturday review/world.
U. L.
2, no.8-
1975-

CKjm 2/24/76 7
NcU St SERIAL

An even worse combined publication was that devised by *Booklegger Magazine* and *Emergency Librarian*. In 1976 the two library science journals produced a joint issue on library education and called it *"Booklegger Magazine*, vol. XIII #3 and *Emergency Librarian*, vol. III #3."

Librarians are as guilty of lack of standardization as publishers, for they use customized order forms, claiming forms, and invoicing stipulations, and they often ask their suppliers to make insignificant changes in the library's mailing address. In fairness, some of this variety is unavoidable because of the need to fulfill requirements of the parent institution, but much of it is unnecessary and attention to the problem can improve the situation.

National and international library groups are working to resolve these problems of inconsistency by creating and publicizing standards. Efforts most closely related to serials are discussed in Chapter 7 as part of the resource sharing response to current economic conditions. Producing and issuing a standard—the International Standard Serial Number (ISSN), for example—requires hard work and compromise, but the development of the standard is only the beginning of the solution to the problem of inconsistency. The difficulty is getting publishers and librarians to apply the standard. With the ISSN, publishers did not want to detract from their cover designs by printing the number there, but when grocery stores demanded barcoding, publishers complied. Now that the U.S. Postal Service requires the ISSN on journals as evidence of eligibility for second class postage rates, publishers are using the standard. In recent years there has been significant progress in standardization of serial identification and library procedures, but only a conscientious and continuing effort by both librarians and publishers will resolve this serial problem.

DEFINITION OF SERIAL

To return to the first of the reasons serial publications are problems, the initial step in developing an understanding of serial management is defining *Serial*. Donald Davinson captures the essence of the problem:

> It would be pleasant to be able to supply a short, neat, all-embracing definition that is unquestioningly accepted universally. It is not possible to do so. To dip even the most tentative of toes into the definitional water is to risk drowning in a sea of conflicting interpretations and variations in terminology.[4]

Nevertheless, it is necessary to define *serial* and related terms such as *periodical* and *series*, because it is only by agreeing upon the meaning of these words that communication is possible. For example, when the government asks for the number of serial orders, the responding librarian must know what the government means by *serial*. Optimum use of a union list of periodicals demands that the compiler and the user define *periodical* in the same way.

There are now and always have been many written definitions of *serial* and related terms. Clara Brown states that serials "contain two ingredients: they are numbered; they intend to continue for an indefinite period."[5] On the other hand, in his *Serial Publications*, Andrew Osborn has a twenty-one page chapter entitled "Definition of a Serial."[6] A succession of written statements over the years has attempted to define serial terms for general purposes; several of them are reproduced in Lynn S. Smith's book, *A Practical Approach to Serials Cataloging*.[7] There are also numerous definitions for special purposes: a union list, a catalog code, or annual compilations of statistics. However frustrating it is to have multiple definitions, it is worse when a union list or a statistics form provides no definition for *serial*, for then there is no way to determine scope, and the validity of the product is questionable.

No standard definition of *serial* exists, but the second edition of the *Anglo-American Cataloguing Rules* (*AACR* 2) defines the term well. The following statement from the code is close to a standard definition for English-speaking librarians:

> A publication in any medium issued in successive parts bearing numerical or chronological designations and intended to be continued indefinitely. Serials include periodicals; newspapers; annuals (reports, yearbooks, etc.); the journals, memoirs, proceedings, transactions, etc., of societies; and numbered monographic series.[8]

Giving credit to the *AACR* 2 wording as "easily the best library definition of a serial that has yet been devised," Osborn adds, "It is still not scientifically sound in the sense that it can be applied to settle all doubtful cases." He then lists eleven qualifications that need to be added.[9]

The *AACR* 2 definition of *serial* is an expansion of Charles A. Cutter's 1904 statement that a serial is "a publication issued in successive parts, usually at regular intervals and continued indefinitely."[10] During the intervening years the qualities of a serial were sharpened to include "under a distinctive title"[11] and "a publication not issued by a government agency,"[12] to suit the purposes of the definer.

Here is Osborn's own practical definition:

> The elements which, by and large, constitute a serial publication are (1) a name and (2) either periodical or serial numbering of the successive parts of a work which appear under the original name or a later name. The qualification "by and large" is significant because at times one element—even both—can be lacking.[13]

Likewise, he says, both elements can be present and the title be treated as a book. At the other extreme, the National Agricultural Library once defined *serial* as: "Any title issued in parts, which is incomplete in the library collection."[14]

In North America, *serial* has traditionally been the term encompassing all types of continuing publications except those having a planned conclusion. In Great Britain, until the publication of *AACR 2*, *serial* was a specific term, comparable to what Americans know as *periodical*. British librarians used *periodical* as the broad term. Davinson explains:

> In the principal British discussion of definitional problems, David Grenfell elects for the term periodical.*
>> The term "serial" is becoming unpopular and a more comprehensive interpretation is being given to the term "periodical."
> It should be noted that Grenfell carefully covers himself by entitling his book *Periodicals and Serials!*[15]
>
> *David Grenfell, *Periodicals and Serials: Their Treatment in Special Libraries*. (London: ASLIB, 2nd ed., 1965).

Thus, the scope of titles included in the *British Union Catalogue of Periodicals* is virtually the same as that of the *Union List of Serials in Libraries of the United States and Canada*. Since *AACR 2* uses *serial* for all continuing publications and has dropped the word *periodical*, American and British usage should be compatible after a short time of adjustment.

The thread running through all the definitions is the continuing nature of the publication, the quality that gives serials the tendency to be problems, to change, to haunt. The continuing nature of serials also gives them their fascination.

TYPES OF SERIALS

Serials are divisible, based on intended frequency of publication, into periodicals and nonperiodical serials. Periodicals are journals and newspapers; all other serials—annuals, conference proceedings, monographic series—are nonperiodical serials. As with the term *serial*, there is not general agreement about the qualities of types of serials.

A periodical, also called journal or magazine, is intended to appear regularly and more often than once a year.[16] Many definitions stop there, but others go on to specify one or more of the following characteristics:

1. A periodical carries numbering, usually of primary and secondary order (volume 7, number 4), so that the collected parts comprise a whole.

2. A periodical is a collection of articles by several persons.
3. A periodical is paid once a year, in advance.

Nonperiodical serials are usually numbered or dated, are published either regularly or irregularly, are usually not paid in advance of publication, and include annuals, conference proceedings, occasional publications, monographic series, and any other title that is intended to continue indefinitely but is not a periodical.

Some definitions of *periodical* include annual serials. From an acquisition standpoint this makes sense because annuals are paid once a year, as are journals and newspapers. However, annuals, although they often are collections of articles, are not issued in parts to be collected into a bound volume as are journals. A practical distinction between periodicals and nonperiodicals may be made on the basis of predictability of publication and of annual price. The cost of journals, newspapers, and annuals, because they are invoiced once a year, can be predicted rather easily. Nonperiodical serials that are irregular in publication cannot be predicted in terms of annual cost, for the number of pieces appearing in a year can vary widely. Some nonperiodical serials have a regular frequency of one volume every three or five years, and their costs cannot be accounted for on a yearly basis. Annuals overlap the two major divisions of serial; in this book they are treated as nonperiodical serials.

One type of serial, the monographic series, is close to being simply a group of monographs, especially if the publisher does not number the series. The library has options for acquisition and cataloging treatment of monographs in series; choices are often determined by whether the library wishes to acquire all volumes in the series or just those of particular relevance to the collection. Whether these works are considered a series composed of monographs or a group of monographs that happen to have a covering series title, catalogers need to treat both aspects of the publication, monographic and serial, because citations are sure to appear in the literature in both forms, and patrons will request these volumes both by author/title and by series.

Some publications are *near-serials*. Osborn describes three types: (1) provisional serials, a nonserial base publication with serially issued updating volumes (encyclopedias having annual supplements); (2) pseudo-serials, "a frequently-reissued and revised publication which quite properly may be, and on first publication generally is, considered to be a monograph" (*Irregular Serials and Annuals*); and (3) continuations, works issued in parts, but having a planned conclusion (foreign dictionaries published in fascicles).[17] Even though these materials are not true serials, their processing is simplified by serial acquisition and, perhaps, cataloging treatment, and they are included in the responsibilities of the serials unit of many libraries.

THE UNIQUENESS OF SERIALS

During the late 1970s, in the context of heated discussion of the proposed second edition of the *Anglo-American Cataloguing Rules*, Dorothy Glasby asserted that "Serials are different!" That straightforward statement about a complex form of communication contains the essence of serials librarianship. Serials differ from other library resources in a number of ways. Most noticeably, serials change. A monograph is a self-contained item; a currently published serial is a living, growing, often multiplying, occasionally ill, and sometimes dying publication. The continuation of a serial depends upon many factors. It must have substantive matter; someone to solicit, select, and organize its contents; a person or a company to produce it; and subscribers to purchase it. All of these contributions are made not once, but again and again, indefinitely. A library's commitment to a serial lasts, so long as the publication is produced, until someone acts to end it. And in this continuing nature of the publication and the library order there is much opportunity for change and for problems.

The most obvious change for a serial is a title change. For several years *Title Varies* has awarded its "Worst Title Change of the Year" prizes at the American Library Association, Resources and Technical Services Division's annual membership meeting. "Winners" have included Williams and Wilkins, who changed *International Journal of Obstetrics and Gynecology* to *International Journal of Gynecology and Obstetrics*; the Economic Intelligence Unit, Ltd., which changed about one hundred related titles beginning *Quarterly Economic Review: [Country]* to *QER: [Country]* and then to *Quarterly Economic Review of [Country];* and the latest winner, the American Association for the Advancement of Science for its publication *Science 79*, which became *Science 80*, then *Science 81*—the second journal named *Science* published by the Association!

A title change in itself is bad enough, but a title change can be a symptom of other changes. Several years ago the *British Journal of Marketing* changed title to *European Journal of Marketing*. Then the publisher changed the title again to *Journal of General Management* and appointed a new editor. The former editor selected a new publisher and continued *European Journal of Marketing*. Subscribing libraries received letters from both journals, each claiming to be the successor of the original periodical and soliciting their renewal order. Most libraries probably took the easy course and subscribed to both journals. Both titles have survived.

In theory, information is communicated more rapidly through serials, particularly periodicals, than through monographs. In many areas of scholarly research, especially in the sciences, serials are the primary means of communication because of the relative speed with which information must and can be disseminated. Newsmagazines and newspapers are the only feasible means of printed communication of current events. Annual reviews are an appropriate means of regularly summarizing the happenings of a year in a popular subject or in a specific field of knowledge. Serials are just as significant a means of communication of developments in popular or esoteric hobbies and other interests; the devotee is kept informed by the publication which arrives periodically. A serial may be significant even though it is not retained by the library; for example, the mimeographed or otherwise rapidly produced newsletter is perhaps the fastest means of printed communication among a group of persons having a common interest.

Producing a journal issue is not ordinarily so complicated a project as publishing a monograph because the journal is geared to regular publication of article-length contributions. Journals are the means for scholars to have information disseminated to their colleagues before it becomes obsolete, just as newsmagazines aim to inform readers about current events while they are still current. Especially good for rapid distribution of scientific information are publications that limit themselves to "letters" and "communications"—brief notices or announcements of results of experiments and hypothesizing, about which a scholar requests criticism and/or supporting evidence. However, with so many scholars, so much pressure to publish, and the cost of periodical publishing so high, even for "communications" there is often a backlog at the most highly regarded journals. Sometimes an author must wait more than two years to have an item published. This situation has led both to new journals being started to take care of the overflow and to fees being charged authors to have their work published. The best journals are refereed; that is, anonymous submissions from authors are criticized by their colleagues on journals' editorial boards and may be returned to the author for more work and polish before publication. This practice upholds the high quality of these journals and bestows extra prestige on authors whose work is published; however, it means even more delay in communicating scholarly work to others in the field. One relatively new American journal publisher felt that he could issue his journals more quickly and inexpensively if he did his own printing, so he invested the time and money to set up such an operation. Naturally, it cost more and took longer than he had anticipated, and all of his journals fell behind in publication. In addition, recent issues show carelessness in typesetting and proofreading. At best this situation is only a period of adjustment; at worst it is a serious decline in quality.

Another feature of serials is that their treatment in libraries requires the full range of library operations, from selection to check-in and renewal, to public service and preservation. Serial procedures may even accommodate monographs if series are included in the serials department. An integrated serials department provides an opportunity for a librarian to gain experience in all the operations discussed in this book. Some persons question whether this range of functions is not too much to include in a single administrative unit, and the topic is open to discussion. However, for the purposes of this book, the range of serial functions is not considered too great for a single department.

THE SERIAL MANAGER

The librarian who accepts responsibility for managing a serial collection may come to the position with some years of experience in serials librarianship, with professional experience in another aspect of librarianship, or directly from school with no prior experience as a professional librarian. In each case, this person needs to arrive at a comfortable understanding of what serials management is, based upon an increasing knowledge of serials librarianship, local library policies and conditions, and his or her own feelings about serials. The ideal serials manager must develop abilities in three areas: (1) supervisory skills, in order to motivate staff members in the midst of constant chaos and exceptions to the rules; (2) accounting principles, to work within the allocated funds and obtain the best service for the lowest cost; and (3) the ability to communicate with departmental staff members and other library personnel, with patrons seeking information contained in serial publications, and with suppliers who ease the acquisition, processing, and preservation of serials. The patience and fortitude of a saint would also be an asset!

The person who approaches the ideal in managing serial processing and service finds the job made easier if he or she is flexible and able to adjust to sudden change, is curious and eager to investigate something that does not seem quite right, and has a sense of humor. Never underestimate the sense of humor and the ability to step back and take a look at the immediate crisis in the perspective of the larger scene.

The larger scene includes not only the entire library, but the universe of library serial operations. Sharing experiences with other serials librarians at state or regional meetings and workshops or at the meetings of the American Library Association is a way to gain a feeling of community as well as practical advice, through either another librarian's solution to the problem one is facing or ideas generated during a brainstorming session around a dinner table or in a scheduled meeting. The ability and willingness to listen, to share, and to speculate is perhaps the most desirable quality of the serials manager.

ORGANIZATION OF SERIAL FUNCTIONS

The manager of serial-related activities may have an opportunity to participate in the organization of the library with regard to serial functions, but it is more likely that tradition and physical conditions have imposed a structure which cannot easily be rearranged. The possibilities extend from a totally centralized serials department to complete decentralization of library processes and procedures concerning serials. The concept of the "integrated serials department" has gained in popularity over the several decades since it was initiated by J. Harris Gable in 1935.[18] Based on the idea that serials could best be treated and made available to patrons by persons familiar with serial idiosyncracies, this organizational structure groups all library functions relating to serials in the same department administratively. The fully integrated serials department contains selection, acquisition, cataloging, preservation and public service. However, many departments include fewer functions; selection may be done by collection development personnel, cataloging by the catalog department or public service by reference librarians. Serials are involved in so much of the library's activity that it may be unrealistic to attempt to restrict every contact with them to one department.

Hans Weber has described and evaluated the range of organizational schemes for serial functions.[19] He joins Gable, Fred Rothman,[20] Beatrice Simon,[21] and Samuel Lazerow[22] in supporting general centralization of serial functions where possible. Weber qualifies his endorsement of the integrated serials department by submitting the level of 5,000 active orders as the minimum for this structure to be optimally efficient. Whatever the specific organization of serial functions, Weber sees the serial record handling receipt and claiming as the core of the unit. Cataloging, he writes, is the function most often missing from a centralized department, although it is of equal importance with the serial record in processing serials.[23] Serial cataloging differs enough from monographic cataloging that most libraries with several catalogers consider serials a specialty and, in either an integrated or a decentralized situation, have one or more catalogers working only with serials. There is some question as to whether it is cataloging or selection of serials which is most often missing from the integrated department. It seems reasonable that, unlike experienced catalogers, bibliographers qualified to work with monographs are qualified to work with serials. At the same time, in many libraries serial selection is done by a committee composed of librarians or of librarians and faculty members, because of the continuing obligation of funds. Often the serials librarian, as well as the bibliographers, has a significant role in the deliberations and decisions of the committee.

Two recent articles have applied specific management principles to serials librarianship and both authors have determined that an integrated serials department is likely to be more efficient than a decentralized administrative arrangement, even in a highly automated library. One article reports Mitsuko Collver's study of James D. Thompson's principles of "grouping for coordination" as related to serials management. Thompson described three types of processing interdependence: (1) *pooled*, use of common resources or facilities (such as a card catalog); (2) *sequential*, a one-way flow of work (monographs moving from acquisitions to cataloging); and (3) *reciprocal*, repeated interaction among functions (the effect of serial cataloging on all serial records).[24] Collver shows that reciprocal interdependence, the most complex to coordinate, describes the relationship among serial functions, because of the ongoing and changeable nature of serial publications:

> Work is done by interaction, and no function can continue for long without reactions from other activities. In this type of interdependence, the cost of coordination is highest, and it receives the highest priority as a criterion for grouping activities. Thus, according to Thompson's theory, all serials-related activities should be grouped into one [administrative] unit for the benefit of maximum coordination.[25]

Collver has applied Thompson's principles to her own library at Stony Brook and reports that the organization is successful and appears particularly suited for an automated situation.

Since the change from manual to automated technical processing of library materials and following the widespread participation of libraries in OCLC and other bibliographic utilities, the momentum for organization of serial functions seems to have swung from integration to decentralization in the interest of efficient use of staff. Margaret McKinley has responded to the current trend by examining, in the context of serial operations, informal communications spanning organizational lines and personal influence strategies. She explains that the library's formal organization chart does not necessarily express reality; it is only a description of "ideal work patterns, communication lines, and supervisory relationships." The intricacies of serial processing demand constant problem solving by means of a communication network involving cooperation and experience—the reciprocal interdependence described above. Where the organizational structure does not match communication needs, an informal communication system must develop. In libraries where functioning serials units have been abolished, the communication system flourishes underground. McKinley points out the advantages to serials specialists of working within the library's formal organizational structure: "efficiency of serials operations would be improved, staff moral would be higher, and a better end product could be delivered to the library's clientele." When the formal library administrative structure fails to coincide with natural communication channels, serials librarians "will inevitably develop and utilize informal communication systems, personal influence, persuasion and, perhaps, deceptive practices, in order to accomplish the library's objectives and the objectives of the serials network within it."[26]

THE FUTURE

This chapter has highlighted some of the problems encountered by librarians in working with serials and by scholars communicating through serial publications. There are responses to these problems which are certain to change the concept of serials management in the foreseeable future. Some of these developments are covered in Chapter 7 of this book, including cooperative acquisition and use of resources. A few publishers of scholarly journals have changed from paper format to microfiche, which is a nearly traditional substitute for the printed journal. Costs of production, distribution, housing, and replacement of serials are lower for microfiche than for printed editions. Another response is the selective dissemination of information, discussed in Chapter 6. The most revolutionary change in serial communication is the potential of the electronic journal. The technology needed for the electronic control and transmission of information exists, and it is being tested and refined on a relatively small scale. It is not perfect and it is not inexpensive yet, but it is available.

Librarians cannot help to resolve the problems of providing access to serial literature by fearing and avoiding the existing and future technological innovations. They must prepare for the time when there is no more Serial Record, no more binding preparation, no more periodicals reading room on the scale at which they are necessary now. It is difficult to turn off the everyday problems of claims, mutilated volumes, and *AACR* 2 in order to think about the future. Nonetheless, we must take the time to discuss and learn and plan for the day when most of the funds now allocated to current subscriptions will be shifted to such uses as online bibliographic services and the acquisition of electronically transmitted data required by a single patron. In addition, we need to make a commitment now to the possibilities which developing technology provides. Librarians acting alone cannot accomplish what is needed for continued satisfactory access to serial information because it takes money— huge amounts of money. Institutional and multi-institutional trial and error are necessary because this is how we learn. It is only in this way that technological possibilities will become workable and economical solutions for libraries.

NOTES

1. *Title Varies* 1 (1974): 29.
2. Clara D. Brown and Lynn S. Smith, *Serials: Past, Present and Future*, 2nd (rev.) ed. (Birmingham, Ala.: EBSCO Industries, Inc., 1980), pp. 23-24.
3. *Title Varies* 4 (1977): 11.
4. Donald Davinson, *The Periodicals Collection*, rev. and enl. ed. (London: Andre Deutsch, 1978), p. 7.
5. Brown and Smith, p. 17.
6. Andrew Osborn, *Serial Publications: Their Place and Treatment in Libraries*, 3rd ed. (Chicago: American Library Association, 1980), pp. 3-23.
7. Lynn S. Smith, *A Practical Approach to Serials Cataloging* (Greenwich, Conn.: JAI Press, Inc., 1978), pp. 1-4.
8. *Anglo-American Cataloguing Rules*, 2nd ed. (Chicago: American Library Association; Ottawa: Canadian Library Association, 1978), p. 570.
9. Osborn, pp. 10-13.
10. Charles Ammi Cutter, *Rules for a Dictionary Catalog*, 4th ed. (Washington, D.C.: Government Printing Office, 1904), p. 22.
11. J. Harris Gable, *Manual of Serials Work* (Chicago: American Library Association, 1937), p. 28.
12. *Union List of Serials in Libraries of the United States and Canada*, edited by Winifrid Gregory, 1st ed. (New York: H. W. Wilson Company, 1927), p. [iii].
13. Osborn, p. 3.
14. Bella Schachtman, "Simplification of Serial Records Work," *Serial Slants* 3 (1952): 6.
15. Davinson, pp. 9-10.
16. The U. S. Postal Service stipulates that a periodical must be issued at least three times a year.
17. Osborn, pp. 16-18.
18. J. Harris Gable, "The New Serials Department," *Library Journal* 60 (1935): 867-71.
19. Hans H. Weber, "Serials Administration," *Serials Librarian* 4 (1979): 144-49.
20. Fred B. Rothman, "Pooh-Bah of the Serials Division," *Library Journal* 62 (1937): 457-59.
21. Beatrice V. Simon, "Cataloging of Periodicals," *Ontario Library Review* 33 (1949): 237-45.
22. Samuel Lazerow, "Serial Records: A Mechanism for Control," in: *Serial Publications in Large Libraries*, ed. Walter C. Allen (Urbana: University of Illinois Graduate School of Library Science, 1970), pp. 108-19.
23. Weber, p. 146.
24. Mitsuko Collver, "Organization of Serials Work for Manual and Automated Systems," *Library Resources and Technical Services* 24 (1980): 307-16.
25. Collver, p. 310.
26. Margaret M. McKinley, "Serials Departments: Doomed to Extinction?" *Serials Librarian* 5 (Winter 1980): 15-24.

Chapter 2

Developing the Serial Collection

Luke Swindler

The hallmark of serials during the last generation has been one of constant growth: growth in numbers, growth in variety, growth in cost, and growth in importance as an intellectual and informational resource. These trends have made the rational development of serials collections much more complex and challenging than ever before, especially during the current period of unfavorable economic conditions.

Unfortunately, comprehensive treatments of serials collection development are practically nonexistent. The standard texts on both collection development and serials invariably fail to give adequate coverage to the subject, while librarian education still concentrates much too narrowly on the book. As a result, most librarians lack a firm understanding of the nature and value of serial publications within the modern configuration of library resources.[1] At the same time, growing demands for greater library accountability and efficiency, expanding user needs, and mounting pressures brought by the dynamics of serials growth make it imperative that all librarians involved in developing serial resources become more knowledgeable than in the past.

This chapter is a discussion of the major issues, factors, and methodologies involved in serials collection development. Beginning with an analysis of the current situation and principal trends in serials publishing from the perspective of a selection officer, the essay goes on to examine some of the basic flaws in philosophy that historically have prevented the creation of effective serials holdings. The third section deals with how one finds out what serials are available for acquisition, concentrating on identification systems and tools. The chapter concludes with segments on selection and evaluation.

SERIALS DYNAMICS

Although there is no general agreement on exactly how many serials are currently being published, the numbers one does come across are astounding: On a worldwide basis the latest editions of *Ulrich's International Periodicals Directory* and *Irregular Serials and Annuals* list 63,000 and 33,000 titles, respectively, while for North America alone the most recent *Standard Periodical Directory* contains 67,000 entries. Indeed, so many serials of value to just the scholarly community now exist that the nation's most comprehensive university libraries maintain current subscriptions in excess of 100,000 titles.[2]

Equally staggering is the proliferation of new serial publications every year: each issue of *Ulrich's Quarterly*, which supplements both *Ulrich's International Periodicals Directory* and *Irregular Serials and Annuals*, now lists 2,500 new and newly added titles. Imposing as these numbers are, this rapid growth represents neither a new nor a temporary phenomenon. The increase in the numbers of journals has been fairly constant over the last three centuries, with the total doubling every fifteen years.[3] Interestingly enough, concern about overproduction of serials and the concomitant fear of being inundated by new titles have been expressed since at least the early eighteenth century.[4] Furthermore, recent studies clearly indicate that the serials publishing industry is generally on a sound financial base and past publishing trends can be expected to continue.[5]

In addition to coping with an ever-expanding pool of current serial publications, librarians charged with collection development face decisions complicated by a growing variety of formats. Although the traditional printed serial is expected to continue its ascendency within the foreseeable future, technological changes, economic pressures, and users' need for the most current information in the most convenient form will result in a proliferation of transformations, supplementary services, and even new products.[6]

A number of these changes have already taken place. In response to financial pressures and the growing inventory of manuscripts waiting to be published, some periodicals, such as the *Journal of Modern History*, have moved to a mixed format, whereby only about half of the articles are actually printed. The other half, supposedly of equal quality but more specialized, are available only on demand. A related development is the synopsis journal, in which just summaries appear, with the articles themselves available only upon request. In both cases there is an optional library subscription to the microform archive. Still other titles are published only in microform, while some, particularly those dealing with current events and business news, are obtainable only on audio-cassette.

Continued advances in telecommunications and computer technology promise even more startling options during the coming years. The electronic serials, in particular, will not only provide a radical alternative to traditional paperbound publishing, but will raise fundamental questions regarding the use of acquisitions funds to provide access to these titles via computer terminals rather than to actually purchase physical entities. How collection developers react to these changes in the nature and format of serial resources will be of critical importance not only in terms of meeting user needs effectively but also for redefining the very nature of libraries themselves.[6]

Along with this growth in the number and variety of serials, there has been an explosive rise in their cost. The increasing expense of traditional publication (including indirect costs such as postage), the greater quantity of articles and other material now found in each issue, and the growing dominance of serials publishing by commercial firms committed to the maximization of profit have all contributed to this situation.[7] As a consequence, for at least a decade the cost of serial subscriptions has grown at a significantly higher rate than other library expenditures. Graphic evidence of this trend is provided by the following periodicals price index:[8]

Year	Average Price of a Serial	Index Value
1967-1969	$ 8.66	100
1970	10.41	120
1971	11.66	135
1972	13.23	153
1973	16.20	187
1974	17.71	205
1975	19.93	230
1976	22.52	260
1977	24.59	284
1978	27.58	319
1979	30.37	351
1980	34.54	399
1981	39.13	452

Such dramatic inflation has, in turn, created a severe financial squeeze on library materials budgets, particularly for research and special libraries because of their need to acquire expensive scholarly titles.[9] For many institutions the last decade has witnessed both a steady growth in the proportion of acquisitions funds going to support serials collections and a reduction in the number of serial subscriptions.[10] Since authorities agree that these trends in serials cost will continue, collection development officers can expect to find themselves in a state of permanent financial siege, especially since most libraries cannot count on sustained increases in funding to cope with serials inflation.[11]

Against this background of dynamic quantitative growth, a subtle but much more significant qualitative transformation has occurred as well. Serial publications have become so important during the last generation that they now represent the prime intellectual and information resource in libraries. Serials form part of the core of reference and general information collections, constitute the backbone of research in most fields of knowledge, and are more heavily used than monographs.[12] Only a few humanities disciplines still present an exception to this trend—and even here the typical researcher reviews several journals each week on a regular basis.[13]

Unfortunately, this fundamental transformation has been neither appreciated nor accommodated. The resultant shortcomings are most evident in public libraries, where serial holdings were found to be almost universally deficient in both quantity and quality.[14] Despite severe financial pressures, the effectiveness of serials collection development at research institutions is also perceived to be poor: Study after study has concluded that there is a low correlation between serial subscriptions and user needs, and that these libraries consistently subscribe to many more titles than can be economically justified.[15]

COLLECTION DEVELOPMENT PHILOSOPHY

The widespread inability of librarians to create effective and carefully controlled serials holdings largely stems from basic flaws in the philosophy of collection development. These deficiencies can be grouped into three major categories: (1) a failure to recognize the primacy of reasonable needs as the basis for a rational collection development program; (2) a failure to appreciate the importance of quality over quantity; and (3) a failure to understand the nature of library resources and to give serials the attention they deserve.

In spite of all the lip service paid to the importance of community analysis in library school, there persists a reluctance to assess and accept actual needs as the basis of collection development programs. With the exception of a few national institutions such as the Library of Congress, libraries are not primarily monuments to culture and erudition existing in a vacuum.[16] Unfortunately, too many libraries forget that they are service organizations designed to support the intellectual and informational needs of their users.

In an important book dealing with research and library resources, Charles Osburn points out again and again how large university libraries in particular have become isolated from the current nature of scholarly research and the library materials it requires. Despite fundamental shifts in the purposes, patterns, and methodologies of academic research in all subject disciplines over the course of the last generation, research collections continue to be built—and often overbuilt—on assumptions from the past and with little regard for actual needs. As a result, Osburn asserts, "it would be difficult to see how, in many libraries, the configuration of collections could be considered a reflection of academic programs."[17] This lack of responsiveness is most serious in the case of serials, because their role and importance in research has changed much more radically than other library resources during the last few decades.

Such neglect of the actual needs of the population supposedly being served is by no means confined to the rarefied atmosphere of selectors in large research institutions. According to Katz, the average public librarian also generally lacks a good understanding of the community, and often is apt to allow tradition rather than demonstrated need determine the scope and nature of the serials collection.[18] In fact, the force of conventional attitudes and elitist prejudices, especially the insistence on subscribing to a wide range of scholarly journals, remains so prevalent that the typical public librarian is more likely to build a serials collection of titles he or she feels patrons ought to read rather than those which users want and need.[19]

Contributing to the widespread failure to build responsive serials holdings is the traditional emphasis on quantity rather than quality. As Paul Mosher observed:

> The literature of librarianship does not even agree on the meaning of the term *good* with regard to collections, to say nothing of providing us with ready techniques for analyzing or evaluating their quality. Often we are told in response to the question how *good*, how *many*, in the rather naive belief that quantity and quality are necessarily equivalent terms when applied to library materials.[20]

Historically, librarians have considered the larger hoards to be the better collections, with completeness as the ultimate goal. As a result, almost all types of institutions have tried to amass the largest accumulations possible.[21] This ideology of massive collection as a substitute for careful selection reached its climax during the affluent 1960s. The consequences of what Osburn has referred to as the "debilitation of the capacity to discriminate," coupled with the tendency to build collections in a vacuum mentioned earlier, were most apparent at well-financed university libraries:

> In the course of rapidly changing events, the relationship between scholarship and the provision of resources for research became blurred; the relationship between the growth of resources of all kinds and the enhancement of library prestige through growth became predominant; and to a considerable extent, the library's mission to serve its constituency deteriorated and became merely lip service.
>
> The point to be made here is that, although library collection growth may have been intended to accommodate the new dynamism of academia, the principles in force and the practices adopted at the time suggest that the development of collections accommodated primarily the growth aspect of that dynamism.[22]

Now that this era of high funding has ended, the traditional philosophy of collection development described above, with its emphasis on maximum acquisitions and its aversion to the realistic assessment of needs, has proven to be fiscally irresponsible. Moreover, it has resulted in the creation of collections than cannot be sustained, especially in view of growing serials commitments that have never been adequately evaluated and now threaten to push many institutions into financial crisis.

The situation demands a more rational philosophy of serials collection development, emphasizing selectivity and quality and firmly based on meeting reasonable needs within an environment of limited resources.[23] Furthermore, quality can no longer be considered synonymous with quantity, but must be redefined in terms of the "utility or benefit of library collections to library patrons."[24] In order for such a strategy to be implemented successfully, librarians must begin to see themselves as selectors rather than collectors, for even in the case of the most affluent institutions serials collection development must essentially involve nonselection from an ever-growing universe of printed and electronic subscription possibilities.

The importance of selectivity and quality as the hallmarks of a successful serials collection development program cannot be stressed enough. Since the ongoing nature of serial commitments translates into certain growth in cost, whereas sustained budgetary increases to cover these charges are at best problematic, a rational collection development strategy demands that serials holdings be carefully controlled. Effective control, in turn, can be achieved only if librarians spend more time systematically developing serial holdings.

Fundamental misconceptions regarding the nature of library resources and the subsequent unwillingness to give serials the attention they require also account for the general failure to build effective serial holdings. In discussing the function of libraries and their relationship to the diffusion of knowledge, Gordon Williams reminds us that they exist "because society has found libraries essential to the dissemination of information," and that the acquisition of books, serials, and any other materials is but a means to achieve this end. He says further that, unfortunately, too many librarians view acquisitions, particularly book purchases, as ends in themselves. Reenforcing this misunderstanding is the habit of considering the number of volumes to be the most important indicator of quality and the prime basis of comparison against other libraries. Since book acquisitions have historically been the focus of collections and translate into the largest number of volumes added, there has been a strong bias toward purchasing as many monographs as possible.[25]

Consequently, until the dynamics of serials growth and the resulting financial crunch forced librarians to alter established notions, serials were quite neglected in comparison to books. In fact, the fixation on books has traditionally been so exclusive that as recently as a decade ago one authority asserted that librarians considered serials to be unimportant.[26] Even today, it is amazing how many librarians charged with collection development continue to see themselves as "book people" and pay only scant attention to serials—or, for that matter, to any nonbook materials. Indeed, a recent study of collection development at large university libraries has once again demonstrated how little attention serials can still receive despite their rapid growth in numbers and cost. One-third of the institutions surveyed had all their serials money in one pot and, therefore, did not know—and presumably did not care—how much they were spending on any given subject area.[27]

Finally, a rational collection development philosophy begins with the realization that funds are allocated to libraries to support specific programs with the most appropriate configuration of resources—and not to purchase, arbitrarily, X dollars worth of materials in format A or Y dollars in format B. Within this context, no one format is necessarily more important than any other. Depending on the programs, serials can be vitally important—often more essential than books in many subject areas and for satisfying certain needs.[28] The tendency of libraries to budget primarily by format not only does not make sense in terms of supporting programs with the most appropriate configuration of resources, but a budgetary model based on format impairs the institution's ability to meet needs equitably, given the traditional bias towards maximizing the number of books purchased and the relatively new trend of arbitrarily setting a limit to how much the library will spend on serial subscriptions. Rather, expenditures should be considered as part of a consolidated budget allocation for the support of a particular program.

On a theoretical level, this view of the nature of library resources demands that serials be fully integrated into overall collection development policies and programs. On a practical level, this philosophy mandates that a great deal of care be given to developing serials resources. Because of the inexorable growth in number, format, and cost outlined above, each serial subscription must be cost-effective: it must involve selection of the most important titles that most clearly meet identifiable needs for a given price, particularly in terms of the core serials that will account for the vast majority of use. Libraries not willing to give serials collection development the attention it deserves will not only end up with poor holdings but will almost certainly come to financial grief.

IDENTIFICATION

The reluctance to devote the requisite attention to serials accounts for the widespread failure to create adequate mechanisms for identification, selection, and evaluation. Libraries typically do not delegate specific responsibility for identifying relevant serials, do not consider subscriptions on a regular basis, and do not treat those titles suggested for purchase with the same attention lavished on book acquisitions.[29] Because most serials—unlike books—are nontrade publications and hence more difficult to isolate, it is especially important that their identification should not depend upon chance.[30]

Effective serials collection development, then, begins with the designation of selectors charged with the identification of titles on an ongoing, systematic, and comprehensive basis. Moreover, this can only be realized if selectors regularly consult a wide variety of identification tools. Although almost all the sources to be discussed have multiple uses such as bibliographic verification, price information, or holdings locations, it is their value to a collection developer for purposes of identification—as distinct from selection or evaluation—that constitutes the basis for inclusion. Furthermore, since this survey is selective, it concentrates on the tools of greatest potential utility in a general American library.

The identification sources fall into three major groups: those for current serials, those for new titles, and those for retrospective acquisitions. These tools will allow a librarian to determine what serials are currently being published, what new serial publications have come into being, and what titles existed in the past and are readily available for acquisition. Successful development of a serials collection ultimately depends more on a systematic view of identification than it does on reliance on a single tool, and the value of any one of the sources discussed below is determined primarily by the needs of the individual library and the particular combination of identification sources used.

Current Serials

A number of relatively up-to-date sources provide comprehensive coverage of the major classes of current serials. Librarians, however, should be prepared to consult more than one source because each varies somewhat in scope, annotations, and searching options.

General Serials

> *Standard Periodical Directory.* New York: Oxbridge Communications, 1964- . Biennial.

The *Standard Periodical Directory* is the most comprehensive listing of U.S. and Canadian serials, providing information on nearly 67,000 titles which appear at least once every two years. It includes magazines, scholarly and trade journals, newsletters, house organs, directories, yearbooks, transactions and proceedings of learned societies and associations, some government publications, and serials issued by religious, ethnic, literary, and social groups.

The serials are divided into 230 subject categories and arranged alphabetically by title within each group. Entries typically include title (including previous titles), publisher's name, address and telephone number, editorial staff, indexing and abstracting information, year founded, frequency of issue, subscription price, circulation, information on physical format, and type of publication. Availability in microform, cassette, or computer tape is also indicated. There is a cross index to subjects in the front and an alphabetical title index in the back.

> *Ulrich's International Periodicals Directory: A Classified Guide to Current Periodicals, Foreign and Domestic.* New York: Bowker, 1932-   . Annual.

Ulrich's contains information on approximately 63,000 periodicals published throughout the world more frequently than once a year. It includes the same varied categories of periodicals as the *Standard Periodical Directory*, but with fewer newsletters and house organs. Although extremely useful, especially for North American and West European titles, *Ulrich's* is often inaccurate, incomplete, or not very up-to-date.

The periodicals are divided into 385 subject groups and arranged alphabetically by title within each category. An entry typically includes title (including previous and alternate titles), Dewey Decimal Classification, as well as a brief subject annotation when the contents are not clear, country of publication and ISSN, a language note when the text is in a language other than that of the country of publication or is multi-lingual, year founded, frequency of issue, subscription price, publisher's name and address, special features such as book reviews and cumulative indexes, and indexing and abstracting information. Notations on back issue and microform availability are also included. There are a number of useful indexes to this tool: subject cross references, publications of international organizations, cessations (since the last issue), and titles.

Irregular Serials and Annuals: An International Directory. New York: Bowker, 1967- . Annual.

This companion source to *Ulrich's* lists about 33,000 serials published worldwide that are issued on an annual or irregular basis. Monographic series are included in its coverage. Its arrangement is modeled on *Ulrich's.*

Although the *Standard Periodical Directory* provides more thorough coverage of North American serials, *Ulrich's* and *Irregular Serials and Annuals* together include 40 percent more titles, provide the international coverage many libraries need, and are more current because they now appear annually.

One of the most exciting recent developments has been the creation of comprehensive serials databases commercially available to libraries. There are now two online sources of information on current serials which are useful in collection development. Although based on printed tools, these computerized sources offer the important advantages of greater currency, more powerful and sophisticated searching options, and a variety of printout formats.

Bowker Serials Bibliography Database (vended through Bibliographic Retrieval Services and Dialog).

Corresponding to *Ulrich's International Periodicals Directory, Irregular Serials and Annuals, Ulrich's Quarterly* (to be discussed in the section on new titles), and *Sources of Serials*, this database contains 102,000 citations and is updated every six weeks.

The wide array of searching and limiting options constitutes the most attractive feature of this database. For purposes of collection development, it is possible to produce lists of serials based on any combination of the following: subject, Dewey number, key words in title or annotation, country of publication, publisher or distributor, frequency, format, circulation, regular inclusion of special features such as book reviews or statistics, where indexed, and by such categories as conference proceedings, monographic series, or international agency publications. Finally, this is a relatively inexpensive database to search.

Select Periodical Data (accessed directly through Oxbridge Communications).

Corresponding to *Standard Periodical Directory, Oxbridge Directory of Newsletters* (to be discussed later), *Directory of the College Student Press in America, Oxbridge Directory of Religious Periodicals*, and *Oxbridge Directorey of Ethnic Periodicals*, this database is continuously updated.

Although probably not as useful to libraries as the Bowker database, *Select Periodical Data* does cover more North American titles, provide some different searching options, and offer more output formats. For purposes of collection development, it is possible to produce lists of serials based on any combination of the following: subject, circulation, frequency, subscription price, type of publication such as newsletter or directory, type of readership such as consumer or trade, geographical location down to zip code, and certain physical format characteristics. Output is available in printout, list, index card, and magnetic tape formats.

Newspapers

None of the general serial sources above includes newspapers. The two most useful and comprehensive tools for finding out what domestic and major foreign newspapers are being published are *Ayer* and *Editor and Publisher*.

Ayer Directory of Publications. Philadelphia: Ayer, 1880- . Annual.

Although technically a source for general serials, the major value of this tool from a collection development perspective is in its coverage of newspapers, which constitute half of the 22,000 titles contained in the latest edition.

Ayer lists serials originating in the United States, Canada, Puerto Rico, Virgin Islands, Bahamas, Bermuda, Philippines, and Panama published four or more times a year. Newspapers are covered comprehensively; other serials more selectivity, based on a subjective judgment of a title's quality and usefulness.

The basic arrangement is by state or province and then city, with all publications originating from a locality arranged alphabetically by title. Each entry normally includes title, publisher and editors, character (especially political orientation), frequency, date established, subscription price, and circulation.

There are numerous classified lists by type of publication: agricultural, college, foreign language, Jewish, black, religious, fraternal, general magazine, and trade, technical and subject class. There are also lists by frequency: daily newspapers, daily periodicals, and weekly, semi-weekly and tri-weekly newspapers. An alphabetical listing by name and place of every publication included is found at the back.

Editor and Publisher International Yearbook. New York: Editor and Publisher, 1921- . Annual.

This work includes statistical and directory information dealing with world journalism, and it is useful in collection development because of its comprehensive listing of U. S. newspapers as well as foreign dailies. The U. S. newspapers are arranged alphabetically within several major groups: daily, tabloid, black, special service (emphasizing business and professions), foreign language, and college and university. The foreign press is grouped by major geographical area, then country, then city, with the individual dailies arranged alphabetically under city. Each entry typically includes title, address, circulation, date established, frequency, and editorial and management personnel. Subscription price and advertising and technical production information are also given for U. S. papers.

Newsletters and House Organs

Although generally ignored as a minor class of serials, newsletters and house organs are growing rapidly not only in numbers of titles but in readership as well, with the serials listed in *Internal Publications Directory* alone having a combined circulation in excess of 160 million. The growing demand for the most current information, together with the proliferation of special interest serials, will undoubtedly increase the importance of newsletters and house organs as library resources.

Oxbridge Directory of Newsletters. New York: Oxbridge Communications, 1979- Biennial.

This is the most comprehensive source for U. S. and Canadian newsletters available. The 1981-82 edition contains 8,000 newsletters, as opposed to only 5,000 in the 1981-82 *Standard Periodical Directory*. The newsletters are arranged alphabetically within 153 subject categories. Each entry includes title, publisher's name, address and telephone number, editor, description of contents, year established, frequency of issue, subscription price, circulation, distribution of readership (e.g., local, national, international), and average number of pages per issue. There is an alphabetical index by title in the back.

National Directory of Newsletters and Reporting Services: A Reference Guide to National and International Services, Financial Services, Association Bulletins, and Training and Educational Services. 2nd ed. 4 parts. Detroit: Gale, 1978-1981.

This source is international in scope and provides information on nearly 3,200 titles, including many not found in other tools. Newsletters of purely local interest and most house organs are excluded. Unfortunately, a number of major U. S. titles that should be included are not to be found.

The newsletters are arranged alphabetically within each part. Entries include title (including previous or alternate titles), name and address of sponsoring organization, description of scope and purpose, frequency, subscription price, and circulation figures. Part 4 contains cumulative title, publisher, and specific subject indexes, with the latter two making this work particularly useful.

Internal Publications Directory. (*Working Press of the Nation*, v. 5.) Burlington, Iowa: National Research Bureau, 1976-   . Annual.

Formerly:
Gebbie Press House Magazine Directory (1952-1975).

This is the most comprehensive source of its type and includes the internal and external serial publications of more than 3,500 U. S. and Canadian companies, government agencies, clubs, and other groups.

The titles are alphabetically arranged by sponsoring organization. Each entry includes name and address of sponsor, title, editor, year founded, frequency, number and size of pages, print method and printer, circulation, and editorial policy. There are indexes by title, industry, and specific subject.

Alternative Serials

Alternative serials are not well covered in the standard sources discussed above. In part this is because such publications, especially when they express unorthodox ideas or have unusual emphases, have traditionally been considered marginal and less pertinent to library collections. Alternative serials are also genuinely more difficult to control bibliographically because they are often short-lived, have limited circulations, and are not integrated into mainline publishing systems. During the last several years there has been an increase in the number of sources that not only provide listings of alternative serials, but also have annotations and indexing arrangements that make them particularly useful and necessary if a collection developer really wants to find out about such titles.

American Library Association. Task Force on Alternatives in Print. Social Responsibilities Round Table, comp. *Alternatives in Print: An International Catalog of Books, Pamphlets, Periodicals and Audiovisual Materials.* 6th ed. New York: Neal-Schuman, 1980.

This important work includes the publications of nearly 2,600 presses, listing many titles that cannot be easily found elsewhere. There is a strong emphasis on dissident publications, especially those advocating social, economic, and political change. The basic arrangement is alphabetical by publisher and then format, with periodicals considered as a separate category. The serial entries include title, subtitle, frequency, language, price, and back issue availability. There are detailed indexes by title (subdivided by format), author, subject, and geographical area.

Carnahan, Don, comp. and ed. *Guide to Alternative Periodicals.* 2nd ed. Greenleaf, Ore.: Sunpark Press, 1977.

The preface states that the "primary focus of these alternative periodicals is on creative, constructive, non-wasteful lifestyles with a reverence for natural harmony and health of body, mind and spirit." A special effort is made to exclude titles included in other related publications such as *Alternatives in Print* and *International Directory of Little Magazines and Small Presses.*

The periodicals are arranged alphabetically by title into broad subject groups such as environmental conservation and alternative energy/appropriate technology. Each entry includes title, address, frequency, subscription price, and a brief annotation on content. There is a title index in the back.

> *International Directory of Little Magazines and Small Presses.* Paradise, Ca.: Dustbooks, 1965- . Annual.

This tool emphasizes literary publications and contains many titles not found in the more standard sources. Entries for serials include title, publisher's name, address and telephone number, editor, type of materials used and areas of interest for review materials, frequency, subscription price, year established, production method and format, average number of pages, circulation, and availability and price of back issues. The arrangement is alphabetical by name of serial or press, with a subject index by broad terms and a U. S. regional index by state.

> Muller, Robert H., Theodore Jurgen Spahn and Janet M. Spahn. *From Radical Left to Extreme Right: A Bibliography of Current Periodicals of Protest, Controversy, Advocacy, or Dissent, With Dispassionate Content-Summaries to Guide Librarians and Other Educators Through the Polemic Fringe.* 2nd ed., rev. and enl. 3 v. Ann Arbor, Mi.: Campus Publishers; Metuchen, N. J.: Scarecrow, 1970-1976.

Although a bit dated now, this is an important and useful source for alternative periodicals. It contains 1,324 publications, almost all in English originating in the United States and Canada. The serials are grouped into generic categories such as libertarian, Marxist-socialist left, radical professional, race supremacist, feminist, gay liberation, anticommunist, with each section prefaced by an essay that describes the field.

Entries generally include title, address, editor, frequency, price, date established, circulation, and information on format. Mention is made if the title is indexed or is contained in the Bell & Howell microform collection of radical periodicals. There is also an informative and nonjudgmental review of the publication, often with a response from the editor of the serial. Each volume has geographical and title indexes (with the latter cumulative) as well as an index of editors, publishers, and opinions.

> Murphy, Dennis D. *Directory of Conservative and Libertarian Serials, Publishers, and Freelance Markets.* 2nd ed. Tucson: Murphy, 1979.

This work includes 222 entries for serials, publishers, bookstores, and book clubs that specialize in conservative or libertarian materials. Not only are all identifiably liberal titles and organizations excluded, but the compiler assures us that he did not knowingly list any "who although, perhaps, considering themselves conservative or libertarian or being so considered by others, favored ratification of the Panama Canal treaties. Those who supported the treaties are too far left to qualify for inclusion in this directory."

Each entry includes name or title, address, short annotation describing content and perspective, cross references to related serials and organizations, and information on submissions. In the case of serials, entries also include frequency, subscription price, and a note stating whether book reviews are contained. There is a subject index reflecting major conservative and libertarian obsessions, for example, fluoridation, gun control, socialized medicine, and, of course, The Conspiracy.

U. S. Government Serials

The federal government publishes many serials useful to libraries, especially in business, economics, and technology. With the exception of approximately four dozen regional depositories that receive every distributed title, all other libraries must select those appropriate to their collections. Because information on government serials is not often included in the standard sources cited at the beginning of this section, selectors must consult additional tools in order to identify all relevant titles.

Andriot, John L., ed. *Guide to U. S. Government Publications*. McLean, Va.: Documents Index, 1973- . Annual (with updates).

Formerly: *Guide to U.S. Government Serials and Periodicals* (1959-1972).

This tool is an annotated guide to current series and periodicals issued by the federal government. It also serves as a complete catalog of all Superintendent of Documents (SuDoc) classification numbers ever issued.

It now appears in two parts: volume 1 includes SuDoc numbers for all agencies currently in existence; volume 2 covers abolished agencies. The arrangement in both parts is by SuDoc classes. There are agency and title indexes in the first volume.

Yannarella, Philip A. and Rao Aluri, comps. *U. S. Government Scientific and Technical Periodicals*. Metuchen, N. J. : Scarecrow, 1976.

Because most librarians find it difficult to identify appropriate periodicals in technical fields, this work can serve as a useful supplementary identification source. It includes information on 266 important U. S. government periodicals, including non-GPO titles issued by federal agencies and federally supported research centers.

Entries include title (and previous title), SuDoc and depository numbers, date established, frequency, issuing organization and its address, distribution policy and subscription price, annotation of scope and editorial policy, indexing and abstracting information, and availability in microform. There are indexes by depository item, SuDoc number, and title/subject.

New Titles

Keeping abreast of new serial publications is difficult because available sources are inadequate in at least one of the critical areas of scope, arrangement, or currency. It is particularly difficult to create a comprehensive system for the early identification of new serials comparable to that for the identification of titles which already exist at any given time. As a result, random identification by means of advertisements and brochures, notices in subject journals, user suggestions, and the comments of colleagues will play an important part in the process. Nevertheless, much can be done to improve the haphazard way librarians currently try to monitor new publications.

Comprehensive Sources

One of the most promising means of identifying new serials is to have periodic computer searches done on either of the two general serials databases discussed earlier. Although such a strategy probably works best for narrowly defined areas in science and technology, a carefully structured profile should identify the vast majority of new titles in almost any field. In fact, because one would be concerned with only publications added since the last search rather than all titles in the system, the searching profile could be quite broad. Given the inexpensive charges for the *Bowker Serials Bibliography Database* in particular, quarterly updating searches would likely be cost-effective for all but the smallest libraries.

With the demise of *New Serial Titles: Classed Subject Arrangement* (Washington, D. C.: Library of Congress, 1955-1980), libraries lost the most convenient and comprehensive printed source for the identification of new titles. Unless one is unfortunate enough to be the sole serials bibliographer for a library collecting in many subject areas, it simply is not worth the time to go through the surviving *New Serial Titles* (Washington, D. C.: Library of Congress, 1953-   ). This monthly, which averaged over 1,000 serials per issue even before its recent expansion to include all CONSER contributions regardless of publication dates, is too massive to be an efficient identification tool. There are, however, a number of other sources that are both more effective and more current.

> *Ulrich's Quarterly: A Supplement to Ulrich's International Periodicals Directory and Irregular Serials and Annuals.* New York: Bowker, 1977-   . Quarterly.
>
> Formerly:
> *Bowker Serials Bibliography Supplement* (1972-1976).

As indicated by the subtitle, this source updates both *Ulrich's* and *Irregular Serials and Annuals.* The scope, arrangement, and searching options are modeled on the main works, and each issue contains 2,500 new and newly added titles. *Ulrich's Quarterly* is the most useful printed tool for identifying new serials because of its comprehensive coverage, its currency, and its arrangement of titles into broad subject categories.

> Library of Congress. *Subject Catalog* (Title varies.) Washington, D.C.: Library of Congress, 1950-   . Quarterly (with annual and quinquennial cumulations).

This source provides subject access to all serials, books, pamphlets, maps, and atlases cataloged by the Library of Congress for which printed cards are produced. It includes publications written in Arabic, Cyrillic, Gaelic, Greek, Hebraic, Indic, and Roman alphabets as well as Chinese, Japanese, and Korean characters. Most titles are new; however, older materials and recataloged items are also included. Entries consist of full MARC records and are arranged in alphabetical order by Library of Congress subject headings.

As the above paragraph indicates, comprehensiveness is the real strength of this tool. There are, however, a number of drawbacks which make this source more useful as a supplemental rather than a primary identification source. In the first place, there is a lack of currency, because inclusion is delayed until the item has been cataloged. Second, the specific subject approach makes this tool practical as a primary identification source only for selectors with very specific collection responsibilties. Third, there are only three quarterly issues and then the annual cumulation, and there is no annual cumulation in the last year of the quinquennial cycle. The lack of a fourth quarterly issue forces one to go through the entire annual cumulation in order to identify titles cataloged during the last quarter, while lack of the fifth annual cumulation for the final year of a quinquennium multiplies the magnitude of the problem.

Libraries receiving proof slips as part of the Library of Congress Alert Service avoid most of these drawbacks. But considering the high cost of this service and the very large number of items received, it is only worthwhile to subscribe if one uses proof slips to identify book materials as well.

Library-Oriented Journals

Reviews and notices of serials appearing in library-oriented journals provide another valuable means of identifying new titles. Inasmuch as the journals to be discussed provide more than just bibliographical information about a title, they are useful in both identification and selection. On the other hand, because only a small number of new serials are listed or reviewed, these tools must be considered supplemental identification sources.

> *Choice: Books for College Libraries.* Chicago: Association of College and Research Libraries, 1964-   . Monthly (except bi-monthly for July-August).

Long, authoritative reviews of periodicals appropriate for undergraduate collections occasionally appear and provide a supplement to the fifth edition of *Classified List of Periodicals for the College Library* (to be discussed in the section on selection). This special column reviews 4-6 titles that are usually 4-5 years old. Generally appended to the end is a list of new serials too recent to be recommended, as they have just begun, but which look exceptionally promising.

Government Publications Review. Part B: Acquisition Guide to Significant Government Publications at all Levels. New York: Pergamon Press, 1980-   . Quarterly.

Formerly:
Government Publications Review (1973-1979).

This source contains bibliographic and ordering information plus a short annotation for important federal, state, municipal, U. N., international agency, and foreign government publications. Many serials, especially annuals, are included. There is a subject index at the back of each issue.

Library Journal. New York: Bowker, 1876-   . Semi-monthly (except monthly for July and August).

LJ features a regular column on new magazines that contains paragraph-length notices on 5-7 titles. Serials in all areas of the humanities and social sciences of interest to a public or general academic library are included, with an entire column occasionally devoted to periodicals in a neglected or unusual field.

New Magazine Review. Las Vegas: New Magazine Publishing Company, 1978-
Bi-monthly.

This is the only tool devoted solely to reviewing new serials. Each issue includes short evaluations of 30-40 periodicals and newsletters, ranging from inexpensive, popular titles such as *The Cook's Magazine* to costly, technical publications such as *Dangerous Properties of Industrial Materials Report.* Although the reviews are solid, it is difficult to envision an audience for this tool. In fact, because *New Magazine Review* contains only a small number of titles covering an exceedingly broad range of levels and subjects, it appears that only a large and well-funded public library would find it sufficiently useful to justify a subscription.

Reference Services Review. Ann Arbor, Mi.: Pierian Press, 1973-   . Quarterly.

There is a regular column on serials "intended to provide in depth, comparative reviews of abstracting services, indexes, serial bibliographies, yearbooks, directories, almanacs and other serial tools that would normally be housed in reference departments." Usually 6-12 titles are reviewed in each issue, although most are evaluations of serials that have been in existence for some time.

Serials Review. Ann Arbor, Mi: Pierian Press, 1975-   . Quarterly.

This source provides evaluations of all types of serials, including regular columns on little magazines, newsletters, government publications, and other major categories. There is usually a feature article discussing serials in some major field. The serials reviews are long and critical.

Small Press Review. Paradise, Ca.: Dustbooks, 1967-   . Monthly.

Almost every issue contains a section on new serial titles. Usually 6-8 small magazines are given one-paragraph notices.

Retrospective Acquisitions

Unlike collection development involving current or new serial titles, retrospective acquisition entails not only the identification of appropriate publications, but also the determination of what is available for purchase. Because the problems and sources of information differ substantially for each process, they will be considered separately.

What Has Been Published

Three basic approaches are available to determine what serial titles have existed. The first strategy involves the consultation of comprehensive library shelflists and catalogs. The Library of Congress, Harvard University, and New York Public Library provide the best examples, both because of the scope and magnitude of their collections and on account of the existence of published access tools.

Library of Congress. *Shelflist*. Ann Arbor, Mi.: University Microfilms International, 1978-1979.

This source consists of 3,200 microfiche representing nearly 7 million shelflist cards, and provides exhaustive coverage of the serial and book literature for almost all fields of knowledge. Access to specific subjects is by means of the individual classification schedules or the subject-keyword volumes of the new *Combined Indexes to the Library of Congress Classification Schedules*.

Harvard University Library. *Periodical Classes: Classified Listing by Call Number, Alphabetical Listing by Title*. (Widener Shelflist, no. 15.) Cambridge, Mass.: Harvard University Library; dist. Cambridge, Mass.: Harvard University Press, 1966.

The Harvard shelflist covers about 26,000 periodical and serial titles in 23 major subject and language classes in the humanities, sciences, and social sciences. It is estimated to include about half the serial titles in the main library at the time it was compiled and complements the Library of Congress shelflist because of the uniqueness of Harvard's collections and its different classification system. The first part of this work arranges all the serial titles by class, and the second part arranges them alphabetically by title.

> New York Public Library. *Dictionary Catalog of the Research Libraries of the New York Public Library (1911-1971).* New York: The Library; dist. Boston: G. K. Hall, 1979-   . (To be completed in 1984; being updated by printed supplements.)

This catalog is projected to run to more than 750 volumes and will contain 9 million author, title, subject, and series entries for Roman alphabet materials in the main collections of the Research Libraries. In addition to providing comprehensive coverage of the serial literature in most of the humanities, sciences, and social sciences, the dictionary arrangement of this tool complements the classed approach of the Library of Congress and Harvard shelflists.

In contrast to this empirical approach to retrospective serials collection development based on the holdings of great libraries, it is possible to find out what serials have been published by consulting lists of serials literature for specific subjects. Theodore Besterman's *Periodical Publications: A Bibliography of Bibliographies* (2 v. Totowa, N. J.: Rowman and Littlefield, 1971) constitutes the basic retrospective guide to such lists, and it may be supplemented and brought up to date by the sources found in the more general guides to reference tools.

One further approach to retrospective serials collection development consists of using older editions of the tools for current serials to identify earlier titles. These lists can often be of unique historical importance, as in the case of the 1947 edition of *Ulrich's*, which is not only a directory of titles being published at that time, but also contains a listing of clandestine serials issued during World War II. By using these methods it should be possible for the enterprising collection developer to build a comprehensive list of all relevant serials publications in any specific field of knowledge.

What Is Available For Purchase

Retrospective serials acquisitions can involve purchase of originals, reprints, or microforms, depending upon availability, cost, space considerations, physical characteristics, perceived user needs, and library preferences.

Originals

In the area of retrospective serials acquisitions, one should not trust statements of availability found in the standard identification tools or even those indicated in publishers' catalogs. These statements tend at best to be incomplete or out-of-date; they are often even erroneous. One should contact the publisher or distributor directly in order to find out what is still in print and the price.

If back issues or volumes are not available from the publisher or distributor, the Universal Serials and Book Exchange offers one of the most efficient means of securing needed titles. This remarkable organization maintains a stock of nearly 4 million issues of approximately 40,000 serials covering all subject areas. USBE members receive annual microfiche catalogs and monthly printed supplements listing the 10,000 most heavily requested titles, which account for nearly 80 percent of the issues on hand at any given time. Nonmember libraries can purchase these inexpensive tools as well as access these titles through the *USBE Database* (vended through Bibliographic Retrieval Services). Moreover, if the needed serials are not in stock, the Universal Serials and Book Exchange will hold a library's requests until the items become available.

A number of commercial dealers also specialize in serial backruns, and a few of them put out extensive catalogs. Although there seems to be a strong bias toward major titles in medicine, science, and technology, consultation of these lists often represents the most economical means of acquiring long runs of serials in the original. As in the case of the Universal Serials and Book Exchange, these published lists tend to include only the most heavily requested titles; consequently, librarians should consider them mainly as indicators of stock and not hesitate to ask about the availability of other titles. If all else fails and a library is determined to purchase originals, it can advertise. This option, however, tends to be expensive in terms of price and staff time.

Reprints

Large-scale reprinting of serials began in the 1960s, and at the same time basic bibliographical tools were published to help control these materials.

Guide to Reprints. Kent, Conn.: Guide to Reprints, 1967-   . Annual.

This source lists serials and other materials available in reprint editions from over 400 publishers worldwide. Serial entries include title, volume numbers covered, years covered, publisher, and price. The basic arrangement is by title or author. For subject access, one must consult:

Subject Guide to Reprints. Kent, Conn.: Guide to Reprints, 1979-   . Biennial.

A companion work to *Guide to Reprints*, this tool provides access to over 100,000 reprints, which are grouped into 136 broad classes. There are separate categories for the major classes of serials such as yearbooks and U. S. newspapers.

Internationale Bibliographie der Reprints: Band 2: Zeitschriften, Zeitungen, Jahrbücher, Konferenzberichte usw. Munich: K. G. Saur, 1980.

This work lists 6,000 reprints of serials by nearly 260 publishers worldwide. Entries are arranged alphabetically by title or corporate author, with many cross references. Under the main entry one finds original publication information, reprint publisher, volumes reprinted, and price. There are indexes by keywords and broad subject classes. This work is updated by the quarterly *Bulletin of Reprints*.

Microforms

Microform acquisitions represent the third major means of retrospective serials collection development and are increasingly being used by libraries in lieu of binding current serials. In fact, many of the major serials publishers now offer special dual subscriptions in both paper and microform as a matter of course.

The inclusion of statements on microform availability in the major directories of current serials provides additional evidence of the growing importance of this format. However, a librarian must still be prepared to make direct inquiries to the publisher or consult other sources because indications of microform availability in the general tools are often inaccurate.[31]

Guide to Microforms in Print. Westport, Conn: Microform Review, 1961- . Annual.

This is a cumulative listing of microforms available from publishers throughout the world. The basic arrangement is alphabetical by author or title. Serial entries include title, volumes available, dates covered, publisher, price, and microformats available, for example, film or fiche. In the case of newspapers, indications of city and state (and country when non-U. S.) follow the title. For subject access one must consult:

Subject Guide to Microforms in Print. Westport, Conn.: Microform Review, 1962/63- . Annual.

A companion work to *Guide to Microforms in Print*, this tool provides subject access under 135 broad classifications, including separate groupings for major categories of serials such as non-U. S. newspapers and general periodicals. There is an index to the subject categories, and an item may appear under two classifications when appropriate.

Although *Guide to Microforms in Print* is an excellent and comprehensive source for retrospective serials acquisitions, it is limited to the products of commercial publishers. This is a significant omission in the case of newspapers since so many titles have been microfilmed by libraries, historical societies, and other noncommercial organizations. When retrospective collection development involves newspapers, one should also consult the following series of tools:

> U. S. Library of Congress. Catalog Publications Division. *Newspapers in Microform: Foreign Countries, 1948-1972*. Washington, D. C.: Library of Congress, 1973.

This source lists 8,620 titles from nearly 2,000 localities based on information supplied by several hundred U. S. and foreign libraries as well as commercial publishers. The basic arrangement is by country and then city, with a title index.

> U. S. Library of Congress. Catalog Publications Division. *Newspapers in Microform: United States, 1948-1972*. Washington, D. C.: Library of Congress, 1973.

This source lists nearly 35,000 titles reported by over 800 libraries and nearly 50 publishers. The basic arrangement is by state and then city, with a title index.

> U. S. Library of Congress. Catalog Publications Division. *Newspapers in Microform*. Washington, D. C.: Library of Congress, 1973-   . Annual.

A companion source updating the two works described above, this tool follows their arrangements. The use of these three sources allows one to find out what newspapers are available in microform and for what years. Since microform masters are also indicated, it is possible to locate the holding organization and request that a copy of the needed title be made, thereby avoiding the expense of making another master.

With the increased concern about the physical deterioration of library materials, more and more institutions are converting their more fragile serial holdings to microform. For information on microform reproductions of non-newspaper serials not commercially available, one should consult the following source:

> *National Register of Microform Masters*. Washington, D. C.: Library of Congress, 1965-   . Annual (with a multi-year cumulation covering 1965-1975).

This tool provides a listing and location of microform masters reported by libraries and commercial publishers. The arrangement is alphabetical by main entry.

In addition to the printed sources cited above, the national bibliographical networks are useful for determining what reprints and microform reproductions exist. Because MARC rules require the notation of reprint and microform, it is now possible to locate these materials through a search of the OCLC or RLIN databases. These online systems, together with the printed sources created during the last two decades, make it easy for librarians to identify and acquire needed serial reproductions.

SELECTION

After relevant titles have been identified, a collection development officer must make actual acquisition decisions. The value of a collection development policy, the major elements in the selection process, and the more critical philosophical considerations and selection criteria influencing acquisitions are discussed in this section. A fuller discussion of evaluation, focusing on the principal means of assessing serials holdings, follows. Selection and evaluation are, of course, closely related processes, especially since the methodologies used to evaluate an entire collection are also used to select a single title. They differ in that each selection decision ideally represents an individual evaluation, while evaluation is collective and looks at the results of many selection—and nonselection—decisions.

The importance of a formal collection development policy must be underscored before discussing actual selection. Such a document, fully incorporating serials along with other library resources, ensures the quality and consistent development of serials holdings that accurately reflect constituency needs and library acquisitions priorities.[32] As Robert Goehlert notes, "Without a concrete collection development policy, one which states clearly the mission and purpose of the library, it is difficult to see how acquisitions are more than a series of unrelated decisions."[33]

A collection development policy is particularly important in the case of serials, because these materials are harder to select and demand more critically informed selection choices than do one-time purchases such as books. A mistake is much more serious because it comes back to haunt one again and again in the form of recurrent and escalating subscription costs. Moreover, as serials budgets come under greater financial pressure with the passage of each year, the necessity of a collection development policy only increases, because there will be less margin for selection error, and it will become more essential that the titles added or even retained be appropriate and useful. Finally, a formal policy not only provides a guide to selection but also furnishes the basis for budget allocations and evaluation.

A deliberate and planned development of serials mandates that selection responsibility for materials in all formats supporting a particular program be vested in the same person(s) in order to ensure the most coherent collection building effort. Ideally, this selector is not only the most knowledgeable person in the library regarding resources in a given field, but also the most competent to assess local needs. Moreover, he or she is in the best position to relate serials to other materials that the library has in support of a given program.

This is not to say that the committees for serials selection that now flourish do not have any legitimate place in the collection development process. They can be useful for suggestions and have a definite role to play in the selection of general and multidisciplinary titles.[34] Indeed, as Katz notes, involvement in the selection process is positive, and it is advisable for the collection developer to listen to constituents and colleagues.[35] This is especially true when dealing with a clearly defined clientele, as in the case of special and academic libraries. There, in fact, user consultation should be a major factor in order to ensure that holdings consist of the most appropriate and relevant titles. However, while seeking advice, selectors must not abdicate actual selection responsibility to either users or fellow librarians.

The manner and timing of choosing new titles constitutes another important element in the selection process. Because funds are rarely sufficient to cover all serial requests, libraries must be content to select only the most valuable serials and hope that budgets will keep up with at least these subscription charges. Within this context, new titles should be considered as a group at specific times during the year, rather than one by one, in order to maximize the chances that a library will subscribe to only the most important serials out of a larger universe of merely desirable publications.

At the same time, it is desirable to anticipate constituent demand by adding new serials as soon as they become known. Indeed, since the number of subscriptions a serial receives in its first year or two often determines whether it succeeds, a library has a special obligation to its users to subscribe to a publication as soon as possible, if it seems particularly worthwhile and fills a definite need.[36] In addition, since print runs of serials, and of new titles in particular, are not much in excess of actual subscriptions, a significant delay in a selection decision may mean that the earlier issues are no longer available and must be secured in the out-of-print market at a cost generally greater than the original price.[37] The periodicity of new serial title selections, of course, depends on the individual situation; however, Davinson suggests that acquisition decisions be made at least quarterly in order to avoid the problems outlined above.[38]

Sample issues also contribute to the high quality selection process that is at the core of effective collection development. Because possession of a sample enables one to make judgments about the scope, contents, format, and overall value of a serial, recent issues should be obtained before actually making subscription decisions.[39] Samples can be obtained easily from the publisher, often at no charge. Moreover, since even the most comprehensive library deals with only a limited number of proposed new subscriptions, the requirement that a sample be secured is not an unfair burden and may actually serve to discourage trivial requests.

Constituent and program needs, given the purpose of the library and the intellectual and informational requirements it is committed to meet, constitute the prime selection factor: all other criteria must be of secondary concern and come into play only if this fundamental consideration is satisfied.[40] Furthermore, demonstrated demand, as evidenced by hard data such as interlibrary loan requests, is superior to perceived needs.[41] Finally, the actual and perceived requirements of a particular library's community take clear precedence over such theoretical considerations as a title's bibliographic accessibility through indexes or a title's citation impact value (both of which are discussed in the next section on evaluation).

Within this framework, a library has a special obligation to make sure that all legitimate serial needs are being met at appropriate levels—and not just those of the more visible segments of its constituency. This is particularly important in public libraries, where serials are often not only considered relatively unimportant, but also selected on the basis of tradition as defined by the supposed interests of middle-class America, regardless of the user population.[42] In order to discharge this obligation adequately, it is generally necessary for collection developers to solicit requests actively.

Once the prime criterion of need is met, then many of the standard selection factors such as authority, accuracy, readability, language, and subjective judgments of quality that apply to books and other library resources come into play. In addition, as in the case of other formats, there are review tools (discussed earlier) and selection guides (to be discussed later) that provide assistance in making acquisition decisions.

In the past price played a minor part in serials collection development. However, the massive inflation of the last decade, especially in science and now business serials, has pushed subscription charges to such heights that above a certain threshold "the quality of the publication, as well as its balance and scope, turn out to be secondary to cost—unless the journal is absolutely essential."[43] A library has to be very careful with reference titles, particularly the electronic serials now coming on the market; otherwise, the excellent bibliographical access these tools provide will be cancelled out by the lack of funds to buy the indexed titles themselves. Moreover, in this age of massive price increases, the cost of serial commitments should be monitored on an ongoing basis. This can be partially accomplished by a system whereby collection developers are notified whenever a price increase goes beyond a certain percentage or a specific dollar amount in order to reevaluate the subscription in light of its new cost.[44]

There are also several essentially illegitimate considerations that may influence decisions. Selectors should never be reluctant to acquire a title just because of the presence of a great deal of advertising matter. As Katz reminds us, "American magazines are built on advertising, and those which are not, are built on high prices. Librarians can't have it both ways."[45] Except in the most extreme cases, considerations of physical format such as binding or ease of handling are also illegitimate grounds for rejecting an otherwise useful and needed title.[46]

Circulation, as measured by global subscription figures rather than use, also fails to qualify as a valid selection guideline.[47] Large circulations simply mean large sales and are not necessarily correlated with any pertinent selection criteria. Both the *National Enquirer* and the *Wall Street Journal*, for example, are among the serials with the largest circulation in this country; yet, they differ dramatically in terms of accuracy and quality. Selectors should not refuse to subscribe to a title just because it has a small circulation, especially since a major trend in serials publishing is the targeting of titles at smaller groups and special interests. In the final analysis, a library collects for a particular group of users and to support specific programs, and these needs can often be met best by a little magazine or specialized scholarly journal having only a limited circulation.

> The profession says the librarian should select material based on positive criteria. No librarian should reject for the sake of rejection. The problem comes from the librarian who sincerely believes he knows what is best for all readers. This librarian is satisfied to believe that his own attitudes are equivalent to the "proper" ones. He is likely to be the first to fight for the status quo and in good conscience deplore any magazine which threatens his sense of morality and taste. He honestly thinks, to repeat Sontag, that he knows what is best for B, and that "B isn't qualified or experienced or subtle enough," to know what is best for himself. Put another way, the avoidance of *Playboy* in many libraries is an expression of the librarian's confidence that he knows what is best for B, all six million of the Bs who read the magazine everywhere but in the library.[48]

As this passage makes clear, tradition and traditional prejudice have no place in the selection process. The widespread failure to respond to community needs, and especially the tendency to build collections of titles readers "ought" to read rather than what is wanted and needed, has been a major obstacle to the creation of effective serials holdings. While personal judgment rests at the center of collection development, selection officers must rise above personal biases and the elitist and censorious attitudes that have so strongly distorted collection building efforts in the past if they are to build responsive serials holdings.[49]

EVALUATION

The American Library Association's *Guidelines for Collection Development* specifically warns against assuming that collections are meeting needs and advises that systematic investigation is required to determine how well holdings meet a library's mission and objectives.[50] In addition to assessing the utility of library resources and the effectiveness of collection development programs, evaluation provides a basis for future planning and budget allocations. Collection evaluation can also serve the politically important function of demonstrating "to administrators that something is being done to change the 'bottomless pit' of library acquisitions budgets."[51] Finally, because the benefits are so great, serial holdings should be evaluated periodically, perhaps even every three years as Osborn recommends.[52]

The collection developer now commands a number of techniques for analyzing holdings, and this section is devoted to a discussion of the principal strategies applicable to serials. The particular approach employed depends upon what information is needed, although available time and staff usually influence choices as well. However, since each method has certain limitations, the most informative and useful evaluations will typically combine more than one approach.[53]

Before discussing evaluation strategies, the question of quantification needs to be clarified. Although librarians traditionally have put a great deal of blind faith in numbers, especially in assuming that the larger collections are ipso facto the better and that the ultimate aim of collection building is to amass the largest hoard of titles possible, one finds a great deal of hostility to the scientific uses of quantification embodied in the newer evaluation methods. This has often been simplistically reduced to a debate over quantitative versus qualitative or objective versus subjective strategies for assessing a collection. As Mosher recently pointed out, these are false dichotomies that miss the point, especially since quantitative data are not necessarily superior to impressionistic information and can also be variously interpreted. He goes on to state that the real issue revolves around judgment: that is, which evaluation strategies are best in terms of gaining the desired information, and what conclusions are to be drawn from this information. Within this context, scientific methodologies provide additional and more precise information that permits the collection developer to make better-informed and less capriciously subjective decisions.[54]

List Checking

Checking a library's holdings against standard selection guides, periodical indexes, bibliographies, and the serial lists of other institutions is a widely used method of evaluation. If a library holds a high percentage of the listed titles, then it presumably is providing a good level of serial support, although it is not known exactly what percentage translates into a good collection. Depending on the type of list employed, this evaluation strategy can also be used to determine the quality of serial holdings. List checking has the further advantage of being an easy procedure to conduct.

On the other hand, this evaluation method has been criticized on the grounds that any such compilation is highly arbitrary and fails to give the library credit for the titles it has that are "almost as good" as those on the list, that the list might not be appropriate to the institution, that the quality of the publications is not fully taken into account, and that the compilation may be outdated. Any discussion of these criticisms must begin with the realization that significant quantitative differences exist between the universes of serial and book titles. While the quantity of books in such major fields as economic history or personnel management is large, with a great many new works appearing each year, the number of current serials in these subjects is comparatively limited, and the titles themselves are fairly constant from year to year. As a result, the use of lists to evaluate serials holdings can avoid many of the pitfalls and limitations inherent when this method is applied to book collections.

In the first place, while selective lists of books can only include a tiny fraction of the total population, those for serials can reflect a proportionately larger and more representative sample, if not the entire world of current titles in a given area. As a result, list-checking methodologies applied to serials tend to be less arbitrary, and failure to give a library credit for titles held but not on the list is likely to be less of a problem.

Second, the smaller universe of titles makes it easier to come up with an appropriate evaluation list for serials holdings, even if this entails the construction of one specifically tailored to a given library. This last course of action, which is considered to be a more effective means of evaluation than relying on standard lists, is usually prohibitively expensive in the case of books.[55]

Third, the much smaller number of serial titles makes it easier to control for quality than in the case of evaluation lists for books. Indeed, a selector is far more likely to be familiar with a list of serials than one of books, while the smaller universe of the former makes it possible for the collection development officer to examine each serial personally to determine its quality and relevance to a particular library.

Fourth, as Broadus points out, "The relative constancy of each periodical means that lists of recommended titles are effective for a longer period of time than are guides to the best books."[56] In fact, not only do serials evaluation lists become dated less rapidly than those for other library materials, but some, such as indexes, are by their very nature up-to-date, since serials evaluation almost invariably deals with current titles.

Although list checking is an extremely useful approach to serials evaluation, it demands a great deal of judgment and discrimination. Before beginning such a project, one must thoroughly evaluate the list to be used, especially in terms of its appropriateness to a given library. After finishing, the results of list checking will require additional interpretation on the part of the selector. The titles identified as not being in a library's collection represent but a pool of potential subscriptions, all of which will have to be individually judged by critical selection standards.

While the numbers of standard guides, periodical indexes, bibliographies, and library serial lists are great, there are now several general guides to basic serials as well as sources for identifying indexing and abstracting services that are sufficiently important to merit specific mention.

General Guides

> Katz, Bill and Berry G. Richards. *Magazines for Libraries: For the General Reader and School, Junior College, College, University, Public Libraries*. 3rd ed. New York: Bowker, 1978.

An authoritative guide, this tool covers approximately 6,500 recommended titles in all subject areas. It includes both general, nonspecialist titles as well as major English-language research journals, balancing the needs of the researcher and of the layman.

The periodicals are grouped into 107 topical categories and then arranged alphabetically by title. Each entry includes title, date founded, frequency, price, editor, publisher and address, information on illustrations, indexes and advertising, circulation, availability of free samples, date volume ends, an indication if refereed, microform availability, indexing information, number and type of book reviews in each issue, and an indication of the audience or type of library for which it is intended. Subjective but generally sound judgments about the value of most of the titles are provided. There is an index of titles and subject cross references in the back.

> Marshall, Joan K., comp. *Serials for Libraries: An Annotated Guide to Continuations, Annuals, Yearbooks, Almanacs, Transactions, Proceedings, Directories, Services*. Santa Barbara, Ca.: ABC-Clio; New York: Neal/Schuman Publisher, 1979.

This is an authoritative companion volume to *Magazines for Libraries* and provides information on approximately 2,000 serials, excluding periodicals, newspapers, and monographic series. It concentrates on the more general English-language titles available in the United States, giving only limited coverage to foreign language serials and titles of interest primarily to research and special libraries.

The serials are grouped into 80 topical categories and then arranged alphabetically by main entry. Each annotation includes title, former title(s), ISSN, date begun, frequency, information on bibliographies, indexes and illustrations, publisher and address, distributor (if different) and address, issue examined, price, audience level, and indexing information. There are author/title and subject indexes in the back.

> Farber, Evan Ira. *Classified List of Periodicals for the College Library.* 5th ed., rev. and enl. Westwood, Mass.: Faxon, 1972.

This is a high quality selection guide for the liberal arts college library. It covers basic periodicals needed to support the undergraduate curriculum and provide general reading as well as titles that permit faculty to keep up with their fields. The serials are grouped into 39 subject categories, and each entry includes title, basic bibliographical information, subscription price, annotations on scope and contents, indexing and abstracting information, and LC card number. There is a title index in the back. This work is supplemented by the reviews of periodicals appearing in *Choice*.

> Richardson, Selma K. *Periodicals for School Media Programs.* Chicago: American Library Association, 1977.

Periodicals for School Media Programs is an important guide to over 500 magazines, indexes, and newspapers useful for satisfying the curricular and leisure reading needs of students in most schools. The titles cover a wide range of reading abilities and areas of interest and include serials appropriate for all grade levels. The entries are arranged alphabetically by title and include publisher and address, suggested grade levels, frequency, subscription price for schools, a descriptive and evaluative annotation, and information on where indexed. There is a subject index in the back. Like the Farber work described above, this selection guide is also useful to public libraries.

Indexes

The use of indexes as guides to serials selection and as a means of evaluation has a long history and has profoundly influenced the development of serial holdings. Librarians have traditionally considered coverage of a title by an indexing or abstracting service to be an indication not only of quality but also of potential usefulness and have made indexed serials a top acquisitions priority.[57] The explosion in the number of indexing and abstracting tools, however, has seriously diminished the validity of these assumptions. The number and percentage of serials now indexed in one or more sources has grown immensely, leaving relatively few titles bibliographically inaccessible.[58] Furthermore, this phenomenon, coupled with the encyclopedic coverage of some indexes, especially in such fields as biology, chemistry, and medicine, has long since ceased to make coverage by an indexing or abstracting service a mark of quality.[59] While indexing and abstracting tools remain useful in serials selection and evaluation, exclusive reliance on them should be avoided.

There are presently thousands of serials indexing and abstracting services, and the determination of which ones exist for a given subject constitutes the initial step in the employment of this evaluation methodology. While a great number of subject specific reference guides to indexes and abstracting services are available, there are two general sources that all collection developers should be familiar with:

> Harzfeld, Lois A. *Periodical Indexes in the Social Sciences and Humanities: A Subject Guide*. Metuchen, N. J.: Scarecrow, 1978.

This is a guide to the major indexes, abstracting services, serial bibliographies, and library catalogs providing coverage of the periodical literature in all areas of the social sciences and humanities. The tools are grouped into 48 subject categories, and each is fully annotated in terms of scope, coverage, and arrangement. An index in the back lists titles, authors, compilers, and the names of institutions publishing or sponsoring the tools included.

> Owen, Delores B. and Marguerite Hanchey. *Abstracts and Indexes in Science and Technology: A Descriptive Guide*. Metuchen, N. J.: Scarecrow, 1974.

Similiar to Harzfeld, this work provides information on 125 basic indexing and abstracting services for approximately a dozen major science and technology areas. Both tools need to be updated to include the database services that are now available.

These guides are selective and concentrate on the principal English-language indexing and abstracting services. For more complete coverage, one should consult *Ulrich's International Periodicals Directory* and *Irregular Serials and Annuals*. A special feature of these two works is the subheading "Abstracting, Bibliographies, Statistics" at the beginning of each major subject group of serials, which makes it easy to identify relevant indexes and abstracting services.

Citation Analysis

While bibliographic accessibility through indexes can provide an indication of a title's potential utility, research shows that users tend to rely more on direct bibliographic citations to locate relevant serial literature.[60] It has also been established that a relatively small portion of the serials in any given area accounts for a disproportionately large share of all citations, especially in the sciences.[61] Taking advantage of user behavior and bibliographic clustering, citation analysis measures the significance of a serial by counting the number of times it is mentioned in footnotes and bibliographies.

The major attraction of citation analysis, then, is its ability to identify current interests and the core and peripheral titles needed to support them. In addition to providing information that can be used to isolate the most frequently cited titles and to construct core lists of serials, this method of collection evaluation also produces data on the temporal aspects of use that are helpful in terms of backrun acquisition and retention. The general availability of citation analysis lists, especially the computer-generated commercial varieties such as the annual citation impact reports put out by the Institute for Scientific Information, as well as the ease of checking such lists have made this a popular method of serials evaluation.

At the same time, the utility of general citation studies and ranked serials lists produced at other institutions has been attacked on the grounds that only locally collected data is truly valid.[62] Citation analyses based on specific user populations avoid this objection, and the computerized databases now available make such lists easy to construct. Indeed, at least one major vendor now offers a special collection development service whereby all the citations produced through database searches are captured, tabulated, and reported by means of ranked serials lists on a semi-annual and annual basis.[63]

Beyond the consideration of biases such as self-citation, co-citation, citation densities, and obsolescence rates, one must keep in mind that this evaluation strategy is most useful when dealing with research serials, where reading is generally purposive.[64] This, in turn, is linked to the fact that although citation analysis is a powerful evaluation technique, it can provide only a partial determination of user needs, since more materials are used than cited.[65] In conclusion, despite the controversy over the validity and utility of this means of serials evaluation, a recent survey of the literature states that "it would seem fair to say that the reliability of citation analysis compares favorably with the reliability of other methods which may be used to make decisions in collection building."[66]

Circulation and Use

In his work on evaluating library services, Lancaster concludes that use represents the supreme test of the quality and utility of an institution's holdings.[67] Use is not only one of the best surrogate measurements of need, but it also constitutes the most accurate means of predicting which titles will be consulted in the future.[68] Statistics on serials use are particularly desirable to gather, because study after study has demonstrated that a very small portion of a library's titles generates the overwhelming majority of use, with 20 percent of the serials typically supplying 80 percent of the use.[69] The financial pressures generated by the serials dynamics outlined at the beginning of this chapter make it more imperative than ever that librarians begin to measure the amount and mode of serials use. Indeed, it is hard to see how the carefully controlled and highly effective serials collections everyone claims to want can be created without adequate knowledge of what readers actually need and use.[70]

Serials use studies are an attractive evaluation method, not only because they relate directly to reader needs, but also because the statistics themselves are generally easy to gather, widely understood, and by their very nature comparative. Flaws in research design, however, constitute the major danger in undertaking any use study, and it is especially important to define exactly what is being measured and how it will be done if the statistics are to have genuine validity.[71]

A major criticism leveled at both use and citation studies is that they simply do not provide sufficient practical guidance. While it is important for a selector to know what titles are heavily used or cited, it would be more useful to have this information in relation to such key factors as subscription price.[72] The desirability of expanding use studies to include such data has been underlined by two recent works, which demonstrate that an analysis of serials use in relation to cost produces very different results from one based solely on use.[73] Since collection developers must live within definite—and often inadequate—serials budgets, such information is vital in building the most effective holdings with a limited amount of money.

Although use studies represent an important means of evaluation, this is a strictly quantitative methodology, one that does not take into account the quality or level of use. In addition, while circulation and use data can be helpful in determining which subscriptions to continue and which to cancel, they will not provide information on how many serials should be acquired.[74] Finally, this evaluation strategy is, by definition, limited to titles a library already has and, therefore, fails to provide information on serials that should be added.

Interlibrary Loan Analysis

Analysis of the materials requested on interlibrary loan can serve as a supplementary means of serials collection evaluation, particularly if employed in conjunction with an overall use study. In addition to representing a simple, economical, and ongoing means of serials assessment, it provides specific information on user needs not readily available else-where. Interlibrary loan analysis not only identifies titles required by users that are not in an institution's collection, but it can also indicate whole areas which are less well served by holdings.[75] Moreover, if statistics are kept on the ages of serials requested, the data can be used as a guide to backrun acquisitions.[76]

As always, the key practical question facing a selector revolves around interpretation of evaluation results: that is, at what point do the data on interlibrary loans justify entering a subscription to a serial title. Studies consistently indicate that as a general rule it is more economical to rely on interlibrary loan services if there are fewer than five requests per year for a title.[77] Excessive reliance on interlibrary loan may not only be uneconomical, but can also result in violation of the fair use guidelines under the new copyright law. Yet, when it comes to judging a specific serial, the cost effectiveness equation must be modified by local economic variables, actual subscription price, and any cooperative collection development or interlibrary loan arrangements.

An institution's philosophy of service and level of funding also profoundly influence the interpretation of any type of serials evaluation. Major research libraries, for example, are expected to meet the vast majority of potential needs and are theoretically funded at a level appropriate to satisfy those needs, even though studies indicate that nearly three-fourths of their journals fall below the critical threshold of five uses per annum.[78] Furthermore, all collection development decisions must go beyond merely the results of serials evaluation and consider user behavior. These quantitative models all assume that serials use is purposive. While this may be true in the sciences and technology, it is probably a less valid assumption in the humanities and social sciences, where the nature of research and generally poorer bibliographical access tools make browsing a virtual necessity.[79] More specifically, models of the cost effectiveness of interlibrary loan versus ownership do not assess user frustration and assume that all users are willing to request the material from elsewhere, even though this is not always the case. In fact, certain major populations, such as users in business and the social sciences as well as students, show a marked reluctance to take advantage of interlibrary loan.

Resources Delivery Tests

As libraries become increasingly dependent upon cooperative acquisition and interlibrary loan arrangements for the provision of the less used and more specialized titles, resources delivery tests are growing in popularity as an approach to serials evaluation. This method typically involves compiling a list of relevant materials in a particular subject area, checking to see if the items are held by the library and on the shelves, and, if lacking, measuring how long it takes to get the them from elsewhere. Such an evaluation strategy has the advantages of measuring not only local holdings but also remote resources and the related services needed to make them available. Although this means of evaluation is biased toward titles used in research, its chief limitation is the amount of staff time required. Moreover, the results of such a study are meaningful only when they can be compared against the performances of other libraries or units of the same library.

Comparative Size and Expenditure Statistics

Comparisons of the number of serial titles and/or the amount of money spent on them in terms of both absolute size and rate of growth constitute another major method of evaluation.[81] While such comparative compilations with carefully chosen libraries provide quick, precise, and significant evaluation information if the areas of measurement are clearly defined, this strategy alone will not provide data on how well a particular institution is meeting user needs.[82]

User Opinions

Although demonstrated needs in the form of hard data such as circulation statistics and interlibrary loans are preferable, user perceptions can also be effectively employed to evaluate serials collections. However, while discrete user suggestions can be valuable in the selection of individual titles, these opinions must be systematically surveyed in order to provide accurate and representative assessments for purposes of evaluation.[83]

User opinion as an evaluation methodology has the advantage of representing a direct assessment of needs and being a practical option in almost all types of libraries. It can also be the most politically acceptable method in the case of academic and special libraries, especially when serial commitments are being reduced.[84] However, user opinions may be subjective, uninformed, and narrowly focused. In fact, surveys of faculty opinions in academic libraries are almost always inadequate because interdisciplinary and general titles as well as the serials most heavily used by students are invariably slighted. This strategy can also be quite expensive in terms of staff time and administrative costs, although it represents a one-time investment, whereas any cancelled titles constitute recurrent savings.[85] This method of evaluation is perhaps most useful as a first step, to be followed and augmented by other types of evaluation.[86]

Direct Examination

Direct examination of serials holdings, although quick and easily performed in any library, remains an imprecise and impressionistic method of evaluation. Though a knowledgeable and alert collection development officer can learn much through direct examination, this strategy is probably best employed as a preliminary technique to help determine what other types of evaluation should be used in order to gain more accurate and detailed information.[87]

Formulas and Standards

Although generally included in discussions of evaluation, the formulas and standards now in existence are almost always useless for assessing serials collections. In the first place, the theoretical and empirical bases used to generate their quantitative recommendations are not generally founded on solid research, and, as a consequence, even some of the most widely accepted models have not been confirmed by independent economic analyses.[88] Second, these formulas and standards typically have been concerned with book holdings and have not paid adequate attention to serials. As a result, even such widely used models as Clapp-Jordan have been shown to seriously underestimate serials needs on the order of magnitude of 100 to 400 percent.[89] Third, the dynamics of serials growth, especially as these resources become more important and consume an ever larger portion of total expenditures, make existing formulas and standards more inadequate than ever before. Fourth, there is always the danger that the minimal recommendations of these models will be considered as optimum levels, resulting in poorer holdings than before.[90]

These, then, are the major methods of evaluating serials holdings. No one approach is necessarily better than any other; rather, the most appropriate technique depends on what information is needed. Moreover, since each strategy has limitations, the most useful evaluation typically will combine more than one approach. The information gained, in turn, should influence future selection decisions. Finally, although much space has been devoted to a discussion of the merits and limitations of various methodologies, one must not overlook the fact that from beginning to end—that is, from the choice of an approach to the interpretation of its results—informed, professional judgment rests at the core of evaluation and is the key factor in the entire collection development process.

ACKNOWLEDGMENTS

Special thanks go to Robert Broadus, Patricia Dominguez, Joan Hubbard, Willy Owen, John Rutledge, and Marcia Tuttle for taking the time to read and criticize earlier versions of this chapter.

NOTES AND REFERENCES

1. See, for example, Siegfried Feller, "Developing the Serials Collection," in *Collection Development in Libraries: A Treatise*, eds. Robert D. Stueart and George B. Miller, Jr. (Greenwich, Conn: JAI Press, 1980), pt. B, p. 497; and Andrew D. Osborn, *Serial Publications: Their Place and Treatment in Libraries*, 3rd ed. (Chicago: American Library Association, 1980), pp. 55-56.

2. With nearly 105,000 titles, the University of California at Berkeley has the largest number of serials—and even this impressive figure represents a jump of nearly 2,600 titles over just the previous year. Association of Research Libraries, *ARL Statistics, 1980/81* (Washington, D.C.: The Association, 1981), p. 36.

3. King Research, Inc., *The Journal in Scientific Communication: The Roles of Authors, Publishers, Libraries, and Readers in a Vital System* (Washington, D. C.: National Science Foundation, 1979), pp. 9 and 11. This growth rate has been typical for both U. S. and foreign serials, although during the last few years American growth has been slightly below the world average.

4. Osborn, *Serial*, p. 35.

5. King, *Journal*, pp. 28 and 106. Even the scholarly press segment of serials publishing is quite sound. See National Enquiry into Scholarly Communication, *Scholarly Communication: The Report of the National Enquiry* (Baltimore: Johns Hopkins University Press, 1979), p. 4.

6. For short sketches of what this world of electronic serials publishing might look like, see especially King, *Journal*, pp. 53-56; and Thomas Hickey, "The Journal in the Year 2000," *Wilson Library Bulletin* 56 (1981): 256-60.

7. King, *Journal*, pp. 11 and 124; National Enquiry, *Report*, p. 55. The impact of commercial firms on the soaring subscription rates should not be underestimated, especially as sales representatives freely admit that their companies make the larger profits from serial rather than book operations, with the latter sometimes barely breaking even.

8. Norman B. Brown and Jane Phillips, "Price Indexes for 1981: U. S. Periodicals and Serial Services," *Library Journal* 106 (1981): 1388.

9. Whereas the non-serial expenditures of research libraries rose by an average of 4.2 percent per annum for the period 1975/76-1980/81, their serials costs soared by 13.8 percent annually during the same period. *ARL Statistics, 1980/81*, p. 5.

10. King, *Journal*, p. 45; Rose Mary Magrill and Mona East, "Collection Development in Large University Libraries," *Advances in Librarianship* 8 (1978): 25; National Enquiry, *Report*, p. 137; Charles B. Osburn, *Academic Research and Library Resources: Changing Patterns in America* (Westport, Conn.: Greenwood Press, 1979), p. 114; and Herbert White, "Strategies and Alternatives in Dealing with the Serials Management Budget," conference paper cited in Coy L. Harmon, "The Impact of Serials on Collection Development: A Report on the Conference Proceedings," *Library Acquisitions: Practice and Theory* 5 (1981): 97. Once again, the most dramatic shift has occurred in research libraries, where the percentage of the acquisitions budget allocated to serials has increased from 46 percent in 1975/76 to 58 percent in 1980/81. *ARL Statistics, 1980/81*, p. 6.

11. King, *Journal*, p. 124; Magrill and East, "Collection," p. 23; Osborn, *Serial*, p. 451;

Osburn, *Academic*, pp. 126-27; and Gordon R. Williams, "The Function and Methods of Libraries in the Diffusion of Knowledge," *Library Quarterly* 50, no. 1 (January 1980), p. 69.

12. Robert N. Broadus, *Selecting Materials for Libraries*, 2nd ed. (New York: H. W. Wilson Company, 1981), p. 157; Donald Davinson, *The Periodicals Collection*, rev. and enl. ed. (London: Andre Deutsch, 1978), p. 163; Bill Katz, *Magazine Selection: How to Build a Community-Oriented Collection* (New York: Bowker, 1971), pp. 5, 8, and 13; Osborn, *Serial*, pp. 49 and 51-52; and Osburn, *Academic*, p. 91.

13. National Enquiry, *Report*, pp. 37 and 43-44. This shift is especially marked in the case of historians, who not only display a growing serial orientation but also "rank inadequate library journal collections among the major communication problems they face as scholars." National Enquiry, *Report*, p. 134. In fact, a recent study indicates that historians use serials almost as much as books. Margaret F. Stieg, "The Information Needs of Historians," *College and Research Libraries* 42 (1981): 549-60, especially Table 3.

14. Katz, *Magazine*, p. 7.

15. Robert N. Broadus, "Use Studies of Library Collections," *Library Resources and Technical Services* 24 (1980): 318; Davinson, *Periodicals*, p. 165; Allen Kent et al., *Use of Library Materials: The University of Pittsburgh Study* (New York: Marcel Dekker, 1979), pp. 2, 57, and *passim*; and King, *Journal*, pp. 49-50.

16. This view is quite standard. See, for example, Robert N. Broadus, *Selecting Materials for Libraries* (New York: H. W. Wilson, 1973), pp. 6 and 11; and Mary Duncan Carter, Wallace John Bonk, and Rose Mary Magrill, *Building Library Collections*, 4th ed. (Metuchen, N. J.: Scarecrow Press, 1974), p. 13. In fact, what is acquired and cataloged at even the Library of Congress is strongly influenced by changing national priorities.

17. Osburn, *Academic*, p. 110. See also pp. 108, 111, 123, and Chapter 4 generally.

18. Katz, *Magazine*, pp. 13-14, 127, and *passim*.

19. Davinson, *Periodicals*, pp. 163 and 169.

20. Paul H. Mosher, "Collection Evaluation or Analysis: Matching Library Acquisitions to Library Needs," in *Collection Development in Libraries: A Treatise*, eds. Robert D. Stueart and George B. Miller, Jr. (Greenwich, Conn: JAI Press, 1980), pt. B, p. 527.

21. Robin Downes, "User Surveys and Development of Journal Collections," conference paper cited in Coy L. Harmon, "The Impact of Serials on Collection Development: A Report on the Conference Proceedings," *Library Acquisitions: Practice and Theory* 5 (1981): 95; Osburn, *Academic*, p. 129; and Williams, "Function," pp. 69-70.

22. Osburn, *Academic*, p. 107.

23. Feller, "Developing," p. 514; Katz, *Magazine*, p. 48; National Enquiry, *Report*, pp. 11 and 21-22; Osburn, *Academic*, pp. 126 and 149; and White, "Strategies," p. 97.

24. Paul H. Mosher, "Collection Evaluation in Research Libraries: The Search for Quality, Consistency, and System in Collection Development," *Library Resources and Technical Services* 23, (Winter 1979), pp. 16-32.

25. Williams, "Function," pp. 69-71. See also Katz, *Magazine*, p. 8.

26. Katz, *Magazine*, p. 141.

27. Wilmer H. Baatz, "Collection Development in 19 Libraries of the Association of Research Libraries," *Library Acquisitions: Practice and Theory* 2 (1978): 92.

28. Feller, "Developing," p. 504; and Katz, *Magazine*, pp. 5 and 8.

29. Davinson, *Periodicals*, pp. 171-72.

30. Osborn, *Serial*, p. 79.

31. Taking a sample of 25 current serial titles from the *Guide to Microforms in Print*, Suzanne Chaney found that *Ulrich's* indicated microform availability for only 31 percent. "*Ulrich's* References to Microform Availability," *RQ* 21, no. 1 (Fall 1981): 70-71.

32. Support for formal statements seems to be very strong, e. g., American Library Association, Resources and Technical Services Division, Collection Development Commit-

tee, *Guidelines for Collection Development*, ed. David L. Perkins (Chicago: American Library Association, 1979), pp. 2 and 5.

33. "Journal Use Per Monetary Unit: A Reanalysis of Use Data," *Library Acquisitions: Practice and Theory* 3 (1979): 98.

34. Davinson, *Periodicals*, p. 173.

35. Katz, *Magazine*, pp. 43-44.

36. Clara D. Brown and Lynn S. Smith, *Serials: Past, Present and Future*, 2nd rev. ed. (Birmingham, Ala.: EBSCO Industries, 1980), p. 80; and Katz, *Magazine*, p. 31.

37. Brown and Smith, *Serials*, p. 80; Davinson, *Periodicals*, p. 172; and Osborn, *Serial*, p. 80.

38. Davinson, *Periodicals*, p. 172.

39. Broadus, *Selecting*, 2nd ed., pp. 158-59; and Osborn, *Serial*, p. 89.

40. This view is quite standard, e. g., Carter, Bonk, and Magrill, *Building*, pp. 1-2. It has been most forcefully asserted for serials by Katz in *Magazine*, pp. 43-44 and *passim*, and most recently reiterated by Edward S. Warner and Anita L. Anker in "Faculty Perceived Needs for Serial Titles: Measurement for Purposes of Collection Development and Management," *Serials Librarian* 4 (1980): 295.

41. For an extended discussion of the relationship of library collection and service configurations to demonstrated and perceived needs, see Edward S. Warner, "Constituency Needs as Determinants of Library Collection and Service Configurations," *Drexel Library Quarterly* 13, no. 3 (1977): 44-51. See also Warner and Anker, "Faculty," pp. 296 and 300; and Edward S. Warner and Anita L. Anker, "Utilizing Library Constituents' Perceived Needs in Allocating Journal Costs," *Journal of the American Society for Information Science* 30 (1979): 326 and 328-29. On the other hand, in another article Warner acknowledges that "data representing constituents' perceived needs, particularly if taken together with data evidencing demonstrated needs, when applied to collection development decision making begins to reveal a 'critical mass' of titles tailored to constituency needs." "The Impact of Interlibrary Access to Periodicals on Subscription Continuation/Cancellation Decision Making," *Journal of the American Society for Information Science* 32 (1981): 95.

42. Katz, *Magazine*, pp. 7, 13-14, 43-44, and 141. As he goes on to state, "The best of all types of magazines must be considered, not simply the best of the coffee table fare of the split-level suburban family." *Magazine*, p. 40.

43. Bill Katz and Berry G. Richards, *Magazines for Libraries: For the General Reader and School, Junior College, College, University, Public Libraries*, 3rd ed. (New York: Bowker, 1978), p. viii. See also Katz, *Magazine*, pp. 28-29.

44. Feller, "Developing," p. 520.

45. Katz, *Magazine*, p. 30.

46. Katz, *Magazine*, p. 30.

47. Katz, *Magazine*, p. 31.

48. Katz, *Magazine*, pp. 84-85.

49. See especially Katz, *Magazine*, pp. 5, 27-28, 36-37, and 39.

50. ALA, *Guidelines*, pp. 9-10.

51. Mosher, "Collection. . .Search," p. 17. See also Jane E. Fowler, "Managing Periodicals by Committee," *Journal of Academic Librarianship* 2 (1976): 233.

52. Osborn, *Serial*, p. 97.

53. ALA, *Guidelines*, p. 10; Mosher, "Collection. . .Matching," p. 531; and Osburn, *Academic*, pp. 146-47.

54. Mosher, "Collection. . .Matching," pp. 530-31; and Mosher, "Collection. . .Search," p. 23. See also Warner, "Constituency," pp. 46 and 48-49.

55. Cynthia Comer, "List-Checking as a Method for Evaluating Library Collections," *Collection Building: Studies in the Development and Effective Use of Library Resources* 3, no. 3 (1981): 29.

56. Broadus, *Selecting*, 2nd ed., p. 159.

57. Broadus, *Selecting*, 2nd ed., p. 160; Carter, *Building*, p. 149; Davinson, *Periodicals*, p. 173; and Osborn, *Serial*, p. 84.

58. Katz, *Magazine*, p. 28.

59. Feller, "Developing," p. 513.

60. Robert N. Broadus, "The Applications of Citation Analysis to Library Collection Building," *Advances in Librarianship* 7 (1977): 307.

61. An extreme example of this clustering is provided by Martyn and Gilchrist's work on British scientific serials, in which they found that 95 percent of the important citations are encompassed by less than 9 percent of the periodicals, and that if a library were content to provide access to only 90 percent of the important citations, this core could be further reduced by a third. Cited in Davinson, *Periodicals*, p. 42. Moreover, Eugene Garfield has estimated "that a combination of the literature of individual disciplines and specialties produces a multidisciplinary core for all of science comprising no more than 1000 journals." "Citation Analysis as a Tool in Journal Evaluation," *Science* 178 (3 November 1972): 476.

62. See especially Maurice B. Line, "Rank Lists Based on Citations and Library Uses as Indicators of Journal Usage in Individual Libraries," *Collection Management* 2 (1978): 313-14; and Maurice B. Line and Alexander Sandison, "Practical Interpretation of Citation and Library Use Studies," *College and Research Libraries* 36 (1975): 393 and 396.

63. For a report on this service and how it can be used in the social sciences, see Celia S. Ellingson and Lori A. Hedstrom, Using Online Databases as a Tool for Collection Development, BRS Brief Paper, no. 15, Mimeographed [Scotia, N. Y.: Bibliographic Retrieval Services], 1981. On the use of database citation statistics in the evaluation of science serials collections, see Barbara A. Rice, "Bibliographic Data Bases in Collection Development," *Collection Management* 3 (Winter 1979): 285-95.

64. Broadus, "Advances," p. 315; Shirley A. Fitzgibbons, "Citation Analysis in the Social Sciences," in *Collection Development in Libraries: A Treatise*, eds. Robert D. Stueart and George B. Miller, Jr. (Greenwich, Conn.: JAI Press), pt. B, p. 321; and Garfield, "Citation," p. 476.

65. Fitzgibbons, "Citation," p. 320; Robert Goehlert, "Periodical Use in an Academic Library," *Special Libraries* 69 (1978): 54-56; Paul H. Mosher, "Managing Library Collections: The Process of Review and Pruning," in *Collection Development in Libraries: A Treatise*, eds. Robert D. Stueart and George B. Miller, Jr. (Greenwich, Conn.: JAI Press, 1980), pt. A, p. 175; and William A. Satariano, "Journal Use in Sociology: Citation Analysis Versus Readership Patterns," *Library Quarterly* 48 (1978): 297-99. For a dissenting view, see Elizabeth Pan, "Journal Citation as a Predictor of Journal Usage in Libraries," *Collection Management* 2 (1978): 31 and 33.

66. Broadus, "Applications," p. 322.

67. F. W. Lancaster, *The Measurement and Evaluation of Library Services* (Washington, D.C.: Information Resources Press, 1977), p. 178.

68. Broadus, "Use," p. 320; and Mosher, "Managing," p. 174.

69. Davinson, *Periodicals*, pp. 165-66; and Lancaster, *Measurement*, p. 183.

70. The importance of this was recognized by the National Enquiry, which concluded that libraries "need to be discriminating in their subscriptions, basing decisions on studies of journal usage." *Report*, p. 11.

71. A number of the more important studies of serials use, especially in terms of methodology, are included in the Annotated Bibliography at the end of this book.

72. Line and Sandison, "Practical," p. 394-96; Goehlert, "Journal," p. 91; and Kent, *Use*, p. 71.

73. See Goehlert, "Journal," pp. 93-95 and 97, especially Tables 2 and 4; and Kent, *Use*, pp. 116-23.

74. Goehlert, "Journal," p. 97. This is not a minor financial consideration since studies indicate that in order to accommodate each 5 percent increase in availability above the 80 percent satisfaction level, the total number of titles subscribed to must double. Davinson, *Periodicals*, p. 166.

75. Doris B. New and Retha Zane Ott, "Interlibrary Loan Analysis as a Collection Development Tool," *Library Resources and Technical Services* 18 (1974): 275 and 282.

76. See, for example, Eugene E. Graziano, "Interlibrary Loan Analysis: Diagnostic for Scientific Serials Backfile Acquisitions," *Special Libraries* 53 (1962): 251-57.

77. Davinson, *Periodicals*, p. 166; King, *Journal*, p. 50; and New and Ott, "Interlibrary," p. 282.

78. King, *Journal*, p. 356. It is, of course, possible to argue that this level of potential needs satisfaction is so expensive and uneconomical that both the expectations and funding of research libraries should be cut back drastically.

79. Davinson, *Periodicals*, p. 167.

80. Davinson, *Periodicals*, pp. 166-67; and Patricia Stenstrom and Ruth B. McBride, "Serial Use by Social Science Faculty: A Survey," *College and Research Libraries* 40 (1979): 430.

81. Lancaster warns that both absolute size and rate of growth must be used because the latter alone can present a distorted picture. He also cites research that shows growth in absolute numbers is a more meaningful indicator of quality than percentage increase. *Measurement*, p. 168.

82. See Mosher, "Collection...Matching," p. 535.

83. Warner, "Constituency," p. 49. See especially the systematic and successful user surveys described in Fowler, "Managing," pp. 230-34 and Warner and Anker, "Faculty," pp. 295-300.

84. Warner and Anker, "Utilizing," p. 326.

85. Warner and Anker, "Faculty," p. 299.

86. See Mosher, "Collection...Matching," p. 533; and Warner and Anker, "Faculty," p. 300.

87. Mosher, "Collection...Matching," p. 534.

88. Lancaster, *Measurement*, p. 171.

89. Lancaster, *Measurement*, p. 172. See especially the charts on pp. 170 and 173.

90. See especially Lancaster's discussion of the experiences of the SUNY system with such an interpretation. *Measurement*, pp. 171-73.

Chapter 3

Acquiring the Serial Collection

Acquiring serials is a complex and exciting responsibility. The work increases and never appears to diminish; patrons abandon the library seasonally, budgets are cut, staff members resign, but still the serials come into the department to be processed. The most notable difference between serial acquisitions and monograph acquisitions is that, while a monograph order produces one easily defined piece or predetermined group of material that is requested, received, paid for, and sent on to be cataloged, the serial standing order or subscription is intended to continue until someone at the library acts to end it. The usual monograph order is a self-contained transaction that is complete when the monograph is received and paid; a serial order carelessly handled can cause repercussions for years.

A serial acquisitions librarian's position provides a continual learning experience because of the changing nature and the variety of both serials themselves and of the ways to deal with serials. Work which on the surface appears to be routine, somehow is never that. Not only do serials change, but collection policies also change, financial situations change, vendors change, means of keeping records change. There is never enough time to keep up with these changes and their documentation in the literature, or to evaluate thoroughly one's own procedures and policies. The variety of types of serials has been shown in the definitions listed in the opening pages of this book; the variety of ways of processing serials will become apparent as this chapter continues and as one reads articles listed in "Research Tools: Acquiring the Serials Collection," a section of the Annotated Bibliography. The result of serial change and variety is an unlimited number of challenges and opportunities for growth as a librarian in serial acquisitions. Those who feel that the preceding thought is overly positive should, perhaps, avoid serial acquisitions; if it is not your thing, there is nothing worse for you or the library.

In this chapter emphasis is not on "correct" procedures, but on the various factors a serial acquisitions librarian must consider in determining local procedures and on the decisions each library must make to assure effective ordering and processing of serials. "Processing" is receiving, checking in, routing, authorizing payment for, claiming, and cancelling serials. Because most libraries with serials departments still use manual, on-site check-in and are likely to do so in the foreseeable future, this chapter emphasizes manual serial records, even though some libraries are able to use one of the locally developed or turnkey automated serial processing systems. A description and evaluation of the OCLC Serials Control Subsystem appears in Chapter 7.

TYPES OF ORDERS

There is a variety of ways to obtain a desired serial. Periodicals—journals and newspapers—are usually paid in advance once a year, or every two, three, or five years if the publisher and/or local accounting system permit. In this book continuing periodical orders are designated as subscriptions. Nonperiodical serials, on the other hand, usually are paid upon receipt, whether they appear regularly or irregularly. Monographic series are nonperiodical serials, as are the annual "advances" and "progress" survey publications. In this book continuing nonperiodical serial orders are designated as standing orders. Continuations or sets—published over a period of years, but having a planned conclusion—are not true serials; they are most easily and economically acquired as serials, however, by means of a standing order.

Subscriptions and standing orders account for the majority of serial orders for a library, but sometimes there is a need for special arrangements. Besides the basic paid subscriptions and standing orders, there are other ways of acquiring serials. These orders are often the responsibility of serial acquisitions for ease in processing: a commitment is made by the library to accept certain material until the agreement is formally ended.

A membership in a society can be the most efficient, and sometimes the only, way to obtain serials published by an organization. Memberships are usually paid annually, in advance, as are subscriptions. This payment may produce not only the journal the library needs, but also newsletters, directories of members, pamphlets, ballots for choosing officers, and registration forms for the annual convention. More significantly, the membership may confer the privilege of purchasing monographic publications at reduced prices or of receiving them at no charge. The serial acquisitions librarian should make an effort to determine the scope of a membership to ensure that marginal items can be

Table 3.1. Types of Continuing Serial Orders

Type	Example	Type of Order	Characteristics
Periodical	Journal Newspaper	Subscription	Published more than once a year Regular publication Paid annually, before publication Usually collection of articles Regularity and annual payment enable some predictability regarding cost and number of pieces
Nonperiodical	Monographic Series Annual	Standing Order	Published irregularly, annually, or less frequently Paid upon receipt Not necessarily collection of articles Unpredictable, as a category, in terms of number of pieces and cost Includes titles published in frequent editions

CONTINUATIONS, OR SETS, ARE MULTI-VOLUME MONOGRAPHIC WORKS THAT HAVE ALL THE CHARACTERISTICS OF NONPERIODICAL SERIALS, EXCEPT THAT THEY HAVE A PLANNED CONCLUSION. THESE PUBLICATIONS ARE EASILY PROCESSED AS NONPERIODICAL SERIALS.

identified and procedures be set up for their disposal, and that other benefits such as members' prices may be used. Some organizations, realizing that libraries neither need nor want every mailing that goes to individual members, have devised the "library membership" which brings only the substantial publications. Such organizations are to be commended for their sensitivity to library procedures. If the library membership were publicized in the appropriate literature and by subscription agents, perhaps it it would be adopted more widely.

A pseudo-membership type of order is akin to the book club: the library must return a notice each time it does not wish to receive a publication or must select from a group of titles and notify the publisher. This procedure has no place in a serial acquisitions unit because of the risk of the library's neglecting to return the announcement on time. Serials work is full of exceptions to the routine. The "book club" type of standing order is an exception which should be avoided by a library.

Serial services, frequently updated publications where currency is essential, are another periodical-like type of publication and are particularly valuable in business administration, law, and other social sciences. Payment is annual or every two years, in advance, usually sent directly to the publisher. The material may be received weekly or daily, perhaps in looseleaf format. These services are not often included in the standard directories and price lists, but most of the large publishers of serial services, such as Commerce Clearing House, Standard and Poor's, and Prentice-Hall, have regional representatives who visit both the library and interested faculty members to solicit renewals and promote new services. The representatives receive a commission on their orders and prefer that the library deal directly with them instead of the home office. This arrangement usually works well for the library, since there is an interested local person with whom to communicate if service is interrupted or duplicated.

Many libraries have blanket orders or approval plans with publishers or vendors so they will receive automatically such classes of material as university press publications, Western European language works in particular subjects, or titles to support a special program. Under the terms of a blanket order the library accepts, with few returns, all works which its vendor selects under an agreed upon profile. In an approval plan, the library receives material with an understood right to return the portion that it does not require. Periodicals are easily excluded from these arrangements and can be acquired by the same means as other periodicals; however, annuals, sets, and numbered monographic series are likely to be received on these orders. There is more than one way for a library to process blanket order and approval plan receipts, and the one chosen may or may not involve serial acquisitions records and staff. When blanket order serials are identified elsewhere in the library and routed to the serials department, they are easily checked in and processed in the same manner as regular orders; claiming should be required infrequently if the program is working smoothly; only the payment is different, since it will probably be handled outside the serials department. On the other hand, serials received through an approval plan are likely to cause confusion when processed through serial acquisitions. The approval plan, with its right of return, is not consistent with standing order procedures, and it should be handled elsewhere in the library.

There are other types of blanket orders that are predominantly serial in nature and can be managed entirely by serial acquisitions. These include publications of international agencies, such as the Food and Agriculture Organization and the Organization of American States; those of research organizations, such as the Rand Corporation and the Brookings Institution; and depository arrangements with the Government Printing Office, the United Nations, or one's own or another state government. Before an order of this type begins to arrive—before it is placed, in fact—those library units involved must determine the appropriate means of processing the material. If it is to be held together as a special collection, such as a documents unit, perhaps shipments should be received and recorded in that section directly, with only the payment being handled by serials. Or, if it is preferable to use a single address, publications received in serials can be routed to the other section for recording of receipt without being checked in on the serial record, on the theory that duplicate check-in is superfluous. If the holding unit does not record receipt of its serials, each piece will then need to be checked in in serial acquisitions. The crucial thing is to plan in advance and in writing how the library will deal with the order before a single piece is received; otherwise that first piece is likely to be passed around until it disappears. Before long the department will be drowning in the bulk of "insignificant" publications for which frustrated patrons are expressing their need in another part of the library. A library which collects heavily in government documents will probably be better off to have all processing and service for these documents done in a central documents department or section.

A library can increase its serial holdings at reasonable cost if it can establish an intelligently administered exchange program. This may be handled entirely within the serials department, by a separate department, by a section of another department, or it may be dispersed among acquisitions and collection development personnel. Whatever the organization of exchange, periodicals and other serials coming on exchange are appropriately received by serials either through the mail or indirectly through an exchange program staff member in another unit of the library. There are two common categories of exchange programs: regular and barter. The first is a simple exchange of available publications between two libraries, with no payment of any kind required of either partner. Except for the absence of payment, these incoming materials may be processed as regular serial orders, so long as the library upholds its exchange obligation by sending to the partner what it has promised. Communication is essential in a regular exchange agreement and involves the receiving and the sending personnel in each library. One detail of this communication is the return of small cards often enclosed in material received from foreign libraries. The card is an acknowledgement of receipt and its return is both a courtesy and an assurance that the next issue will arrive. Disregarding this task may quite justly lead to the end of the exchange agreement.

The second type of exchange occurs when one library subscribes to serials that are mailed to the partner library, usually a foreign library with no funds to acquire American serials. That library in turn either subscribes to equivalent serials published in its country and has them mailed to the American library or sends titles to which it has free access. In this barter type of exchange, payment is involved, but the payment is made to a source other than the one from which the library receives compensatory material. A check-in card will serve to record serials received on this kind of exchange, and a payment card is needed for documenting payments for publications mailed to the foreign library. The outgoing material is most easily handled, from the library's perspective, if it is mailed to the foreign library by the publisher. If the serials are shipped directly to a foreign library by the publisher, the local library cannot confuse the exchange serial with its own. The purchase of a domestic title for shipment to a foreign library is a fertile area for problems, so a direct order with the publisher is preferable to an order with the library's subscription agent. Sometimes, however carefully the library has acted, there are problems of nonreceipt, and the only solution is for the local library to collect issues and volumes and reship them to the exchange partner.

In the barter exchange program good communication is even more crucial than in the regular type. Exchange records need to show complete terms of the exchange, full addresses, and cross references to related serials. This is the place to go overboard with detail in records, rather than to risk losing essential data. All specifics need not be on the receipt record, so long as there are current full records available to serial acquisitions personnel. If those records are outside the serials department and are not adequately detailed, more facts are needed on the check-in and payment records in serials. This is not a luxury!

Enlarging the library serials collection through gifts is similar to the exchange programs, but simpler. Gifts come either unsolicited or as a result of a request from the library that it be placed on the mailing list for a publication. Gift subscriptions and standing orders can be checked into the serial record in the same manner as paid orders, except that there is no payment record. Unfortunately, because of economic conditions, many publishers who had gift lists are cutting back or eliminating gifts entirely. Sometimes they inform the library, sometimes they do not. In either case, when a serials department staff member realizes that a title which has been received as a gift is available only for a price, he or she needs to notify persons responsible for collection development, so that they can decide whether to subscribe or to place a standing order, or to stop receiving the title.

Since the procedures for processing both gifts and exchanges are similar to those for paid orders, the specific ways of handling these special orders are discussed later in this chapter, along with regular subscriptions and standing orders. In all respects except payment, they are virtually identical. Details of all these special arrangements vary from library to library. The agreement may be all-encompassing, or it may be tailored by the library or the supplier to conform to certain characteristics of the library, such as the scope of its collection or the internal division of responsibility.

All the types of serial receipts discussed until now are continuing orders: the title should be received until someone acts to end it. Two kinds of serial orders are not continuing, but are one-time orders for specific items; they are similar enough to monograph orders that some libraries place them through the monograph acquisitions department. *Replacement orders* are for specific issues, volumes, or pages that have been received but were lost or damaged. *Serial backfile orders* are for issues or volumes that the library has never owned. Both types of orders (1) may be for recently published material that is easily obtainable from the publisher or a back issues dealer, (2) may be available only in a reprint edition or in microform, or (3) may be out of print, unavailable in reprint, and difficult to acquire. Work with these orders requires a different knowledge of the book trade than that for continuing orders for current serials; there is an entire network of publishers and vendors for these types of orders, and there are unique procedures for determining the best source for an order. Further, the Duplicates Exchange Union, sponsored by the Resources and Technical Services Division of the American Library Association, circulates lists of available material and supplies back issues and volumes to its member libraries. The Universal Serials and Book Exchange (USBE; formerly United States Book Exchange) is often a fruitful source for these items as well. USBE has available, at no charge, a publication titled "Your Guide to USBE Service," which is listed in the Annotated Bibliography.

WHAT TO DO WITH THE MAIL

Every day the mail comes. It comes whether anyone is around to open and distribute it. It comes on weekends and legal holidays and during school vacations. The mail must be processed accurately and promptly before it becomes an overwhelming mess. Serial acquisitions receives two types of mail: (1) packages of books or journals, most of which have been ordered and can be checked in; and (2) "letter mail," a euphemism which includes not only letters, but invoices, claim responses, ads, requests for funds, publishers' catalogs, questionnaires, contest entry blanks, and, often, communications addressed to some other part of the library, someone in another library, or someone totally unrelated to any library—especially at Christmastime. Some person must look at every piece of this mail and make a decision as to its disposal. In their book *Serials: Past, Present and Future*, Clara Brown and Lynn S. Smith have a lively chapter entitled "Mail Information," which discusses all the things that can happen to mail before it gets to the library.[1] This section concerns what happens to the mail after it has survived the hazards Brown and Smith mention.

There are decided advantages to having the nonletter mail delivered to the check-in area unopened. Addresses on wrappers can aid in resolving problems of duplicates or titles for which there are apparently no check-in records. Sometimes it seems that the local post office workers see a magazine and throw it in the library pile. It is not unheard of for a serial acquisitions department to receive properly addressed journals destined for a library across the country. Nearly every staff member has his or her version of the "University of California, Cambridge MA" garbled address! This only compounds the chance that the serial will be delivered to the wrong library. Even when both copies of a duplicate issue are addressed (and delivered) to the department, the addresses are frequently different and the mailing labels probably have different numbers at the top. These labels can be the key to a publisher's correction of the problem and should be retained when there is trouble. In both a large check-in area where the serial record is divided among several persons and a small one where a single staff member processes all incoming serials, the person who records the receipt of a title learns quickly to recognize it and to make sure that it goes to the correct destination. Longstanding problem titles, those which have taken much searching time in the past, are easily recognized when the mail is opened by check-in assistants.

Likewise, a seasoned staff member needs to review the letter mail. Experience teaches this person to distinguish between invoices and statements, ads and renewal notices, publishers' catalogs and newsletters, and it teaches him or her to realize when something is not quite right and to question and investigate. He or she develops a sense of what to throw away and what to keep, what to route to collection development and what goes to monograph acquisitions. Opening the mail does not sound like a very responsible task, but accurate sorting and evaluating of the mail requires experience and care. Curiosity is a valuable quality in any staff member, but it is especially beneficial in the one who processes letter mail.

Each serials department can reduce letter mail problems by establishing written procedures based upon local library organization and stated division of responsibility. Much of the bulk of this mail is ads—ads for journals, series, monographs, audiovisuals, conventions, automobile seat covers, and worse. What can be thrown away at once? And where is the rest routed? If there are duplicate ads, is one discarded or is it sent to a different person than the first copy? The same staff member who evaluates the ads can decide what to do with sample copies of serials which arrive unsolicited. Is the subject matter of the piece within the scope of the library's collection? If so, which librarian or faculty member should see it?

There is often a fine line between an ad and a renewal notice. Some of both are complicated by special subscription offers, which are nearly always for arbitrary time periods, such as forty-one weeks or seventeen months. These offers, if accepted, probably cost the library more in confusion than is saved in the price, because library records are geared to regular, annual cycles, not artificial terms. If a communication from a publisher says, in effect: "Your subscription is about to expire," it probably is a renewal notice. If the library has no orders direct with the publisher, the notice can be discarded after the expiration date on the mailing label is seen to correspond to that on library records. But if there are direct orders, it is safer to have the notice examined more carefully by the proper acquisitions assistant for possible payment. If the notice arrives well after the renewal invoice has been processed for payment, it should be investigated fully.

Invoices and statements, likewise, can be practically indistinguishable. An invoice is to be paid; a statement is a record of what has been invoiced and should already have been processed for payment. But some publishers do not recognize these definitions and reverse the terms. Publishers may print "INVOICE—DO NOT PAY!" or other contradictory messages on the form that contains a figure to be paid. Whatever the communication is called, one should not ignore it. Institutional red tape delays payment several weeks, so staff members need to process invoices quickly. Statements that list outstanding invoices serve as a means of identifying unpaid charges. Partially approved invoices can get buried in a mail basket, lost at the photocopying center, or misplaced outside the serials department before the check is sent. It is unlikely that all such mishaps can be avoided, but care in evaluating and processing the mail can reduce missed payments and, thus, the patron and staff frustration that occur when serials do not arrive because the invoice has not been paid.

In summary, it pays to be overcautious when checking the mail. Communications that turn out to be extraneous can be discarded at whatever point this is verified. There will be occasions when an invoice or other notice is discarded in error, and every serial acquisitions unit will plead guilty to the emotional charges made by faculty members or other patrons unjustly deprived of research material or of the latest issue of *Playboy* or *Road and Track*. The likelihood of such a situation, even though it is an excellent learning experience, can be minimized by written procedures designed to promote careful evaluation of the mail.

SERIAL ACQUISITIONS SYSTEM: AUTOMATED OR MANUAL?

When librarians began to consider the uses they could make of computer technology, serial acquisitions appeared to be a natural area to convert from manual to automated operations: periodicals are published regularly, they are numbered consecutively, and their processing requires much routine and clerical labor. All of this is true; but any person who has worked with serials will characterize their processing not as routine, but as "fraught with irregularities!" or some equally emphatic phrase. Indeed, it is the problems and the unexpected happenings that make serials work fascinating. These same things make the intelligence and flexibility of human beings necessary to successful serial processing. None of the early automated serial check-in or serial management systems has swept the library world, although some systems, most notably those of Northwestern University Library[2] and the Biomedical Library at the University of California at Los Angeles[3] have successful local online check-in. A few networks, such as PHILSOM and OCLC, have developed somewhat satisfactory cooperative systems, which are used by a limited number of libraries. Many libraries have automated ordering and most now include searching some database as a part of their preorder processing. Computer output microform (COM) catalogs of serial holdings are in vogue now. The local database may include more than location and holdings—for instance, accounting information—and can, therefore, be considered an automated serials management system. The check-in aspect of acquisitions is so far the least successful computer application to serials work. In the 1980s it appears not to be technology that is responsible for the slow development of automated check-in systems, but the funds required and the low priority library administrators have given to this aspect of computerized library operations.

The public service function of a serial system is an area which could be revolutionized by freeing librarians from consulting the manual check-in and binding records, or better still, by providing a terminal for patrons to use in determining whether the serials they need have been received, bound or claimed. Unfortunately, most systems in use today are not yet able to extract and display public service data in a form that is meaningful to the patron. It is all or nothing, and "all" is so complex that it is unrealistic to expect patrons to recognize what they need and to interpret these data.

Automated serial check-in does exist, and an increasing number of libraries is using some version of it; but because of cost and stated priorities for most libraries, the manual, visible file will be around for many years. For this reason, most of the following discussion deals with a manual serial check-in system.

SERIAL CHECK-IN RECORD

"Central Serial Record." The term is tossed around and is universally understood by serial acquisitions personnel. Or is it? Are we all talking about the same thing? To some the central serial record contains everything the library has to say about all its serials; it is the one place to look for answers to questions about serials; it identifies each serial publication in the collection, gives specific holdings, date received, cost, source, publisher, subject, call number/location, binding specifications, historical data, and so forth. And it is "current," which in this context means "today." To other persons the central serial record is a tool that has evolved from a succession of separate files in which current serial receipts were recorded: periodicals, series, gifts, exchanges, memberships, replacements, and so on. In still other libraries the central serial record is a public card file which contains the catalog record of every serial title held by the library system, with complete holdings including multiple copies and notices of lost and replaced volumes.

The tool described in the first definition above is one that is not practical in manual format in a library of any size. The larger or more specialized the library, the more record conscious it is, and the more unwieldy this "central serial record" must be. Picture the following scene: While check-in assistants try to process the day's mail (let's make it a Monday mail), binding staff members want to prepare volumes to send to the bindery, a reference librarian needs to know where various copies of *Scientific American* are shelved, and patrons are in line waiting to look up call numbers. This is not an efficient way to run a serials department!

The final record described above is broader in scope than serial acquisitions and, as such, is not a practical means of recording receipt of parts of volumes. A public record giving such detailed information requires so much time to maintain (part of which is duplicate recording of information, since a check-in file is also needed) that it is considered expendable by most libraries and has been widely replaced by the COM catalog. The accurate, complete recording of serial receipt is so complex and difficult that the persons who are responsible for this function should not have their work space crowded with other staff members and patrons. They do not need their detailed check-in records filled with colored marks and sliding tabs which mean nothing to them but are significant to the person who carries out another serial function. Nor is it fair to make other employees' work dependent upon their ability to interrupt gracefully or catch the check-in assistant away from the serial record.

The second definition of "central serial record" describes a file that exists in many libraries. It can be a workable control over the masses of incoming serials and a means of tracking them to their ultimate locations. However, because the term "central serial record" is ambiguous, it will not be used in this chapter; instead, the file containing a library's record of serials received will be referred to as the "serial record." For most libraries, that is still a visible, manual file of five by eight inch cards commonly known as the "Kardex." "Kardex," though, is not a generic term, but the copyrighted name given by one manufacturer to its visible files.

In an automated serial system there could conceivably be a central serial record as defined in the first case above, because there are no problems of limited space on cards or people crowding around a work station. All relevant data about serial titles can be entered on one comprehensive record with access through multiple terminals designed for varying types of use—cataloging, recording receipt, public service, binding preparation. At this time, however, there does not appear to be a cost-effective automated serial management system available that will serve all these purposes for any but small libraries.

The manual serial check-in record needs to contain enough information about the standing order or subscription that the order can be identified. The amount of this information will vary with the size and complexity of the library; smaller academic and public libraries will be able to manage with fewer details than large academic and special libraries. The serial main entry—title or corporate body—is what determines where a record is filed in an alphabetically arranged check-in system, and that is what shows on a visible record. The official, cataloged main entry should be unique, so that identical titles are distinguished by publisher, place of publication, or some other identifier. In libraries where serials are not cataloged, the publisher's name and address on the check-in cards can distinguish between identical titles. The International Standard Serial Number (ISSN) is increasingly used as the means for identifying one title among the universe of serial literature. At times, notes on the record facilitate identification of the material: "pink cover," "be sure volume says 2nd edition," and so forth.

The check-in record must show certain bibliographic details, so that one can verify that a specific item has been received. Foremost among these data is numbering; the record must be flexible enough to provide for whatever numbering system the publisher has chosen to use. The most common methods of numbering serials are volume, volume and issue, sequential number, or date. All of these appear in various ways and in many languages. They can be made more comprehensible to a check-in assistant who lacks extensive language skills if there is at hand a multi-language or polyglot dictionary of terms used in the description of serials and in the book trade.[4] When a monographic series is received and entered in the serial record, it is most useful to have the card provide a space for author and title of each monograph as well as for the series number, if there is one. Then, when a patron who knows a volume only by series title and number fails to locate it in the public catalog, the serial record links serial title to the title of the individual volume.

A third category of information on the serial record is related to payment. At a minimum, this includes the source of the order (to ensure that payment is made to the proper vendor), the amount charged, the period or numbers covered by the payment, and the date on which payment was processed. It is useful to note the invoice number on the serial record, so it can be cited as documentation of payment. Use of the vendor's own identification number for the title eases communication in correspondence concerning payment or nonreceipt. Finally, if the library's budget for serials is divided by subject, or in some other way, this information is needed on the check-in record so it can be transferred to the invoice to let accounting know which fund is to be charged.

Other details about the serial and the library's order will prove useful if they can be listed on the check-in record. Some libraries enter date of receipt for all serials on the check-in card, which means the card gets filled faster than if this were omitted. Other libraries datestamp journal issues instead, which means that one must examine the piece to know when it arrived. Each practice and every variation of it has advantages and disadvantages, so a serial acquisitions librarian must decide what to sacrifice and what is needed at hand. Internal routing of serials needs to be on the card for composition of routing slips and for aid in retrieval when a piece has strayed along its route. Of increasing importance is the access number to the local record in the database. Check-in assistants may prepare some serials, such as softbound annuals, for binding; if this is the case, binding specifications need to be available on the record. It is useful if the intended frequency of the serial is noted. This may be done through words or symbols, or it may be accomplished through a method such as color coding the check-in card. Often a note on the record calling attention to some peculiarity of the serial, such as "two years late," or "return card acknowledging receipt," will prevent unnecessary claiming or other problems. Notes, such as "Issue no. inside back cover," aid in recording receipt.

All of the above seems an overwhelming amount of detail to place on one five by eight inch card, and all of it is not required in every library or for every title. However, it can and should be done if needed for accurate, speedy processing of serials and invoices. Local use of the serial record will determine what items can be omitted. For instance, if the record is used for public service as well as check-in, such data as call number, monograph title, and publisher's full address are of greater significance than if it is not.

It is important, even essential, for the serial check-in record to show payments, as well as receipts. If these two acquisition functions are not held together in the same place, it means that two records should be, but probably are not, consulted before each claim is sent and each invoice paid. This consolidation of data can be done on one card or on two cards, both of which are visible when the record is consulted. Having the two together reduces the likelihood of a title's being paid year after year, but never being received. It also alerts the claimer to request an invoice as well as current issues when a lapsed title has not been paid. A library that uses a single vendor for all, or nearly all, its orders may try using the annual invoice or a vendor-generated printout of payment records as the official verification of payment, instead of entering the data on each check-in record. If this shortcut is to be successful, the annual invoice must be examined very carefully when it arrives, to make certain that all charges are valid. When a library does not have prices of serials entered on a check-in record, price increase trends are not so easily apparent, although at least one subscription agent notes on the annual invoice those titles which are supposed to have increased in price since the previous billing.

A notation of claims placed and responses from publishers is useful for follow-up purposes and for answering questions from patrons and other library departments. In subsequent claims or claim letters, specific information lends weight to the complaint. Claiming is discussed in detail later in this chapter.

For ease of communication with patrons and other library staff members the manual serial record should contain the same form of entry as the card catalog and/or COM catalog. Consistency can be the rule if preorder searching includes verification of entry in a database such as OCLC or in a Library of Congress publication. This ensures that the entry under which a serial is ordered will be, in most instances, the entry under which it is later cataloged. Differences between the two records can be reconciled quickly if there is a procedure for communication— perhaps a special form or a copy of the catalog record—between serial cataloging and serial acquisitions, whether they are in the same department or not. This communication has become more crucial with *AACR* 2 in effect, for preorder searching turns up records cataloged under *AACR*, which are changed by the cataloger using the new rules. Consistency of entry is more important to libraries having manual files than to those having automated records because of the availability of multiple access points in computerized systems. In a manual check-in record the liberal use of cross references serves the same purpose as multiple access points to a database. Cross references enlarge a serial record, but they save time and money.

Closely related to the serial check-in file is the serial order file. It is so closely related that it can easily and efficiently be combined with the serial record by placing a copy of the new order in the visible file, attached to a card which gives minimal data—entry, copy number, and date ordered are enough; other details are on the order itself. When the first piece of a new serial arrives, it is identified as a new order from the unique card in the serial record. Either at the time of receipt of the first piece or, secondarily, at the time of cataloging, a permanent check-in record can be made. Some libraries also place a copy of each new order in the public catalog so patrons can have direct access to an order file.

The efficient check-in file contains records for current orders only. If a title is no longer received automatically as issued, the retention of its check-in card makes a very active record grow to an unnecessarily awkward size. Dormant or dead records occupy valuable, expensive space, which usually cannot be justified. However, a nearby ceased/cancelled/completed file, to which noncurrent order records are retired, is a great timesaver for identifying occasional very late and irregular problem pieces of material. The serial record is neither a source from which to determine the library's holdings of a title nor one for identifying which volumes have been bound. It is a record of receipt and payment of ordered material, not of everything the library contains of a title. The detail needed for acquisition purposes is reason enough to keep binding and complete holdings records elsewhere.

In a manual system there are other records that are useful to serial acquisitions staff members when these records are located near the serial check-in. They include:

1. A file of copies of orders in numerical arrangement, to be consulted when an invoice gives an illegible entry but includes the library's order number;

2. a source file, arranged by agent or publisher, again to be used when identifying invoice charges or entry of materials, or when transferring all orders placed with one vendor from that vendor to another;

3. a file of invoice copies, arranged by payee, to assist in identifying (from the previous year's invoice) mysterious charges; and

4. a problem file with instructions for the disposal of problem or ephemeral material.

Related to the last file is the practice of keeping a "discard card" in the serial record—it could be a plain white card with red letters—for unwanted gifts which the publisher will not stop sending. A small library or a library using a single agent will not need all of these supplementary files and, indeed, more and more of the assistance received from such records can be obtained from the database. Some day automation will make most of these adjunct files obsolete. An exception is one library's "status-change file," which contains a copy of all notifications to serial cataloging of title changes, cessations, mergers, cancellations, and so forth.

PREPARING AN ORDER TO BE PLACED

When a library places new subscriptions and standing orders, it is most efficient to determine certain facts about the serial in question before the order is sent, to (1) ensure that what is requested is what is received, (2) ensure that the title ordered is actually being published, and (3) record facts about the serial that will be useful to the cataloger. Searching and verification are the two procedures by which one determines this preorder information and records it. Each order being prepared should be represented on a separate order card or form that has adequate space for symbols and notes. This working card is best retyped before the request is mailed to the vendor, since it is likely to become marked to the point of illegibility during the preorder procedures.

Searching

When an order request arrives in serials it needs first to be searched; that is, it needs to be checked against library records to see if the title is already on order or if the library has any portion of it. There are two reasons for searching. Primarily, one wants to ascertain that there will be no inadvertent duplicate orders. If, however, the request is intentionally made for a second or third copy, the information on the new order card should be consistent with that already in the serial record and card catalog or database. If a new order is to duplicate an existing subscription or standing order, we want to know it, because this linking makes processing and cataloging more efficient. A second reason for preorder searching is its function as precataloging searching. All data that can be passed on to serial cataloging about the new title's relationship to library holdings will save time and effort.

The logical starting point for a preorder search is the serial record. If the title appears there, publisher, price, and source can be verified or added, and the searching procedure may be complete. If orders for specific issues or volumes of serials are placed by the monograph acquisitions department, that order file should be checked for duplication and for the purposes of communication. The only remaining task for additional copies is to determine whether a duplicate is needed.

In most cases the title being requested will not appear in the serial record as an active order. The next step is to check the COM catalog, serial catalog, public catalog, or database, whichever record is the official union catalog of systemwide serial holdings. The library may previously have had an order for the title or may have received some volumes of it as a gift. Part of a series may be cataloged as a monograph and not be in serial records; it can be identified from a series added entry or access point in the public catalog. If earlier volumes of the serial in question are already in the library, an indication on the order card of the call number (for all except classed separately monographic series) and holdings will speed processing when the new order begins to arrive, since the title has already been cataloged. Finally, the searcher must determine whether any part of the serial is currently on order but not yet received. If the serial record or public catalog serves as an order file for every kind of serial order, then this final step has already been taken. When one-time serial orders are placed by monograph acquisitions and not recorded in the public catalog, a search of the monograph order file is needed. If such an order is located, recording pertinent information ensures that the two orders are brought together for processing when they arrive; otherwise, the title may be cataloged twice, or part of the holdings may be cataloged while the rest sit indefinitely in the backlog.

Sometimes serials arrive at the library without having been searched, for example, gifts from patrons and material which comes as part of a membership or blanket order. These can be searched quite easily before cataloging, using the same procedure as for preorder searching. The advantage here is that the searcher has in hand a volume or an issue of the title.

Verification

After it has been determined that an order request is not a duplicate in the library system and that no part of the title is in the library or on order, the serial needs to be verified. That is, the title and publication information must be checked against an authority—at best, Library of Congress cataloging in the OCLC, RLIN, or other database, *New Serial Titles*[5] or the *Union List of Serials*[6]—to ensure that it is consistent with what has been accepted as a standard. An order needs to show not only the title, but also the place of publication and the publisher, the beginning date, the ISSN, and (for encumbering funds by accounting) the approximate price.

Much of the verification procedure for serial orders takes place today at the computer terminal. Records that have been "authenticated" by the National Serials Data Program (NSDP) at the Library of Congress (for United States publications), the National Library of Canada, or another ISDS Center, have listed in the record a key title—a title unique to that serial—and the ISSN. In most cases, this should be enough to identify the specific title one is going to order. Such a record will also supply the publisher, place, and beginning date, as well as other information necessary for cataloging, for example, subject headings and linking notes. Some very complete records even give publisher's address and price, although only a price entered recently can be accepted as accurate, since most serials increase in price each year.[7]

Many of the serial records in the OCLC database have not yet been authenticated because NSDP has not been able to keep up with the volume of records entered by the CONSER project and by local libraries. For this reason there is a good chance that the record one locates will have been entered by a CONSER participant or another American or Canadian library, but will not yet have been authenticated. Most of these records have accurate data for verification purposes, so long as they have been cataloged by successive entry and not by latest entry.[8] The major deficiency of these nonauthenticated records is the omission of information, not the presence of inaccurate data.

Should the title requested not be in the database, or should the details be insufficient for verification, one can go to the standard manual sources— the pre-1981 *National Union Catalog*[9] for Library of Congress cataloging or cataloging from a cooperating library; *New Serial Titles* or the *Union List of Serials* for records contributed to this international union catalog by major libraries; *Ulrich's International Periodicals Directory*[10] or *Irregular Serials and Annuals*,[11] Bowker's companion lists of serials; or other national or subject lists of serials, examples of which are listed in the Annotated Bibliography. Periodicals and other serials that have begun publication very recently will not have had time to appear in printed sources, so the procedure for verifying new titles may be abbreviated. Before abandoning the search, however, one may check certain vendor publications, such as the *EBSCO Bulletin of Serials Changes*,[12] which list new titles soon after they begin or even before publication.

At times during the verification process, the searcher finds information that changes the entry under which the title is to be ordered. Whenever this happens, it is necessary to re-search the title under the new main entry.

Final Preparation of Order

The final order, as sent to the vendor or publisher, should identify clearly what title the library wishes to receive, when the order is to begin, the shipping and invoicing address(es), the library's order number, and (as inconspicuously as possible) essential data for internal use, such as fund, routing, and searching history. This internal information can confuse the vendor, so separate it as clearly as possible from the bibliographic data and instructions to the agent or publisher. The best location for local use data is on the back of an order form or on a copy of the order that remains in the library.

Unless the library's serial orders are prepared by computer, there is nearly always a need to retype the order before sending it to the vendor. In the searching and verification procedures, corrections and additions will have been made, and a newly searched order is generally cluttered and confusing to everyone except the searcher. A library places comparatively few serial orders each year, so there should be time to make this effort to reduce the possibility of misinterpretation by the vendor.

Committee Z39 of the American National Standards Institute has a subcommittee working on a standard order form. It is not certain yet whether this single form will be appropriate for continuing serial orders, or whether a second standard form for serials will be needed. The publicizing, acceptance and general use of such a standard form should go far toward eliminating the misunderstandings that occur between library and vendor because of ambiguous order forms.

SUBSCRIPTION AGENT OR NOT?

The decision whether to use a subscription agent or standing order vendor as an intermediary in the purchase of serials, or to deal directly with the publisher, is one each library must make based on its own needs and priorities. This decision may be a blanket policy governing all serial orders, or it may be made for specified types of orders or for each order individually. The size and scope of the serial collection are major factors in the decision. The policy that the library follows needs to be continually evaluated as computer technology and library budgets change and as vendors and their promised services change.

Until recently, many American journal publishers gave to subscription agents discounts that were not available to libraries. The agents were able to pass on savings to the library customer. Rising costs and serial publishing practices have reduced or eliminated agency discounts. The vendor now must add a service charge to the cost of publishers' prices for the library's list of titles in order to cover his expenses and make a profit.

The service charge by American vendors is usually a percentage of the total list price of the periodicals, although some companies may make other arrangements for the highest priced titles, for example, many indexes and abstract journals. Foreign vendors have customarily included an unspecified service charge in the price for each periodical title, but they now appear to be turning to the American practice of adding a percentage to the total of list prices. Libraries ordering direct from the publisher may receive the same discount for nonperiodical serials as an agent and may simply get a lower discount when ordering through a vendor.

In this era of the necessary service charge, agents compete not only on the annual cost of subscriptions, but also on the service they give. The largest agents are extensively automated and can provide almost any information or special handling the customer wants, such as customized invoicing, management data for single or multiple years, automated off-site check-in and processing by the vendor, or union lists. How much of this service an agent will provide and how much will be done without additional cost depends largely on the company's willingness to please the customer, that is, how much the vendor wants the library's business. One agency may provide a great number of services at no charge but be unwilling to do something slightly different for a single library. Another agency may charge for certain services but be quite flexible in what it will do for an individual customer, both for a fee and at no charge.

The two largest American subscription agents, EBSCO and Faxon, publish annual catalogs of titles for which they have orders.[13] The preliminary pages to these catalogs describe the services the agencies provide their customers. Other domestic vendors issue smaller catalogs listing the most popular serials they supply. All these catalogs are useful reference tools, since they give a number of facts about the titles listed. The Faxon and EBSCO catalogs are published at different times during the year, so first one and then the other is likely to be more nearly accurate regarding price and latest title. Both are kept current by other publications: Faxon's *Serials Updating Service*[14] and the *EBSCO Bulletin of Serials Changes*. Examination of the two catalogs and their updates reveals several differences between them, such as form of entry, listing of prices, and special notes. While there is duplication between the Faxon and EBSCO catalogs, they very definitely complement each other, and both should be readily available to the serial acquisitions librarian and staff. Both Faxon and EBSCO now make their databases available online to subscribers.

Blackwell North America, a supplier of nonperiodical serials and sets, produces a monthly microfiche catalog of activity in the titles it handles. Features of the BNA listing include volumes published (with prices and dates), next volume expected, notice of completion or cessation, and frequency. Much of BNA's data is in natural language and useful for recognizing lapsed orders and dead wood in the serial record. The catalog is available at no cost to qualified customers and for a subscription fee to others. Information recorded on the BNA microfiche is reliable, but it is occasionally not current, since data are added only in the course of supplying the company's orders. Still, the reliability and detail of its contents make this catalog a valuable bibliographic tool for standing orders and a supplement to the EBSCO and Faxon catalogs or databases.

Good working relationships depend on good personal relationships. Having one person in the agent's office who is familiar with the library's account promotes a comfortable business relationship. Only one telephone call to the vendor during which no one seems to recognize the library's name, much less the account, is damaging both to the caller's ego and to the relationship with the vendor. Personal contact is the best way to assure the communication which can promote a good working relationship. Visits to the library by interested and informed sales representatives of the subscription agencies and publishers are influential in securing and increasing the amount of business a serials department does with a vendor. Sales personnel who best understand the library's concerns are those who have been practicing librarians.

Vendors adapt their procedures and services in response to the requirements of library customers, discovered during sales visits. Several years ago the F. W. Faxon Company, which had never used regional representatives, hired first one and then a number of other persons to visit serials librarians. Otto Harrassowitz, a West German agency, has not only employed its first American representative, but is also providing more and more of the services not customarily given by foreign vendors. Both of these companies responded to librarians' needs. The competition among American vendors forces them to be creative and sensitive to the needs of their customers and potential customers. This competition has recently extended to foreign titles, and is forcing nondomestic vendors to offer services previously restricted to American subscription agents.

Some libraries elect to place orders directly with the publisher instead of with one of the subscription agencies. When service charges were new, some customers objected to paying for "service" which was not apparent to them, and changed their orders to direct transactions with the publishers. Instead of paying a percentage of the serials' cost, libraries absorbed the labor, postage, checkwriting, and other costs of ordering and renewing. Busy serial check-in assistants either absorbed the work or were given additional help.

When many subscription agencies automated their records and procedures during the late 1960s and early 1970s, there was a period of adjustment for vendor, publisher, and library, while the computer programs were debugged. During this confusion, some libraries bypassed the agent and dealt with the publishers. After a few years, the automated agencies were able to offer much more efficient processing of orders and detailed management reports than in the years before computers, and many libraries returned as customers.

Both sales representatives and promotional literature mailed to libraries by the subscription agencies make claims about service that the company cannot fulfill. The promise of one annual invoice and a single payment for all serials is not realistic. Annual journal price increases are becoming the norm and the increase decision may not be made by the publisher until shortly before the new volume begins. Agencies are invoicing earlier than ever so they can earn interest on library money until they pay the publishers. These two trends ensure that the vendor will have to send the library supplementary invoices for added subscription charges.

Claiming is another area in which the subscription agent cannot always fulfill promises. The agent is an intermediary between the library and the publisher in claiming, as in ordering, and this service is one for which librarians believe they pay. But the intervention of the account representative slows the transmission of the claim to the publisher and sometimes garbles the message so that it becomes meaningless. Both the routine, computer-generated claim and the procedures to which office employees adhere may cause deletion or misinterpretation of crucial claiming information transmitted by the library. However, when a library's claim is the latest of many the agency has received for a specific issue or title, the response can be given from the database immediately without involving the publisher. In fact, the largest agencies may already have given the claim response in one of their periodical publications on serial irregularities. EBSCO and Faxon distribute the computer-generated bulletins mentioned earlier, which list both changes in serials (such as title changes, frequency changes, suspensions, and mergers) and publication delays reported to them by the publisher. Some other agencies and publishers such as Pergamon or Gordon and Breach have a similar reporting system for their customers. Much of the dissatisfaction expressed about claiming through the subscription agency could be eliminated if both parties were more careful about the claims. The library staff member can reduce the number of claims by checking the vendor publications which report delivery problems, and the customer service representative can reduce the ineffectiveness of agency claims to the publisher by paying attention to the information the library has sent about the problem. If either party feels a telephone call is needed, he or she should call. There is often reason for libraries to be dissatisfied with the overall claiming service they receive from their vendors, but there is much the library can do to ameliorate the situation.

In 1975 Bill Katz and Peter Gellatly published a book length study of librarian/subscription agent relationships, *Guide to Magazine and Serial Agents.*[15] Although the book needs to be revised to take into account the benefits of agents' sophisticated computerization, it is invaluable to both the new serials librarian who is without experience in the selection of vendors and to those who are evaluating vendor performance and assessing their policies concerning the sources of continuing orders. The book explains differences among subscription agencies and contains a rating of vendor services, based on a sample of various types of libraries. Katz and Gellatly's treatment of this topic is more detailed than this chapter can be, and it should be required reading for all serial acquisitions librarians.

When a decision has been made to place all or part of the library's serial orders with an agent or with several agents, the librarian has several choices to make, which should be formalized in written policy statements. For many libraries the ideal situation is to place all serial orders, including both subscriptions and standing orders, with one vendor, particularly if the list of orders is relatively standard and predominantly American. The only orders not placed with the agent would be those for which the publisher will not accept orders from agents, such as the H. W. Wilson Company titles. This consolidation permits the library to process the fewest number of invoices and to deal with only one agency. If the vendor's computers compile management data, that information will be more useful than if the orders are divided among several sources, since it will include nearly all of a library's current serial orders. Claims could, with few exceptions, be sent to one source.

In spite of all these positive factors there are those who say a library should not restrict itself to a single agent. That company, they believe, will come to take the library customer for granted and will cease to compete for the library's business; performance will drop and service charges will increase, because it would be an impossible task for the library to move its orders to another vendor or to place them directly. A recent article by Doris New indicates that such a change may not be as difficult for the library to effect as agents insist.[16] There is evidence that when a library serials department monitors the performance of its vendors and gives new business to the one(s) which rate highest, the agencies involved respond with improved service.

There are other, more substantive reasons for libraries, particularly research libraries, to use more than one vendor. Every agent has strengths and weaknesses, and it is to the library's advantage to recognize and use an agency's strengths. Variables to be considered are type of material (journals or nonperiodical serials), subject of material, and geographic location of the publisher. Some vendors restrict themselves to, for example, standing orders, a single language or scientific serials—whatever they do best. Many others will accept an order for any title and do their best to supply it. This is commendable, but a library with a strong collection of German or African serials should have more success with a vendor in the country of origin, or at least one specializing in that region, than with a general domestic subscription agency. The more reliable foreign agents will correspond in English, eliminating the language problem. American subscription agents often use a foreign vendor themselves, adding another step between library and publisher. The loss in scope of management data with the use of more than one vendor may not be a problem as computers become more economically feasible and more libraries develop their own automated management systems.

When a library consolidates its subscriptions and standing orders with a single, domestic vendor, it may have a lower service charge than when the agency handles only its periodicals, because the agency discount is still the rule for nonperiodical serials. Even so, there are likely to be disadvantages to the use of one vendor. Periodicals and nonperiodical serials are different types of publications with differences in pattern of appearance, and billing and fulfillment procedures. An American subscription agent, highly automated, often attempts to apply routines which are successful for periodicals to other serials, and they do not work. Irregular publications cannot be paid annually in advance, but are invoiced by the publisher to the agent and, in turn, by the agent to the library upon publication. Libraries combining subscriptions and standing orders with one vendor should prefer and should demand separate invoicing for serials. Experience and careful attention can minimize the foul-ups, but vendors have personnel turnover just as library serials departments do, and the risk of orders not being filled is significant when standing orders are placed through a periodical subscription agency. It is better to have a separate source for each type of order and to place standing orders through a vendor specializing in that form of serial, unless the number of a library's current serials is small and the list is uncomplicated.

There are valid reasons for libraries to place certain subscriptions and standing orders direct with the publisher, even if most orders are through an agent. Some commercial publishers give the same discount to libraries as they do to vendors. In this situation the library has to decide whether a lower price is worth the loss in consolidation of orders. The American Mathematical Society gives members as much as a 50 percent discount for journals ordered direct, but charges full price when the orders are placed through a subscription agent. At least one agency is trying to convince societies that follow this practice to extend member prices to orders placed through vendors. Another society will give the member discount if the agency provides evidence of the library's membership, a more workable situation for the library.

A decision to use no subscription agent should be examined as carefully as the decision to use one or more agencies. The savings in service charge and possible savings in time for orders to begin and claims to reach the publisher must be weighed against the need to process approximately one invoice a year for each title received, the costs of writing separate checks and postage to send the checks to the publishers. With inflation making all cost figures invalid before they appear in print, there will be no attempt here to calculate the expense of processing and paying an invoice; rest assured it is significant, for recent figures range from $8.00 to $25.00. And there is no difference between the local payment procedure for *Chemical Abstracts* and for a $3.00 newsletter.

For serial acquisitions personnel who do not have direct experience with a variety of vendors, and for those who have reason to consider changing or adding agents, two books provide guidance. The Katz/Gellatly *Guide to Magazine and Serial Agents*, previously mentioned, reports the results of a survey in the early 1970s of 850 libraries of various size and type. *International Subscription Agents*[17] is a work which is revised every few years. The latest edition has expanded the definition of "international" to include many American vendors who accept orders for serials published in foreign countries, even though the bulk of their business is with American publishers. Those agents should not be used for a large number of foreign serial orders, because their procedures were not established for this type of order, and the library is taking an unnecessary risk of not receiving the material it orders. Otherwise, the directory is quite useful, for it is based on recent questionnaire responses by both librarians and vendors, and it contains a geographical index.

In summary, each serials librarian needs to decide the source that is best for his or her library's situation—one agent, several agents, or no agent. There is justification for each choice, because every library is a unique institution with individual requirements. Each librarian must set priorities and decide what is best for the library. New's article and one by Harry Kuntz[18] have checklists containing questions a serials librarian should ask of prospective subscription agents. Two categories of questions emphasized by both authors are cost and service. Cost includes not only service charge, but also possible fees for such exceptions to the rule as cancellations and rush orders. Among service details are the time required to process orders and claims, agency claim forms, invoicing flexibility, and various reports. In addition to investigating cost and service, Kuntz's checklist questions the management, fiscal condition, and facilities of the company. Serials librarians are glad to talk about their own experience with the agencies they use or have used, and such discussion is a valid aspect of the vendor selection and evaluation process. A sales representative presents his or her agency in the best light. A questionnaire or letter of inquiry sent to serial acquisitions librarians working with a collection of comparable size and scope to one's own will either support or refute what one learns from the company itself.

CLAIMING

A library claims, or asks for, a serial that was ordered and should already have arrived but has not. Serial departments place continuing orders—subscriptions and standing orders—so that they can receive each part of the serial automatically upon publication. When the material does not reach the library, someone needs to ask that it be sent. Claiming missing issues and volumes is one of the most time-consuming and neglected aspects of serial acquisitions. Few libraries are able to give enough attention to claiming.

There are five categories of claims, each of which requires its own investigation within the library and its own procedure for communication with the publisher.

1. *Skipped Issue.* The most obvious claim and that most easily apparent is the skipped issue or volume: number nine is being checked in, but number eight has not arrived. Frank Clasquin states that claims for "single missing issues" accounted for 74 percent of all claims received by Faxon during a study made several years ago.[19] This type of claim can be processed routinely.

2. *Lapsed Subscription.* Sometimes a periodical stops coming, either at renewal time or during the course of a volume. This type of claim must be recognized either through systematic review of the manual serial record or at a patron or staff member's request, since there is no reason to examine the check-in card when processing the daily mail. The first action to take when one becomes aware of a lapsed subscription is to look at the title's payment record to make sure that it has been renewed. If payments are entered in the serial record, their consultation becomes automatic and details of the payment can be transferred to the actual claim message.

3. *Dormant Standing Order.* This type of claim is similar to the lapsed subscription, but it is not as obvious, since most standing orders are for irregular publications. In systematic review one would question a standing order in which significantly more time has elapsed since the arrival of the most recent volume than between the next-to-last and last volumes. Monographs in series and annuals are often listed in publishers'

catalogs, national bibliographies, and catalogs of in-print books, so the necessity for a claim can sometimes be confirmed for standing orders by verifying that the missing volume has been published.

4. *Inactive New Order.* There is necessarily a delay of several weeks to several months in receiving the first piece of a new serial order, but sometimes titles have not been received a year or more after the order is mailed, even though payments have been made. A file of order copies, arranged by date, facilitates monitoring of new orders. If the first piece has arrived, the copy of the order can be discarded.

5. *Replacement.* A different category of claim is a request for replacement of a serial that is imperfect or that was damaged in transit. Sometimes this condition is apparent to the check-in assistant, but occasionally the defect is not noticed for several years. As a rule, the quicker the claim, the more willing and able the publisher is to supply a replacement.

As described above, claims originate in several ways: in the process of recording receipt; as a result of a request by a patron, a serials department staff member, or a departmental library staff member; when a missing issue is noticed in the bindery preparation procedure; and during a systematic review of the serial record. Systematic claiming is an examination of the serial record entry by entry to discover claims needed. An increasing number of orders and additional duties assigned serial acquisitions staff members have caused many libraries to reduce or eliminate systematic review and to rely on other library units to inform them of needed claims. Libraries which have automated check-in systems do not have this problem, for either the computer program can produce a list of possible claims, or there is no efficient way to review the orders.

Preparation of the actual claim message is done by the check-in assistant or by a staff member who processes all claims for the serial record. Consistent with the low priority often given to claiming, libraries that assign this responsibility to one person usually classify the position at a lower grade than that of check-in assistant positions. To be sure, many claims, particularly those for skipped issues, are routine, but much of the work requires a decision about whether a claim is needed, using bibliographic resources, and the resolution of long and complicated misunderstandings. This kind of claiming is as difficult as serial check-in and processing of invoices. Since claiming demands knowledge of the title's publication pattern, and since claims can easily develop into full-scale acquisition problems, the job is done better by the check-in assistant. A clerk or student assistant can prepare routine claim messages once the check-in assistant has determined that the claim is a straightforward one.

All types of serials work are governed by the uncertainties of serial publication, and the procedure for timing of claims can be only a set of guidelines based on experience. Publishing delays are not unusual and many times there is no explanation or warning from the publisher. The length of time publishers or their distributors retain back issues varies, with a positive correlation between size of publisher and quick disposal of earlier issues. One must also take into account political disturbances, mail and transport strikes, the weather, and even the reading preferences of library mail room personnel. Whatever guidelines a serial acquisitions unit employs to determine timing of claims, it seems certain that some inquiries will be too early, risking publishers' anger, and some will be too late, requiring expensive replacement orders. Some claims, both because of chance and because of care and common sense, will be timed correctly and will produce the missing serial at no extra cost. Developing and following guidelines with respect to the timing of claims will increase the library's rate of successful claims.

The library can follow certain principles to improve its success in claiming. Above all, the claimer should use common sense in following the rules for timing of inquiries. One does not claim the 1979 *Proceedings* if earlier volumes have corresponded to even-numbered years. If the 1980 *Annual Report* arrived in June 1981, then February 1982 is too early to claim the 1981 edition. An awareness of the date of receipt of the latest piece of the serial and of the past pattern of publication can nearly eliminate inappropriate claims. If there are published citations to the serial in question or if a volume is listed as available in the publisher's catalog, then certainly a claim is in order—whatever the previous schedule of publication. Occasionally, serials that fall behind pick up the pace again, but one cannot assume this will happen.

At times a publisher actually distributes issue number five before issue number four and often sends a message stating this fact. Unfortunately, the publisher sometimes undoes this good work by inserting the notice inside the serial, where the check-in assistant will not find it. Even when there is a separate announcement about out-of-sequence issues or a delay, the piece of paper may be inadvertently discarded or separated from the check-in record, so the claimer does not know that the problem has been explained. However, the lost message is probably reported in one or more of the vendors' computer-produced updating lists. If the agent has already received a claim response from the publisher, this information has been entered in the vendor's database and subsequently reported in the updating list. In this way the agent replies to librarians' claims before they are aware of the problem.

All this information is of no use to the claimer unless he or she uses it. The investment of time required to consult updating lists brings a reduction in both total number of claims and number of inappropriate claims sent. If there is adequate time for claiming activities, the best use of these tools is to enter relevant data on the check-in record in pencil or on a slip of paper (attached *securely* until it is no longer needed). This task may be done by a full-time claimer, the check-in assistant, a clerk, or a student. Perhaps it is more practical to check all potential claims against the list or lists before preparing the claim form. When an explanation of a problem is found, it should be transferred to the check-in record to prevent premature initiation of later claims and to provide an answer to patron enquiries.

Every library has an occasional clash between the serial acquisitions unit's claiming guidelines and the needs of public service staff members. One of the benefits of an integrated serials department in which staff members do both public service and technical processing is the understanding of the other person's job. Those who produce accurate and informative check-in records use these records to respond to patrons' questions. Persons whose primary job is assistance to patrons experience the difficulty of creating serial check-in records. Even in a library where the serials department personnel do no public service, a brief exchange of jobs with reference staff members may be worth the expense. A pre-crisis program of staff development should minimize resentment of special requests and help limit them to urgently needed serials. It is especially in the claiming situation that a reasonable sense of humor can ease tension.

The claimer can increase the rate of success by reading the library's communication from the publisher's or agent's perspective. Can the recipient tell what is being requested? Vagueness, illegible handwriting, and misspelled words are not conducive to positive responses. Nor are clutter, several remotely related questions in the same letter, and bad grammar in a foreign language. The ability to see claims from the recipient's point of view improves the success of the effort to acquire missing serials.

The entire claiming system depends upon the library's knowing the approximate date of arrival for each serial. This equalizes differences between foreign and domestic serials, between air mail and surface mail, and between on-schedule and behind-schedule titles. Timing of claims is based on the interval between issues, not the date on the cover. The chart which follows gives guidelines for the timing of claim requests for periodicals. It is more appropriately used by the staff of departmental libraries and binding preparation sections than by serial acquisitions claimers, because there are many more factors to consider in sending a claim than merely a delay in receipt. Notice that a serial is late, according to these guidelines, can alert the claimer to investigate further to determine whether a claim is appropriate. The staff member responsible for placing claims needs to have an awareness of world events, such as strikes and revolutions, that delay mail delivery, and the realization that there is no agreement among vendors and among librarians as to timing of claims.[20]

Table 3.2. Number of Days to Wait for First Claim
After Expected Arrival Date

Frequency	Domestic	Foreign
Daily	30	75
Weekly	45	105
Monthly	90	150
Bimonthly	120	180
Quarterly	150	210
Semiannual	240	300

For second claims allow six weeks to two months after the first claim for domestic titles and three months for foreign titles.

These guidelines can be ignored for rush claims. However, the claimer or a supervisor should evaluate immediately each request for an exception to claiming policy and determine both that special action is required to obtain the serial and that this action has a good chance of being successful. When a rush claim is appropriate, the telephone is a far better means of communication than the mail, unless it is necessary to claim from a foreign country. American representatives of European subscription agencies can relay a rush claim overseas more effectively than the local claimer.

The variety of claim forms being used by library serials departments is nearly as large as the number of libraries times the number of types of serial orders, plus the number of agents. Volume three of *Manually Maintained Serials Records*[21] contains page after page of examples of claims on postcards, letter-sized stationery and multi-page printed forms. All of them state that the library has not received a specific serial and ask that it be sent. Some of the letters are preprinted forms that can be used for purposes besides claiming. Libraries that have automated ordering can also have computer-produced claims. This variety of forms may soon be reduced, for an ANSC Z39 subcommittee has drafted a standard claim form which, if approved, can be either purchased or made the standard format for a locally produced manual or automated claim. General use of such a claiming device would go far toward facilitating communication between serials departments and the suppliers of their material. For the present, when one constructs a new serial claim form or revises an obsolete one, there are several types of information that should be provided.

1. *Title of Serial.* A claim must state what serial the library is requesting. In the past librarians and nonlibrarians have often used different forms of entry, since publishers and agents are not concerned with corporate entry and consistency of library records. It is easier for the claimer

to copy the library form of entry from the check-in record than to change it. The use of the official entry means that the claim response can be assigned quickly to the correct record. An exception to the use of main entry on claims is the enquiry sent to a vendor such as EBSCO, whose orientation is masthead title. Claiming under that form of entry will make things easier for the agent's staff and will result in more successful claims for the library. Use of corporate entry in this case will probably cause the library trouble. With *AACR* 2 this is not so great a concern, because there is less frequent use of corporate authors than before.

2. *Library Order Number.* The use of the library's order number is for the benefit of both the library and the vendor. It enables each party to identify the title and copy, if relevant, being claimed.

3. *What is Missing.* State the specific issue(s) or volume(s) and date(s) the library is claiming. If the request is for a lapsed subscription or new order that has not begun, this situation can be explained concisely.

4. *Payment Details.* Evidence supporting the payment for material claimed is appropriate for standing orders and inactive subscriptions, but it is not needed for skipped issue claims. Specific facts a library can report are date and amount paid, period covered by payment, and invoice number. When payment details are recorded on the serial record, they can be transferred easily to the claim form. When a claim is for a serial that has not been paid, the absence of payment is as significant as proof of payment and signals the claimer to ask for an invoice.

5. *Date of Claim.* The date a library sends a claim can tell the publisher when the claim was made too early. Date is particularly important for claims to foreign vendors, where the delay caused by serials dispatched by sea mail must be taken into account.

6. *Library Address.* Each claim should contain the serial acquisitions unit's complete address, exactly the way mail is to be sent. This address should not be hidden or be in very small print but should be obvious to the person who responds to the claim.

Some libraries claim through their agents, using either the agent's form or their own, and some send all claims directly to the publisher. Claiming is covered in the vendor service charge, and the agency is able to send a copy of its cancelled check as proof of payment (when necessary) much faster than the usual institutional library. Still, the claim does not reach the publisher quite as quickly as when it is mailed direct from the library. One librarian tested his suspicion that claiming through the agency was not as efficient as claiming with the publisher and found that there was an identical success rate in his study.[22] If a local experiment gives this result, the library may take advantage of the agent's claim service, but if direct claims are significantly more productive, then the library should claim from the publisher, or consider changing agents. Claims for foreign titles will almost certainly be sent to the agent, since the freedom from language problems is one of the strongest reasons for using an intermediary.

It is as important to know what not to claim as to know what to claim. Serials that were not ordered should not be claimed. This seems obvious, but many times the acquisitions unit receives a request to claim a volume that appeared before the library's order began, and the claimer will not notice that it was not included in the order. A little care in processing the request would have shown the discrepancy. However, in defense of claimers, there are times when the library has changed vendors during the course of an order and the exact point of the change is missing or unclear on the check-in card, so the claimer can be blamed only for not questioning.

Libraries do not need complete files of all serials. Titles whose latest edition updates the earlier one, such as *World Almanac* and *Encyclopedia of Associations*, are examples. Likewise, serials which are not retained by the library, such as some newsletters, need not be claimed unless the order has lapsed. Titles which are held for only a year or two do not need to be complete.

The library needs to keep a record of claims so the work will not be duplicated. The record should show date of first claim and issue(s) or volume(s) claimed; agent's or publisher's response, unless the transaction was completed by receipt of the claimed material; follow-up claims and dates; and notice of composed letter sent and location of letter copy. This record should be retained as long as the claim is active, but it may be discarded when all requested material is received or declared unavailable from the publisher. "Out-of-print" claim responses should be noted in the serial record and a decision made about an out-of-print order.

Libraries differ in their preference for location of the claim record, and each system has advantages and disadvantages.

1. *On the Check-In Record.* If claim information is kept on the check-in record it is accessible immediately to any person who looks at the card. One does not have to go to another file to verify that a serial has been claimed. But the notice can become detached and lost if it is a separate card or piece of paper. Unless this method is supplemented by a chronological file, follow-up claiming is not handled systematically.

2. *File of Duplicate Claim Copies.* This file can be arranged by main entry, which facilitates verification of a claim, or it can be arranged by date, which provides a simple way to monitor unresolved claims. Its disadvantage is that no record of the claim appears on the check-in card, unless some signal is attached to the card.

3. *Claim Diary.* A list of claims sent, with dates and issues, may be a practical record for a small library to keep, but it is a time-consuming

procedure and is not efficient for a library having a large number of active serials. The diary also has the disadvantage of being separated from the check-in record. One librarian suggests that keeping a claim diary temporarily to monitor vendor performance is a worthy project and that the information revealed justifies its expense.[23]

The library need not restrict its record of claims to any one of the above methods; it can use two or all three of them, or it can keep two or more copies of claims filed in different arrangements. Whatever works for the library is the best claim record.

Several of the problems associated with serial claiming have been discussed earlier: the difficulty of timing the request, the need for particular alertness in evaluating potential claims, the time and care required to keep informative records of claims sent, and the frustration of having the claimer's careful work ignored by an agent's customer service representative. In addition, a claim can cause a library to receive duplicate serials. A second copy of a $1.50 newsmagazine is no real problem, but when the duplicate is a $75.00 yearbook, the check-in assistant needs to act. The obvious course is a letter to the agent or publisher acknowledging the duplicate and asking permission to return it. If there is an invoice with the volume, there should be arrangement for its cancellation. Sometimes there is no response to the letter, and the serial may stay around for years, unless another letter is sent stating that if no direction is received by a certain date, the library will dispose of the duplicate. The presence of an invoice assures that the vendor will not ignore the situation, so long as the library does not pay. Duplicates that the publisher does not want returned may be added to the collection as second copies, sent to USBE, put on the library's duplicates list, or sold to a back issues dealer.

The claiming aspect of serial acquisitions links library, agent, and publisher in a common effort to resolve a problem. Several works cited in the Annotated Bibliography explore this three-way relationship, and an earlier section of this chapter discussed library/agent relations. But what is the publisher's reaction to library claims? In the first place, supplying missing issues to libraries is not the publisher's main purpose. It is expensive for him to respond to claims, just as it is expensive for the library to initiate claims. Customer service personnel have received inappropriate claims which careless library staff members and agency clerks have sent, just as library claimers have received thoughtless answers from publishing companies. In other words, we are all human and make mistakes and get angry. Large publishers often seem less than human, because of the difficulty of working with their highly computerized operations. In fact, many large publishers have transferred the distribution of their periodicals to "fulfillment centers," which are located at some distance from the editorial offices and which depend so heavily on automation that it is nearly impossible to break into their routine.

According to Frank Clasquin, publishers estimate that 50 percent of library claims are premature.[24] He does not explain whether "premature" means before actual publication or before expected publication based on past performance. Clasquin states that a publisher's attention to library claims is in proportion to the amount of library business it has.[25] He cites examples of publishers to whom library subscriptions are significant who fill without question single issue claims. Investigation into the problem is reserved for lapsed subscriptions because of expense.

In a study of the reasons for library claims, European publishers listed poor postal service, postal and transport strikes, and misdirection of mail within a large company or university, all beyond the control of the publisher. Only one reason was suggested for which the publisher might be blamed: poor wrapping.[26] There was no recognition of garbled mailing labels, unannounced title changes, publication delays, or any of the other publisher practices that prevent the serial from reaching the library and being recognized. There is a need, probably within the Serials Section of ALA/RTSD, for a forum for open discussion of the mutual problems of libraries, subscription agents/standing order vendors, and serial publishers. Claiming would probably be the first topic on the agenda.

It is not easy to determine an acceptable percentage of titles requiring claims, because librarians have not published many articles on claiming. Katz and Gellatly suggest 5 to 8 percent per year of the number of periodicals as a reasonable rate[27] and cite three studies to support their statement. What does a serials librarian do if claims exceed an acceptable percentage? The first step to take, before blaming outside factors, is to look at the department's procedures, records, and staff performance. Agents and publishers should know the exact address to which serials are to be mailed, and it should be given them in a format that will fit computerized label requirements. Although there is at this time no standard computer label, it is better for the librarian to abbreviate a long address than to leave the decision to the vendor. Receipt of a correct mailing address does not guarantee that the publisher will use it, though, and sometimes repeated requests for correction have no effect.

At times the difficulty is not with the check-in record but with the check-in assistant. Careless recording of serials and failure to investigate every possible entry for an apparently unordered piece cause both inaccurate records and claims for serials the library has received. The latter problem is alleviated if the supervisor reviews incoming serials for which no check-in record has been located. Carelessness in claiming, including inaccurate or insufficient information on the request, also results in more claims than necessary, since each request must be done again when the wrong material arrives.

Library mail often comes through the Postal Service, the institutional mail system, and the library mail room. At any of these points a serial may be misrouted or held out of the mail until it can be read, then returned to the process. The most likely place for intentional delay to occur is within the library, because the volume of mail is smallest there. Misrouting is corrected more quickly after, rather than before, mail reaches the library. However, mail room personnel are held responsible for serials reaching the acquisitions area and are valuable allies; most of them have no interest in delaying the mail.

United States mail service appears to be slowing and a noticeable amount is misrouted, but reports indicate that mail service in many other countries is far worse.[28] Rough handling of packages and single periodical issues causes them to be separated from their address labels and sometimes to arrive in the library damaged. Unless mail is wrapped and labelled securely, it may not reach its destination and have to be claimed. Currently United States Postal Service employees are making a sincere effort to determine the destination of damaged mail.

Occasionally lapsed subscriptions and standing orders result from poor service by the agency. It is the subscription agent's responsibility to enter the library's order with the publisher and to pay the publisher promptly. The agent's instructions should reflect the library's requested starting volume and date and correct address. Anything less than this is poor service and causes excessive claiming time and expense for the library and the agency.

One possible reason for excessive unsuccessful library claims is the use of inappropriate check-in records. The card should indicate what is expected (frequency) and what is received. If a journal changes from a monthly to a bimonthly, or vice versa, replacing the old card with one designed for the new frequency shows clearly what is to come. A second cause of unsuccessful claims is too little time given to claiming by staff members. Claims that are delayed may reach the publisher too late for the missing piece to be available. The ninety-(or fewer) day limit publishers impose is not an arbitrary one; it is the length of time they keep back files before shipping them elsewhere for sale.

CANCELLING

Even in times of adequate funding libraries cancelled serial orders; now such action is becoming almost routine. Each library needs to establish policies and procedures for cancelling orders. In general, the most satisfactory time to end a continuing commitment for a periodical is at the conclusion of the term already paid or agreed to. When library requests for refunds can be minimized, relations with vendors and publishers should not be strained by cancellations. Many agents send automatically or upon request a list of all periodical orders held, for the library's approval of renewal. Usually the renewal list arrives a few months before new orders are to be placed by the vendor. This is an excellent time for a review of the collection, or that part of it covered by the vendor's list. It is even better if cancellation decisions have been made from the previous year's renewal list, in anticipation of the new list, so it can be returned immediately with instructions about which titles are to be renewed and which are to be cancelled. Unfortunately, many cancellation decisions result from large price increases on the annual invoice, when it is usually too late to cancel until the next year. Some libraries have, or wish they had, their own mechanism for periodical review and do not rely on renewal lists. These libraries especially need to consider the timing of their cancellations, because cancellation instructions to the supplier after the renewal process has begun are likely to be ineffective and can create an angry flurry of messages.

Cancelling standing orders smoothly can be either easier or more difficult than cancelling subscriptions. Since standing orders are paid upon receipt, an arbitrary future termination of the commitment (such as at the end of a calendar year) can be set. Flexibility and the willingness to accept an occasional extra volume eliminate the expense of correspondence, returns and refunds. On the other hand, if the vendor has confirmed cancellation of the library's order and continues to send and invoice succeeding volumes, the library should insist upon returning the serials and receiving credit. Usually such actions are inadvertent, but sometimes they are deliberate and will continue as long as the library tolerates them.

Whichever order is being cancelled, for everyone's protection—serial acquisitions, departmental library, vendor, and publisher—the request needs to be in writing, and the cancellation should be confirmed in writing. In this way all parties can keep a copy of the transaction if questions or misunderstandings should arise in the future.

Transfer of orders from one agent to another or from the publisher to an agent or vice versa are best treated as cancellations followed by new orders. The library can retain both a written confirmation of cancellation from the first source and a copy of the new order with its own order number. Having these records at hand simplifies resolving the problems of duplicate receipts. Transfer demands that serial acquisitions carefully mark its internal records concerning the change, so that there are no loose ends. When two agents are involved, the old and the new, accurate recordkeeping is even more necessary than when one order is or has been direct. Serial acquisition records involving cancellations and transfers are the place to go overboard on detailed recordkeeping.

MANAGEMENT RECORDS

The collection development librarian wants to know the subject breakdown of the current serial budget. The botany librarian needs to know the total amount spent annually during the past five years for botany periodicals. The reference librarian asks for a list of all German language periodicals. The library director must tell the university president the percentage of increase in foreign serial prices since last year. The serials librarian believes it would be more efficient to consolidate foreign orders with one vendor and needs to know what foreign serials the library receives and what the source is for each order. If the library has a functioning automated serial management system these requests may be filled easily. The amount of time and the degree of effort required to produce manually the pertinent information depends upon the type of management records the serials department has, as well as the size of the serial record.

A manual visible record of the receipt of serial orders is a management record when it contains data beyond the entering of issues and volumes received. Examples of these data are (1) payment information, including invoice number or date, period or volumes covered by the payment, amount, and date paid; (2) publisher's name and address, source of order; (3) fund and classification number or routing instructions. With these kinds of facts at hand it is possible to describe the serials collection according to subject, country of origin, source, cost, or any combination of two or more of the above, and to document pricing trends by using payment data over two or more years. But the larger the collection, the more cumbersome is an analysis made from the manual serial record. The time required to identify, from a visible record of 20,000 entries, Swiss titles placed with non-Swiss vendors is likely to cost more than the value of the data or savings resulting from a projected consolidation of orders.

A second approach to management records is to have multiple files, each with a specific kind of information—source file, shelf list, holdings list, fund lists, and so on. Each of these files describes the collection from one aspect and can be examined with less human effort than the complete serial record. But the group of single purpose files not only occupies space, but also requires a significant amount of labor for maintenance. Chances are, not one of the files contains data that could not be entered on a manual visible record if desired, except for full cataloging.

The question here is the selection of the appropriate means of manipulating—extracting, arranging, and analyzing—the data available. Even for a traditionally labor intensive operation, costs in staff time are enormous if analysis is done manually for a large collection. Computerization is the only answer for efficient management records. Fortunately, this does not always require the library to invest in a crash program of entering its serial records into a new database. Libraries that have placed all their orders with one of the large American subscription agents can benefit from its management system. A growing number of European vendors can now provide management data. Many such services are provided upon request at no extra charge to the library; some will be available only at additional cost. For libraries using more than one vendor, partial information is useful, but it is possible to have a single agent provide data for a library's total list, even for titles placed direct or through another agent. Some vendors can provide total serial processing as well as management records, for instance, Faxon's LINX and EBSCO's EBSCONET. With computerization established and highly sophisticated in the offices of commercial subscription agents, there appears to be no limit to the uses of their databases for serial management. Whether a vendor's database, one of the bibliographic utilities or a local database is most practical, serial management records will be increasingly automated and will provide data which have been too expensive to extract from manual records.

THE FUTURE

Serial acquisitions is in a transitional situation, which is not an unusual condition for this area of librarianship. Much is possible through automation, even with the irregularity of serial publication and receipt. The progress made in the near future can have as dramatic an impact as that already made on other library operations. But on the other hand, there is the problem of money: inflation raising the cost of everything from salaries to scotch tape; instability of the dollar creating even faster increases in the cost of European titles than of domestic serials; competition within the library and within the parent organization for priority in funding for materials, staff, and automation. Automation brings no staff reductions, but it usually means that more can be done using existing staffing. These things are no more than serial personnel have faced before and to which they have adapted. This need to adapt and explore is one more reason why serial acquisitions will always be a challenge to serials librarians and support staff.

Librarians and publishers are predicting that, ultimately, scholarly information will not be published in serials or in paper format, but will be available electronically upon request. When and if this happens, serial acquisitions personnel will be required to adapt to drastically changed conditions. Until that time, however, the need for accurate, written manual or computer acquisition records will retain its importance. Flexibility and curiosity, as well as accuracy, are the personal qualities that will enable staff members to meet the challenge of serial acquisitions.

NOTES

1.   Clara D. Brown and Lynn S. Smith, *Serials: Past, Present and Future*, 2nd (rev.) ed. (Birmingham, Ala.: EBSCO Industries, Inc., 1980), pp. 253-64.

2.   William J. Willmering, "On-Line Centralized Serials Control," *Serials Librarian* 1 (1977): 243-49.

3.   James Fayollat, "On-Line Serials Control System in a Large Biomedical Library," *Journal of the American Society of Information Science* 23 (1972): 318-22, 353-58, and 24 (1973): 80-86.

4.   For example, Jerrold Orne, *The Language of the Foreign Book Trade*, 3rd ed. (Chicago: American Library Association, 1976).

5.   *New Serial Titles: A Union List of Serials Commencing Publication after December 31, 1949* (Washington, D. C.: Library of Congress, 1953-   ).

6.   *Union List of Serials in Libraries of the United States and Canada*, 3rd ed. (New York: H.W. Wilson Company, 1965).

7.   Norman B. Brown and Jane Phillips, "Price Indexes for 1980," *Library Journal* 105 (1980): 1486-91.

8.   See Chapter 4 for a discussion of successive and latest entry cataloging.

9.   Not all volumes of this work have this title. See Sheehy AA 92-99 for a thorough discussion of the history of this publication.

10.   *Ulrich's International Periodicals Dictionary*, 1-   1932-   (New York: R. R. Bowker Company).

11.   *Irregular Serials and Annuals*, 1-   1967-   (New York: R. R. Bowker Company).

12.   *EBSCO Bulletin of Serials Changes*, 1-   1975-   (Birmingham, Ala.: EBSCO Industries, Inc.)

13.   EBSCO Subscription Services, *Librarians' Handbook*, 1-   1970/1971-   (Birmingham, Ala.: EBSCO Industries, Inc.); F. W. Faxon Company, Inc., *Faxon Librarians' Guide*, 1931-   (Westwood, Mass.: F. W. Faxon Company, Inc.).

14.   *Serials Updating Service*, 1-   1972-   (Westwood, Mass.: F. W. Faxon Company, Inc.).

15.   Bill Katz and Peter Gellatly, *Guide to Magazine and Serial Agents* (New York: R. R. Bowker Company, 1975).

16.   Doris E. New, "Serials Agency Conversion in an Academic Library," *Serials Librarian* 2 (1978): 277-85.

17.   Nancy Melin Buckeye, *International Subscription Agents*, 4th ed. (Chicago: American Library Association, 1978).

18.   Harry Kuntz, "Serial Agents: Selection and Evaluation," *Serials Librarian* 2 (1977): 139-50.

19.   Frank F. Clasquin, "The Claim Enigma for Serials and Journals," in *Management Problems in Serials Work* (Westport, Conn.: Greenwood Press, 1974), p. 76.

20.   Katz and Gellatly's *Guide to Magazine and Serial Agents* has a helpful discussion of the differences which appeared in agencies' responses to their questionnaire. See pp. 137-38 and 171-73.

21.   American Library Association. Resources and Technical Services Division. Serials Section. *Manually Maintained Serials Records: Report of the Ad Hoc Committee to Study Manually Maintained Serials Records* (Chicago: American Library Association, 1976), pp. 266-338.

22. Calvin D. Evans, "An Experiment in Periodicals Claiming," *Stechert-Hafner Book News* 25 (1970): 26-27.

23. Katherine R. Smith, "Serials Agents/Serials Librarians," *Library Resources and Technical Services* 14 (1970): 11.

24. Clasquin, "Claim Enigma," p. 75.

25. *Ibid.*, p. 70.

26. Paul Nijhoff Asser, "Some Trends in Journal Subscriptions," *Scholarly Publishing* 10 (1979): 285.

27. Katz and Gellatly, *Guide to Magazine and Serial Agents*, p. 134.

28. Asser, "Some Trends," p. 286.

Chapter 4

Cataloging the Serial Collection

Nancy I. White

The description of change distinguishes serials cataloging from monographic cataloging. A serial begins publication without a foreseeable end, and most serials are published in more than one issue. This multiplicity of issues produces the possibility of change in each of the elements of bibliographic description.

It is obvious that most publishers of serials have never given any thought to the problems for libraries created by changes in their serials. Although it is easy for sorely tried serials catalogers to picture some publishers as diabolic, in reality most of them are simply unaware. They publish their products for individuals, not for libraries. It may be possible to educate the larger publishers in the problems of libraries, but most serials are not issued by large publishers. Even groups of librarians, when acting as publishers, change titles and numbering with abandon. For peace of mind, the serials cataloger had best look on the vagaries of publishers as creating job security.

Cataloging serials is easier now than ever before. The shared cataloging of the OCLC system brings much information to the cataloger that formerly was not available. The change from latest entry to successive entry cataloging, which occurred with the publication of the *Anglo-American Cataloging Rules* (*AACR*) in 1967 and was adopted by the Library of

Congress in 1971, means that the cataloger no longer has to attempt to catalog earlier titles of the serial in hand, titles which the library may not possess. With the second edition of *AACR* (*AACR* 2) has come the further improvement that the cataloger can describe the earliest issue in hand, make a note of which issue is being described, and have done with attempts to catalog issues not in the library.

This chapter assumes that the cataloging will be done on the OCLC computer system and according to *AACR* 2.

AIDS TO CATALOGING SERIALS

The minimum tools necessary to catalog the smallest collection of serials are the second edition of the *Anglo-American Cataloguing Rules*[1] and the Library of Congress *Cataloging Service Bulletin* (*CSB*).[2] The *AACR* 2 should be annotated with references to the relevant *CSB* number and page to refer to Library of Congress interpretations of specific rules. An index to the *Bulletins* is most helpful, and should be kept up to date by added references to newer bulletins. It is advisable periodically to read again both rules and bulletins, both for deeper understanding and for the knowledge that there is a rule or interpretation for a given problem.

The *OCLC Serials Manual*[3] is, of course, another necessary tool. The Library of Congress interpretations of the uniform title (*CSB* 11, pp. 46-49) should be added to either this manual or the *AACR* 2. The OCLC field numbers should be added to the appropriate paragraphs in the *AACR* 2 serials chapter. The Library of Congress decision on cataloging microforms for previously published books and serials (*CSB* 11, pp. 15-16), should be added to the OCLC serials manual as well, because it differs from *AACR* 2. These annotations are timesavers. At first the cataloger will spend a great deal of time referring to the rules, the manual, and the bulletins. Eventually the most-used rules will be learned, but many rules are used so infrequently that these references will continue to be needed.

Any library except the smallest should have as tools *New Serial Titles* (*NST*) and the *Union List of Serials* (*ULS*). *Ulrich's International Periodicals Directory* and *Irregular Serials and Annuals* are useful sources of ISSN.

For establishing corporate body names, *World of Learning, International Handbook of Universities*, and the *Commonwealth Handbook of Universities* are valuable. A geographic dictionary and English/other language dictionaries are necessary. In small libraries one copy of these publications will be used for both reference and cataloging, but in large libraries catalogers may reasonably expect to have separate collections of working tools.

The serials cataloger will also use the standard tools of catalogers, the

Figure 4.1: OCLC Bibliographic Record

```
Screen 2 of 2       ¶
▶16 265      ATA National Office, 1000 Vermont Ave., N.W., Washington,
DC 20005 ¶
 ▶17 300      v. ‡b ill. ‡c 26 cm. ¶
 ▶18 350      $15.00 ¶
 ▶19 362 0    v. 31-   Mar. 1979- ¶
 ▶20 550 1    Vols. for 1979-   edited under the auspices of the
University and College Theatre Association. ¶
 ▶21 690  0   Dramatic criticism ‡x Periodicals. ¶
 ▶22 690  0   Drama ‡x History and criticism ‡x Periodicals. ¶
 ▶23 690  0   Theater ‡x Periodicals. ¶
 ▶24 650  0   Drama ‡x Periodicals. ¶
 ▶25 710 20   American Theatre Association. ¶
 ▶26 710 21   University and College Theatre Association (U.S.) ¶
 ▶27 780 00    ‡t Educational theatre journal ‡x 0013-1989 ‡w
(OCoLC)1567630 ¶
 ▶28 901      ‡c Ser ¶
 ▶29 936      Mar. 1979 ¶
```

```
Screen 1 of 2       ¶
▶NO HOLDINGS IN XXX - FOR HOLDINGS ENTER dh DEPRESS  DISPLAY RECD SEND
OCLC: 4799124      Rec stat: c Entrd: 790330      Used: 801001 ¶
▶Type: a Bib lvl: s Govt pub:    Lang:  eng Source: d S/L ent: 0
Repr:    Enc lvl:    Conf pub: 0 Ctry:  dcu Ser tp: p Alphabt: a
Indx: u Mod rec:    Phys med:    Cont: ^o  Frequn: q Pub st:  c
Desc:    Cum ind: u Titl pag: u ISDS:    1 Regulr: r Dates: 1979-9999 ¶
 ▶ 1 010      79-643622 ¶
 ▶ 2 040      XBM ‡c XBM ‡d MUL ‡d HUL ‡d DLC ‡d NSD ‡d DLC ‡d OCL ‡d DLC ¶
 ▶ 3 012      4 ‡b 3 ¶
 ▶ 4 019      6073221 ¶
 ▶ 5 022 0    0192-2882 ¶
 ▶ 6 035      1621174 ‡b MULS ¶
 ▶ 7 042      lc ‡a nsdp ¶
 ▶ 8 050 0    PN3171 ‡b .E38 ¶
 ▶ 9 082      792/.05 ¶
 ▶10 090      ‡b ¶
 ▶11 049      XXXM ¶
 ▶12 222 10   Theatre journal ‡b (Washington) ¶
 ▶13 245 10   Theatre journal. ¶
 ▶14 246 17   TJ ‡f 1979- ¶
 ▶15 260 01   [Washington, ‡b American Theatre Association] ¶
```

National Union Catalog and the *Library of Congress Subject Catalog, Library of Congress Subject Headings,* and the classification schedule appropriate to the library. Figure 4.1 reproduces, as an aid to this chapter, an OCLC bibliographic record used in the *OCLC Serials Manual.* With tools available and annotated rule book at hand, the cataloger is now prepared to approach a serial.

WHAT THE RULES DO NOT TELL YOU

The serial to be cataloged should first be searched in the OCLC database. In a large library material will probably be searched before it reaches the cataloger, but if much time has elapsed between searching and cataloging, the search should be repeated. Most serials the cataloger searches will already be in the database. On the OCLC serial record, first establish that the record is for the serial in hand by comparing title, issuing body (if any), dates (if any), and place of publication (if any). Then look in the fixed field area at the successive/latest entry designation. Only a "0" or successive entry record may be used, although the information on a latest entry ("1") may be useful in making a new record. Next, consider the Reproduction designation. Only a record with the appropriate designation may be used, although again an unsuitable record may be useful in making a new record.

If the record on the screen still seems to match the material to be cataloged, or if it may be useful in making a new record, make a printout of the record. Serials cannot be cataloged efficiently without a printer, and attempting to do so is uneconomical in most libraries. Serials do not lend themselves to at-terminal cataloging. A good OCLC serial record will contain almost all the information needed for cataloging, but if the record was entered before 1981, several changes will be necessary to make the record conform to *AACR* 2. Unless the cataloger is equally familiar with old and new cataloging rules and expects to remain so, it is better to change all records to *AACR* 2 rules in all respects. The serials chapter of the *AACR* 2 rules can serve as a checklist to ensure that no elements of the description are forgotten. Among the elements often missing from OCLC serial records are the collation, frequency, and numerical and/or chronological designation. It is easy not to notice the absence of one of these fields unless one uses a checklist. So, go through the rules one by one, considering whether each applies to the serial in hand.

Title

The first element of the description to be determined is the title. The description is based on the title page or title page substitute (both known as "chief source of information") of the first issue—not volume—of the serial, or the first issue in hand. Most periodical issues do not have title pages. If a page which would otherwise be a title page has contents on it, it is considered an editorial page. Do not use an editorial page as a title page substitute unless it is the only place the title appears. Most periodicals are cataloged from the cover. Some monographic series carry the series designation only on a half-title page which must serve as the series title page.

Once the chief source of information is established, the title proper is determined. Read the examples of titles and subtitles in chapters 1 and 12 of *AACR* 2. It is usually readily apparent where the title stops and the subtitle begins. Subtitles are often in smaller or different type than titles; they are usually more specific or explanatory than titles. A cataloger new to serials who is having trouble distinguishing between titles and subtitles may be helped by studying as examples the cards in the catalog under a heading such as "Geography - Periodicals" or "American Poetry - Period-icals." *AACR* 2 uses the more inclusive term "other title information" instead of subtitle.

Use the subtitle in two instances only: (1) when it contains a statement of responsibility (. . .journal of the American Gem Society), or (2) when the title proper is an initialism and the subtitle is the full version, or vice-versa. Library of Congress practice is to use the full version as the title and the initialism as the subtitle unless the initialism is "the only form consistently presented in various locations other than the chief source" (*CSB* 11, p. 16). Some monographic series have no titles, but do have series numbering (for example, Missouri Historical Society. 12). In such an instance, the name of the issuing body is used as the title: "If the series is entered under title, assign a uniform title that consists of the title qualified by the term '(Series)' even if there is no conflict" (*CSB* 14, p. 10). Supplied titles in brackets are not used.

If the title appears in more than one language, use the title in the language of the content as the title proper (*AACR* 2, 1.1B8). Titles in other languages are recorded as parallel titles. Occasionally a scholarly journal has text in several languages and titles in several languages. The title in the largest type should be used as the title proper, or, if all the titles are in the same size type, the first title should be used.

If a serial has a title proper made up of a title common to a number of sections and a section title, and a parallel title for the section title only, repeat the common title as a part of the parallel title. In other words, place equal parts of the title on either side of the equals sign:

Acta Universitatis Gandensis. Sociology studies = Acta Universitatis Gandensis. Etudes sociologique.

Statement of Responsibility.   Record statements of responsibility appearing prominently in the item in the form in which they appear there (*AACR* 2, 1.1F1). If no statement of responsibility appears prominently in the item, neither construct one nor extract one from the content of the item (*AACR* 2, 1.1F2).

Main Entry. At this point the cataloger should decide whether the entry is to be a title entry or an author/title entry, basing the decision on rule 21.1B2. Most serials are title entries. The most common author/title entries are for annual reports of the activities of an organization, directories of the membership, catalogs or catalog supplements, official statements of position (white papers, etc.) and conference proceedings. Many records in the OCLC database as author/title entries must be changed to title entries under *AACR* 2. Also, many author/title entries with truncated titles must now be title entries with the titles extended to their full length. Applying *AACR* 2 results in some title entries for titles which were not even traced under earlier rules. For example: American Gem Society. *Journal* becomes *Journal of the American Gem Society.*

Uniform Titles. The serials chapter of *AACR* 2 would be unworkable without the addition of the Library of Congress guidelines for the treatment of serials entered under title (*CSB* 11, p. 46). Under *AACR* 2 most serials and almost all monographic series are entered under title. Many serials have the same common or generic titles. Library of Congress policy is not to anticipate conflict, but other libraries may find it more practical to anticipate conflict and to add unique identifiers to each generic or common title. Conflicts may exist in a library's database that are not immediately apparent because of older cataloging practices which did not require title added entries for generic titles. Retrospective conversion programs which include conversion to *AACR* 2 entries will uncover many conflicts of generic titles which can be resolved only by use of uniform title guidelines.

If a serial is a separately published section of another serial, and the title common to all sections requires a unique qualifier, place the qualifier after the title common to all sections, not after the section title:

> Annales (Université de Toulouse). Geologie.

not

> Annales. Geologie (Université de Toulouse).

Edition Area

This area, which is not much used in serials cataloging, has not been troublesome in a year of *AACR* 2 cataloging. One serial cataloged by the author did require the use of the edition statement in the title proper. The last example in *AACR* 2, 2.1B1 was helpful.

Numbering and Date Area

This area is sometimes forgotten when a cataloger is adapting a record already in the database. The designation and punctuation rules have changed. Some more examples may be useful. The date should be placed with the numbering system with which it best fits if there are alternative systems. For example:

Año 56- = Vol. 137- = No. 2837 (abril 1972)-

If an alternative numbering system starts after the first system, this situation may be shown in this way:

Bd. 33 (1840)-Bd. 76 (1850) ; Bd. 77 (1851)-Bd. 168 (Apr. 1873) = Neue Reihe, Bd. 1-Bd. 92.

Remember, the numbering on one side of the equals sign must equal that on the other side.

Occasionally a publisher will decide that his journal, now at, let us say, v. 35, is a direct descendant of an earlier journal which had 30 volumes. Accordingly, his v. 35 is followed by v. 66. Usually, but not always, the publisher will issue an explanation of such a change. Other publishers quietly change the date of founding or beginning publication and let the cataloger guess at the journalistic ancestry now being claimed. Under the *AACR* 2 rules for describing numbering it is relatively simple to show changes:

Vol. 1 (1925)-v. 35 (1959); Vol. 66 (1960)-

This area is one in which cataloger's judgement must be exercised. Some catalogers will prefer to place most numbering description in one statement, while others will prefer to use notes to explain intricacies and eccentricities in numbering. As long as the explanation is clear, either system is acceptable.

Place of Publication

If the place is not on the chief source of information, record it in square brackets. Always give the state or country if it appears with the city, and supply it in square brackets if the city needs further identification. Check the abbreviations list in *AACR* 2 Appendix B14 to see which places may be abbreviated. If no place of publication can be determined, use the abbreviation [S.l.] (*AACR* 2, 1.4C6; note capital "S").

Publisher

The name of a well-known publisher may be given in abbreviated form. If the publisher's name already appears in the description, it may be given in abbreviated form (The Association, or La Société). If the publisher is not named on the chief source of information, bracket the publisher. If the publisher is not determinable, use [s.n.] (note lower case "s"). Many periodicals are businesses and publish themselves. In such a case, use the title as publisher, with "Inc." or "Ltd." (note capitals) if such a designation exists. Usually there is no such designation. If there is no publisher information, list the printer if available. (See *AACR* 2, 1.4D3.)

Date of Publication

The date of publication can usually be determined for a serial. If it cannot, Library of Congress practice is to use a comma after the publisher. Some libraries may prefer to use a period for esthetic reasons (cataloger's judgement).

Collation

Numbered rather than physical volumes are described in the collation, and only the designation "v." (rather than "no.") is used. The cataloger should note the fact that volumes are oversized on all temporary records immediately after measuring. Failure to do so can lead to production of cards marked "Folio" while volumes are not, a waste of time and money.

Series Area

Place series statements after the collation only when all the volumes of the serial are in the series. If only part of the volumes of the serial are in a series, describe the situation in a note. Remember that most author/title series entries have now changed to title entries.

Notes

It is in the notes that serials cataloging differs most from monographic cataloging, for the notes describe the changes which characterize serials. *AACR* 2 specifies that a serial is described from the first issue in hand. All available issues are examined, and any changes in the description are detailed in the notes, except those changes which make a new catalog record necessary.

Most of the examples in the rules are self-explanatory, but some comments may be helpful. Notice that the wording of frequency notes is different in *AACR* and *AACR* 2. These changes are easy to forget when adapting a record. The terms "bimonthly" and "semimonthly" are ambiguous and are best avoided. "Two issues monthly" and "Six issues yearly" are clear.

Some OCLC records use the note: "Title from cover." This note is unnecessary when the cover is the chief source of information.

Among the notes shown for variation in title, one deserves special attention: "Sometimes published as: . . ." This note can be used for what the Library of Congress calls a "flip/flop" situation. The *Yale Literary Magazine*, or *Yale Lit*, is an example of a "flip/flop" title. The magazine has had each title two or more times. Library of Congress practice is to have one record for such a serial instead of several. This cataloger's judgement is that the journal will still require recataloging when the title changes so that the one record will be for the latest title. Otherwise the publisher could settle on one title, and the cataloging record would be under the wrong title on a long-term basis. One cataloging record rather than several does seem easier on library patrons. *Brigham Young University Studies*, sometimes published as *BYU Studies*, is another example. In this instance the publishers probably have not intended to change the title, but they certainly have done so, repeatedly.

Do not use a "Subtitle varies" note unless a subtitle is included in the description.

Notice that dates in a statement of responsibility note come at the end of each statement, rather than at the beginning.

In relationship notes, use uniform title, title proper, or key title in that order of preference.

The index notes in the cataloging rules do not have enough examples, and some of the examples in *AACR* are still useful. The most common problem with indexes is the index covering two or more successive titles. Parenthetical notes can be used: (Includes index to earlier title), (Includes index to: Southern mansions), (Includes index to later title), (In index to Southern mansions), or (In index to later title). The first three examples require an added subject entry for the index, while the latter two do not. For an online catalog, the index note without an added subject entry is preferable.

CATALOGING SERIALS ON THE OCLC SYSTEM

As stated above, new material coming to the cataloger should be searched in the OCLC database. It is most advisable to have a printer and to make printouts of OCLC serial records. It is not economical to attempt to catalog serials at an OCLC terminal in any but the smallest library. If there is any competition at all for terminal time, serials cataloging should be done away from the terminal, with only searching, input, and production taking place at the terminal. A printer enables the cataloger to make efficient use of time at the computer terminal. The printer should be set to double space so that changes can be made easily and legibly on the printout. For this reason, the ability to double space should be a requirement of any printer considered for purchase. Printouts should be made of Library of Congress records for a title, even of an unusable latest-entry record, and also of any other records matching the material in hand. The LC call number, subject headings, and information can be used even though the record itself is unsuitable. For the first three or four years after the change to *AACR* 2, most of the serial records on OCLC will reflect older cataloging codes. While the OCLC system permits older LC records to be entered with only the access points changed to *AACR* 2 form, it is simpler for the serials cataloger to use one code only, and to do all cataloging, original and adaptive, by *AACR* 2.

Since older codes required description of the latest issue in hand, with earlier information in notes, and *AACR* 2 requires the exact opposite practice, most older records require some modification.

In using the *OCLC Serials Manual*, it is wise to read the introductory material carefully. Then, after some experience in using the manual, it is helpful to read that same material again.

The fixed field area is quite straightforward. The cataloger does not need to guess any of the information, and "u" can be used for unknown information. The country code may need a change if the place of publication has changed. The Descriptive cataloging form (Desc:) should be coded "a" for *AACR* 2. In the dates, remember that a split year date such as 1975/76 is expressed as the latter year, 1976.

This discussion will cover adapting first an *AACR* record for original printed material, then a record for a reprint, and finally a microform record.

010. If the record being adapted does not reflect LC cataloging, and the Library of Congress has cataloged the title, add the LC card number in the 010 field.

022. Add the ISSN if it is available in one of the tools mentioned early in this chapter. The publication may contain an incorrect ISSN. Some publishers do not realize that the ISSN changes when the title changes, and they retain the ISSN assigned to a superseded title.

041. Notice that for *multilingual* titles, language codes are entered in order of their predominance, while the *languages of summaries or abstracts* are entered in alphabetical order.

049. Use of this field differs from library to library. Two cautions pertain to its use. Caution 1: a word in a holdings statement that is too long to go in the margin of a catalog card will mean that the text of the card will start below that word. Very little text will get on each card, and

the resulting pack of useless cards will be large and expensive. For instance, if a library's cards have a nine-space margin, the word "Chemistry" will occupy all the margin with no space between that word and the text. If "Chemistry" is part of a holdings statement that reads "Also in Chemistry," which comes below a call number, the text will start four or five lines lower than it should. Caution 2: eighteen lines of space are available down the margin, including the call number and empty spaces between the call number and various holdings statements. Attempting to put too much information in the margin will result in no cards being produced. The cataloger may not know why the cards were not produced and may try again and again to produce this record before receiving a letter from the network explaining the problem.

Call number fields. A library's OCLC profile determines what type of call number will print on that library's cards. The call number of the selected classification (LC or Dewey) which is lowest on the record or screen is the one that prints. It is prudent to delete unwanted call numbers. If the library has the "x suppression option," cards can be produced without call numbers.

100. Few serials have personal name authors, but an occasional directory or guide of this sort does appear. Check the author's name for *AACR* 2 form. The Library of Congress announced an intention of cataloging under personal author serial reports which, though emanating from government bodies, have the names of individuals attached. One hopes that by now this policy has been reconsidered. In such cases, a title entry seems more useful.

110. Many serial records now in OCLC have author/title entries which should be changed to title entries. In such a case, change the 110 to 710. Be sure the name of the corporate body is in *AACR* 2 form. At the same time, look at the 245 field and delete coding for a title added entry.

111. Again, check for *AACR* 2 form of entry. Most conference publications will remain author/title entries; most will also be treated as monographs.

130. The cataloger should have incorporated in the manual or the rules the LC guidelines on uniform titles from *CSB* 11, p. 47. In choosing which category of qualifier to use, sometimes the question of an indication of subject content seems very uncertain. In such cases choose the corporate body as the qualifier (cataloger's judgement).

212. At present the variant access title is a perfectly useless field, with neither indexing nor the ability to generate a note. If the information in the field is valuable, change the field to 246 39 for a note and indexing or 246 29 for indexing alone.

222. If this field is present in the record, be sure the 022 field contains an ISSN. Otherwise a strange note appears on the catalog cards:

= Journal of the . . .

240. This field will seldom be used for serials. Parliamentary debates which have been issued with differing titles over the years may be brought together here and differentiated by date. Such an arrangement is useful to library patrons.

245. Remember that the coding for both designation and name of parts and sections has changed and that most subtitles must be deleted. If the subtitle seems to contain useful information but does not meet the LC guidelines for inclusion in the 245 field, put the subtitle in a 500 note. The #c statement of responsibility must be added to pre-*AACR* 2 records. Some older records have parallel titles only in the 246 field. In such a case add the parallel title in the 245 field.

246. Both subtitles containing statements of responsibility and parallel titles which were added after the first issue can be placed in the 246 field and tagged to generate added entries or notes.

260. The punctuation must be changed on old records. The name of the publisher can be added to some records and abbreviated on others. On many records, the change to describing the first issue will require changing either or both the place of publication and the name of the publisher. The date of publication can often be added.

300. The punctuation must be changed. Again, a caution: if the library's profile specifies that volumes over 30 cm. are Folio, be sure the physical volumes are indeed marked Folio, because the computer is going to ensure that the cards are marked Folio.

310 and 321. The 310 field must often be added to the record. If a 321 field is also present, do not capitalize the first word in the 310 field. Do not punctuate these fields. Delete any punctuation in the field being adapted. Be sure the phrasing is in *AACR* 2 form.

The OCLC manual's instructions about not entering a frequency in the 310 field when that frequency is in the fixed field should be ignored. The 310 and 321 fields are in illogical order. It would be nice if OCLC would someday reprogram these fields in order and clean up the capitalization and spacing oddities. Remember, if the record has 3 frequency notes, they should be in this order:

> 310 latest (not capitalized)
> 321 Earliest (capitalized)
> 321 middle (not capitalized)

362. The phrasing in this field has changed with *AACR* 2. If the first issue is not available, the cataloger may have to change from v. 1-   to a 362 1 note: "Began publication with . . ." and a "Description based on

..." note in a 500 field. If the 362 field ends with a hyphen, add three blanks and a period. Caution: using the wrong delimiter in this field will result in unusable card sets, with the "Began publication ..." note following the title.

400 and 800 fields.   These fields are the same as for monographs. On adaptive records they require considerable change. Only 440 and 490 are used now. 440 produces a series added entry. 490 requires an 830 field if an added entry is desired.

5xx: Notes.   OCLC order of notes does not match the *AACR* 2 order of notes. While the manual states that notes should be entered in tag order, the cataloger may prefer an order more closely resembling that in *AACR* 2. Some changes are possible to improve the situation. Within the 5xx fields, except for the 555 index note, the notes print in the order in which they are entered. If a note pertains to the index, it should appear on the card below the index note. If a note pertains to a microform reproduction, it should appear on the card after the microform note.

If the *AACR* 2 serials chapter is annotated with field numbers by each note, the cataloger can easily keep the notes in approximate *AACR* 2 order.

510:   Citation note.   This note seems more logically placed after the 555 index note. The citation note is not a part of *AACR* 2.

500:   Description based on.   This note ordinarily should be the last of the 5xx fields (cataloger's judgement).

555.   One peculiarity of the 555 field is that the use of a colon or semicolon results in the end of a line on the catalog card, whether the cataloger wants the line ended or not.

580.   Many records have linking entries in the 580 field which can be generated by the 780 or 785 fields. In such cases, delete the 580 field and change the indicators in the other linking entry fields to produce the appropriate notes.

6xx: Subject headings.   Subject headings containing proper names of any sort should be checked to determine that the entry is in proper *AACR* 2 form. Subject headings should routinely be checked to see if they have become obsolete.

7xx: Added entries.   The same concern about whether the entries have changed applies to added entries. In addition, there will be some author/title entries in the 7xx fields which must be changed to title entries under *AACR* 2. An added entry which becomes a title entry should be changed to the 730 field.

7xx: Linking entries.   Many linking entries on existing records are in author/title form, and must be changed to title entries, some to uniform title entries. Remember, the order of preference of titles is uniform title, title proper, and key title. Many changes in linking entries are necessary to reflect that order.

Reprints

In the fixed field "Repr:" is coded "r" for reprints. All other areas in the fixed field describe the reprint except the dates, which describe the original. In the variable fields, the reprint is described, and the original is then described in a 580 note. A 775 field for the original title is made. Any notes after the 580 field should refer to the original. If a reprint of a serial requires a uniform title, the qualifiers should describe the original. Occasionally a library will need to differentiate between reprints of a journal with a uniform title (see *CSB* 14, p. 52). As an example of how reprints can be handled, consider *The Spectator*, by Addison and Steele. *Union List of Serials* lists twenty *Spectators*, four of which were published in London. A large academic library might have over a dozen reprints of the *Spectator*. The original journal would have the uniform title:

Spectator (London, England : 1711)

The reprints would be differentiated as follows:

Spectator (London, England : 1711) Reprint (1930)
Spectator (London, England : 1711) Reprint (1897)
Spectator (London, England : 1711) Reprint (1809)
Spectator (London, England : 1711) Reprint (1803)

"Reprint" in these examples corresponds to the second definition in the Glossary of *AACR* 2: "A new edition with substantially unchanged text."

Microforms

In the fixed field "Repr:" is coded "a" for microfilm, and so on. All other areas in the fixed field describe the microfilm, except the dates, which describe the original. In the variable fields, the original is described, and the microfilm is then described in a 533 note. A 776 field for the original is made. Any notes after the 533 field should refer to the microfilm. Caution: when a microfilm of a newspaper is being cataloged, the #c in the collation (the 300 field) of the original should be deleted. Otherwise, if the library's profile automatically marks oversized items "Folio," cards will be produced for "Folio" microfilm.

CHANGE AND RECATALOGING

So far this chapter has been concerned with new material and cataloging from the first issue. Now we shall consider change, the distinguishing feature of serials. Any element in the description of a serial is liable to change, and when a serial is recataloged for any reason, most of the changes should be noted on the new record. Three changes will precipitate recataloging of a serial: (1) a change in title; (2) a change in the issuing body or in the name of the issuing body of an author/title entry; and (3) a change to Folio size from non-Folio.

Many libraries have reclassification programs which, with serials, usually involve complete recataloging. Other libraries are engaged in retrospective conversion projects which, with serials, must involve considerable recataloging, For whatever reason, much recataloging of serials goes on constantly.

Recataloging starts with a copy of the old catalog card. A search of the OCLC database is made for the old entry and for any other entries mentioned in a "Title varies" note or an "Issuing body varies" note on an author/title entry. Unless one of the records in hand at this point is an LC record, the *National Union Catalog* should be searched for an LC record. Now *Union List of Serials* and/or *New Serial Titles* should be searched for any further information about the serial. More information, especially ISSN, may be found in *Ulrich's* or *Irregular Serials and Annuals*. The cataloger should have in hand at a minimum the first issue available, the last issue of the old title (for a title change), and the first issue of the new title. In reclassing, the cataloger will have the whole run of the serial, making the process of cataloging easier. The first issue of the initial title should be examined at the start. In older serial volumes the covers of the issues are often missing, so, while the first issue is available, it may be minus both a title page and a cover. Sometimes the cataloger can feel certain of the numbering scheme without the cover and sometimes not. Even though the library has the first issue, the cataloger may wish to use a "Description based on:" note for a later cover or title page. Having described the earliest issue in hand, the cataloger now compares that issue with the latest one available. If the two differ in any of the details in the description, the issue where the change occurred should be located, and the change should be described in a note, with the appropriate dates. Recataloging often involves separating a record for a long run into two or three titles, each with a separate record. Truncated titles must be written out in full, author/title entries must become title entries, subject headings are changed to modern wording, and the names of issuing bodies are changed to *AACR* 2 form. Sometimes two author/title entries should be combined into one title entry. If there are two author/title records in the OCLC database for the title, use the record describing the earlier volumes. Sometimes the cataloger finds that following *AACR* 2 results in a change in the title proper. A serial may have been cataloged from the title page of a volume, or from an editorial page, when according to *AACR* 2 it should be cataloged from the cover of the first issue. The title proper may be on the old record as a cover title in the 246 field.

The simplest recataloging involves a newly cataloged serial with a title change. On the record for the old title, close the dates in the fixed field, close the numbering and the dates in the 362 field, close the dates (if any) in the 260 field, and create a 785 field for the new title. For the new title, if there is a record in the database, that oddity, a serial exact-match record, is occasionally found. If no record is found in the database, the cataloger must create a new record. In some libraries original records are more likely to be added to the database for title changes and recataloging than for new acquisitions. When dealing with a title change, a cataloger works from the first issue of the new title, while in dealing with a new title, the cataloger probably will not see the material until a bindable unit is accumulated.

ORIGINAL RECORDS

To create an original record the cataloger needs a serials workform. If the library does not have such a blank form, call up the serials workform on OCLC, get a printout, and use this form as the basis for creating a form of your own. Probably the first version of any new form will need some changes, so a small number should be produced for use until the workform has been tested. Adding new records to the database seems daunting at first. It is well to remember that mistakes can be corrected, and that cataloging errors are not life and death matters.

If a cataloger reads newly received OCLC cards before they are filed, he or she will find some errors. On original records, errors can usually be corrected before anyone else has used the record; however, if another library has used the record, send an error report to OCLC, and get the correction made. The error report does not count against the library's performance record if the perpetrator reports the error before anyone else does.

A cataloger starting to use the OCLC system is well advised to produce and examine some adapted records before entering any originals. Misunderstandings about how to enter records can then be cleared up before they are apparent to other OCLC users.

PHYSICAL DISPOSITION OF MATERIAL

New material comes to a serials cataloger from the serial record where standing orders are received, or from the acquisitions unit, where individual orders and gifts are received. Information about the extent of local library holdings should accompany all new material. If there is no system to ensure that the cataloger receives adequate information with each serial, a search of the catalog is required for each item, to avoid cataloging added volumes as new titles.

After new material is cataloged it must be prepared for use. Bound volumes may receive the same treatment as newly cataloged monographs, having labels and pockets affixed. Unbound material must be prepared for binding, and the serials cataloger is often the most logical person to separate the material into bindable units and create binding specification records, to ensure that future volumes will be bound in matching color and size units.

The cataloger should not receive added volumes. Having cataloged a serial, the cataloger should not see that publication again until there is a change that necessitates recataloging.

COMMUNICATION

In cataloging a new title, the cataloger must make a temporary shelf list and a binding specification record (if the material is unbound). Information about the correct entry, the call number, and the library's holdings of a new serial title should move in routine fashion from the cataloger to all other persons who maintain serial records. A form letter should be employed for this purpose. The same letter can be used to transmit change information to ensure consistency in all serial records.

When recataloging a title, even more temporary records are involved. In addition to the records mentioned above, a temporary main entry should be filed in the public catalog immediately, and if volumes are being moved from one call number to another, a sign should be taped to the shelf where the volumes used to be housed, explaining concisely what is happening. The sign should show the new call number, the date the volumes were removed, and the initials of the person who removed them. It is impossible in the present state of the art to change all records instantly, but the cataloger can leave an almost-instant trail enabling a public service librarian, if not a patron, to track down the needed serial. Material in the library building should be accessible to patrons at all times, no matter in what stage of processing it may be. A backlog of uncataloged material should be indexed, and the index should be understood by and accessible to public service librarians. The serials cataloger should be sensitive to the problems of public service librarians and give some priority to correcting cataloging that is inadequate from a public service point of view.

If the library has a serials list on microfiche and if the serials catalogers are up to date in their work, some patrons will never need to look in the catalog for a serial. The patron who knows the title of the serial he or she wants gets the call number from the microfiche list and is on the way. The patron who consults a periodical index for a group of references can move directly from the serials list to the stacks. These patrons are making indirect use of serials cataloging. The reference structure that tells the patron that one title is continued by another was created by a cataloger, and the call number that puts a serial near similar material was supplied by a cataloger, but the patron can use these products without using the catalog. The patron who takes a subject approach to material which is not in current indexes is going to make direct use of the catalog. The patron who found a reference in a fifty-year-old bibliography is going to need the catalog and perhaps the services of a librarian to determine whether the library has the material. Catalogers must stay aware of how patrons are finding or not finding serials. While *AACR* 2 promises to be more easily understood by laypersons than previous codes, the changes and transition are likely to prove trying for a year or two. Many personal names, corporate body names, and series-added-entries have been changed by *AACR* 2 from forms previously used in the catalog, and a reference structure must be provided to ensure that material is accessible under old and new forms of entry.

CORPORATE BODY HEADINGS

Serials catalogers do not often encounter titles having individual authors, but they must of necessity become very familiar with corporate bodies. Just as serials change titles, corporate bodies change names. While title changes are dealt with by linking entries on catalog records, name changes must be handled through linking references. A special sort of see-also reference can show the relationship:

> [Name of earlier body]
>   For works by this body under its later name see:
> [Name of later body]

When a corporate body has had more than one name change, make references to and from only the closest names: with names 1, 2, and 3, make references between 1 and 2, and between 2 and 3, but not between 1 and 3.

With a fairly complex reference structure already necessary to describe the relationships of corporate names, catalogers must also deal with rule changes which change the form of corporate entries. There are three basic choices for handling changes in form of entry:

1. Split files, leaving old entries under the old form of name, putting new entries under the new form, and making see-also references between the two files.

2. Interfiling. If the two forms of name do not differ a great deal, they can be put in one file, with a see-reference in the place where one file would have been. The integrated file can be under either the old or the new form of the entry. It is easier to integrate the file under the old form and better to integrate it under the new form.

3. Changing all the cards in the old file to the new form. This option is obviously the best from the point of view of users of the catalog; it is also obviously the most expensive.

A combination of all these ways of linking new and old forms of names is quite workable. Some files are so large that moving them and changing all the entries would be a major undertaking requiring rearrangement of much of the catalog. Other files are so small that only a few minutes are required to change all the old entries to the new form and to make the references. When a corporate body has changed its name a time or two, it is better to change all the catalog cards to the new form of each name, because references between old and new forms of earlier and later names are so intricate they are practically worthless.

If public catalog reference cards are taller than regular catalog cards they are easier to see and use. See-also references for corporate names are easy to miss in a catalog, and a "raised" reference is definitely preferable. Raised reference cards are useful for all types of references. In the past catalogs may have had few references for series-added-entries, but the rule changes have required that catalogers pay more attention to monographic series.

MONOGRAPHIC SERIES

Many monographs, particularly scholarly ones, are published in numbered series. To make this material fully accessible through the catalog, each monograph must be cataloged as a separate unit, and as a part of the series, through either a series-added-entry or a set of cards for the series as a whole, or both. A decision must be made either to class each monograph in the series separately or to class all the volumes in the series together. If the Library of Congress has already cataloged some of the monographs, it is usually practical to follow the pattern set by LC, because added volumes can be cataloged more economically if the library can make full use of Library of Congress cataloging. LC practice now is to class each volume of a monographic series separately unless the volumes are closely related in subject matter. In the past, LC often cataloged two copies of each volume of a monographic series, classing one copy separately and the other together with the other series volumes. A few years ago this practice was abandoned, and the Library of Congress began classing both copies in the same way, with a goodly majority of monographic series being classed separately. Libraries which had been classing many series together have had to make some troublesome changes. Some libraries have opted for continuing to class many series together. Others have changed in mid-series, using a note on the series card:

Vols. 20 -   classed separately.

An extension of that note can be typed on the series main entry card only:

Vols. 20-   classed separately; see following cards.

Then the series main entry card, which shows the call number for the first 19 volumes is followed by series-added-entries for volumes 20 on. Sometimes older volumes have been reclassed to achieve consistent treatment for a whole series.

Series Authority File

Whatever is done with a series, the treatment should be recorded in a series authority file in order that later volumes may be treated exactly as earlier ones have been. *AACR* 2 has engendered many, many changes in series entries, because almost all monographic series entries are now title entries, many of them uniform title entries. With all catalogers adding entries and changes in the series authorithy file, filing above the rod in that file is advisable, with one or two persons responsible for checking the filing before dropping the cards.

Series-Added-Entries

Some libraries make a set of cards for the whole series, whether it is classed together or not, and a series-added-entry for each volume, whether it is classed separately or not. Other libraries make a set of cards only for the classed together series and series-added-entries only for the classed separately series. The fuller cataloging has obvious advantages, but considerations of catalog drawer space and of economy may dictate the decision. Online catalogs will be free of these constraints.

With *AACR* 2 changing series-added-entries for many continuing series, both the catalog and the series authority file need see-references from the old form of the series-added-entry to the new form. It is possible to split the files of series-added-entries and employ see-also references between the files, but it makes for a simpler reference structure to change all the series-added-entries to the new form at the time the new form is determined. The change to *AACR* 2 has some added benefits in that a whole file of series-added-entries is examined at once, and some peculiarities can be eliminated from the catalog.

Serial/Series

A discussion of monographic series would not be complete without mention of the serial which suddenly becomes monographic and its reverse, the monographic series which becomes a serial. The former instance does not pose much of a problem. A note of the new treatment in the series authority file and a letter to the serial record so that future volumes will be cataloged as analytics will suffice. When a monographic series becomes a serial, the same treatment is appropriate if the series is classed together. But if the series is classed separately, it constitutes a nuisance. Two treatments are possible: (1) the monographic volumes can be recataloged and classed together, with a serial record starting with volume 1, or (2) the same serial record can be made with a note added:

Vols. 1-5 classed separately.

The main entry can have an added note:

Vols. 1-5 classed separately; see following cards.

If only a few volumes are involved, reclassing them is the neater solution to the problem.

OTHER PROBLEM MATERIAL

There are certain types of publications which are a little out of the ordinary and which are recurring problems simply because they are not routine. Here are ways of handling a few types.

Monographs and Sets Continued by Serials

Sometimes a monograph, especially a bibliography, is continued by a supplementary serial. The serial should be given the same class number as the monograph and the Cutter number of the monograph with a "2" added so that the serial stands on the shelf right beside the monograph:

Cutter no. of monograph	*Cutter no. of serial*
.C65	.C652

Some catalogs are issued as multi-volume sets kept up to date by supplementary serials. Each numbered supplement may be in several volumes, but if the supplements are numbered or dated, they can be treated as serials. The serial has the same Cutter number as the set with "Suppl." as the third line of the call number:

Set:	*Set vol.:*	*Supplement*	*Supplement vol.:*	*Supplement vol.:*
Z999	Z999	Z999	Z999	Z999
.C65	.C65	.C65	.C65	.C65
	v.5	Suppl.	Suppl.	Suppl.
			no.1	no.1
				v.1

Supplements

A monograph issued as a numbered supplement to a serial is part of a supplementary monographic series which can be either classed together or classed separately, depending on the subject matter of the series, as any other monographic series is handled. A monograph issued as a supplement to a serial issue, if it is of little lasting significance, can be bound with the issue to which it is a supplement. If a monographic supplement is important enough to be cataloged, it is classed separately with an added entry for the serial as a whole (if the monograph supplements the series as a whole), or with an added entry for the particular serial number (if the monograph supplements a particular number.) See *CSB* 14, pp. 23-24 for examples.

Single Issues

Sometimes a single issue of a periodical is purchased because of a single article it contains or because the entire issue is on one theme. Such material is best handled as a monograph and as an extract from a journal. The irrelevant parts can be ignored or even removed and discarded. An article can be cataloged under its author/title, and an issue can be cataloged under its title or, if there is no title, under an assigned title reflecting its theme. The material is thus cataloged to reveal the purpose for which it was purchased. Even if the library has a complete run of the journal, it is still a good idea to analyze or class separately the piece ordered for a special purpose. Presumably, someone empowered to order library material did not know the library already had the needed article or issue, so it will save time and tempers to make the material accessible and get it out of cataloging. To sum up, a whole issue on one topic can be analyzed or classed separately; a single article is best classed separately. An added entry for the serial and volume (and pages) is made in either case.

Dictionaries Issued in Parts

A dictionary is not a serial but a dictionary issued in parts is a binding problem, and serials catalogers sometimes get involved with such material, often after some parts have been bound oddly. Each library should establish a policy for handling such material; instructions for handling should be in the serial record. Some dictionaries are published over a period of fifty years or more, and it may take ten years to cumulate a single volume. Publishers of multi-part dictionaries usually issue title pages, and the library's binding instructions should include waiting for the title page. The covers of the parts often show the publication plan and also show which parts have been published. All this information makes binding very simple. The problem arises from the fact that the material is not a serial and is being handled by people who are not accustomed to material received in unbound parts. The solution is to prevent premature binding of incomplete or mixed volumes by having clear instructions in the serial record.

Serials Issued Together

Some journals have issued with them annual surveys or directories in related fields. These annuals may or may not be numbered as parts of the more frequent periodical. Often they start out numbered as issues of the parent journal and become independent later. Also, they may get bound with the parent publication whether or not they are independent. If the annual directory is a numbered part of the parent journal, make both a note about it and an added entry for it on the catalog record for the parent. If the annual directory is not numbered as an issue of the parent journal, catalog it as a separate journal. If some of the issues have already been bound with the parent, make a 590 note:

Vols. for 1960-1965 bound with: Parent (Call no. of parent).

If the independent directory was issued earlier as a part of the parent, make a 580 note of that fact:

Continues an annual issue of: Parent.

Serials Issued with Parts of Monographs

Some journals, mostly in philology or linguistics, have parts of dictionaries issued with them. These parts should be removed before binding and cumulated as stated previously. Bibliographies are also sometimes issued in separately paged parts with serials, sometimes as serials themselves and sometimes as monographs. If the worst occurs and such issues get bound together, the situation can be remedied with an Exacto knife and some muscle power.

CLOSING THOUGHTS

The cataloger has some responsibilities broader than cataloging individual items.

Supplies

In a new job a cataloger should find out immediately his or her responsibility for supplies. No matter who actually orders supplies, the cataloger must anticipate routine needs and should determine as soon as possible what items will be needed in what quantities and how long it takes to get them. A system should be devised for reordering in time to keep a continuous supply of needed items. Find out immediately how long it takes to get a stencil made, how long it takes to get new mimeographed forms, how long for printed forms.

Policy Decisions

There are decisions about cataloging to be made in every library based on the library's clientele, its size, its staff size, and its budget: (1) Should periodicals be classed or not? If they are not classed, how are they shelved when a title changes? Should all volumes be put under one title and a reference dummy under the other, or should the volumes be split by title with a dummy with each title? (2) When a title changes, should the old title be recataloged to close the entry or ignored? (3) When an old entry is changed by new rules, should the spine titles be changed to correspond to the new entry? (4) In *AACR* 2 corporate body authority work, which files will be changed, which will be interfiled, and which will be maintained as split files? There are no absolute answers to these questions; in most cases a compromise between the theoretical best solution and the most economical solution will be necessary.

Quality Control

Quality control can best be maintained by having each record examined more than once. Even in a one-person operation, a time lapse between steps in cataloging can ensure a fresh look at the record. Records can be cataloged in one step, entered into a save file in a second step, and produced in a third step, whether by one person or by three. It is desirable that all catalog cards be revised by a cataloger before going into the catalog.

Cataloging serials is a complicated, often clerical operation. The change involved in the job increases its difficulty but also increases its interest. Just when I thought I had seen every eccentricity of which serial publishers were capable, a colleague showed me *The New York Spanner*. The publisher proposes to distinguish between the issues of this journal not by number or by date, but by varying the color of the wrench on the cover! The ability of publishers to create new challenges appears to be infinite, as does the ability of serials catalogers to cope.

NOTES

1. *Anglo-American Cataloguing Rules*, 2nd ed. (Chicago: American Library Association; Ottawa: Canadian Library Association, 1978).

2. *Cataloging Service Bulletin*, 1- Summer 1978- (Washington, D.C.: Library of Congress Processing Services).

3. OCLC, Inc., *Serials Format* (Columbus, Ohio: 1980). (On-Line Systems. C80-4).

Chapter 5

Preserving the Serial Collection

Preservation of library serials consists of three aspects—binding, microforms, and security—and it encompasses the various functions of serials management. Preservation is, first, a collection development responsibility; also, it is affected by network relationships and cooperative agreements; it influences the selection of options in acquiring and cataloging; and finally, it determines the means of access chosen for serials.

Before the 1960s most libraries practiced one type of serial preservation: binding. Loose journal issues were combined in a buckram, cloth, or cardboard volume, and single-piece paperbound volumes received the protection of a more substantial cover. Then, with growing space and money problems came the popularity of microforms. Today some libraries are more concerned with binding, some with microforms. The emphasis depends upon the local policy for retention of serial backfiles. During the 1970s librarians recognized a number of ways to preserve their collections; these include care in selecting among the types of microform, studies of the acidity of paper, the use of electronic security systems, and the development of disaster-response plans and preservation standards.

A library's policy concerning preservation of its resources should be coordinated with other aspects of collection development so that the written statement reflects the purpose of the library. For instance, a branch of a public library system may restrict its funds to current serials, because the main library can supply older volumes when they are needed. A research library needs both current and retrospective serials in the fields in which its patrons are working, so a portion of its materials and equipment budget must be dedicated to preservation, includng storage and security.

Each subscription and standing order should be evaluated in terms of the collection development policy to determine what must be retained and in what format. When the decision is made as part of the selection process, no title will be retained without evaluation. The decision can also be made or reviewed as part of precataloging procedures. The advantage to the latter practice is that the evaluator will have recent issues in hand. Factors to consider in the retention decision are, in part, those used for initial purchase, discussed in Chapter 2.

Few libraries are able to finance the optimum degree of preservation and must reach a balance between acquiring and preserving. Not all preservation costs can be isolated in budgeting, for they are often hidden in the materials funding when an item is purchased on acid-free paper or when a silver halide microform is chosen over vesicular or diazo. Preservation is expensive, and a commitment to it requires financial support. For this reason libraries must frequently compromise and sacrifice optimum preservation in order to acquire a greater number of resources.

The preservation of library materials is currently a lively topic in librarianship. It fits well with energy conservation and ecology, matters of concern to librarians and nonlibrarians alike. The Resources and Technical Services Division of the American Library Association had, for many years, a Preservation of Library Materials Committee. In 1980 this committee was raised to sectional status and formed its own committees and discussion groups. Fifteen hundred RTSD members joined the new section in its first year. In this era of concern for the continued existence of material things, preservation of serials is a legitimate interest.

There is an increasing amount of published material to aid librarians in their efforts to preserve the collection, and several sources are included in the Annotated Bibliography. One of these is the series of concise *Preservation Leaflets*, published by the Library of Congress and available without charge.[1] Each leaflet covers a particular type of material (newspapers, photographs, leather bindings), a preservation problem (mildew, insects), or some other aspect of the topic (marking, literature of conservation). The series is intended for the practicing librarian who needs basic information, and leaflets are written in response to specific requests made of LC's assistant director for preservation.

BINDING

Commercial binding is the most widely used method of preserving serials. An understanding of the options a library has and the procedures used by the binder should be included in the training of serials librarians. Binding has traditionally been a labor intensive industry, but now many processes can be computerized and others can be performed by sophisticated machinery. Not all commercial binders have been willing to accept automation and mechanization at the same rate, so there are differences in the way they process serials.

Not all libraries bind serials. Some libraries, usually small ones, elect to retain periodical issues unbound (perhaps for a stated number of years) either loose, tied and stored, or boxed. Others prefer to retain some or all of their periodicals in microform. Still other libraries purchase pre-bound complete volumes for retention and dispose of worn individual issues. Every library must consider and resolve the question of binding: Shall we, or shall we not bind serials? How can we best serve our patrons? What are the costs of each alternative? The cost of binding is rising along with the cost of obtaining materials, and the binding budget must be recognized by the library as an increasing, continuing commitment just as the serial allocation is. Not only is the price of a bound volume rising, but increasing costs of paper and postage have forced publishers to cut expenses wherever they can. They have narrowed margins and are using a poorer quality of paper, changes that mean fewer issues can be bound in the customary way. A typical weekly newsmagazine, for instance, may have been bound in one or two physical volumes a year initially; later it required quarterly volumes. Now the title must be bound bimonthly or monthly if all the text is to be readable and copyable. In this case, binding costs have at least tripled, without considering increases in cost per volume. Library binders are dealing with these problems, but at binding time, the librarian must evaluate each title and decide on expensive hand sewing, retention in microform, or discard.

Most academic libraries will bind or otherwise routinely draw together in volumes every periodical title that they retain. If a serial is worth keeping, it deserves treatment better than leaving issues loose. Unbound nonperiodical serials, which usually appear in large pieces appropriate for binding separately, are exempt from the problem of loose issues, but policy regarding their retention is also needed.

Although at least one library's binding manual is available for purchase,[2] no library should accept without question any other institution's practices. Binding policy depends upon the function of the library. Does it collect current serials and dispose of older volumes? Does it support the parent institution's curriculum and, perhaps, limited research? Or is it a research library which collects exhaustively within an explicit profile? Is the library a regional or national resource with a heavy interlibrary loan and photocopying program? The function of the library determines the degree of permanence necessary for its serial collection and the subject emphases that guide binding policy.

If a title is recognized to be of value to the library collection, there is a limited number of binding alternatives from which to choose. It can be bound by a commercial binder, according to Library Binding Institute (LBI, discussed later in this chapter) standards, and become a permanent part of the library's holdings. A serial of questionable retrospective value can be bound commercially in a semi-permanent binding, placed in boards, or otherwise drawn together in the library, or it may be retained unbound until it falls to pieces or is lost. Even for a library that has elected to preserve serials in their original format, there are times when microform is appropriate, such as for titles produced in newsprint. Finally, the serial may be discarded at a specified time, perhaps after one year or two years.

Types of Binding

When a library selects a member of the Library Binding Institute as its primary binder, it has a right to expect certain standards of quality, as specified by LBI, and to expect a variety of choices within the Class A Library Binding. This binding provides for a buckram cover and for the stitching of serial issues together. The most commonly used stitching is *oversewing* (Figure 5.1), which is defined in the LBI Standard as "the process of sewing, by hand or machine, through the edge of each section in consecutive order, using preformed holes through which the needle passes."[3] The thread travels diagonally through the back of each section of the book, taking up at least one-quarter inch of the inner margin; this loss is in addition to what was ground or cut away to separate the book into single leaves. Oversewing prevents the volume from lying flat when opened. If a serial volume with inner margins of less than one-half inch is oversewn, any use, but especially photocopying, is likely to lead to broken stitches or torn pages as the reader attempts to see words close to the inner margins. Thick volumes require much wider inner margins than thin volumes if they are to be readable after they are oversewn. As journal margins become narrower because of publishers' attempts to cut expenses, oversewing becomes less satisfactory as a means of stitching issues and signatures together. The amount of space required by oversewing makes rebinding virtually impossible.

An alternative to oversewing is *hand sewing* (Figure 5.2), a procedure in which the binder uses a saw to cut notches in the spine edge of folded signatures or issues and sews the book to cords placed in the notches. The hand binder uses a good quality linen thread to stitch the leaves and issues together and to the supporting cord. The notch enables the bound volume to be opened flat, so that even the innermost words are visible. Hand sewing is more expensive than machine sewing.

The commercial binder may also offer *Smyth sewing* (Figure 5.2), or through sewing, a machine method of sewing through the folded signa-

Figure 5.1: Oversewing

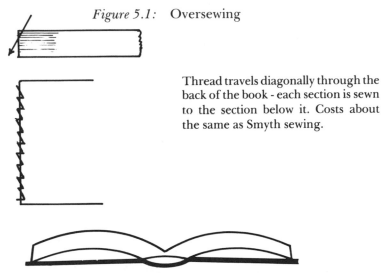

Thread travels diagonally through the back of the book - each section is sewn to the section below it. Costs about the same as Smyth sewing.

Opening is somewhat restricted. The back of the book is moderately flexible, but a minimum of ½-¾" margin is necessary. A wider margin is needed for thick books or for books on thick paper.

Figure 5.2: Sewing Through the Fold

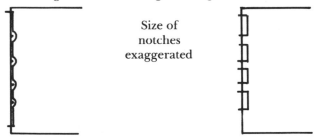

Size of notches exaggerated

Hand Sewing

Thread travels across cords placed in grooves sawn in spine. Suitable for material which cannot be Smyth sewn. Most expensive sewing.

Smyth Sewing

Independent loops of thread join sections to each other. No sewing supports. Costs about the same as oversewing.

Opening is quite free. The back of the book is flexible and should arch upward when the book is opened. Pages with very narrow margins are still readable. If volume is not already in sewable sections (ie. single-section issues) preparation is expensive.

Figure 5.3: Side Sewing

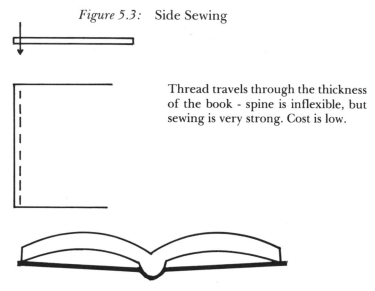

Thread travels through the thickness of the book - spine is inflexible, but sewing is very strong. Cost is low.

Opening is greatly restricted. Margin of ¾″ needed for books on thin paper - more for books on thick paper. Suitable for the thinnest books only.

tures. Smyth sewing is used by some publishers. The thread used by the binder will be that specified by the manufacturer of the machine used and may be cotton, nylon, or polyester. Smyth sewn volumes require less inner margin than oversewn volumes and lie relatively flat when open.

Thin books may be stitched by the *side sewing* (Figure 5.3), or Singer sewing, process. The stitching is similar to that done by a home sewing machine, and it is used for many children's books. This is the strongest type of sewing available, but the spine of the book is completely inflexible, so the maximum thickness of the piece is one-quarter inch.

A commercial binder should be able to offer each of the above methods of sewing a volume, as deemed appropriate by the library, based on the volume's thickness, width of inner margins, and projected use. It is the binding librarian's responsibility to select the best method of stitching.

Use of bound serials causes some common and predictable types of wear that can and should be anticipated when writing binding specifications. For example, it is standard for the binder to use cloth jointed endpapers to compensate for the weak joints inherent in cased books. It is not standard for him to reinforce the inner fold of a Smyth sewn volume, and this should often be specified, because, in a magazine printed on thin, coated paper, its omission leads to a definite weakness in the binding. A strip of repair tape over the inner fold should not cost much to apply at the bindery and should pay for itself by saving repair time and expense while reducing the number of missing pages to be replaced later.

Some serials do not need the durability of Class A Library Binding. In addition to the various types of sewing, commercial binders should offer a non-Class A adhesive binding, accomplished by using the *double fan* method. On a machine, inner edges of a volume are slightly spread and passed across glued rollers on first one side and then the other. Binders have individual names for the process. Gluing does not make as strong a binding as stitching, but it does not require more than a one-sixteenth inch margin and has been proven satisfactory for low use serials. A second glued binding, called *perfect binding*, is often used for paperbacks. This is not as strong as the double fan method, because the glue reaches only the outside edge of pages.

For low use titles, a cloth cover may be selected instead of the standard buckram; the volume within this case may be either sewn or glued. Single issues of serials and thin single-piece volumes which will not be used heavily are often stapled or glued between cardboard covers. This binding is frequently done within the library, and can be considered either permanent or temporary. Some librarians glue the serial's cover to the outside of the front cardboard; many use a typed label. Other types of binding that can be done within the library include *spiral binding*, in which pages are held together by a plastic or metal ring backing; *post binding*, where metal or plastic fixtures are inserted through holes in the material; and *portfolios*, folders that hold together loose issues or pages.

Among original-format alternatives to commercial or in-house permanent binding are boxing, which at its best includes the purchase of acid-free boxes and at its worst, Princeton files or cartons from the grocery store; bundling, trussing with cotton string or tape; and placing loose issues between cut-to-size cardboard and tying them securely. The above are methods of retaining serials; by no means can they be called preservation.

Every library has some material that will be used for so brief a time or so seldom that it does not warrant the expense of permanent binding; guidelines will be determined by the individual library. Most libraries provide for on-site repair and temporary binding, involving cardboard covers, tape and staples. There is need for local processing of materials that do not need commercial binding because of low projected use or low cost. The type and amount of binding (sometimes combined with repair) done within any library can vary from simply taping and/or stapling between cardboard covers to the use of devices which punch and sew, available from library suppliers, or even the use of some types of specialized binding machinery. So long as the in-house treatment does not require expensive equipment justified only by heavy use, it is probably an economical means of preserving some materials. Serials that do not have to leave the library to be bound are more quickly available for use, and the procedures employed within the library, being less sophisticated than a commercial binder's, are more quickly completed, provided there is not a large backlog. It is important to remember that any local binding that is considered to be temporary must not preclude permanent binding in the future. Temporary binding must not alter the piece to the extent that it cannot be bound commercially if the need arises.

When to Bind

The appropriate time for binding serials varies according to both library priorities and subject of the material. For instance, a library with low patron use for a specific period during the year, such as a library at a high school where there are no summer classes, may hold all unbound issues and volumes until that low use time to ensure that serials will always be available to patrons. A library having more consistent, year-round use may bind whenever the volume is complete, sacrificing patrons' immediate access for the relative security of hard covers. Some libraries make a special effort to have certain subject categories of journals available at a particular time; for example, university library education journals may be kept on the shelf (either bound or unbound) during summer school when public school teachers are enrolled. One library sends a volume to the bindery as soon as the last issue arrives, while another feels it is important to wait until the first piece of the next volume appears, so the most recent issue will be available to patrons. Certain titles that are published in bindable units, such as annuals, may be held for review by a faculty member, or they may be shipped immediately to the commercial bindery.

Every library system should be able to work out a procedure whereby multiple copies of a serial are sent to the bindery in succession, not all at the same time. One library can be designated the first to send a volume of a multi-copy subscription, and the other holding locations agree to wait until notified that the first copy is back from the bindery before they send their copies. This ensures that a patron will always have access within the system to a title that is used heavily enough to justify more than one subscription.

When should a serial be rebound? As soon as possible after someone realizes that it needs rebinding. The longer the wait to rebind a deteriorating volume, the more the risk of loss and permanent damage to the pages. Rebinding must be scheduled to fit the cycle of library use in the same way as the initial binding was.

Repair of a serial volume may provide a temporary resolution of the problem, but it must be done carefully for materials that will go later to the commercial binder. Tape, holes, trimming, and staples can cause the binder problems both by mutilating the piece so badly that it cannot be rebound and by damaging binding machinery. A library may want to consider limiting the availability of a deteriorating volume through closed shelving instead of risking more damage by "repairing" it.

At the time a serial volume is sent for rebinding, the librarian may want to consider splitting the piece into two physical volumes. Heavy use, particularly copy machine use, of a volume more than about two inches thick, even with three-quarter inch or larger inside margins, can cause damage quickly. It is more economical to rebind in two volumes that will survive heavy use than it is to rebind in a single volume that will neither last nor take rebinding again.

Binding policies and their details are unlimited, and each library will determine the optimum time to send journals to the bindery by considering such variables as public service, security, cycle of use, budget, and binder's schedule. Whatever the specifications of the written policy, it will prove beneficial to retain enough flexibility to account for unexpected situations—a change in the school calendar, an international institute meeting on campus, patrons' publishing deadlines, and equipment breakdowns at the bindery.

Bindery Preparation

Many of the routine operations used a generation ago in preparing serials for binding are no longer considered practical by some libraries. Such tasks as removing advertising, collating every unit to check for missing pages, and deciding for each title whether to retain or discard covers have often been dropped in the interests of economy and efficiency through standardization. Even the choice of color and lettering may be made once, for all a library's serials, instead of for each title.

What remains essential is the collecting of pieces of a title that comprise a volume, not necessarily corresponding to a bibliographic volume; arranging them in numerical order, top to bottom; securing them temporarily with cotton string, tape, or rubber bands; marking the bundle so the binder can identify the title; and recording that the volume is being bound. These things should be done according to guidelines which support the library's public service and collection development objectives; thus, the guidelines will vary from library to library.

The first step in preparing a serial for binding is to get it to the staff member responsible for the succeeding steps of this operation. A one-piece volume may be routed from the serial record to the correct staff member, or the check-in assistant may do the preparation. The latter practice may gain a few days' time, but it probably sacrifices the care that would be taken by a person whose chief responsibility is binding preparation.

Periodicals that have accumulated and are ready to be bound can be gathered by a clerk or student assistant working from either binding records of these titles or notices sent by check-in assistants reporting that a volume is ready to be bound. As the clerk gathers the issues, he or she can easily place them in chronological and numerical order and check to see that all pieces are present. When there is a missing issue or the subscription appears to have lapsed, the supervisor can be notified in writing so a search can be made and a claim or replacement order can be placed if needed.

It is at this point that a trained binding preparation assistant should take over the procedure and examine each volume according to the library's guidelines. If pages are missing, photocopies can be ordered and inserted when they arrive. Replacement pages are usually obtained in front-and-back photocopy with binding margins. There are problems with this method of replacing pages even before binding, for sometimes the copying is done carelessly and is out of register. If this was done within the library, rephotocopying can be done quickly. If the pages came from another library, one must decide whether to delay binding until an acceptable copy can be obtained, to go ahead and use what is at hand even though the copy extends beyond the page edge or into the inner margin, or to bear the expense and time required to have the pages carefully recopied within the library. Stolen pages contain articles that people use, and the replacement pages will be read and photocopied and, perhaps, cut out and stolen again. One wonders whether it would be practical to keep a master file of replacement pages for particularly high-risk articles.

In libraries where advertising pages and covers are removed before binding, now is the time for this operation. It is likely that in-house removal is less expensive than leaving this to be done at the binder's. Also, the library staff member may take more care than the bindery employee. This procedure saves money if the binding budget is tight, for the cost of removing covers and ads is paid from the personnel budget. If, however, the personnel budget is tighter than the binding budget, the library may prefer to have ads and covers removed at the commercial bindery.

Sometimes a volume cannot be completed, at least not in paper format. When an issue is not available from the publisher or a second-hand dealer and when a photocopy is too expensive, the librarian may decide to bind the volume in its incomplete state. Sometimes there is a request for the binder to "stub" the volume, so the missing issue, if it is ever located, can be bound in, but often there is so little chance of this happening that stubbing is not necessary. For essential missing issues it is preferable to purchase a microform copy and forget about acquiring a paper issue.

Once the binding assistant has determined that a volume is complete or has decided to bind it incomplete, the issues are tied together and are ready for preparation of a binding slip. The form that accompanies a serial volume to the bindery may be manually or computer produced, depending upon the binder's and library's capabilities.

In addition, the binding assistant needs to record at every appropriate location the titles and volumes that are at the bindery and the date they left the library. If there is a serials department public service point, the record should be close by, so patrons can be informed as to the status of volumes. Some libraries elect to make this information a part of the central circulation file. Whichever location is used, it is important that staff members know where to direct patrons to confirm that a specific volume is at the bindery. When this record is kept within the serials department, it is possible also to record the date the piece returned from the bindery. This information can help locate a recently bound serial, which may travel through a number of checkpoints before it reaches its place in the stacks. A review of such records can also alert the staff to initiate an enquiry about serials that have been sent to the bindery but have not been returned within a reasonable time.

A library must decide whether centralized or decentralized binding preparation is best. If there is a backlog in a library binding unit, it benefits patrons for individual issues to be available at their unbound location as close as possible to the time when they leave the building; this can be done best if binding is prepared at the location of the unbound issues. On the other hand, if there is not sufficient staff at these interim locations to prepare the volumes for commercial binding, centralized processing is efficient. In either case the library with several locations for unbound serials must have one place at which the binder's truck picks up and delivers the shipments. This station can have adequate staffing to give a final check to materials being sent and an initial review of volumes being returned.

Guidelines for Selecting a Commercial Binder

The first thing a library should require of its binder is that the company be a "certified library binder," a member of the Library Binding Institute. Without the assurance of this professional association and support, the librarian has no way of knowing that the binder's work will be satisfactory and no recourse if it is not. If a commercial binder is not a member of LBI, the library customer is taking an unnecessary risk with its materials requiring binding.

Even though they may be certified library binders, commercial binders are not equal. Prices, equipment, procedures, and services all vary among binders. There is general agreement in the literature that it is the responsibility of the librarian in charge of binding to select the binder; the decision should not be made by an institutional purchasing agent or a library bindery staff member. If the binder is selected on the basis of a bid, it is again the librarian and not someone outside the library who must have the knowledge to select the competitors. In comparing binders, each should be evaluated upon several points. Samples of their work will be available for examination and, if it is necessary, for evaluation by LBI. Visits to the binderies and observation of their procedures and equipment are also recommended. Other libraries using the binderies under consideration can advise as to reliability, treatment of the library materials, length of time volumes can be expected to be away from the library, flexibility in adapting to terms set by the library, and other aspects of service such as computerized binding slips and insertion of security system strips. Price quotations from competing binderies must be examined carefully, for there may be charges for lettering, collating and so on, which one binder lists separately and another includes in the basic price. Not least, the library, and particularly the librarian in charge of binding, must be certain to take great care in writing the specifications for the binding of serial volumes. The instructions must be explicit and obvious. The binder cannot be expected to follow directions that are vague and do not spell out the library's needs in detail.

The choice of a binder or the process of changing from one binder to another is an occasion when the binding librarian should communicate with other such librarians and with the Library Binding Institute, if need be, for it is a crucial decision. Changing from one binder to another is perhaps more disruptive of processes and more expensive to the library than changing subscription agents.

Some libraries have all their binding done by a local bindery in the library or elsewhere on campus. This is an impractical course in most cases because, even if there is no question of quality, there is a loss of the economies of scale. Modern bindery equipment, particularly where some parts of the operation are automated, can be efficient only with high volume; the machines must be kept operating. Unless a local bindery can reach the volume of work that will make the equipment cost-effective, something few libraries can do alone, the cost of permanent binding done in-house will be significantly higher than work done by a commercial binder.

Standards and Quality Control

The Library Binding Institute is an association of commercial binders whose business is primarily with libraries, and their suppliers. This institute was established in 1935, when binders who were specifically *library* binders left the Book Manufacturers' Institute (BMI) to form their own group. Since that time LBI has worked to formulate, revise, and promote standards for various types of book and serial binding done for libraries. This group has worked closely with the American Library Association and its Library Technology Project and with the Special Libraries Association, to their mutual advantage. As early as 1923 there were "specifications" for library binding; the ALA/BMI-sponsored "Minimum Specifications for Class 'A' Binding" is the basis for current standards. The specifications were based on materials and methods of manufacture of the binding and were widely adhered to in the industry. The 1933 Specifications and a 1939 document, "Standards for Reinforced (Pre-Library Bound) New Books," were the foundation for the "Library Binding Institute Standard for Library Binding" and the "Library Binding Institute Standard for Pre-Bound Books." These were issued in 1958 and revised several times, until they were combined into one standard, "The Library Binding Institute Standard for Library Binding," revised last in 1981. LBI publishes a periodical, *Library Scene*, covering binding matters and broader library topics. Its predecessor, *Library Binder*, dealt more specifically with the binding industry.

The following is a statement of the ways in which the Library Binding Institute members work to implement the Standard. The Institute

A. Has established a certification system to inform librarians which binders can do work in accordance with the Standards, are reputable, have been recommended by librarians, and carry insurance to protect their customers' property.

B. Maintains a Free Examination Service for librarians to determine whether binding has been done in accordance with contractual requirements.

C. Sponsored the promulgation by the Federal Trade Commission of Trade Practice Rules to insure the highest possible standards of equitable and fair dealing in the industry and to protect librarians against deceit and misrepresentations.

D. Maintains a continuous program of research and education involving binders, their customers and suppliers.

E. Has established the use of a warranty on invoices of Certified Library Binders, stating that work complies with the LBI Standard for Library Binding unless otherwise stated thereon.

F. Established a Quality Control Program whereby the plant of each Certified Library Binder is periodically examined for adherence to a carefully planned quality control program.[4]

The work of the Library Binding Institute, the national library organizations, and the certified library binders has greatly benefitted libraries by virtually abolishing nonstandard commercial library binding that lacks the library's consent. However, the standard for "Class A Library Binding" is only the minimum required for routine binding. Its value is, in part, as a means of communication between the librarian and the commercial binder. Both understand that binding will meet Class A minimum standards unless some other arrangement is made; if the library requires a higher quality binding or a lower quality binding than the standard, it must work with the binder to determine mutually acceptable standards.

The librarian who works with the commercial binder to establish local standards has a responsibility to become knowledgeable about the binding process through visiting the binder and attending workshops and seminars on library binding and preservation. He or she should examine the binder's work occasionally to be sure the binder understands the library's instructions. The librarian can flag certain volumes to examine when they are returned to the library.

Matt Roberts, writing in *Special Libraries*, supports the preceding suggestions by urging librarians not to let their concern with binding end with the completion of the binding slip, but to learn to recognize and treat materials, especially those having special binding problems, and to evaluate the work of the bindery. While the owners and officers of the commercial bindery may be far more knowledgeable about their work than a librarian can expect to be, Roberts reminds his readers that these persons are not the ones who actually bind the library's serials. The persons who handle the material are likely to be employees who have less overall binding knowledge than the owner and less time to examine each volume than the librarian. And, Roberts writes, the mechanization of the binding process makes this handling even more superficial, for the cost of the machinery requires that materials be processed as rapidly as possible. One cannot expect the binder to correct the library's mistakes.[5]

Roberts offers guidelines for the librarian to work with in setting the library's standards for commercial binding. The Library Binding Institute has published a handbook for librarians which includes recommendations for proper handling of library material to be bound.[6] Most recently Maurice F. Tauber has compiled the third edition of *Library Binding Manual*,[7] a comprehensive work encompassing the history and projected future of binding, as well as guidance in selecting a binder and recommendations for bindery preparation by the library. Tauber also has covered the steps in binding a volume and has given pointers for evaluation of the finished work.

There is evidence that libraries are turning from the Class A Library Binding to a nonsewn binding that permits material with narrow inside margins to be held together without loss of text. There is concern among some librarians that the risks in using this "standardized" binding are great, because there are no standards for its use. A recent article by Don Lanier urges that librarians and the library binding industry work together to develop standards for this type of binding so the details of the process will be clearly understood by both parties.[8] Several years ago Paul Banks made a similar point about the significant number of materials falling into the gap between Class A binding treatment and expensive handwork. He called for a binding standard for the "permanent research value" category of material. This would be an extra-cost, nondestructive binding for valuable works for which expensive hand binding cannot be justified.[9]

Librarians need to work with their binders to establish specifications for materials that should have different treatment from the Class A standard. Binding instructions can specify more than just the color of the cloth and lettering; they can specify sewing or gluing instructions based on the librarian's decision for the individual title. The binder can supply the librarian with a number of different specifications stating what types of sewing are available, so that the librarian can elect hand sewing, Smyth sewing, or some type of stitching other than oversewing. The binding form can list a number of options, with boxes for the librarian to check. This compensates for the lack of national standards by creating a set of local standards that are easy to change if it should be necessary. In addition, this experience gives librarians practice in the development of standards that may lead to national standards.

MICROFORMS

Many libraries, particularly those that have developed during the past few decades, have chosen to retain some or most of their periodicals in microform, rather than bound or otherwise maintained in their original format. Some libraries have had no realistic alternative, for much retrospective material is available only in microform or expensive reprint. Established libraries, outgrowing their stack space and/or facing the problem of mutilation, have turned to microform as a solution. The companies producing the microfilm and microfiche, and equipment for using them, have become convincing in their promotion of these products. They have also kept the prices of current volumes of periodicals in microform at just about the cost of binding. Prices for backfiles are higher than for current subscriptions, and, until recently, each periodical in microform was available from only one company. Now various microform producers have begun to offer titles formerly available only from one of their competitors, so there is a possibility that backfile prices may come down as a result of competition. Some libraries have the equipment to do their own filming of serials that are not available commercially. Local filming is valid as part of a larger preservation effort, but it is almost prohibitively expensive for a library to film its own serials individually, unless there is a market for the filmed product and the library promotes its availability.

At present there are three types of microform processes on the market: silver halide, diazo, and vesicular. Of these diazo is clearly unacceptable for library preservation use because of its relatively short shelf life. The inexpensive diazo is adequate for short-term use in COM catalogs that are replaced periodically. Silver halide is the archival standard film, but it is expensive and subject to scratching with repeated use. Recent studies indicate that silver halide film may not be as long-lived as had previously been thought. The polyester vesicular process has been controversial but is apparently perfectly acceptable for copies of serials that will be used by patrons. Vesicular microforms are tough, inexpensive, and likely to last as long as silver halide in a library situation. For archival purposes silver halide is still the recommended medium, but few libraries will be concerned with archival microform serials, since most will purchase copies from commercial dealers who will maintain their own archives in the form of the master negative copies.

When a library develops a policy about serial retention in microformat, it must proceed cautiously and not neglect the costs and space requirements of factors other than the microform itself: mechanical readers and copiers; service and replacement parts; staff to assist readers in locating, using, and copying the material; and the attitude of the library's patrons. The physical characteristics of specific serials and their local use are so significant in this decision that each type of material needs to be considered individually.

Daily newspapers are unquestionably best retained in microform because of the poor quality of their paper, the awkward size of bound newspaper volumes, and the amount of shelf space required. Binding newspapers is not a form of permanent retention. If a library decides to collect backfiles of newspapers, the cost of microform equipment and staff assistance has no alternative, and it must be calculated during the decision-making process.

On the other hand, most periodicals, particularly scholarly publications, will not fall to pieces after a few years of use. The library has more leeway in determining its treatment of them. Some periodicals use as poor quality paper as newspapers; if their content is of permanent value to the collection, the costs of microform are justified. Heavily used periodicals retained only in microform can create congestion in the area of mechanical readers, a situation which leads to frustration among users. At the same time, a patron who finds all the articles on a term paper topic cut or ripped from volumes or who finds entire volumes missing will be at least as angry and frustrated as the one who has to wait for a reader. A case can be made for the conversion of backfiles of little used journals to microform or for the original purchase of the title in this format. This policy will generate less use of equipment than would converting more heavily used titles, and it frees stack space for more often consulted material. When a library is able to have microform subscriptions to back up bound subscriptions to popular and much used periodicals, the cost may be justified by the elimination of the frustration caused by mutilation, assuming the microform copy is not lost or stolen. But this is a luxury most libraries have to use selectively, for ordinarily funds can be better spent on titles that are not available in the library in any other format.

It is possible to alleviate somewhat the congestion that occurs when many patrons want to use microform readers. Commercially produced readers for both microfilm and microfiche are becoming more reasonably priced and give better images than earlier models. Their presence can lead to a more positive attitude toward microform on the part of users who object to being restricted to a dark, crowded room. The alternative of taking the microform and a circulating reader to one's office or home and studying it at leisure appeals to many patrons.

With all the benefits of microform serials, there are some types of material which are not suited to any format except the original paper. Journals which have long articles are more easily read in paper format, because most persons' eyes are bothered more by long hours of reading microform than by reading paper. Periodicals where colored illustrations are a significant part of the articles, such as those with color-keyed charts and maps, are not acceptable on microform, often not even on colored microform. Reference tools, such as indexes and bibliographies, until recently have not been successful in microform. However, the increasing dependence of librarians upon collections of, for instance, telephone directories and college catalogs on microfiche has brought a change in the appearance of reference collections. Many more reference works are acceptable in microformat than heretofore.

Traditionally, libraries subscribing to periodicals in microform have preferred reel film, the most popular reason being that microfiche is easily misfiled and, thus, lost. It appears now that microfiche is gaining in popularity because of its ease of use, reproduction and replacement. The mechanical equipment required to use microfiche is simpler, and therefore, easier to use and to repair, than that for microfilm. It is likely that the wide use of computer output microfiche for libraries' public records of serial holdings and the experience of patrons of libraries that ventured to retain their periodicals on fiche have outweighed the fears of confusion in refiling sheets of microfiche. Despite the general acceptance of fiche, the misfiling problem remains and single fiche continue to be lost.

Often there is a choice to make between positive and negative microform. When a patron reads a positive copy, the printing is dark on a light background, as is a printed work. When this positive microform is copied on a reader-printer, the reproduction usually comes out as a negative copy; that is, light printing on a dark background. With negative microform, the copy is positive. There are machines capable of printing a positive copy from a positive microform; however, a negative microform produces a noticeably better print than a positive one. Negative microforms, thus, are the preferred medium for copying and will also cause users less eyestrain. Patron resistance to negative microforms, however, is higher than that to positive, especially when there are photographs or illustrations in the material reproduced.

Whatever the characteristics of the material that is copied, the print on paper is not as good in quality as the copies made from printed material on a coin paper copier. The quality of reader-printers is vastly better than it used to be, but there is still much room for improvement. One must keep in mind also that certain illustrations such as plates and colored photographs do not show up well in microform and do not copy satisfactorily on reader-printers because of the chemical composition of film designed to achieve the sharpest contrast between print and paper. Maps and plans lose their calibrations when they are copied, because most photocopies are not exact size reproductions, and copies from microform are one more step away from the original. The amount and importance of illustrative matter is a definite consideration in the decision to bind or purchase microform.

SECURITY

Security, another aspect of preservation, involves circulation, exit control, and the housing of paper serials and multi-media supplements to serials. Deciding whether to circulate serials for use outside the library is a public service question with broader implications than security alone, so it is discussed in Chapter 6. Restricted access to serials within the building is a preservation concern because of the serious problem of mutilation of journals. Too often the decision to restrict access to a specific periodical is made after much of it has been cut out and stolen, instead of at the time of purchase. Just as each serial should be evaluated for retention as a permanent part of the collection, so it should be examined for high risk of mutilation and theft. Some serials are more likely to be damaged or lost: those treating current controversial topics in a popular way, education and particularly physical education journals, newsletters and journals devoted to a single author, and popular culture serials. Local additions to this list of categories will become apparent to the staff member who must order replacement pages and issues, so that new titles fitting the high-risk profile can be restricted from the beginning. Unless the library's policy requires that all unbound journals be shelved in a closed storage area, the number of restricted titles should be kept to a reasonable minimum, because of both staff time required and the reduction in number of periodicals available for browsing. It is unfair to the patron to take away all the journals attracting his or her attention, leaving only those which hold no interest. A reading room filled with grey journal covers in foreign languages is probably very secure and very little used. Each library will find a balance between security and accessibility.

Exit control deters theft and stops inadvertent removal of library materials if it is done well. A staff member who examines briefcases and armloads of books can be effective, but this job does not appeal to or challenge many persons. It pays little, it places one in unpleasant confrontations with patrons or fellow staff members who feel that they should be trusted, and often it exposes the checker to cold winds blowing through the door each time a patron leaves the building. Most persons who can and will do this job conscientiously are able to handle a higher level position and are soon promoted. Unfortunately, many checkers prefer to read or talk with their friends rather than to examine volumes leaving the library. Some libraries attempt to make unbound periodicals easier to spot by putting colored stripes on the edges of three sides of the issues, but this is effective only if the checker looks for it.

Many libraries have installed one of the electronic security systems available. Although they are expensive, their cost can probably be justified by savings in salary or wages of exit control personnel and in replacement of books and serials. Selective treatment of library materials combined with publicity directed toward patrons should be nearly as effective as preparing every volume to sound the system's alarm. Some library binders will include this preparation in their operations. The wisdom of treating journal issues that will be bound together later has been questioned. It is one more task for busy staff members, and some bound volumes may have twelve strips, where one would do. However, the replacement costs of serials are so high that a few issues retained will pay for many issues to be treated. In the future it is likely that subscription agencies will offer the preparation of periodical issues for security systems as a part of their off site check-in and processing services. It would be unrealistically expensive to have an electronic security system for a periodicals reading room alone, so patrons will continue to take journals to the far reaches of the bookstack as they have always done.

Electronic security systems can stop inadvertent theft, but some persistent patrons will circumvent the best control. One university library staff queried students and identified and interviewed periodical mutilators, in an attempt to develop a program to combat destruction of materials. The investigators determined that their best recourse was a publicity campaign, combined with obvious penalty warning signs.[10] No library has yet found a total solution to the security problem. In addition to publicity and warnings of penalties, a serials reading room should have only one public exit, with unobtrusive observation, as a deterrent. This single exit, of course, can be a problem when the fire alarm goes off!

The availability of low cost, efficient coin photocopy machines probably reduces both mutilation and theft. At the same time, the presence of the self-service machine works against preservation efforts because of the chance of damage to the volume as it is held on the machine by a patron who is thinking only of getting every word copied. Even salaried operators of sophisticated copiers in a library photographic laboratory may not take time to handle volumes carefully. It is becoming increasingly difficult to copy without hurting the volume, because of narrow margins and poor quality paper; that is reason to educate both staff members and patrons in the proper way to treat a bound volume.

The security problems just discussed—theft, mutilation, and inadvertent damage to volumes—can be nearly eliminated by retaining serials in microform. For some titles this policy would only exchange one set of problems for another, but it may be a viable alternative for many serials if administered with care. Mutilation of microforms occurs only rarely and inadvertently in a well-run reading room; photocopying (printing) produces no more strain on the titles than does reading, and theft is almost nonexistent.

Every library needs to have a policy concerning disposition of multimedia supplemental materials received with printed serials. *National Geographic* publishes maps that accompany the monthly issues; other journals supply sound recordings, slides, charts, games and so forth, placed inside or attached to issues. Some of them require equipment for use, others do not. Libraries with closed serial stacks may elect to place this supplementary material in a pocket at the back of the volume. Otherwise, that part which must be used with audiovisual equipment may be kept with other recordings, tapes, and so forth, in a part of the library near machines for its use.

In open stack collections, leaving this nonbook material with the bound volume or the unbound issue is asking for it to be misplaced or stolen. A map is more secure in a map collection than in the pocket of a book. If it is worth keeping, it is worth preserving in an appropriate manner, and the library has this obligation. For ease in locating supplements housed away from their parent volumes, a written or printed notice in the volume directs patrons to the material. Serial public service staff must be aware of the policy too, because some readers will not see the notice. A library that has no map room and no audiovisual collection may prefer to store all serial supplementary material in a restricted area of the periodicals reading room or reference department, so patrons may charge it out as they would reserve materials. The essential point is that there must be a policy and procedure so these items will not have to be treated as problems. Lack of policy can easily lead to supplements' being misplaced by staff members before patrons can have an opportunity to use them. Cataloging and acquisition records, in accordance with the policy, should clearly reflect the presence of this material and its exact location, if different from the parent title.

ACKNOWLEDGEMENT

The author wishes to express her grateful appreciation to Peter Schledorn, Periodicals Binding Supervisor, UNC-CH, for his invaluable assistance in the preparation of this chapter.

NOTES

1. Library of Congress. Administrative Department. Office of the Assistant Director for Preservation, *Preservation Leaflets* (Washington, D.C.: Library of Congress), no. 1- 1975-.

2. S. K. Lakhanpal, *Library Binding Manual*, rev. ed. (Saskatoon: Serials Department, Murray Memorial Library, University of Saskatchewan, 1972).

3. Maurice F. Tauber, ed., *Library Binding Manual: A Handbook of Useful Procedures for the Maintenance of Library Volumes*, 3rd ed. (Boston: Library Binding Institute, 1972), p. 77.

4. Library Binding Institute, *Library Binding Handbook* (Boston: Library Binding Institute, 1963), pp. 10-11.

5. Matt Roberts, "The Role of the Librarian in the Binding Process," *Special Libraries* 62 (1971): 413-20; reprinted in *Library Scene* 2 (1973): 26-30.

6. *Library Binding Handbook* (1963).

7. Tauber, *Library Binding Manual* (1972).

8. Don Lanier, "Binding—Is Standardized Standard?" *RTSD Newsletter* 5 (1980): 33-34.

9. Paul N. Banks, "Some Problems in Book Conservation," *Library Resources and Technical Services* 12 (1968): 332.

10. Clyde Hendrick and Marjorie E. Murfin, "Project Library Ripoff: A Study of Periodical Mutilation in a University Library," *College and Research Libraries* 35 (1974): 402-11.

Chapter 6

Serial Public Service

"Has the fall issue of *Economic Geography* arrived?" "I can't find the 1980 volume of *Parks and Recreation*." "Where is *Asian Folklore Studies* indexed?" "What library has *Paris Match*?"

Serial public service is the assistance given by staff members to library patrons who want to identify, locate, and use serials. The process usually involves serial records, other bibliographic tools, and the serials themselves. Serial public service consists of reference and a variety of other functions, many of which are often not administered by the serials department. The library's reference department, circulation department, branch libraries, and other units routinely provide public service related to serials. Thus, the activities discussed in this chapter are not limited to staff members who work only with serials. Much library service involving serials is either circulation or reference, and it is often difficult to separate the two. However, in this chapter on serial public service, there is an attempt to distinguish between the handling function—circulation—and the investigating function—reference. In addition, three special types of service require treatment here: copyright restrictions, assistance for handicapped patrons, and microform public service.

STAFFING

The number and classification of staff members involved in serial public service are determined by the library administration's priorities and the services it offers, by the decisions it has made about housing the collections, and by its definition of the scope of employees' responsibilities. For instance, if the library collects heavily in document serials, subscribes to online bibliographic databases or has purchased sophisticated equipment for reading and copying microforms, it will have provided staff to support the use of these materials and equipment. If serials are housed in closed stacks, the library must have staff to retrieve volumes requested by patrons.

An integrated serials department, which includes both technical processing and public service functions, is a natural situation for using staff members in both types of work, since each aspect of serials work depends heavily upon the other. Administrators who use technical service personnel part time for public service responsibilities and vice versa have more staff members involved in direct contact with patrons using serials than those who limit personnel to one function. This management attitude requires a greater financial investment in training, because each employee has broader responsibilities than he or she would have if restricted to a single function. However, in serials work the investment is sound, since it makes use of the expertise of acquisitions and cataloging personnel in giving service to patrons. An acquisitions assistant may not agree with the policy of recording the arrival date of each journal issue until a patron asks when the next issue of a quarterly is expected. In answering the question the benefit of knowing the arrival pattern for the title makes the extra check-in effort meaningful to the staff member who records that information. Providing details such as arrival date on the serial record and issue-specific holdings statements on permanent records requires time and attention; these procedures demand much of a staff member. Any resentment at producing such records is likely to disappear when that staff member uses these detailed records to respond to a patron's question. Likewise, the public service employee benefits from the knowledge gained by creating acquisition and cataloging records which contain the answers to patrons' questions. This experience promotes conscientious service to the library patrons and gives department personnel a fuller appreciation of their work, which can led to improved ways of performing tasks that have become routine. Even when some aspects of serials work are allocated to other departments, the investment in extra training is worth the time, expense, and effort. The staff member who knows the entire range of library serial functions is more valuable to the library than one who has a narrowly defined position. A broader view of library operations and the implied trust of the individual accompanying this opportunity often lead to an increased sense of responsibility and foster leadership capabilities among staff members. An extra benefit is a pool of employees to cover service points in emergencies.

CIRCULATION

A large share of the public service work in a serials department is, broadly defined, circulation; this includes handling, locating, and retrieving serials. The usual conception of library circulation is charging materials for use outside the building and maintaining records of the locations of these materials. However, a great many libraries do not permit serials to be removed from the building, so serial circulation work includes collection maintenance: helping patrons locate volumes, interpreting library records, searching for missing serials, shelving, and recognizing volumes that need to be repaired or replaced. Sometimes it is difficult to separate the circulation and reference functions of serial public service: "Has the summer issue been published?" "Did the library ever receive 1976?" "Do we have an index to the *American Sociological Review*?" The lack of a clear delineation between circulation and reference is support for an integrated serials department.

Written Policy

One decision which every library must make concerns the charging out of serials to patrons—both removing bound volumes and unbound issues from one location in the library to another, and taking these items outside the building. "Do serials circulate or not?" There is no way to avoid answering this question. Each library can make its serials staff members' jobs easier by having a written policy describing the circulation of all types of serials. This policy should be concise and easy to understand, it should be publicized, and it should be enforced. The policy should have few exceptions; specific exceptions should be stated in writing: "Journals may be checked out for class use for one half hour longer than the class period." The availability of such a written circulation policy provides support to staff members when they are asked about checkout rules and, especially, when they are asked to circulate serials in ways contrary to policy. When these situations arise, a strong and immediate response based upon a written policy is more effective than hesitation, uncertainty, and consultation.

The content of a serial circulation policy is determined by the library's collection, its function and its patrons. Which serials, if any, circulate depends on four conditions: (1) type of library (research, college, public); (2) type of serial (journal, monographic series, annual review); (3) cataloging and binding practice (analyzed issues bound together or retained separately, back volumes in microform); and (4) category of patron (faculty member, town official, student, research assistant). For any library there is probably a case to be made for both circulation and noncirculation of periodicals and of nonperiodical serials. Consider the following:

1. Is it better for a scholar to have both monographs and serials together for research outside the library, or should serials remain in the building in case another patron needs them?

2. Should periodicals be retained unbound so they can be circulated without removing a year's worth of articles from the library? These issues may become worn through being transported outside the building, but they may not be exposed so often to the destruction of careless photocopying.
3. Does free circulation of journals deter mutilation?
4. Does the availability of inexpensive photocopy machines reduce the perceived need to use serials outside the building?
5. Should analyzed series be circulated differently from classed separately series?
6. Should journals be retained on microfiche so they can be reproduced inexpensively for patrons who have outside access to mechanical readers, thus bypassing the question of circulation?

The list could go on indefinitely; all of these aspects of the question and others which apply to the local library must be examined in formulating a written circulation policy for serials.

Nonperiodical serials—annuals, monographic series—can be treated differently, and more liberally, than periodicals. They are less likely to be a collection of articles or essays, and they are not as apt to be covered in periodical indexes and abstract journals. In current practice research libraries do not circulate journals, while college and public libraries permit all serials to be used outside the library. With a limited and highly specialized clientele, special libraries, including university departmental libraries, often compromise by circulating journals and other serials in the immediate vicinity, such as in adjacent offices, where they can be retrieved quickly if needed.

Whatever the library's decision about the circulation of serials, and in spite of the previous emphasis on a written policy with few exceptions, there should be limited flexibility in practice. There will be times when noncirculating materials must be used outside the library, just as there will be times when circulating materials must be kept immediately available on reserve. The exception to policy is most often determined by a special need, although a special person—a mayor or a chancellor—may merit an exemption. When weighing a request for a circulation policy exception, try to determine the best course of action for the whole group of library patrons.

Housing

The library's policies about housing the serial collection constitute one aspect of circulation. The best treatment of serials is determined by the configuration of the library building and by the balance of accessibility and security considered appropriate for each library. Often the serials librarian has no choice in the location and arrangement of serials and must accept what has been practiced for many years. Sometimes there is opportunity for evaluation and change, for example, when the library is planning a new building, when there is a major stack shift, or when a serials department is created. A discussion of the options in housing the serial collection must take into account four factors: (1) Are the serials in question bound volumes or unbound issues? (2) Are they periodicals or nonperiodical serials? (3) Are the library stacks open to all patrons, or are they closed? and (4) Is the serial collection classified or arranged alphabetically? This section does not cover housing of microforms; that is discussed later in this chapter.

Bound Volumes. Many libraries, particularly research libraries, treat bound serials and monographs alike with respect to housing. They catalog and classify each title and interfile bound serials with monographs in a single stack area. Other libraries arrange all serials except monographic series in alphabetical order, with or without a class number. Still others shelve all nonperiodical serials with monographs and alphabetize bound journals. A final option is to classify all serials, but segregate them from monographs.

The first decision to make about housing bound volumes is how to treat periodicals, because they comprise the largest number of serial volumes and are a high percentage of the total collection in many special and academic departmental libraries. Since they are usually collections of articles, periodicals are used differently than monographs. More than other serials, they are accessible through indexes and abstract journals. On the other hand, periodicals contain information, just as the rest of the collection does; to some librarians and patrons, format is not valid justification for different shelving treatment.

The appropriate means of housing bound periodicals is determined by the needs of patrons and staff members. If the bookstack is closed to patrons, their need is only that staff members locate a volume quickly. In open stacks patrons are able to browse in their subjects of interest and have a larger base for examination when all volumes are together regardless of format. However, most periodicals cover a wider range of subjects than monographs and are given general classification numbers. This causes a large group of periodicals to be shelved together in those general numbers. For example, periodicals on American literature and twentieth-century fiction are likely to contain articles on Fitzgerald, but only a journal restricted to studies of this author is classified with monographs about his work.

New and infrequent library users may need guidance to the location of specific periodicals. It is easier to direct them to an alphabetical periodical collection than to a classified bookstack where there is a possibility of the patron's not understanding the classification scheme. A segregated periodical stack also permits fast reshelving of volumes which have been used, especially if there is a class number to eliminate the need for guesswork. This means of housing periodicals works best in a small library.

There are problems with an alphabetical arrangement of journals. The most obvious problem heretofore has been that of generic titles with corporate authors. With *AACR* 2 corporate authors will gradually disappear and the number of entries beginning "Journal" and "Bulletin" will increase, thus relieving the corporate author problem, but creating large groups of periodical titles which begin with the same word. A decision must be made about filing initials and prepositions. The library may elect the traditional word by word alphabetizing, or it can use "computer filing," in which prepositions and articles are ignored and acronyms are filed as words. After years of learning exact titles, such as *Journal of THE History of Ideas* and *Review of EconomicS AND Statistics*, librarians may need to adapt gracefully to filing titles in a sequence designed for the way nonlibrarians think.

Bound periodicals housed separately from monographs and kept in alphabetical order may be easier to work with than a classified arrangement. There is no need to look up a call number to locate a journal. When a title changes, the new title, once cataloged, can be shelved under its own title, the name by which it will be requested. The growth of the collection can be calculated more accurately if journals, which expand quickly and somewhat predictably, are segregated from the irregularly expanding monographs.

A library shelving bound volumes in closed stacks can use compact shelving if it is short of space. This shelving can be used in open stacks if patrons are familiar with its operation, but it is more suitable for closed areas because of the equipment movement involved. An additional benefit of closed stacks is the ease and increased validity of any use studies the staff conducts. With all use of serials controlled through a checkout station, attendants can be sure of recording each consultation of a serial. Libraries with closed periodical stacks also have the option of shelving by size, which conserves space. Here, especially, the use of a class number is essential. The serial public service staff that has a choice must weigh the pros and cons of each arrangement and determine the combination of options that will be most suitable to the local situation.

The same options are available for housing nonperiodicals, and the same factors should be considered. When periodicals are interfiled with monographs, all nonperiodical serials will be interfiled also; if periodicals are housed separately from monographs, each type of nonperiodical serial must be considered individually. Monographic series classified separately are not a concern for serial personnel after the volumes have been received and cataloged; they belong with other monographs in a classified bookstack. Analyzed monographic series consist of volumes that can stand alone, but they are given the same call number because they are closely related in content. Since many libraries circulate volumes of analyzed series as if they were monographs, they fit well into a classified collection. In libraries where analyzed series do not circulate, the decision may be to house them with periodicals if there is a separate periodical stack. Annual reviews, proceedings and other nonperiodicals that are collections of articles require more study before their shelving location is determined. In general, if they do not circulate, they may be treated as periodicals; if they circulate, they may be shelved with monographs.

Whatever is decided, there must be written procedures and guidelines so the library staff understands the arrangement and can explain it to patrons, guide them to journals they seek, or retrieve quickly a bound volume. An alphabetically arranged periodical collection with public access benefits from cross references in the form of wooden or heavy cardboard "dummies" showing relationships between titles: "*Zetetic* changed title to *Skeptical Inquirer* with vol. 2, no. 3. For later volumes see that title." Many librarians consider this detail a luxury, since the public record of serial holdings makes the relationship clear, but not all patrons use the official record. A library may choose to employ such aids only in collections of bound volumes shelved in a periodical reading room, although in the long run, the use of dummies saves staff time.

Unbound Issues. This section covers only periodicals, because other serials are either received hardbound and go directly to their permanent location or are processed individually as soon as they arrive. In a library displaying unbound issues of periodicals, some of the same considerations apply as with bound volumes, for example, the question of whether the arrangement is to be classified or alphabetical. Arrangement is also influenced by whether the collection of unbound serials is on open or restricted shelves, because this determines whether the order is for the patron's or the staff's convenience. The author is a confirmed alphabetizer, although she realizes that there is another point of view. Presumably every library user and staff member knows his or her ABCs; not everyone is able to comprehend the Library of Congress Classification or the Dewey Decimal System without guidance. To be sure, numerous faculty members would have all the journals of interest to them gathered together, in an alcove perhaps, but to do that satisfactorily would require more duplicate subscriptions than use can justify, given the interdisciplinary nature of so many heavily used periodicals. Unbound journals in an open shelf reading room should be arranged by title or other main entry. If the collection is too large for the prime space allotted, it is necessary to select titles which will not be heavily used and shelve them in a location nearby. Although this practice is not ideal, it is preferable to breaking up the collection by subject or to using a strict classified arrangement.

Some libraries may place the latest issue of selected titles, perhaps protected in plastic covers, on a display rack. Others will shelve all unbound issues on bookcases. A third alternative is use of the type of shelving which displays a single issue and stores other recent issues beneath that one.

A library providing a reading room for patrons using current periodicals will probably have lounge furniture, especially if newspapers are a part of the collection. There will also be tables and individual carrels for persons doing research. If space permits, there can be an area for conversation and communal use of periodicals, although the location of such a grouping must be one which will ensure that talking does not disturb other patrons.

If unbound issues of periodicals are not displayed on open shelves, they may be stored in a closed area, or they may be shelved with the bound volumes if those are also in closed stacks. The latter arrangement works best with a small journal collection and helps to keep retrieval time brief. For this same reason one might decide to keep unbound issues of selected high use titles close to the service point. When volumes and individual issues are housed together a page needs to look in only one place to locate the material and does not have to check binding records first. Even where open stacks are used, volumes and issues can be shelved together, provided the serial public service staff and library administration are able to deal with the consequences of the lack of security for recent issues. This is not a recommended arrangement because, with the larger space involved, it is virtually impossible to ensure that much used periodicals will remain in the vicinity of their shelf location.

Public Service Records

Whatever decisions the library makes about housing and circulating serials, there are occasions when staff members must rely on manual or automated records to determine the current location and, therefore, the availability of an item. One of these is the serial record, discussed in Chapter 3. Another heavily used tool is the binding record, which is mentioned in Chapter 5. Both of these technical processing files are crucial for serial public service, because from them one can quickly answer the questions: "Have we received it?" and "Is it at the bindery?" Since these two questions and their answers constitute a large percentage of serial public service communications, the proximity of both of these records to the service point is desirable and is another strong reason to have an integrated serials department.

Whether library policy is to circulate serials outside the building or not, there is occasionally a need to charge out some serials. The circulation record reveals whether a specific item is in use at the time it is requested and tells what serials are overdue to be returned. For this file each issue may have its own checkout card; a transaction slip may be used which requires the notation of title, date and borrower's identification; or some other manual or automated system may be used. At the University of North Carolina at Chapel Hill a simple mimeographed form is used for inhouse circulation of material that usually does not circulate. It shows title, volume or issue, current date and assistant's initials. Attached to this form as a sort of deposit or hostage is the patron's student ID or library card. When he or she returns the material, the patron gets the ID back. The system is not without minor problems— some patrons forget to pick up their IDs, others invariably come to the library without identification—but it works better than any other circulation method that has been tried.

Reserve

Sometimes a serial reserve is necessary, in addition to and separate from the library's main reserve collection. Many journal articles are too long to copy for reserve. Occasionally an entire periodical issue is devoted to one topic. A professor mentions an article in class and twenty-five students want to read it the next day. These are examples of situations in which the person responsible for serial public service can retrieve a volume from open or closed stacks and circulate it for short periods from a service point. In spite of the fact that patrons must make an extra effort to obtain the material, the security often means that all those who need to use it are able to do so. When only a short or medium length article is needed, it is best that it be included as a part of the regular reserve collection, provided it can be photocopied legally and without damaging the journal. The article will be conveniently located with other class reading on reserve, and the bound volume is available to other patrons in its place in the stacks. Only when the photocopying cannot be done and a reprint is not available should a volume be removed from its usual place, charged to serial reserve, and put on that shelf.

Maintenance

A final aspect of the circulation function of serial public service is maintenance of the collection. There is little that is challenging about keeping bookstacks and reading rooms orderly, but no library can function without this care. Someone must reshelve the items which have been used and retrieve volumes and issues from other parts of the library. As issues accumulate, someone must identify those ready to be bound or replaced by microform and send them to be processed or discarded. Periodicals, especially newspapers, get misshelved and scattered; these must be straightened. Lost, not-yet-received, and mutilated pieces must be identified and acquired. Stacks must be shifted more often than anyone would think. These necessary tasks point out the labor intensive state of serial circulation work. Some of the operations can be done or assisted by computers, but it seems unlikely that the time will ever come when some maintenance will not be done by human beings. The persons who perform maintenance tasks and their supervisors are essential to the successful operation of the serials department.

Another aspect of serial maintenance is the provision of directional and instructional signs. In addition, patrons appreciate handouts describing the serial collection and services and giving instructions in the use of the department and its resources. A typical brochure describes the arrangement of the public areas of the department, type of assistance available, and reference tools at hand for patron use. Many libraries must post visual guides that are phrased in the negative: "Materials may not be removed from this room" and "Use coin copiers at your own risk." With the apparent increase in mutilation of library material, it is often beneficial to display a sign giving the state law concerning destruction of property and the accompanying penalty; it serves as a deterrent and as an aid when a patron has been observed tampering with library material.

REFERENCE

Serial reference was defined earlier as the investigating function of serial public service. This discussion of serial reference service considers six phases of the topic: (1) the selection, identification, and use of indexes and abstract journals; (2) sources used for verification of bibliographic information and interpretation of abbreviations; (3) location of serials within the library or library system; (4) location of serials in other libraries; (5) interlibrary loan; and (6) selective dissemination of information and current contents services. The arrangement of these subtopics is deliberate. The patron first identifies the article he or she needs, then learns the title of the journal which has published the article. Next, in most cases, the patron locates the journal and volume within the library, then reads and/or photocopies the relevant article. Journals which are not available in the library can be located elsewhere, and the interlibrary loan service is used to obtain a photocopy of the article. Selective dissemination of information and its less ambitious alternatives constitute an outreach program which the library may provide for those who request it.[1]

Indexes, Abstract Journals, and Bibliographies

"Does *The Journal of Marriage and the Family* have its own index? Well, where is it indexed?" A popular category of serial public service questions concerns the availability of index coverage for periodicals. There are standard tools to identify indexes and abstracting journals but according to a recent study none is fully accurate and complete.[2] *Ulrich's International Periodicals Directory* is a good place to begin to look for current coverage, because journals indexed in certain popular sources are so noted. *Indexed Periodicals* by Joseph V. Marconi is a source for retrospective indexing of domestic and foreign titles covered by thirty-three standard American indexes before 1973. Katz's *Magazines for Libraries* contains indexing availability for the titles included. Subscription agents' annual catalogs are another source for indexing information. This has been a feature of the F. W. Faxon Company's *Librarians' Guide* for several years. EBSCO is beginning to enter this item in its database, so the *Librarians' Handbook* will become more useful for this purpose each year. Some journals list their index coverage on the contents page or elsewhere in the front matter of each issue, but not enough of them do so to make it practical to check there first. This may change, however, since one proposal for consideration by the subcommittee revising the ANSI standard on "Periodicals: Format and Arrangement" is "that information be provided on the abstract journals and the bibliographic databases carrying abstracts or references to articles in the publication."[3] At least once a year, if not in each issue, the indexes themselves print a list of titles included, so a good guess as to which source will index a specific periodical can provide the answer quickly.

In selecting periodical indexes and abstract journals for purchase, the reference librarian needs to know what proportion of the titles included are currently received or are likely to be added to the collection. The match should be high to avoid having patrons frustrated by not being able to examine articles they have found cited. However, it is not necessary for the library to subscribe to all the titles indexed or abstracted, because many are available through interlibrary loan and other library cooperative programs, and because some periodicals covered in the index may be only remotely related to the library's areas of interest. Scholars may use indexes to establish that a topic has not been covered in the literature and proceed with their research with greater assurance of breaking new ground. In general, the scope of the index being considered for purchase should match closely the curriculum of the institution or the interests of the community supporting the library. If the index is acquired, it should be used. It should be relatively easy to use and to show patrons how to use. The service being evaluated needs to be examined in relation to other resources in the library or in nearby libraries. Finally, unless the index is new, one should take a look at its track record. Is it up to date? Is the list of titles covered increasing or at least stable? Are reviews of the index available? Serials are expensive and place a continuing and increasing obligation on the library materials budget; indexes are expensive serials and must be purchased with particular care.

Much of the information in this section applies to serially published bibliographies as well as to periodical indexes and abstract journals. In recent years these secondary resources have increased in number and in the diversity of their physical characteristics. Not long ago the majority of American periodical indexes, and certainly most of those found in public and college libraries, were published by the H. W. Wilson Company: *Reader's Guide to Periodical Literature, Education Index, Business Periodicals Index*, and so on. There were other publishers; *Music Index* and *Public Affairs Information Service Bulletin* are examples of standard non-Wilson periodical indexes. Research libraries subscribe to appropriate abstract journals, serial indexes which give, in addition to the bibliographic data, a summary of the content of the article. *Chemical Abstracts, Biological Abstracts*, and *Psychological Abstracts* are examples of established titles. Many scholarly disciplines have national or international associations which sponsor an annual bibliography of articles in journals and *Festschriften*, such as the *MLA Bibliography, Writings in American History*, and *L'Année Philologique*.

As serial literature increased in volume in the second half of the twentieth century, as scholars began to specialize in more specific areas than before, and as federal grants gave libraries additional purchasing power, a market evolved for indexes, abstract journals, and bibliographies of increasingly narrow scope, for example, *Deafness, Speech and Hearing Abstracts* and *Electrical and Electronics Abstracts*. Wilson's *Social Sciences and Humanities Index* was divided into *Social Sciences Index* and *Humanities Index*.

A trend beginning in the mid-1960s leads back toward resources with a broader scope, possibly because of the automation of indexing and the practice of Key-Word-In-Context (KWIC) indexing. Institute for Scientific Information was a trailblazer of this period with, first, *Science Citation Index*, then *Social Science Citation Index* and, recently, *Arts and Humanities Citation Index*, all of which employ the concept of citation analysis to evaluate journals. Several of the older abstract journals became available on magnetic tape and were purchased in this format by large libraries and consortia that could justify the high price.

The next step was online bibliographic services, such as Lockheed's DIALOG and Bibliographic Retrieval Services, Inc. (BRS), through which subscribers can access several databases, one at a time, by the use of a search strategy. Terms can be included and excluded in the search, and a search can be made more specific by combining concepts (for example: advertising + children). Patrons can see online a list of the articles that the search has identified—a bibliography tailor made to a person's research needs—and they can obtain a printout of the references. At additional cost the patron can often acquire copies of the articles cited. Thus, currency and speed are available to scholars and other researchers for a price. The online bibliographic services in academic libraries are presently used most often by graduate students who are beginning the literature search for their theses and dissertations.

It seems safe to speculate that online services will increase in popularity but will never totally replace the printed indexes and abstract journals, because the cost, even if it should drop sharply, cannot always be justified. An undergraduate doing a class term paper seldom requires the speed that money can buy; the comparatively inexpensive *Reader's Guide* and similar printed indexes serve well for that term paper. In addition, the person who identifies references and locates articles manually is learning to do research. There will be time later for data to be provided by a machine, if that is necessary. Many libraries do not need to support the kind of research for which the online bibliographic services are designed, and they would waste funds that could be used to better advantage in some other way. But for those whose need for current data can justify the cost, the online bibliographic services are irreplaceable. Most members of the Association of Research Libraries have online searching available to their patrons, as do special libraries. The systems are currently spreading to large public libraries. Online databases will become more crucial for libraries to access in their support of scholarly research. *Psychological Abstracts*, for instance, has more sources of data available online than are available in the printed index. In addition, online databases now include newspapers such as the *New York Times* and the *Washington Post*. Some periodical indexes, such as *Magazine Index*, are available only online or on microfiche. The *Magazine Index* covers all periodicals included in the *Readers' Guide* and more, and a complete new cumulation of the microfiche edition is provided monthly.

In the last two decades indexers have given increased attention to material other than journals. The *New York Times Index* has been published in book form for many years, but except for the indexes to *The Times (London)*, the *Wall Street Journal* and the *Christian Science Monitor*, there was no other serially published commercial newspaper index until recently. In 1972 Bell and Howell began a current paper index to four newspapers for which they sold the microfilm edition: the *Washington Post*, the *Chicago Tribune*, the *Los Angeles Times*, and the New Orleans *Times-Picayune*. The existence of the index made the newspaper film more attractive to libraries and provided access to columns, editorials, and news stories which had previously been lost. Bell and Howell indexes other newspapers was well, particularly those contained in their ethnic and cultural microfilm collections. Additional microfilming companies have followed this lead. When Research Publications was awarded the right to film the *Washington Post*, it began to publish a printed index to the newspaper which, apparently, was so successful that Bell and Howell gave up their index. An expansion of the practice of indexing newspapers is making available the contents of television news programs. For example, Microfilming Corporation of America (MCA) publishes microform transcripts of CBS news broadcasts and special news programs and of the "MacNeil-Lehrer Report." MCA issues printed indexes to both series.

Book reviews appear in serials and are included in some periodical and newspaper indexes. For many years reviews meeting certain criteria have also been indexed by the H. W. Wilson Company's *Book Review Digest*. Within the last twenty years other works, such as *Book Review Index* and *Index to Book Reviews in the Humanities*, have added to the bibliographic control of book reviews published in serials. Until the last decade few reviews of serial publications existed, and there was no reference work which provided access to reviews which were printed. Now *Serials Review*, issued quarterly since 1975, gives both original reviews of serials and an index to reviews of serials (predominantly periodicals) appearing in other publications. *Serials Review* fills what was a noticeable gap in serial public service. Another source, *New Magazine Review*, began publication as a monthly periodical in 1975.

The indexes and abstract journals already discussed have been commercial publications. An index to a single journal, distributed as a part of the subscription, or a cumulative index to a journal, available from the publisher, is usually more a service and less for profit than the indexes noted above. To the patron looking for articles on a specific topic, indexes to individual journals are less useful than an index covering many periodicals. However, self-indexes can be valuable for serials which are not covered in commercial indexes in the library collection, for identification of an article when the source journal is known, and for a historical study or an analysis of the content of a single journal.

Indexes and abstract journals may be housed either with the periodical collection or in the reference department, in both places, or in some other location which suits the library's needs. Wherever these works are located, there should be staff assistance. This guidance is particularly important for the basic indexes used by high school students or undergraduates, because training in the best use of a standard, general periodical index is the groundwork for later use of complex indexing and abstracting tools. The library's physical facilities and its patrons' level of sophistication in library use are both factors in determining the optimum location for indexes. Self-indexes are conveniently shelved with the journal, so the patron is not required to search elsewhere for the periodical after the citation is located, as he or she must do when using commercial indexes and abstract journals or printed indexes to microform serials.

Sources Used for Verification of Bibliographic Information and Interpretation of Abbreviations

No effort is made here to list comprehensively the tools one uses in answering identification questions about serials. The Annotated Bibliography lists many such sources, particularly in the acquisition and public service sections of Part I, but even that compilation is highly selective, giving examples only. The reference collection is not limited to works housed in a single department, but extends to the entire range of library resources. Part of the satisfaction and joy of reference service is discovering (preferably with the patron along to share the excitement) that obscure work which answers exactly the question being asked.

Records assisting in the identification of serials and the verification of title, price, address, and other facts about a serial fall into several groups: directories (*Ulrich's International Periodicals Directory*), union lists (*Union List of Serials in Libraries of the United States and Canada*), subject guides (*Writings in American History*), catalogs (*National Union Catalog*), bibliographic utility databases, and a huge miscellaneous class. When one is using these tools, and especially when evaluating conflicting information, one must consider the authority of the person or organization responsible for the contents. American librarians generally accept the work done by the staff members of the Library of Congress as the best authority in the area of cataloging and bibliographic control. Works or databases reproducing LC cataloging, such as *Monographic Series*, may be taken as accurate unless there is reason to question the cataloging, such as an obvious typographical error or transposed letters in a call number. The Library of Congress also publishes works that reproduce the cataloging of a number of other research libraries, for example, *New Serial Titles* and the *National Union Catalog*. It is easy to recognize cards representing LC cataloging in the *NUC*; those are the printed cards with LC card numbers. In *NST*, however, only the appearance of the Library of Congress as a holding library assures that the cataloging as it is printed was done by LC. The responsibility for cataloging the serials listed in *NST* was not indicated; only in the "Changes in Serials" section was the contributing institution named. For this reason *NST* (like *ULS*) did not have quite the authority of *NUC*. Beginning in 1981, *New Serial Titles* is produced from CONSER tapes showing the complete bibliographic record in catalog card format entered into the database by LC, the National Library of Canada, the National Serials Data Program, and other CONSER participants. At the same time *NST* dropped its union catalog function, the "Changes in Serials" section, and the post-1949 starting date requirement. The first issues of *NST* in its new format contain only Library of Congress cataloging, much of which is partial (lacking call number and subject heading) and/or not according to *AACR* 2. While the 1950 to 1980 volumes of *NST* are a valuable resource, the recent issues are of little use to the serial public service librarian who has access to the OCLC database.

The R. R. Bowker Company publishes several directories and other serial reference sources, including *Ulrich's* and *Books in Series in the United States*, which use the *Anglo-American Cataloguing Rules* in determining the main entry. The Bowker publications also make liberal use of cross references from earlier and variant entries. In 1981 the Bowker database became available online. The fact that the Bowker serial database was selected to assign the first group of ISSN bestows further authority upon that company. The H. W. Wilson Company in the United States and certain publishers in other countries have a similar relationship to the library community.

For reference questions concerning subscriptions and other types of purchases, the date of information is a crucial consideration in determining authority. Serials occasionally change title and publisher, but price is the aspect of a periodical which changes most rapidly, and today a printed source more than a year or two old cannot give a reliable approximation of price. The cutoff dates for printed listings in *Ulrich's*, *Standard Periodical Directory* and similar works is a year or more before publication. It is possible that prices in the Bowker online database will be current. There is additional help for this type of question in the form of subscription agents' catalogs, which are published annually and whose prices reflect very recent information, because the vendor has placed orders for the publications listed. The accuracy of price and the other information in the catalog is determined by, first, how reliable and current the vendor's database is and, second, how many months ago the catalog was printed. In the United States both EBSCO Subscription Services and the F. W. Faxon Company produce good, extensive catalogs. They are updated (in details other than price) by computer format periodical publications which relay corrections within a few months of the changes. The agents' databases are available online to subscribing libraries, for up-to-the-minute information. All of these tools are discussed more fully in Chapter 3.

Two kinds of sources of abbreviations aid the patron who needs to determine the full name of a serial: abbreviation dictionaries and lists of abbreviations used in specific publications. One of the most useful book format collections of abbreviations, compiled from many periodical indexes and annual bibliographies, is Leland Alkire's *Periodical Title Abbreviations*.[4] Alkire does not include chemical serial abbreviations, because this field has an excellent guide to its literature in *Chemical Abstracts Service Source Index*.

Most periodical indexes, subject bibliographies and similar works either contain a list of the serial title abbreviations they use or state that standard abbreviations, such as those of the Modern Language Association, are followed. Most lists are not long and are usually included in each issue or at least in one issue a year. A librarian might assume that the patron would expect to find a list of abbreviations for *Education Index* in the publication itself and would locate and use it, but patrons do not always reason the way librarians hope they will. However, when a patron presents an abbreviation from one of the standard indexes and asks for help, there is a great opportunity to teach library use. One method is to have a photocopy of the list of abbreviations at hand and to explain its use; another is to accompany the patron to the index and assist him or her there. As a diehard "Teach-Them-to-Use-the-Library-for-Themselves" advocate, the author opposes simply answering the title identification question without showing the patron how to find the full title for him- or herself next time.

Location of Serials Within the Library or Library System

This is the aspect of serial reference that bears most resemblance to circulation. It is a function of reference service to enable the patron to determine where a serial should be; if the material is not there, the query becomes a circulation matter. In serials work the same library staff member often assists in both cases. The tool used to determine the permanent and, sometimes, temporary location of a serial is the library's holdings list. Formerly, in most libraries this was in card form, either interfiled with cards for monographs in the public catalog or segregated in a serial card catalog. When the library received a bound serial or when a collected volume returned from the bindery, part of the internal processing was changing the holdings record on the card, either by erasing the pencilled final volume number and/or date and supplying the new one, or by checking the next date or volume on a holdings card.

Some libraries still use this card record as either the official record of holdings or a supplement to a computer output microform (COM) catalog or automated system. In either case this method of noting serial holdings is expensive, a labor intensive luxury. Yet there are times when only this record will give the answer to a patron's question; there is something reassuring about a check mark made forty years ago. Or not made! It may be that this card record is the only one which provides complete bibliographic information about a title, for the early automated catalogs of serials often gave no more than title and, perhaps, place of publication and beginning date, along with summarized local holdings. There were no standards, no OCLC, no CONSER. Each library set up its own system and tried to produce a serial holdings list as inexpensively as possible. More recently the existence of the MARC-S format, the reduced costs of computer hardware and software, and the necessity and desirability of interlibrary cooperation have worked together to improve the quality and usefulness of many computerized serial holdings lists. Assistance is available in the form of ANSI standards: Serial Holdings at the Summary Level (1980) and Serial Holdings at the Detailed Level (in process); others may follow. These standards are evidence of an increased awareness on the part of the library and scholarly world of serials' value to research and of problems in bibliographic control of serials. The impact of these standards depends upon their voluntary use by librarians, just as the impact of other standards such as the ISSN and ISBN have depended upon their use by publishers.

The serial acquisition check-in record is also a reference tool, provided one asks the right questions. It is most reliable when consulted for recent information. The definition of "recent" depends upon several library policies: Are all received serials entered on the serial record? How long are these records retained? There are other questions that help to define the usefulness of the serial record as a reference source: Does this file include serials received for the entire library system? Are binding records kept in the check-in file? Is the record arranged by main entry or in some other way? The discussion of the serial record in Chapter 3 presents other factors to consider for reference use. But the simplest and probably most asked serial reference question is: "Has the library received the [latest] issue?" And that is what the serial record is all about!

The Location of Serials in Other Libraries

Since no library can or wants to own every existing serial, there are times when a patron or a staff member needs to know what other library holds a specific title and which volumes it has. A union list of serials is a single source designed to answer questions about serial location and holdings in several specific libraries. The scope of contributors to the union list may be national, as is the *British Union-Catalogue of Periodicals*; international, as is *New Serial Titles*; regional, as is the *Minnesota Union List of Serials*; or local, as is the catalog of the serial holdings of all libraries on a university campus or in a municipal library system.

With the economic necessity for cooperation among libraries, union lists of serials have proliferated and currently appear in various formats: cards, printed books, microform, and automated (both batch and on-line). In 1980 the American Library Association's Resources and Technical Services Division's Serials Section formed a committee to establish guidelines for creating union lists of serials; ANSC Z39 has one new serial holding standard and a subcommittee at work on another. Libraries are seeking and receiving federal and private grants to fund projects leading to union lists of serials. Subscription agents are able to produce union lists for both customers and noncustomers, the bibliographic utilities have realized that they must deal with the question, and OCLC has activated its union listing capability.

The value of union lists of serials, both for locating a specific title in a library and for purposes such as verification of bibliographic data varies widely. At one extreme is the uncomplicated finding list with title, location, and holdings; at the other is the online union list which attaches the issue-specific holdings record to a full current cataloging record. Most union lists of serials fall somewhere in between and, used together, complement each other. When conflicting information appears, one may tentatively resolve the problem by considering the authority of the compiling institution, the purpose of the union list, and the currency of the data.

There are other sources for locating a serial in another library. Several individual libraries have published catalogs of their holdings, among them Harvard's Widener Library and the British Library. G. K. Hall has published the shelf lists of many special collections, which include at least the catalog card record of serials. Sometimes a letter or telephone call of inquiry is the only way to determine that a library holds an item, but published guides can direct the searcher toward the most likely location.

Interlibrary Loan

Closely related to locating serials in other libraries is interlibrary loan service. Years ago it was not uncommon for libraries to send serials, including bound periodicals, through the interlibrary loan system. Gradually, most libraries changed their circulation policies and made serials noncirculating, even to their local patrons. Their reasoning was that removing an entire volume from the library so one person could use a small portion of it was unfair to other patrons who needed to see other small portions. And if local patrons could not take a serial from the library, why should a patron of some other library be able to borrow it? There is risk involved in every circulation, especially interlibrary loan, and in general it is more difficult and more expensive to replace a serial volume than a monograph. Another factor in the decision not to lend serials to other libraries was probably the slowing of the service, both within the libraries and through the mail.

At the same time technological advances enabled manufacturers to produce better and less expensive photocopy machines. Healthy competition among these manufacturers helped bring prices down. Librarians preferred to substitute a photocopy of a periodical article for the actual volume on interlibrary loan, either free of charge or at a cost of ten to twenty-five cents a page. All was well for a while, until the cost of labor, paper, and postage forced libraries to increase their photocopy prices by adding handling charges and an increasing minimum amount to each order. The copyright section later in this chapter discusses the implications of the new copyright law for interlibrary loan.

Interlibrary lending of serials, or substitution of photocopies, is primarily a circulation function, except when the bibliographic citation received from another library is incorrect. The routine transaction involves retrieving the serial from the stacks, copying the requested article, recording the action and mailing the photocopy to the borrowing library. Added to this may be billing and receipt of payment. On the other hand, interlibrary borrowing of serials, or request of a photocopy, requires that a staff member verify the citation reported by the patron and determine which holding library is the best choice for the request. This is serial reference work involving a variety of bibliographic tools and in some libraries is entrusted only to librarians.

One way to deter the effect of rising prices for interlibrary loan is to enter cooperative and reciprocal agreements between and among libraries. The scope of the agreement may be determined by proximity (North Carolina's Triangle Research Libraries' Network), subject (medical libraries), or nature of library (Research Libraries Group). The agreement usually is not limited to interlibrary loan but also involves cooperative collection development, use of computer facilities, or other expense-cutting projects. For a research library, cooperative acquisition, cataloging, and reference are necessary to long-range survival as a responsible institution. The various aspects of interlibrary cooperation are discussed fully in Chapter 7; particularly relevant to serial reference are the Center for

Research Libraries, the bibliographic utilities' union catalog functions, and planning for a national periodicals system.

Selective Dissemination of Information and Current Contents Services

In the future it is likely that there will be fewer journals issued in the format we know now. Production and distribution costs are reaching levels that prohibit many libraries from continuing the most expensive and marginal subscriptions. There is a growing feeling that scholarly information will eventually be communicated routinely by the selective dissemination of information (SDI). That is, the scholar will have displayed on a computer terminal bibliographic citations with abstracts or complete articles and will order electronically produced copies of the texts of relevant works. The proliferation of esoteric journals will diminish and cease; libraries will no longer have to subscribe to periodicals which are consulted by only one or two patrons. When this evolution has matured, the cost of electronic communication will still be higher than that of today's interlibrary loan, but the delay in receipt of the information should be significantly shorter—no longer, perhaps, than the time required to locate a volume that is not in place on the shelf. This change will not come quickly, and it may not come to all libraries. It will probably begin in special libraries and those academic libraries where funds are available for experimentation and/or where the need for rapid retrieval of information is great. Then the electronic selective dissemination of information will spread to other academic and large municipal or county library systems as costs decrease. The time may come when only recreational and other mass circulation journals retain the paper format. Serial public service librarians will need to continue to adapt to the changing technology, however it develops, so that they can meet the needs of their patrons by utilizing the best aids available.

Many libraries have a current awareness service for patrons through which photocopies of title pages or abstracts from selected journals are sent regularly to those who request them. In special libraries this service may be offered free of charge, but in many other libraries there is a fee to cover at least the photocopying costs. This is an almost impossible activity for serial public service librarians in a general academic or public library to attempt for their patrons because of the subject knowledge required to select and abstract and the amount of time consumed by this service. It might be feasible to permit faculty members and graduate students to submit lists of journals for which they will purchase copies of contents pages, if the financing can be arranged. Patrons who enjoy browsing among recent journals might not be attracted, but there will be a market for this service if it is offered. Alternatively, the library may prefer to subscribe to one or more subject sections of the Institute for Scientific Information's weekly *Current Contents*, which reproduces journal contents pages. *Current Contents* may be held in the library or it may be circulated to faculty members or other researchers.

COPYRIGHT

In 1976 Congress passed a copyright law to replace both the 1908 law and the "Gentlemen's Agreement" of 1935, which defined the concept of "fair use" regarding photocopying of materials under copyright. The development of rapid, inexpensive copy machines and of computer technology has created a volume of library photocopying which could not have been imagined in 1935. Congressmen, assisted by librarians, authors, and publishers, worked for nearly twenty years to write a law that would be fair to all parties. The result is somewhat ambiguous and provides an opportunity for the scholarly and artistic communities to work with it, interpret it, and test it. The results of the early use of the law will be included in a report to Congress by the Register of Copyrights in 1983.

At the implementation of the new copyright law (PL-553) in 1978, librarians did not know whether their continued adherence to the principles of fair use—one copy for scholarly purposes—would be in jeopardy. The law required librarians to post warning signs at public copy machines. These statements of copyright restriction transferred the responsibility for compliance to the patrons using the unsupervised copiers. Interlibrary loan librarians had to keep records of the number of copies made from each journal published within the previous five years. Library photocopy centers were required to post a warning notice/disclaimer and to have the patron sign a statement that the material was to be used for scholarly purposes and would not be resold. Otherwise, librarians could only begin to work under their interpretations of the provisions of the law and, on the basis of their experience, assess the effect it had on their photocopying of library materials. One review of the copyright law indicated that it had not had any great effect on copying practices of either libraries or their patrons.[5] Continued observation of the law has appeared to support this hypothesis. It is not photocopying which has changed, only recordkeeping.

The journal publishers' practice of charging libraries a subscription rate significantly higher than that for individuals has become the norm for scholarly journals, and librarians have complained by means of articles, letters to publishers, and face-to-face discussions in professional meetings. However, the dual pricing structure is continuing. Many publishers now list a subscription price, then offer a greatly reduced rate for individuals who state that the journal is for their own use. This is just a public relations gesture to avoid the label "Institutional Rate." Often the statement of the price that libraries must pay is followed by an explanation that this amount includes the right to make either unrestricted or limited photocopies of the contents, without permission of the publisher or payment of a fee. Sometimes this offer carries meaning, but often it adds no privilege beyond that already granted by the copyright law. At the bottom of the first page of each article, many scholarly journals now print a coded line that identifies the article and gives the price to be paid for photocopying it. This should not intimidate librarians who are exercising their legal rights but should be observed when it applies.

Certain commercial journal publishers have attempted to convince serials librarians to subscribe to contracts which claim to permit unlimited copying and to free library staff members from the necessity of recording and paying for each reproduction of the publisher's serials. Each of these "offers" from publishers must be examined carefully by the librarian to determine whether it is either necessary or a bargain. The library has a responsibility to observe the copyright law, but it must not hesitate to reject expensive ploys that take advantage of this still untested law by attempting to charge libraries for photocopying that should be free. If a librarian feels that he or she cannot interpret adequately these communications from publishers, advice may usually be sought from the institution's legal counsel.

SERVICES TO THE HANDICAPPED

Within the last several years the library profession, along with other service occupations, has on its own and by necessity become more aware of the difficulties that physically handicapped persons face in an environment designed for the majority. Statutes now require that public institutions be accessible for all persons. Unfortunately, the cost of compliance within existing buildings prohibits remodelling in most cases, and new construction is slow to replace the old. The library's overall policy on service to handicapped patrons determines such things as access to the building and facilities and the width of aisles in the stacks. Serial public service staff can do much to promote the use of serial resources by those who are immobile, sight or hearing impaired, or otherwise restricted in their use of the library. Many of these special services can be grouped under the policy of relaxing the rules: permitting serials to be checked out to carrels, providing typing rooms and a Kurzweil Reader, if available; retrieving volumes from the stacks for those who cannot do so for themselves; arranging furnishings in the best way possible for wheelchair patrons. Some institutions offer sign language courses for their employees; a staff member able to communicate in this way with a hearing impaired patron is a decided asset to the library and to the community. Equally as important as written policies on service to handicapped patrons is a good staff attitude, one characterized by a willingness to ease, with respect, the difficulty of using the library. This necessary flexibility does not differ for serial public service from any other area of the library; it is a consideration that must not be neglected or denied.

MICROFORM PUBLIC SERVICE

Chapter 5 discusses the factors to consider in deciding whether to retain serials in microform. This section suggests ways of providing public service for whatever titles the library has chosen to preserve in this format. Serials in microform, like bound volumes, can be housed in a number of ways. It is efficient to house all microforms together, whether serials or monographs, because of the mechanical readers and copiers necessary for patrons to use them. Much microform public service is instruction in use of the reader; operating the reader printer, which is not likely to be coin operated; and limited machine maintenance, such as replacing light bulbs and unjamming the focus. The library gives best service to the user by bringing together microforms and mechanical readers in the same unit. This arrangement promotes use of microforms, deters patrons from scattering microforms all over the library, and facilitates timely reshelving. A separate serials stack within a large microform area means that the serial microforms are concentrated in a smaller area, thus making use and service simpler.

If bound and microform serials are interfiled, either there must be readers throughout the stack without staff attention at hand, or microforms must be taken to the area(s) of the library in which the readers are located. Another possibility is circulating microforms and portable readers for use outside the building, provided the library is willing to maintain these readers.

Microforms can be placed on open shelves with printed serials, but this sacrifices both shelf space and the means of protection from climate, dirt, and loss. ANSI standards recommend a temperature of 60-70 degrees Fahrenheit, with humidity between 40 and 50 percent. These conditions are difficult to obtain in open stacks under the best conditions. In addition, the acid content of most nonarchival paper is even more destructive to film than it is to the paper itself.

There are many types of microform storage units, and special adaptations of regular shelving exist. Some libraries simply put the stack shelves five inches apart instead of twelve in areas where they have a large amount of reel microfilm, but if the library has made a commitment to preserve its resources in microform, then it may have invested in special cabinets. This equipment is expensive and is not used to best advantage if it is scattered, partially filled, through a library's bookstack. For the storage of microfiche there is no better method than special cabinets, but for microfilm, storage in cabinets may present problems for uninitiated patrons and can damage film containers. Special five by five inch shelving appears more inviting to the patron and can be easier on the film, but this form of storage needs to be braced across the top, since it is high and narrow.

For optimum use of space and equipment, all or most microforms the library owns should be kept in one location with machines and staff. This arrangement separates serial microforms from bound volumes, but the need for microform staff to be trained specifically in serial public service really does not exist. Once the patron identifies the article needed, he or she rarely requires assistance from serials staff. Thus, there is no need for microform service to be a part of the serials department. However, if microforms are part of the serials unit, serial public service staff must be familiar with machine maintenance procedures, as well as with serials work. If there is a separate microform reading area, microform staff members need know little about serials, provided they are able to communicate quickly with serial personnel.

Microform serials that are collections of source material on a theme or transcripts of network news programming often create problems for users and require staff assistance. Some of these sets have indexes. For instance, University Microfilms International's *American Periodicals Series* has a finding list and *CBS News Television Broadcasts* has a full name and subject index. Many collections have no index. The proper location for the indexes that do exist can be a controversial matter when microforms are segregated and housed away from professional public service staff. If there are two copies of the index, one can go with the microforms and one can be kept in reference; if there is only one, there must be a policy about location. Having the index in reference, away from the set, can lead to a feeling on the part of staff that the microform must be used with instruction and therefore must be moved out of the microform area into the reference department, undermining the policy of grouping microforms for most efficient use of readers and space. When the lone copy of an index is located at any distance from the microform, patrons may need to run back and forth and become disgruntled. The best policy is to order two copies of the index to a microform set. When there is an index housed with the microform collection, microform staff members should be trained to use it.

Some publishers have attempted to provide catalog cards with their microform sets; individuals have begun to catalog and sell cards to some sets; there has been talk of entering microform publishers' catalog records for microform sets into the databases of the bibliographic utilities. So far nothing has happened on a large scale to relieve the problem of inaccessibility. The Association of Research Libraries has studied the situation and has commissioned a consulting firm to conduct a thorough investigation of the bibliographic control of microforms, intended to lead to cooperative, online records. Serial public service librarians are among those watching the progress of the study in the hope of participating in a project which will bring to the scholarly community resources that have been buried too long in dusty boxes, in cataloging backlogs, or in unused cabinets and on shelves.

CONCLUSION

Many aspects of the serial public service function of the library have developed in the past few years—online bibliographic service, selective dissemination of information, and circulation of microforms with their readers. It is reasonable to expect that more and better ways of assisting patrons in the use of serial resources will be possible in years to come. There will begin to be less traditional public service as described in this chapter and more assistance tailored to the individual patron. Nonetheless, it will be many years before reference sources and human assistance are replaced by machines, if that time ever comes.

NOTES

1. Some of the reference works mentioned in this section do not appear in the Annotated Bibliography. Most of these may be verified in Paul Vesenyi's *An Introduction to Periodical Bibliography* (Ann Arbor: Pierian Press, 1974).

2. Cynthia Swenck and Wendy Robinson, "A Comparison of the Guides to Abstracting and Indexing Services Provided by Katz, Chicorel, and Ulrich," *RQ* 17 (1978): 317-19.

3. *Voice of Z39* 2 (1980): 23.

4. Leland G. Alkire, Jr., ed., *Periodical Title Abbreviations*, 3rd ed. (Detroit: Gale Research Company, 1981).

5. John Steuben, "Interlibrary Loan of Photocopies of Articles Under the New Copyright Law," *Special Libraries* 79 (1979): 227-32.

Chapter 7

Data and Resource Sharing Functions of Serial Management

In the decade of the 1980s there are so many users and so many serials that library materials budgets cannot provide total support for everyone's research at his or her institutional library. A library can make better use of its funds than supporting the specialized research of a single faculty member when a neighboring collection has these resources. In all disciplines serials can be shared to the benefit of the entire community of scholars, although management science specialists recognize that the need to share resources is a condition often resulting in conflict. The requirement that one person or organization consider the needs of another demands a willingness to compromise, to accommodate, and to redefine what is meant by local resources.

The successful sharing of serials among libraries depends upon good communication. For fullest cooperation each library must know what serials others own and the specific holdings. Communication has evolved through printed lists and catalogs, but these tools are expensive to maintain and become outdated very quickly. Effective resource sharing on a large scale becomes possible only with the development of computer technology and its application to library processes. Automation of serial management can be discussed only generally in this chapter, but the Annotated Bibliography contains a number of references to specific projects and expands the topics covered here.

A generation ago when librarians initiated plans to apply computer technology to library processes, they assumed that serials work would be one of the first areas to be automated. Manual serial procedures, especially check-in, are more labor and cost intensive than other library procedures and appeared to be suitable for the application of computer technology, but automation experts and librarians learned that the wealth

173

of detail and frequent exceptions to the rule prevented the successful conversion of serial check-in from a manual to a computerized system. This setback caused administrators to turn to other library operations more suited to computerization: accounting, circulation, and cataloging. Even with today's sophisticated hardware and programming, there are few successful automated serial check-in systems. The existence of these systems proves that the technology exists; the obstacles are funding and library priorities. The only area in which serials work could be automated easily was the union list of serials. Union lists, in turn, depend upon national and international standards if they are to be of real use throughout the library profession.

UNION LISTS OF SERIALS

Union lists of serials began as manually compiled holdings lists for individual libraries; some were only abbreviated replicas of receipt file information that could be distributed to locations distant from the check-in center. In a library system with branches, the list probably originated as a union list for all or part of the system. Universities belonging to a multi-campus system and public libraries belonging to a city or county system compiled union lists of the holdings of all member libraries. Later, groups of libraries began to work together, forming networks and consortia. Some of these cooperative groups formed primarily because of a desire to produce a union list of serial holdings.

As serial costs continue to rise faster than overall inflation, there is a growing need for cooperative collecting and use of resources, so the need for union lists of serials increases.[1] Advances in automation techniques have enabled librarians to create complex and detailed access tools to meet today's requirements.

Librarians performing union-listing operations must understand serial control and recognize the intricacies of serial identification. Nationally acceptable bibliographic records are essential and so is control over the pieces that comprise a bibliographic unit. Some union list designers were not fully knowledgeable before they produced their lists, or they concentrated primarily upon bibliographic details and to some extent cataloging problems, while neglecting holdings and location statements. What makes a union list of serials effective is both the identification of the title and a holding structure composed of two elements: one designating the library owning the serial and the other indicating the specific pieces that library has. Many union lists began with centralized editorial control, diminishing the problem of lack of standardization, but now, with online entry by many libraries, there is a greater need for standards that can be adhered to by all participants. The American National Standards Institute Committee Z39 Library and Information Sciences and Related Publishing Practices (ANSC Z39), discussed later in this chapter, is filling a major need with its work.

The *Union List of Serials in Libraries of the United States and Canada (ULS)*, originally published in 1927, was the first nationwide or international list of serial titles and holdings. The preface to the third edition, published in 1965, contains a fascinating account of the preparation of each edition; it is worth reading. One is struck by the labor intensiveness of the project and by the increasing cost of producing each edition. Also impressive is the growth in number of serials listed, growth not primarily because the scope of the list was expanded, but because new serials appeared and more libraries contributed their titles and holdings. The first edition of *ULS* listed 75,000 titles, nearly twice as many as anticipated, and holdings for 225 libraries. When the second edition appeared in 1943 it had 115,000 titles from 650 libraries, and the third edition (with a cutoff date of 1949) contained over 156,000 titles and holdings from 956 libraries.[2]

By the time the third edition was underway, the cost of continuing *ULS* had become prohibitively expensive. Further, in 1951 the Library of Congress had begun to issue a list of its newly acquired serial titles. Beginning in 1953 LC's list was expanded to include coverage of other American libraries and was renamed *New Serial Titles (NST)*. The scope of *NST* was limited to serial titles first published after December 31, 1949, and received by LC and cooperating libraries. Unlike *ULS*, *NST* was able to report bibliographic and holdings data on a current basis, because it was issued monthly, with quarterly, annual, and multi-year cumulations. In 1973 the R. R. Bowker Company published a twenty-one-year cumulation to *NST* for the years 1950 to 1970, enabling libraries to replace multiple alphabetical lists with one.

Beginning in 1981, *NST* dropped its union list function, along with its valuable "Changes in Serials" section. It now reproduces the CONSER bibliographic records created within the period of coverage. Each current issue is larger than in previous years because *NST* is no longer restricted to titles beginning publication after 1949, and because the entire catalog record is reproduced in card format, similar to records formerly included in the *National Union Catalog*. For librarians and patrons with easy access to the OCLC database, *NST* is now redundant as a source of current information since each record appears online well before it is distributed in print. OCLC members also have access to the symbols of libraries holding newly cataloged serials and, for union list participants, to standardized summary holdings statements.

The value to American libraries of the *Union List of Serials* and *New Serial Titles* has been immense. They have provided in convenient format a guide to the location of serial literature throughout the country. Local and regional union lists are more useful for popular titles such as *Redbook* and *American Historical Review*, because the expense of borrowing or obtaining photocopies of articles is less from a nearby library and there are often reciprocal copying or borrowing agreements among institutions in the same geographical area. For the lower circulation titles, however, the national union lists have served a need well. The lists have been used not only for interlibrary loan purposes, but also for verification, because their bibliographic information is among the most authoritative available. The third edition of *ULS* followed Library of Congress cataloging, but *NST* carries that authority only if LC is listed as a holding library. Other *NST* entries are those submitted by the library that catalogs the title and contributes the notice, and so their authority equals that of the contributing library's cataloging. Current issues of *NST* list the cataloging library—LC, National Library of Canada, or another CONSER participant.

Editors of and contributors to local and regional union lists of serials face many of the same problems as compilers of the national lists. Both the absence of standards for reporting holdings statements and the differences in library cataloging policies and detail have made centralized editing and quality control a thankless job in manually produced lists. With the growing number of online union lists possible on the local level and through the bibliographic utilities, editing is likely to be decentralized and quality control is even more difficult unless standards are determined and adhered to.

There has been significant progress toward the goal of a uniform holdings notation, because an ANSC Z39 standard entitled "Serial Holdings Statements at the Summary Level" was published in 1980.[3] Some librarians are using this standard for union list holdings statements, including those participating in OCLC's Union Listing Capability, but others are not satisfied that it is adequate for their needs.[4] Another Z39 subcommittee is working on "Serial Holdings Statements at the Detailed Level," which should be more nearly what individual library systems and regional union list members need to display specific serial holdings.

Librarians responsible for producing regional union lists of serials have felt a need for further guidance in the absence of an adequate range of standards. In 1980 they campaigned successfully for the creation of the Ad Hoc Committee on Union Lists of Serials, a committee within the ALA/RTSD Serials Section. Its charge is to "solicit information from appropriate groups regarding the creation, production, and maintenance of union lists of serials."[5] The resulting document is to be published by RTSD and should resolve many of the uncertainties concerning the production of both automated and manual union lists of serials.

CONSER

The cooperative serial cataloging effort known as CONSER (CONversion of SERials to machine readable format) is perhaps the most significant development in serials resource sharing. Certainly its association with OCLC makes the combination of CONSER and OCLC serial cataloging of premier significance to serials librarianship. CONSER originated at the 1973 ALA Annual Conference when a group of librarians met informally to discuss their concern about: "1) the lack of communication among the generators of machine-readable serials files; 2) the incompatibility of formal and/or bibliographic data among existing files; and 3) the apparent confusion about the existing and proposed bibliographic description and format 'standards.'"[6] The librarians, led by Richard Anable, named themselves the Ad Hoc Discussion Group on Serials Data Bases. In a position paper the group called for a solution to the problems it had identified, by means of revising projects that already existed and suggesting new projects. The group was expressing its frustration over the many delays with and inconsistencies among the existing serial automation programs, including the National Serials Data Program, which was widely endorsed by the library community. A steering committee, including an NSDP representative, met to establish a procedure for converting and communicating machine readable serial data and to design a retrospective conversion project for creating a serial database. Subsequent meetings produced a proposal for a cooperative conversion project using OCLC facilities. The primary use of the resulting database was to be that of a union list of serials. The Annotated Bibliography lists several sources that describe in detail the evolution of the Ad Hoc Discussion Group on Serials Data Bases into CONSER. The major events in this early period were the decision to use the Minnesota Union List of Serials (MULS) as the basis for the project, the commitment of support and management by the Council on Library Resources, and the agreement of OCLC to be the conversion vehicle.

The following statements and the accompanying diagram by Lawrence G. Livingston (Figure 7.1) illustrate the interrelationships among the parties involved in the project. While the number of CONSER participants has increased, most of the relationships are still valid.

The following statements are keyed to the diagram in the chart:

1. The interim responsibility for the management of the CONSER project rests with the Council on Library Resources. The Council also provides partial funding for the project. During the project, a more permanent arrangement will be made. [The Council on Library Resources withdrew primary support for the project in 1977 and, since LC was not then in a position to assume

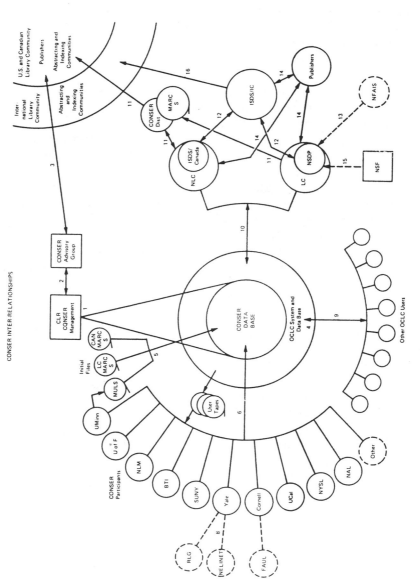

Figure 7.1. CONSER Interrelationships.

administration as planned, OCLC accepted and retains the responsibility until LC can take over.]

2. There is two-way communication between the CONSER Advisory Group and the CONSER management staff at the Council on Library Resources. [Since 1977 the CONSER Advisory Group has worked with OCLC.]

3. It is the responsibility of the CONSER Advisory Group to inform the U. S. and Canadian library communities, the publishers, and the abstracting and indexing communities in both countries. The Advisory Group is also responsible for informing CONSER management of the reactions to CONSER from these communities.

4. The Ohio College Library Center's system is the interim host site for the CONSER data base. OCLC's staff and management work closely with the CONSER management, Centers of Responsibility, and the Advisory Group to implement the project.

5. The initial files are loaded from magnetic tape in a batch mode. Shown are the Minnesota Union List of Serials, the LC MARC serials, and the Canadian MARC serials. There may be other initial files.

6. After the initial files are loaded from tape, the CONSER participants shown in the left semicircle begin their input on-line.

7. Periodically, on prior arrangement with OCLC, each user institution may get tapes of its own records from OCLC. These may differ from other CONSER records in that they contain local data.

8. This shows that Yale is also a member of the Research Library Group and NELINET. Cornell University is a CONSER representative of the Five Associated University Libraries System.

9. Other OCLC users who are not CONSER participants also input serials records to the data base and have on-line access to these records. [The *MARC Serials Editing Guide, CONSER Edition* enables other OCLC users to enter records according to CONSER standards.]

10. After the initial files are loaded, there is a constant interaction between, on the one hand, OCLC and, on the other, the Library of Congress and the National Library of Canada. These two libraries input their own serials records; they receive separate tapes of their MARC serials records for MARC distribution. They also act as Centers of Responsibility for certain bibliographic content of the records. [The International Serials Data System assigns national or regional Centers of Responsibility, whose purpose is to assign ISSN and key title. Beginning in 1981 CONSER records are distributed in catalog card format in *New Serial Titles*.]

11. Periodically during the project and at its end, the Library of Congress and the National Library of Canada will receive the CONSER files and distribute them as they do their MARC serials. [Distribution is by means of a CONSER "snapshot" including both authenticated and unauthenticated records in the file. July 1981 is the latest produced. Future changes will be distributed monthly by LC.]

12. The National Serials Data Program (NSDP) within the Library of Congress, and the ISDS/Canada within the National Library of Canada, provide re-

cords from CONSER to the International Serials Data System (ISDS) International Center in Paris. In addition, these two activities receive from the ISDS records prepared by other national centers and by the ISDS Center itself. These records become part of CONSER. The NSDP and the ISDS/Canada have the responsibility for providing the ISSN and Key Titles to CONSER records for serials published in the two countries, and for authenticating and locking these data elements. These two centers also provide to the CONSER records additional data elements required by the international system.

13. The National Federation of Abstracting and Indexing Services provides input to CONSER by way of the National Serials Data Program, and receives CONSER records in the national distribution system.

14. The Library of Congress and the National Federation of Abstracting and Indexing Services inform U. S. publishers concerning CONSER and request their assistance in using the International Standard Serial Number. The National Library of Canada has the same relationship with Canadian publishers. The International Serials Data System in Paris and other National Centers perform this function for foreign publishers.

15. The National Science Foundation provides some of the funds and guidance for the National Serials Data Program so that it may satisfy the requirements of the abstracting and indexing services primarily and of the scientific and technical community generally.

16. The ISDS Center in Paris is responsible for communication with the international library and abstracting and indexing communities. It has other functions not related to CONSER.[7]

CONSER adheres to American and international standards so that the project can accommodate both existing and past standards, rather than setting new ones. Both successive and latest entry cataloging were accepted at first, with successive entry preferred. A later decision mandated that only successive entry cataloging was to be used for titles published after 1967, the year of publication of *AACR*. Records are supposed to be updated by the participants to reflect changes in the serials and are based on a minimum set of MARC-S requirements. Participants are encouraged to enter records as fully as possible.[8]

An original objective of CONSER was to convert 2,000,000 serial records to machine readable form during a two-year period, beginning with the 75,000 MULS records. The target number of records proved to be unrealistically high; CONSER depends, on the one hand, upon the commitment and financial support of its member libraries and, on the other, upon authentication of the records by the National Serials Data Program, where the workload has been strained by the volume of records and surrogates (photocopies in lieu of title pages and mastheads) generated by serial catalogers. CONSER was conceived as a project which would end in two years. However, there is no sign of an end to the building of the database seven years into the project, although it seems reasonable to expect retrospective conversion to begin to level off in number of records added and in time required to upgrade partial records. In late 1981 the CONSER database contained more than 383,500 records, 125,000 of them authenticated.[9]

Currently a group of representatives from the Association of Research Libraries, the National Federation of Abstracting and Indexing Services, LC, NLC, and OCLC is being supported by a grant from the Council on Library Resources to devise a program "for enriching the CONSER data base with information about coverage by abstracting and indexing services." If approved and funded the project will "1) ensure that the CONSER file includes records for all titles currently abstracted or indexed by the major abstracting/indexing (A & I) services in the U. S. and Canada; 2) ensure that information about where these serials are indexed is included in the CONSER record; 3) develop a mechanism for continued updating of information about A & I coverage in the CONSER file."[10] The A & I program should be only the first of a series of projects designed to enhance this resource so that it can meet the varied serial control needs of librarians and library patrons.

CONSER specialists at OCLC issue a quarterly newsletter entitled *CONSER*. Available upon request, it contains news items, statistics, sketches of related activities at participating libraries, and occasional brief articles, all of which inform interested readers of progress and changes in the project. Certain CONSER libraries are adding special subject collections to the database. Articles in *CONSER* describe Cornell's work with law and agricultural serials and with New York Public Library titles; Boston Theological Institute's entering of theological serials; and Indiana University's Title II-C conversion project, including unique collections in music and folklore.

The purpose and objectives of the CONSER Project appeared in its newsletter in 1979.[11] Enough time has passed since the beginning of the project to evaluate its success in meeting the objectives listed.

Objective 1: To provide a reliable and authoritative serials data base to meet the needs of library patrons, other users of information and the developing national and international bibliographic networks. The key words here are "reliable" and "authoritative." The decisions to build the database in MARC-S format and to adhere to national and international standards ensured that the resulting file would be authoritative; reliability depends on the quality of cataloging contributed by each participating library and on the concern and accuracy of individual catalogers. Participants were selected originally on the basis of their serial cataloging. The opportunity for one member library to edit another library's records helps control the quality of cataloging. The utility of the CONSER database increases as it grows and as participants add to and amend its individual records. Fullness of description has improved noticeably in the past few years.

Objective 2: *To assist the national libraries of both Canada and the United States in the establishment and maintenance of a machine-readable serials data base.* There is no question that the work of CONSER participants assists the national libraries by presenting already-constructed records, with surrogates, for authentication. The fact that the validation procedure is backlogged is evidence that LC and NLC could not have built so useful a database alone. The many brief records in the original MULS list, substandard records that some libraries entered later and duplicate records are being upgraded and/or deleted by NSDP and ISDS/Canada and—since authenticated records have been unlocked to CONSER participants—by catalogers at CONSER libraries. The 1979 policy change allowing CONSER catalogers to enhance authenticated records online has speeded the process of authentication by eliminating at NSDP and ISDS/Canada much paperwork formerly required to change validated records. Non-CONSER libraries can now request enhancement of records not only from the National Center, but from one of the CONSER libraries.

Objective 3: *To provide a source data base for use within the International Serials Data System.* Authenticated CONSER records are transmitted to the ISDS International Center in Paris for inclusion in the ISDS machine readable serial file.

Objective 4: *To support local, regional, and union list serial activities.* CONSER participants may receive tapes of their own records for local and regional use, including union lists; other libraries using CONSER records in their cataloging have these records on their own OCLC archive tapes. For libraries building union lists within the OCLC system, CONSER records to which they have attached their local data record form a significant part of the bibliographic file.

Objective 5. *To ensure the use of nationally and internationally accepted standards, rules, and conventions for building and maintenance of serial bibliographic records.* CONSER participants' adherence to such standards, rules and conventions, together with the locking of authenticated records by NSDP or ISDS/Canada, ensure that this objective is met.

Objective 6. *To identify deficiencies in the data base such as subject, language, and retrospective coverage and to implement appropriate remedies.* This objective can be interpreted in two ways. Its intended meaning probably relates to the overall balance of the serials in the database. Participants would identify any subjects, languages, and time periods not adequately represented and would ensure that these deficiencies were corrected. If there were subject and language access to the CONSER records, it would be easier to determine which areas needed to be strengthened. If users had subject and language access, it would be more important that balance be attained. Objective 6 may be interpreted at another level, that of treatment of omissions and errors in existing records. There are specific rules and procedures for correcting this type of deficiency.[12] In either instance, CONSER participants and management appear to have given lower priority to Objective 6 than to the preceding five. This policy is wise because building the database to minimum standards is a more urgent need than remedying its deficiencies, either large scale or small, despite the user frustration they may cause. With the completion of retrospective conversion projects, it seems reasonable to expect that participants will be able to devote more time to fulfilling their sixth objective.

Most libraries are not CONSER participants. What is the impact of the project on the work and services of this majority? Most obviously, the presence of CONSER records in the OCLC database makes their serial cataloging easier, faster, and less expensive, because they can use existing records instead of having to create new ones. The serial database is much larger and more nearly standardized than if the CONSER libraries and many nonparticipating libraries had not made the commitment to build at the rate of growth and quality of bibliographic data specified. How much easier, faster, and less expensive the local library's cataloging actually is depends upon its willingness to forego local standards of excellence in some cases and to accept most CONSER records as they stand, trusting that the records will eventually be expanded or corrected. Each catalog department must determine to what degree this compromise is feasible. The CONSER database is not perfect, but limited personnel resources make perfection in catalog records a more impossible goal than ever before.

For members of the nation's largest bibliographic utility, the CONSER database is available online not only for cataloging but also for preorder verification of serials, for interlibrary loan, for union listing activities, for collection development decisions, and, if desired, for serial check-in. The records are available to members of other networks and to individual libraries on tapes distributed by the national libraries and through *NST*.

STANDARDS

The foregoing discussion of union lists of serials and the related CONSER project has referred to the need for and the use of standards. Communication among librarians and between librarians and patrons is possible only when each party understands what the other is saying. For communication to occur, the sender and the receiver of the message must define their terms identically. Between two libraries within a city or institutional system, understanding is not often a great problem, particularly when interaction by telephone is feasible. However, nationwide or international communication through printed or online catalogs requires that every person involved enter and interpret data in the same way. To ensure uniformity, standards are created. The CONSER project, for example, adheres to cataloging standards so that its records will carry the same meaning to all librarians and patrons who use them. It is difficult to establish standards in the face of old and varied procedures and with the knowledge that standardization is sometimes achieved only at the expense of the special and unusual.

There are many sources of the standards used in serials work. Library of Congress cataloging is generally accepted as a standard in the United States, and certain divisions of ALA have authority to create standards in their areas. Many other countries have national standards-making bodies, and, at the highest level, there exists the International Organisation for Standardisation (ISO). This discussion focuses on the American standards-setting body and on its work with national and international groups to develop the International Standard Serial Number, perhaps the standard most visible to serials librarians.

American National Standards Committee Z39

American business has long recognized the need for mass produced goods conforming to specific industry standards so that these products may be offered at the lowest cost to consumers. Following this line of thought, four American library associations petitioned the American Standards Association in 1939 to form a committee on library standards. The resulting committee, Z39, was responsible for setting standards pertaining to library, information science, and related publishing practices. Its current purpose is "to develop and promote standards for information systems, products and services."[13] The parent organization is currently named the American National Standards Institute (ANSI), and the committee is American National Standards Committee Z39 (ANSC Z39).

ANSI is a nonprofit corporation embracing over 160 technical, professional, and trade organizations representing some 1,000 companies. It is the national clearinghouse for voluntary standards agencies in the United States and, through membership in the International Organisation for Standardisation, participates in preparing standards at the international level. The sixty-five organizational members of Z39 represent libraries; professional, technical, and educational associations; abstracting and indexing services; publishers; government agencies; and commercial and industrial organizations. Its executive council is composed of a chair, vice-chair/chair-elect and three councilors from each of the three major areas of concern—libraries, information science, and publishing. This group sets goals and priorities for standards development activities. Each member organization appoints a representative to work, comment, and vote on proposed standards. Briefly, the standards-setting procedure is as follows:

> Within Z39, standards are developed by subcommittees made up of professionals in the specific areas of concern. Draft standards developed within these groups go out to the members of Z39 for comment. During this procedure any conflicting opinions are resolved. The draft standard is then submitted to the Z39 members for vote and announced for public review by ANSI through its bi-weekly publication, *Standards Action*. Once public review and member representative voting is complete, the proposed standard is submitted to the ANSI Board of Standards Review (BSR), along with the record of the voting, pertinent documentation, and certification that the ANSI procedural requirements have been met. BSR approved standards are then prepared for publication by ANSI. ANSI requires that all published standards be reviewed as to suitability and applicability every five years. The same procedures are applied to this review process as outlined for new standards development.[14]

ANSC Z39 publishes a quarterly newsletter, *Voice of Z39*, which includes a report from the committee chair, brief news notes, and updates on the work of its subcommittees. Z39 has issued more than 35 standards; many relate to serials, including these: "Periodicals: Format and Arrangement" (1977), "Abbreviations of Titles of Periodicals" (1974), "International Standard Serial Numbering" (1979), "Criteria for Price Indexes for Library Materials" (1974; now being revised), "Compiling Newspaper and Periodical Publishing Statistics" (1979), and "Serial Holdings Statements at the Summary Level" (1980). More standards are in process: "Serial Claim Form," "Single Title Order Form for Library Materials," and "Serial Holdings Statements at the Detailed Level." Three proposed standards relate to serials: "Journal Article Identification Code," "Interlibrary Loan Forms and Procedures," and "Serial Holdings Statement Format for Information Interchange." All of these complete, draft, and proposed standards are described in an ANSC Z39 booklet.

By devising and making available its national standards, Z39 performs an essential service for librarians and others involved in any work with serials. However, adherence to these standards is voluntary, and their impact depends upon familiarity with the standards and recognition of their value by librarians, publishers, vendors, and others. The work of the National Serials Data Program in promoting use of the International Standard Serial Number, discussed below, is an example of the effort that is required after publication of a standard to ensure that it actually resolves the problems for which it was created. The cooperation of representatives from all sectors of the information industry works for the benefit of all.

In 1980 Z39 issued a standard entitled "Serial Holdings Statements at the Summary Level." Some union lists, such as those constructed through OCLC, observe the standard; others do not. When this standard is reviewed in 1985, it probably will be changed to make it more generally acceptable. As it exists now, the standard provides for three levels of detail in summary holdings statements, all of which must be linked to a standard identifier such as the ISSN. Level 1 requires only an institution code attached to the bibliographic record. Level 2 calls for the addition of a "General Holdings Data Area" to include date of report, completeness code, acquisition status code, and nonretention code. Level 3 adds a "Specific Holdings Data Area" composed of enumeration (volumes or equivalent) and chronology (years).

International Serials Data System and National Serials Data Program

The International Serials Data System (ISDS) was created in 1972 within the UNESCO/UNISIST program as an intergovernmental organization.[15] Originally given the charge of creating an international register of scientific periodicals to facilitate standardization of citations to science and technology journal articles, the overall objective of ISDS has been expanded "to provide a reliable registry of world serial publications covering the full range of recorded knowledge and containing essential information for the identification and bibliographic control of serials."[16] ISDS has published *Guidelines* to describe its governance, policies, and procedures. What is particularly important for resource sharing is the ISDS responsibility for managing the International Standard Serial Number program, in conjunction with the network of national and regional centers of responsibility. These national centers and the International Center for the Registration of Serials in Paris form a two-tier structure:

- On the one hand, each National Centre contributes its bibliographic expertise and knowledge of the serials published within its territory. It keeps in close contact with the users and publishers and also acts as focal point for national and regional networks.

- On the other hand, coordination and file building on the international level ensure common policies, uniform operational procedures, coherence and constant maintenance of ISDS standards, rules and formats.[17]

The National Serials Data Program at the Library of Congress is the national center of responsibility for ISDS in the United States; ISDS/Canada, at the National Library of Canada, is the center for that country. In 1980 the network included 44 operational centers covering approximately 80 percent of the world's serial publications.[18] The ISDS International Center in Paris assigns ISSN for serials published in countries not having national centers.

The National Serials Data Program provides an example of the service offered by the ISDS system.[19] It is charged with registering and numbering all serials published in the United States, as well as with promoting ISSN use and filling requests for the standard numbers. The office receives information from a variety of sources: the three national libraries provide worksheets, magnetic tapes, and aperture cards; CONSER participants send catalog records and surrogate photocopies of serial title pages; publishers send journal issues or photocopies. NSDP assigns an ISSN and a standard "key title" to each separate serial. NSDP has a significant role in the CONSER project, for it places the stamp of authority, called "authentication," on CONSER records by assigning the ISSN and key title.

The International Serials Data System and its centers of responsibility provide both the standardization required to support automated union lists of serials and the communication necessary to keep union lists effective. The primary means of communication are the work done by the national and international centers and the publications they issue giving the standard number and key title. Various products are generated by the ISDS machine readable file. The *ISDS Bulletin* is published bimonthly on microfiche and has a cumulating index arranged by ISSN, key title, and variant title. Each issue of the *Bulletin* lists some 4,000 new and amended records. The annual *ISDS Register* cumulates entries in the *ISDS Bulletin* and previous editions of the *Register*; an *ISSN-Key Title Register*, derived from the ISDS database, was issued in 1978. The International Center maintains the International Organisation for Standardisation's list of periodical title abbreviations. A 1971-1976 supplement to the ISO list is available for purchase, and annual supplements from 1977 to date are free of charge.

In 1975 ISDS, with UNESCO and the International Council of Scientific Unions Abstracting Board, issued *Guidelines for the Coded Bibliographic Strip for Serial Publications*.[20] The designation includes ISSN and/or CODEN to be used as a title code, volume and issue identification, pagination and nominal date of publication. A similar system is included in *American National Standard for Periodicals: Format and Arrangement* (ANSC Z39.1-1977). The *Guidelines* includes the procedures for calculating check characters for CODEN and ISSN. Guidelines and national level standards often evolve into international standards that reconcile slight national differences and carry added authority.

International Standard Serial Number

The International Standard Serial Number is an eight-digit number, two groups of four numbers separated by a hyphen and preceded by the letters "ISSN." For example, the ISSN for *Special Libraries* is ISSN: 0038-6723. The ISSN is used worldwide as a unambiguous code to identify a specific serial publication. The last digit of the ISSN is a check digit, effective in detecting transposition errors, and so the number cannot be broken down into meaningful digits, as can the International Standard Book Number.

The need for a unique serial identifier had long been recognized by the time of the development of the ISBN, and ANSC Z39 had in draft form a standard entitled "Identification Numbers for Serial Publications," which it had submitted to both the British Standards Institution and the ISO's Technical Committee 46—Documentation, for consideration as an international standard. In 1974 the latter group issued for ratification a draft standard for International Standard Serial Numbers; it was accepted by members and published in 1975.

Even before final approval of the ISSN, the R. R. Bowker Company was authorized to assign the standard numbers to both its own database of serial titles and to titles being included in its publication of the 1950-1970 cumulation of *New Serial Titles*. The mammoth project was completed with relatively few difficulties. There were instances of one title being assigned two ISSN or one ISSN being attached to more than one title, which led to all the numbers being considered provisional until they had been validated by NSDP or another ISDS national center. On the whole, however, the fact that numbers had been assigned to titles prior to adoption of the standard encouraged use of ISSN from the beginning.

The national centers are responsible for promoting use of ISSN, because its success depends upon consistent worldwide use by publishers, librarians, subscription agents, and scholars. To that end NSDP provides publishers a brochure packed with information about the significance and proper use of ISSN, including an application form for the publisher to return for the free-of-charge assignment of an ISSN. Included in the brochure for publishers is a list of eight advantages of ISSN use:

1. ISSN provides a useful and economical method of communication between publishers and suppliers, making trade distribution systems faster and more efficient.

2. The ISSN results in accurate citing of serials by scholars, researchers, abstracters, and librarians.

3. As a standard numeric identification code, the ISSN is eminently suitable for computer use in fulfilling the need for file update and linkage, retrieval, and transmittal of data.

4. ISSN is used in libraries for identifying titles, ordering and checking in, and claiming serials.

5. ISSN simplifies interlibrary loan systems and union catalog reporting and listing.

6. The U. S. Postal Service uses the ISSN to regulate certain publications mailed at second-class and controlled circulation rates.

7. The ISSN is an integral component of the journal article citation used to monitor payments to the Copyright Clearance Center, Inc.

8. All ISSN registrations are maintained in an international data base and are made available in the ISDS Register.[21]

Thus, the ISSN benefits those who produce serials, those who process them and those who read them. Serials librarians are probably the group of ISSN users most pleased by the standard, because it brings specific identification of titles to every area of their work.

The success of the ISSN was virtually assured in the late 1970s: at the urging of the National Federation of Abstracting and Indexing Services, the Association of Research Libraries, and other groups, the U. S. Postal Service began to require that most serial publications adopt and display the ISSN as USPO's official registration number, as qualification for second-class postage rates. NSDP set up a branch office in the main Washington, D. C. post office and, with the assistance of CONSER participants and the support of a grant from the Council on Library Resources, identified and registered the serials involved.[22]

Associated with the ISSN and inseparably linked to it in the files of ISDS is a corresponding "key title," which is "based upon the title as it appears on an issue or volume, with the addition of an author statement if the title consists of a generic term [and] qualifying information [if necessary] to create a unique citation."[23] If the key title of a serial changes according to rules stated in *Guidelines to ISDS*, a new ISSN is assigned. The earlier ISSN remains as the unique identifier of the serial under the former title. Many key titles were assigned before the implementation of *AACR* 2 and would be different if they were assigned today, because assignment was formerly based on latest issue while now it is based on first issue.

In resource sharing efforts and particularly in union lists of serials the ISSN eliminates problems created by use of more than one cataloging code. This unique serial identifier minimizes errors in transmission of bibliographic data from a local cataloger to a union list editor or from one collection development officer to another. Interlibrary loan requests carrying an ISSN no longer go unfilled as a result of garbled references. Finally, the ISSN is a much more satisfactory means of accessing a database than truncated title or other main entry, because it retrieves a single serial title. With the proliferation of serial publications and the frequent revision of cataloging codes, it is now difficult to imagine working with serials that lack the International Standard Serial Number.

Other Standards

The *International Standard Bibliographic Description for Serials*, known as *ISBD(S)*, is one of a series of programs sponsored and published by the International Federation of Library Associations for the purpose of promoting consistency among descriptive cataloging codes throughout the world. In *A Practical Approach to Serials Cataloging* Lynn S. Smith has included a detailed study of the early developments and interplay of various groups and concerns prior to the 1977 publication of the "1st standard edition" of *ISBD(S)*.[24] Neal Edgar and Patricia Rice published complementary review articles of the standard.[25] Edgar lists the three primary purposes of *ISBD(S)*: "to make records interchangeable among libraries and other bibliographic agencies; to insure reliable interpretation of bibliographic elements in unfamiliar languages; and to assist in converting bibliographic records to machine-readable form."[26] The principles of the standard were incorporated in the *AACR* 2 chapter for serial description.

MARC-S is the acronym for a machine readable cataloging format for serials developed by the Library of Congress in the late 1960s. It consists of a list of "content designators," often referred to as "tags," for each item of bibliographic data and is used as the basis for most automated cataloging systems. MARC-S was influential in the design of *AACR* 2. The Library of Congress has distributed tapes of MARC-S cataloging for nearly a decade. These tapes now include the CONSER records, which are in MARC-S format.

Standards are developed in response to specific needs. They are used and amended or abandoned as required, and new standards are created to fill new communication needs. The acceptance of international standards is a positive response to the need for worldwide sharing of resources. The national standards organizations have a significant dual role in the international scene: they identify where standards are needed and develop preliminary ones which then are tested and revised, and they promote existing international standards. Their success depends upon the degree of acceptance and use by persons and agencies concerned.

BIBLIOGRAPHIC UTILITIES

A highly visible response to the need for resource sharing was the creation of the bibliographic utilities—OCLC, RLG/RLIN, UTLAS, and WLN. Among all the means of cooperation available from the utilities, shared cataloging has had the greatest effect. In fact, in all except OCLC, cataloging is virtually the only developed serial function. This section introduces each of the utilities and describes its existing and planned serial features. It concludes with an evaluation and with speculation about the future role of the utilities in serials management.

OCLC (Online Computer Library Center), Inc.

OCLC, Inc., originally the Ohio College Library Center and now the Online Computer Library Center, evolved from a consortium formed in 1967 by colleges and universities in Ohio. It is a private, nonprofit organization financed by annual library membership fees and use charges and governed by elected representatives from its member libraries. In 1981 OCLC had about 2,500 library members, many of which joined through regional networks such as NELINET (New England Library Information Network), PALINET (Pennsylvania Area Library Network) and SOLINET (Southeastern Library Network).

OCLC has concentrated on providing cataloging services for its member libraries, initially for monographs and, since October 1977, for serials as well. The central database can be searched for bibliographic verification and its records used for cataloging, with or without card production. Access to the database is by OCLC control number, ISSN, ISBN, CODEN, LC card number, title, or author/title. A search can be limited by type of material and by beginning date. Both of these features are especially useful when searching serials by title because one can now eliminate most records from the search by excluding all except serials. New records can be entered by a cataloging library if it does not locate a suitable record already in the database of over 7,500,000 entries.[27]

The OCLC Serials Control Subsystem is the only check-in system available now or in the foreseeable future from any of the bibliographic utilities. The OCLC system is not the only online check-in system available, but it is the most readily available to the general library belonging to OCLC. Over one hundred library members are using the automated check-in system in 1982.

An OCLC member deciding whether to use the Serials Control Subsystem needs to evaluate it on several levels and in light of local needs and priorities. Harry Kamens has written an excellent essay that provides guidance to librarians contemplating use of the OCLC online check-in system.[28] He lists five areas to be studied:

1. Institutional commitments to OCLC, including what the library expects from OCLC and what it is willing to invest in the system.
2. A comparison of the library's existing serial system with both the one currently offered by OCLC and the one OCLC can be expected to offer in the future.

3. The amount of work involved in implementing the OCLC subsystem.
4. The staffing required for the conversion of cataloging and holdings records and for temporary maintenance of parallel check-in systems.
5. The library's financial commitment to the Serials Control Subsystem.[29]

Kamens discusses these questions from the background of his experience in implementing the subsystem at Kent State University Library, so he is able to present specific problems encountered in the conversion, as well as opportunities for correcting and standardizing local records.

Use of the Serials Control Subsystem is separate from use of the Cataloging System and requires its own authorization. However, serials control depends on the Cataloging System, because OCLC requires that each holdings record (Local Data Record or LDR) be linked to a cataloging record showing the serial's bibliographic data. A library having more than one active order for a title will create a separate LDR for each copy. Access to serials control records is by means of the same search keys as those used for the bibliographic record, although OCLC number is the most efficient means of retrieving a specific record. Libraries participating in the OCLC Serials Control Subsystem must first enter bibliographic records for each active title before creating LDRs. If there is already a record in the database, the task may be quick and easy, or it may be very slow, depending upon the completeness of the database record and the library's cataloging standards. When no record exists, the cataloger must add a bibliographic record to the database. Early reports from libraries preparing to use OCLC's Serials Control Subsystem indicated that the bibliographic record was already in the database from 60 to 90 percent of the time, depending on the complexity of the library's serial collection. Now, several years later, nearly all titles should be in the database in some form, except for ephemeral serials and items of strictly local interest. After the library has accepted, amended, or entered a bibliographic record, it must construct an LDR for each active order. No library can use another's LDR or even examine it unless the operator knows the other library's authorization number. Thus, building a file of LDRs is usually a slow, expensive process. Kamens reported a creation rate of 6 to 8 an hour at Kent State.[30]

Figure 7.2 reproduces an OCLC serials control record screen. Note that it is linked to the catalog record by the OCLC number given in one of the fixed fields at the top. The variable fields, with mnemonic symbols, contain the data about a single library order (or inactive serial run), the same data that are traditionally found on manual check-in records and other manual files. These include the call number, location within the library system, fund, dates received, and current and retrospective

Automatic Check-In - Issue Received

```
¶
American Society for Information Science. ⊢
Journal of the American Society for Information Science. ⊢
ISSN: 0002-8231  CODEN: AISJB6  OCLC no: 1798118  Frequn:  b  Regulr:  r
¶
▲ Hld lib: TRNG Copy: 1    Repr:    Subsc Stat: a Loan: 3 DAYS ¶
¶
▲ 1 CLNO    Z1007 ‡b .A477 ¶
▲ 2 LOCN    Faculty Library ¶
▲ 3 FUND    7789-2279 ¶
▲ 4 RMKS    Preceding entry: American documentation; a quarterly review of⊢
ideas, techniques, problems, and achievements in documentation (#1479779) ¶
▲ 5 RMKS    This record is to be used for training purposes only. ¶
▲ 6 DEFN    ‡v vol. ‡p no. ¶
▲ 7 NEXT    ‡v 31 ‡p 1 ‡d 800525 ¶
▲ 8 DTRD    791122 ????? 800318 ¶
▲ 9 CRHD    ‡v 30 ‡p 1,3-4,6 ‡y 1979 ¶
▲10 RTHD    ‡v 23-29 ‡y 1973-1978 ¶
```

Figure 7.2.   OCLC Serials Control Subsysten Check-in Screen

holdings. A repeatable "Remarks" area exists for information needed to supplement that in the other fields. One field predicts the enumeration and arrival date of the next expected piece, based on the enumeration definition, given in a separate field. The Date Received field lists only the six most recent pieces. When a new volume or issue arrives, the earliest receipt date is deleted and the latest one is added.

When the serial holdings records are entered in the database and online check-in begins, the library must decide whether to maintain the manual serial record. Parallel check-in is expensive, yet most libraries prefer to continue manual check-in until their adaptation of the online method proves sufficient for their needs.

Central Michigan University Library was one of the first libraries outside of Ohio to implement the OCLC Serials Control Subsystem. An article by Nancy Melin Buckeye describes and evaluates the experience.[31] Harry Kamens has reported on the conversion from manual check-in to OCLC check-in at Kent State University Library and included a breakdown of the approximate number of hours required for the process.[32] Both of these accounts are useful to librarians considering the Serials Control Subsystem because, except for the larger number of serial bibliographic records in the OCLC database, little has changed. One possibly significant difference from the mid-1970s is the wider use of the ISSN on serial publications, making the standard numbers available and useful as a means of access to the database.

There are advantages for OCLC members in using the OCLC Serials Control Subsystem instead of a manual check-in or some other available online check-in systems. Kent State wanted to provide its patrons direct access to check-in data and purchased a terminal for this purpose.[33] Kamens's article does not discuss difficulties arising from patrons' attempts to call up and interpret the LDRs. One advantage of the OCLC system is that the check-in/holdings entry always agrees with the OCLC catalog entry, often a problem for manual systems, because the LDR is attached to the library's bibliographic record. However, the OCLC record is not necessarily identical to the local library's card record, because the library may have adapted the database record before ordering catalog cards.

The disadvantages of OCLC's system appear to outweigh the advantages substantially. Most obvious are the components that are missing: claiming, binding, and financial data. Some libraries have devised their own adaptations for these deficiencies by using the remarks field for local purposes. However, OCLC discourages this practice, in spite of offering no alternatives. The reason for this dissuasion is probably the future difficulty of changing to an OCLC standard approach and the likelihood that many libraries will continue to use their own adaptations.

Currently the claiming function is nearly ready to be tested, and financial management is promised as a part of the acquisitions subsystem. A binding field, once reserved for future use, was dropped when the Union Listing Capability was activated.

An additional disadvantage of the OCLC serials subsystem is lessening in severity with time; this is the presence of incomplete bibliographic records to which to attach LDRs. Some libraries accept skeletal records in the expectation that these records will be expanded and updated eventually; other libraries will not make this compromise. The appearance on the OCLC archive tapes of records that do not meet the local library's standards causes difficulties for libraries using them.

Down time, both scheduled and unexpected, has caused some libraries to bypass the Serials Control Subsystem. There is no service on Sundays, traditionally one of the days of heaviest activity in academic libraries. Scheduled down time frequently lasts longer than planned and announced. Related to down time is the history of poor response time for the utility as a whole. OCLC has indicated that improvements in these areas are among its top priorities, so the situation may change.

The time expended in building the OCLC check-in records was discussed above. Other expenses include the actual charges for using the subsystem each time a serial is received. Future costs will include additional fees for using the claiming and financial modules. In addition, one must add the cost of the telephone line to Dublin, Ohio, often via the regional network headquarters. More subtle costs appear in (1) the extra staff time studies seem to show is required to use any online system over a functioning manual check-in system, (2) time to locate the LDR through an index of OCLC numbers, and (3) time to answer patron inquiries when the system is down. The OCLC serials check-in system will not permit every title to be checked in automatically. Since the automatic feature is based on predicted date of arrival, titles having any irregularity in publication schedule, such as a September to May monthly, must at times be checked in manually. Kamens's article reveals how often his library had to adapt the subsystem to meet special needs, thus losing the automatic check-in capability much of the time.[34]

The financial and public service impact of these disadvantages to the OCLC Serials Control Subsystem must be balanced against its advantages and the degree of the library's commitment to the OCLC system. Buckeye and Kamens both point out the opportunity a library has during the start-up period to update and standardize its check-in records.[35] However, libraries to which the above would be the most significant advantage might want to consider it as a special project for their manual systems and not relate it to online check-in.

In summary, at this time libraries with relatively small and general files of active serial orders are the ones that can make best use of the OCLC Serials Control Subsystem. However, these libraries and others should evaluate carefully the cost and benefits of OCLC's online check-in system for their local situations before adopting it.

There is an alternative that would resolve many of the problems associated with OCLC's check-in system. This is local library or consortium use of the OCLC archive tapes for bibliographic records, with a locally designed online check-in system. The archive tapes give the library its own bibliographic records as it has expanded or corrected the OCLC records, an important consideration for public service as well as for serials control. At the same time the flexible local check-in system could accommodate claiming, binding and financial data, while eliminating the OCLC, regional network, and long distance communication charges. The check-in record could be designed exactly as the local library needs, and it could support displays for both staff and public use. The database containing only local check-in records would be smaller than the OCLC database, and so response time could be significantly faster. System down time could be reduced, and the hours during which the database could be accessible would be suited to the library's schedule. However, a local system would have significant start-up and maintenance expenses for programming and hardware, and staff capable of the development work would have to be available. Similarly, library members of the other bibliographic utilities can use tapes of their serial cataloging to create local systems. When one or more local serial control systems has developed, it is likely that software will be available for purchase by other libraries or consortia. The alternative just discussed is available currently. It is possible that in the future a library will be able to transfer its OCLC or RLIN records directly to the local database without the need for archive tapes.

Other alternatives to the OCLC Serials Control Subsystem are developing or purchasing online check-in software from a library that has developed its own system independently of OCLC, and creating a local online check-in system not based on the OCLC bibliographic records. For OCLC members both of these options are less desirable than the archive tape system, because they do not benefit from OCLC cooperative cataloging.

OCLC announces its enhancements and changes of policy and practice in a series of *Technical Bulletins*. For instance, *Bulletin* no. 96, dated September 15, 1980, described several new features in the Serials Control Subsystem that permit greater flexibility and increased compatability with other subsystems. Among the changes are several that simplify use of the subsystem by permitting the operator to eliminate steps in going from one screen or record to another (for example, automatic interaction with the cataloging subsystem, screen number request, holdings display requests, and local data record request).[36] Such continued refinement of OCLC procedures and capabilities is necessary to attract more libraries to the Serials Control Subsystem.

OCLC has an online Union Listing Capability available to member libraries and to nonmember libraries that enter contractual agreements with an authorized union list group agent. Union lists use the Local Data Record, originally designed for the Serials Control Subsystem but expanded for union listing. Libraries do not have to participate in the Serials Control Subsystem to use the Union Listing Capability. Users enter summary holdings information into the LDR according to ANSC Z39.42-1980, "Serial Holdings Statements at the Summary Level," at one of three increasingly detailed levels. They can call up a title and retrieve either a Union Listing Group Display, showing summary holdings for all libraries within a union list group, or a Union Listing Institution Display, showing copy-specific summary holdings for a single institution.

The OCLC Interlibrary Loan Subsystem permits online requests for a volume or photocopy. Users may search by title, author/title or ILL transaction number. Borrowing libraries are able to retrieve records by patron name or identification number. On a workform provided by the system, the borrowing library can specify up to five potential lending libraries. The system circulates the request to the libraries selected and transmits the lender's response (restrictions, changes, etc.) to the borrowing library. Lending libraries can retrieve records by their own call number. Messages are stored online for each library. Libraries may also search the file for their current lending and borrowing partners.[37] An OCLC booklet describes three improvements to the Interlibrary Loan Subsystem being developed:

> Statistical analysis of each participant's loan activities; interface with Name-Address Directory, giving names, addresses, and institution policies [the Name-Address Directory is an online file containing names, addresses, and other communication and policy information about libraries, publishers and vendors]; and interface with Serials Union Listing, giving holdings information about individual issues of journals.[38]

Several OCLC publications are available to members and other interested persons. Among them are *OCLC Newsletter* and *Research Libraries in OCLC*. OCLC staff members also participate actively in professional meetings and publish articles in relevant journals.

Research Libraries Group/Research Libraries Information Network

The Research Libraries Information Network (RLIN, formerly BALLOTS: Bibliographic Automation of Large Library Operations using a Time-Sharing System) originated at Stanford University as that library's own system. In 1978 three members of the Research Libraries Group (RLG)—Yale and Columbia Universities and the New York Public Library—joined Stanford in a new bibliographic network designed for research library purposes:

> to provide the capacity by which research universities, their libraries and major independent research libraries may work together to determine the means of providing information required by the scholarly process. The justification for creating such a network is two-fold. First, both in the short and long-term, the research libraries of this country have a special mission within their universities that demands a unique and effective form of inter-institutional cooperation.... Secondly, the agencies, both public and private that support library related projects, have been clear that they will no longer fund discrete, non-interrelated activities.... Research libraries must create an operating federation that balances local, regional and national activities if any significant resources are to be made available to support their needs.[39]

A development plan produced in late 1978 listed RLIN services to be made available by Spring 1979: *searching* by personal name, corporate/conference name, title word, LC card number, RLIN identification number, local call number, subject headings, and ISSN; *cataloging support* for monographs, serials, maps, manuscripts, sound recordings, scores, and films; *acquisitions support*; *online union catalog*; and *databases*, including MARC records from 1972, MARC authority records, and contributed cataloging from RLIN libraries. Other services were planned for later years.[40] As with OCLC, not all services predicted have been activated on schedule. One can search the serial database by ISSN and CODEN, and the system allows author/title and subject searches using Boolean logic. The first serial catalog cards were produced in April 1980. Although no services beyond cataloging have been implemented specifically for serials, RLIN has plans for a full serial system. The database contains more than 460,000 serial records, including over a quarter of a million CONSER records.[41]

Currently more than one hundred libraries participate in RLIN's shared cataloging system, administered by the twenty-six members of RLG. Two supplementary membership categories are available. *Special members* are single-focus research libraries, represented by law and art libraries; special members take part primarily in their own programs. *Associate members* have access to RLIN, but do not participate in its governance. On December 19, 1979, an RLG News Release announced a program permitting cooperative purchase of expensive items and serials, the first component of a cooperative collection development program. The memo states that

> all RLG members with installed RLIN terminals can now search a special in-process file in the RLIN data base which will contain records of all recorded items having a

value of more than $500 and all new serials on order at any member institution. . . . The system permits selectors at any RLG institution to search the file before placing orders so that the purchase of items not required locally may be deferred or avoided, and access assured through RLG's Shared Resources Program.

While the number of research libraries abandoning OCLC and joining RLG/RLIN increased steadily during the late 1970s and the early 1980s, not all of them jumped on this bandwagon. One midwestern state university librarian determined, after an exhaustive study, that it was best to remain an OCLC member, at least for the time being. One of the reasons was related to serials:

> The RLIN serials records pose problems for us. The *California Union List of Serials*, making up the major portion of the database, contains minimal level bibliographic records. The records will require extensive changes. The CONSER tapes are not scheduled to be loaded in RLIN until July, 1980. . . . Even after the CONSER tapes are loaded, we are told that they will be in a static file. A library using the CONSER records would have to input information from the static file into the RLIN database prior to adding to the bibliographic record.[42]

A January 23, 1981, RLG press release announced that RLG and UTLAS (University of Toronto Library Automation Systems) had signed a memorandum of understanding concerning international cooperation, including "sharing data bases, collaboration on programs to support ongoing functions at their respective libraries and shared system development projects." Specifically, UTLAS would "produce page form catalogs for RLG member libraries from machine-readable data supplied by [RLIN and] carry out the conversion of RLG authority tapes from current formats to an RLIN-defined format."

University of Toronto Library Automation Systems

The University of Toronto Library Automation Systems (UTLAS) has been described as "the Canadian counterpart of the Ohio College Library Center."[43] It was designed at the University of Toronto Library to serve not only that university but the general library community, and since 1973 has served an increasing number of libraries, primarily Canadian. UTLAS has more than 200 institutions and members of consortia in its online user network. More than 600 individual library clients (or subscribers; they are not called "members") have access to the Catalogue Support System (CATSS), an online database of more than 10 million records, either directly or through Canadian networks.

A promotional booklet describes UTLAS features that enable libraries to maintain flexibility as individual institutions while sharing those functions that can be shared. Within CATSS, clients establish and maintain individual files representing their cataloged collections. Records derived from the total database can be modified to meet local requirements. Online authority control is optional. Libraries own their data and receive paper, microform, or magnetic tape records. UTLAS programs enable the client to create a variety of products from the records held in its files. One subscriber may access another's file only with that library's permission. The flexibility of CATSS is shown in its modular approach to automation; each library chooses the functions it wishes to use and pays only for those. Because it is Canadian, UTLAS is accessible in both English and French.

UTLAS is dedicated to developing integrated distributed processing, believing that certain functions—such as online searching, circulation control, and collection management and analysis—belong in the library and are best carried out at the local level. The goal of UTLAS processing is

> to distribute as much of the data processing and communication activities as is economically advisable to locally situated minicomputers. Through the minicomputer system, libraries have access to a full range of automated library services, from cataloguing to serials check-in and local accounting systems. The processing power of the large central computer supports the local minisystem by performing functions not technically possible or economically feasible on the minicomputers.[44]

To supplement CATSS, UTLAS offers its Library Collection Management System (LCMS), a preprogrammed minicomputer system that stores data derived from CATSS and provides for local data and services. The local online catalog permits user searches and browsing: "The user has the option of inputting complete or partial information with any key. The system also allows the use of Boolean operators."[45] LCMS can serve as a circulation system and can provide certain statistical and administrative data. It can also be used for union listing. Serials ordering and check-in are scheduled for implementation, but no target date is available. When serial management functions are developed, UTLAS's LCMS should provide a subsystem that eliminates the necessity of accessing the central database to update a local record, as OCLC serial check-in users must do.

Although no date has been set for UTLAS's Serials Control module, an undated handout, entitled "Development at UTLAS: Acquisitions and Serials Control," describes its projected functions:

Preorder searching: comprehensive searching, which takes advantage of other clients' data, and simple searching, which uses precise or browsable access.

Ordering: of all monographic and serial orders in any format.

Receiving: with or without invoice, of complete or partial shipments.

Invoice Control: for all invoices in any currency, with totals in client-determined currency.

Fund accounting: for allotments, adjusted allotments, encumbrances and expeditures; conversion tables.

Claiming: with automatically produced claim notices, according to a date reminder table.

Cancelling: orders cancelled and reordered, with reasons for cancellation given; automatic production of cancellation notices.

Serials check-in: of daily receipt, including multi-volume sets and monographic series.

Subscription renewal: with a renewal alert, projecting the approximate cost.

Binding: with automatically produced binding notices.

Routing: with automatic generation of notices.

Management and statistical information: monitoring the flow of materials.

Access points: through multiple search keys, including ISSN, title, browsable author/title, vendor, purchase order number, publisher and fund.

Individualized products: such as purchase orders or tapes, claim and cancellation notices, vendor performance reports, fund reports, buying patterns, cost and holdings lists.

Other features: a large database with source and user files, links to cataloging system, accommodation of vendors and publishers, as well as libraries, and an online vendor name and address file.

Certain features of the Acquisitions and Serials Control System are already operative, but those related to serial acquisitions are not yet implemented.

The REFCATSS module, designed for public service staff use, serves a type of union listing function in that the client's records are linked to parent bibliographic records. When the user retrieves a linked record, all holding locations are displayed. Presumably this is true for serials as well as monographs.

Washington Library Network

The Washington Library Network (WLN) is a government agency coordinated by the Washington State Library Commission. The network's objectives are to

1. expand the availability of library materials throughout the state;
2. reduce unnecessary duplication of cataloging effort among libraries;
3. improve control of the accuracy and completeness of bibliographic records;
4. improve interlibrary loan communication and delivery; and
5. develop the capability to interface with other computer utilities in a national network.[46]

After a brief pilot project, WLN began using its own cataloging subsystem in July 1977. Fifty-six libraries, located in Alaska, Oregon, Idaho, Montana, and Arizona, as well as Washington, are members of WLN. Having expanded beyond the borders of Washington State, the network hopes eventually to encompass all automated services, although there are no definite plans for a serials control subsystem. Cataloging is strictly monitored, with central editing. MARC-S records and data entered by WLN participants amount to more than 150,000 serial records, and there are brief records for additional serials in the system. An acquisition and accounting system, already in operation, can be used for serials as well as monographs, and a union list function is available that gives summary holdings.

Some OCLC-member networks have purchased WLN software to adapt for their own uses. In March 1979, WLN and RLG announced "a plan to share data bases and to engage cooperatively in development projects." Programs to be undertaken jointly include "the functional and technical specifications for serials, acquisitions, authorities, and interlibrary loan."[47] A press release in 1981 announced that WLN and OCLC would work cooperatively on certain unspecified projects. In the current search for the means to link the bibliographic utilities' databases, the Washington Library Network has always been an active participant. The present economic crisis within the Washington state government indicates that WLN's survival depends upon close cooperation, perhaps to the extent of merger with another network.

The Future of the Bibliographic Utilities

The four active bibliographic utilities in North America provide or promise many of the same services, but they differ in constituency, governance, philosophy, and stage of development. Each utility fulfills some needs of its member or client libraries, but none is maturing into the complete service required by American librarians and library users, most of whom have become dependent upon resource sharing for at least the cataloging of incoming materials.

As the cost of sharing resources through the bibliographic utilities continues to increase, many libraries find it easier to fund automated processes and services than to add human resources. Furthermore, they receive a greater return on their financial investment in computerized networks than on their investment in staff members. Cost is an increasingly serious problem; as library budgets are cut across the board, online users are insisting on even more value for their money.

The most widely discussed change that may occur in the existing situation is cooperation among the networks, particularly the sharing of their databases and development programs. The Washington Library Network, smallest of the utilities, has entered reciprocal agreements with both RLG/RLIN and OCLC, but the latter two organizations are still competitors, each with huge development costs. OCLC was hurt when many research libraries changed to RLIN, but it has offered remaining members additional services such as the formation of an advisory group of research library administrators. Research libraries do indeed have common needs, but RLIN members are seriously handicapped by the inaccessibility of CONSER records online. UTLAS offers individualized participation in resource sharing, but its cost for libraries in the United States is significantly higher than that for OCLC. Nonetheless, the agreement between UTLAS and RLG/RLIN is one step toward the type of cooperation that is necessary.

A source of further conflict is the role of the regional networks. This group played an essential part in the expansion of OCLC from a state to a national network by coordinating organization and training, but this need no longer exists. In their struggle to survive financially, some regional networks seem to have evolved into competitors of the primary utilities by developing unique services to be offered nationwide. The economic climate is wrong for this tactic, and several of the regional networks are in serious financial difficulties. Questions about the future role, if any, of the regional networks must be resolved. If they have served their purpose, libraries should not continue to support them financially; instead, that money could help to develop cooperative programs of far greater benefit.

There are services bibliographic utilities should not provide. A network cannot be all things to all its members. For instance, the national utilities should not develop centralized circulation subsystems and they should not offer serial check-in through the central database. They should not print order forms, claim forms, or binding forms centrally. These functions are more efficiently performed at the local level. The UTLAS concept of the Library Collection Management System is worthy of study and perhaps adoption or adaptation by OCLC and/or RLG. A system which accommodates local needs is more expensive than a single program for all, but it may be necessary for survival.

The utilities must cooperate on another plane. They should work with commercial vendors of circulation and serials management systems to ensure that the vendors develop products that are compatible with the programs of the central utility and that, therefore, may be added to a local library's integrated system. Subscription agents are testing and marketing serial management systems that they have developed more or less independently of the online networks' systems. Purchase of a serials system that cannot interact with the central library system may be prohibitively expensive and wasteful for a library because of duplicaton of data and labor.

In summary, libraries are dependent now upon resource sharing through the bibliographic utilities, but they require more services and more return on their financial investments. Cooperative development of these services is essential. The utilities must cooperate with each other, with their group and individual members and with commercial vendors of products and services if they are to remain within the financial reach of North American libraries.

In 1978 the Council on Library Resources established the Bibliographic Service Development Program (BSDP) with funding from both the National Endowment for the Humanities and several private foundations. The objective of BSDP is "to help bring about a nationwide bibliographic record service in order to serve the needs and demands of the library user in the mid-eighties and beyond."[48] BSDP commissioned "a short-term study...that would examine a fixed number of link alternatives for a fixed number of services."[49] The Battelle Columbus Laboratories was awarded the contract for this study and submitted to BSDP a report in September 1980 that included BIBLINK, a computer model designed to support linking of the bibliographic utilities' databases. The Battelle report was widely criticized for its methodology and resulting recommendations, so BSDP continued to receive proposals from others throughout the country suggesting methods of linking the LC, RLG, OCLC, and WLN databases for the benefit of American libraries. To date nothing has been resolved, and the utilities are still competing for members. However, BSDP continues to search for a feasible means of linking the bibliographic utilities.

OTHER RESOURCE SHARING EFFORTS

Other national level resource sharing efforts are evolving. For serials librarians, two of the most significant are the Center for Research Libraries and the proposed National Periodicals System with its National Periodicals Center; they are highlighted in this section.

Center for Research Libraries

The Center for Research Libraries (CRL, originally named Midwest Interlibrary Center) was established in 1949 by ten midwestern libraries as "a nonprofit organization operated and maintained by its member institutions for the purpose of increasing the library materials available to their readers for research."[50] Membership in CRL is open to any institution maintaining a library of at least half a million volumes and having a five-year average materials budget of at least $200,000; also required are the approval of the Center's Board of Directors and payment of an annual fee based in part on expenditures for library materials. Libraries not meeting both criteria may become associate members.[51] The founders recognized that some research materials could be held at a location remote from the library, for their use would not be frequent and the probability of their having more than one user at a time was very low. Thus, the collection of over three million volumes consists in part of monographs and serials weeded from member libraries' collections. CRL also purchases research materials that are available to members, either by direct loan or by photocopy.

Among these materials are subscriptions to approximately 14,000 journals, paid in part by grant money from the National Science Foundation and other sources. CRL has substantial runs of both foreign and domestic newspapers and administers the Association of Research Libraries Foreign Newspaper Project, whose membership is separate from CRL membership. In addition, the Center holds collections of university and college catalogs, foreign doctoral dissertations, and foreign, federal, and state documents. For access to even more material, the British Library Lending Division serves as a backup and provides speedy photocopy service. The Center does not want, however, to depend indefinitely upon BLLD, which provided more than 85 percent of the articles supplied to users in 1979/80.[52]

In a press release dated April 13, 1981, CRL announced that its Board of Directors had approved unanimously the Center's participation in both OCLC and RLG/RLIN; all newly cataloged titles will be entered into the databases, and retrospective conversion will be undertaken as funds permit. The press release continues:

> At the present time, the Center's *Book Catalogue*, numbering 16 volumes, is the most complete record of Center holdings now available to its members. Since the time that the most recent supplement was completed in mid-1977, 70,000 records for monographs, serials, newspapers and other materials have been created. . . . To provide even a relatively current bibliographic record of all the materials which the Center holds would require a one to two volume supplement to the *Book Catalogue* each year.

> Not only will the Center's joining OCLC and RLG/RLIN make immediately accessible a significant portion of its collection to its members, the on-line systems will also provide magnetic tape of the Center's bibliographic records to member libraries for entry into local bibliographic systems. In addition, machine readable records will be used to produce microfiche catalogs and printouts for individual member use.[53]

On May 1, 1981, the Council of the Center for Research Libraries was presented a three-phase program

> to allow the orderly implementation of the Center's journal holdings as space and funds became available. The first phase of the program will be the addition of a group of new titles now frequently ordered for Center members from the British Library Lending Division. About 800 new subscriptions, primarily foreign science and technical journals selected on the basis of a year-long study of periodical transactions at the Center, will start in January 1982. The second phase of the program is dependent on the completion of CRL's new facility—now planned for the summer of 1982—so it is likely to be January 1983 before more new subscriptions can be added. While initial planning will allow the first two phases to be implemented on internal funds, the Center will also be seeking outside funds to help make the second phase operational by spring of 1982. One possible approach might be for a CRL member institution to purchase the first few years of a periodical and then give the backfile to the Center. The third phase is not yet as well articulated as the first two. This phase, essentially a rapid influx of a large number of new journals to allow the Center to function as a national periodical service function, would require substantial outside funding.[54]

National Periodical System/National Periodical Center

In the past the research library attempted to supply from its own collection virtually all materials its patrons needed. Increasingly libraries have turned to interlibrary loan to supplement their collections as the growing volume and cost of books and journals made it unrealistic for any library to be independent of other libraries. In recent years, photocopies of articles are sent instead of the actual periodical requested on interlibrary loan, and a charge is usually assessed to cover copying, service, and postage charges. However, by the mid-1970s, the volume of serial requests, the cost of obtaining the photocopy and the time required for the transaction had all so increased that the traditional system was no longer satisfactory.

Great Britain has a very successful program for lending and photocopying articles, administered by the British Library Lending Division. This system, originally the National Lending Library for Science and Technology, subscribes to over 50,000 serials and holds, in addition, technical reports, conference proceedings, and translations of foreign language articles. BLLD lends volumes domestically and supplies photocopies for foreign requests, many of them through the Center for Research Libraries. In 1977/78 BLLD received 2,241,000 domestic and 393,000 foreign requests and supplied 82.9 percent from its own holdings. Use of other collections reduced the unfilled rate to 5.9 percent.[55]

In 1977 the Library of Congress, acting on a recommendation of the National Commission on Libraries and Information Science (NCLIS), asked the Council on Library Resources to devise a technical plan for a National Periodical Center (NPC), to be operated by the Library of Congress, to house certain journals and to provide libraries with copies of articles in lieu of interlibrary loan. Completed in August 1978 under the direction of C. Lee Jones, the *National Periodicals Center: Technical Development Plan* recommends a three-tier National Periodicals System, of which NPC is the middle level. Tier one is the local and regional level and tier three is NPC referral to specified research and special libraries. NPC would be

> a centralized collection of periodical literature directly accessible to libraries through-out the nation. Initially projected at 36,000 titles... the collection would continue to grow prospectively (adding more titles) and retrospectively (acquiring back files) according to an established strategy and in as timely a fashion as possible.... Eventually the collection may number in excess of 60,000 current titles, but it will never contain all of the estimated 200,000 currently published periodicals.[56]

Other details presented in the technical plan concern (1) the existence of a "finding tool" organized by ISSN and key title, (2) establishment of a deposit account for each library or consortium having direct access to NPC, (3) provision for compliance with copyright legislation, (4) internal processing and transportation of requests, (5) funding, and (6) governance.

After reviewing the CLR technical plan, NCLIS encouraged reaction from all those concerned and held an open forum attended by 190 persons. The NCLIS 1978/79 Annual Report states:

> The forum, as well as some of the letters and statements received in response to NCLIS' solicitation of comments, revealed that a certain amount of doubt and skepticism existed, primarily within the private sector, on such questions as: whether a national periodical center was, indeed, needed; whether it should be subsidized through federal funding; whether new technology would make outmoded a service based on physical collections; whether the present concept adequately exploits private sector capabilities; whether copyright liability was properly addressed; whether the proposed center's collections should duplicate commonly held titles and whether the center needed to develop new finding tools.[57]

One librarian's dilemma on the subject is revealed in the following statement:

> The Center... would eventually have any part of any journal on all subjects except clinical medicine available to any library, within a 24-hour period, with even copyright problems settled.... With a program such as this one, along with the better coordination of the networks, where will the challenge come for that special breed of people called serials librarians?[58]

While the debate continued, NCLIS commissioned and received from Arthur D. Little, Inc., a report entitled *A Comparative Evaluation of Alter-*

native Systems for the Provision of Effective Access to Periodical Literature, which described three levels of access systems but did not make a firm recommendation. In the meantime a Periodicals Legislative Drafting Team of NCLIS had prepared a draft bill creating a federally subsidized National Periodicals System, of which the Center was to be a part. NCLIS voted to support this draft plan.

Efforts continued to have legislation passed creating a National Periodical System and in late 1980 Congress approved the amendment and extension of the Higher Education Act of 1965. Part D of Title II provides for a

> National Periodical System Corporation, which shall not be considered an agency or establishment of the United States Government.... The corporation shall assess the feasibility and advisability of a national system and, if feasible and advisable, design such a system to provide reliable and timely document delivery from a comprehensive collection of periodical literature.[59]

Unfortunately, funding of Part D depended upon full funding of Part A, Part B, and Part C, which did not occur, so there the matter ended. It is not likely that a National Periodical System will ever develop from this legislation. If government policy toward library funding changes, a detailed procedure for setting up an NPS exists, but the plan would have to pass Congress again in this or another form. Other factors are working against this particular system, such as the lack of wholehearted support from the library community, the opposition of publishers and the ambitions of other groups to fill this purpose. It is fair to say that librarians have become aware of the need for greater accessibility of periodical articles and will not let the matter drop. Whether the answer will come by means of an agency created specifically for this purpose or through use of an existing collection of journals, such as the Center for Research Libraries, remains to be seen. The system may not even use printed journals as the basis for its service, for many persons believe the electronic dissemination of scholarly information is right around the corner.

SUMMARY

This discussion of serial resource sharing has reviewed more than a dozen national and international programs. Some of them, such as the bibliographic utilities or the National Periodicals System and the Center for Research Libraries, appear to be in practically direct competition. Others, such as ANSI, NSDP/ISDS, and CONSER are working and growing together. All are evolving and the situation changes rapidly. Although the business of providing serial information to library patrons is a continuing struggle, it is holding its own against an uncertain economy and the proliferation of information. Nonetheless, ultimate success is impossible without considerably greater standardization, automation, and cooperation among libraries.

ACKNOWLEDGEMENT

The author gratefully acknowledges the assistance of Lynn S. Smith in the preparation of this chapter.

NOTES

1. Michael B. Kronenfeld and James A. Thompson, "The Impact of Inflation on Journal Costs," *Library Journal* 106 (1981): 714-17.

2. *Union List of Serials in Libraries of the United States and Canada*, 3rd ed. (New York: H. W. Wilson Company, 1965), pp. [iii]-[vi].

3. *Serial Holdings Statements at the Summary Level*. (New York: American National Standards Institute, 1980).

4. See Kathleen Bales, "The ANSI Standard for Summary Holdings Statements for Serials: The RLIN Implementation," *Serials Review* 6 (October/December 1980): 71-73.

5. American Library Association. Resources and Technical Services Division, *Procedures Manual, 1981-1982*, p. V-12.

6. Richard Anable, "The Ad Hoc Discussion Group on Serials Data Bases: Its History, Current Position and Future," *Journal of Library Automation* 6 (1973): 207.

7. Lawrence G. Livingston, "CONSER Inter-Relationships," *Library of Congress Information Bulletin* 34 (1975): A87-89.

8. For a discussion of problems created by shared cataloging of serials and the means of resolving these problems see Patricia O. Rice, "CONSER from the Inside," *Title Varies* 3 (1976): 13, 20-22.

9. Minna Saxe reported these figures in her talk, "Going Online with Serials," at the First Annual Serials Conference, Arlington, Virginia, October 30, 1981.

10. *ARL Newsletter* 108 (1981): 11.

11. *CONSER* 2 (May 1979): 1.

12. See Patricia Rice's article, noted above, for examples of when and how this is done.

13. American National Standards Committee Z39 has published a booklet describing the purpose and procedures employed by the committee and listing current, in-process and proposed standards. This section is in part a condensation of information in that booklet.

14. Ibid.

15. A detailed account of the development and specific objectives of ISDS is presented in Lynn S. Smith's *A Practical Approach to Serials Cataloging* (Greenwich, Conn.: JAI Press, 1978), pp. 321-24.

16. UNISIST, *ISDS Guidelines* (Paris: 1973), p. 1.

17. *ISDS Publications & Services*, 1980.

18. Ibid.

19. See Smith, *Practical Approach*, pp. 329-44, for a detailed account of the development of NSDP.

20. *Guidelines for the Coded Bibliographic Strip for Serial Publications* (Paris: United Nations Educational, Scientific and Cultural Organization; International Council of Scientific Unions Abstracting Board; International Serials Data System, 1975).

21. *ISSN Is for Serials* (Washington, D.C.: National Serials Data Program, 1979).

22. A detailed discussion of the plan to register these serials appears in *CONSER* 1 (1978): 1-2.

23. Mary Sauer, "National Serials Data Program," *Drexel Library Quarterly* 11 (June 1975): 46.

24. Smith, *Practical Approach*, pp. 347-52.

25. Neal L. Edgar, "ISBD(S): A Descriptive Evaluation," *Title Varies* 4 (1977): 33-34; Patricia Rice, "ISBD(S): A Review," *Title Varies* 4 (1977): 32.

26. Edgar, p. 33.

27. For a more detailed description of cataloging on OCLC, see Chapter 4.

28. Harry Kamens, "Serials Control and OCLC," in *OCLC: A National Library Network*, ed. Anne Marie Allison and Ann Allan (Short Hills, N.J.: Enslow Publishers, 1979), pp. 139-54.

29. Ibid., p. 140.

30. Harry H. Kamens, "OCLC's Serials Control Subsystem: A Case Study," *Serials Librarian* 3 (1978): 54.

31. Nancy Melin Buckeye, "The OCLC Serials Subsystem: Implementation/Implications at Central Michigan University," *Serials Librarian* 3 (1978): 31-42.

32. Kamens, "OCLC's Serials Control Subsystem," pp. 43-55.

33. Ibid., pp. 43-44.

34. Ibid., pp. 48-51.

35. Buckeye, p. 42; Kamens, "Serials Control and OCLC," pp. 143-44.

36. *OCLC Technical Bulletin* 96 (September 15, 1980): p. 1.

37. "OCLC Online Library Systems," booklet dated June 1981.

38. Ibid.

39. Memo to Directors of Research Libraries, from Edward E. Shaw, dated January 4, 1979, p. 1.

40. Research Libraries Group, Inc., *A Plan for the Development of a Research Libraries Information Network*, rev. and abr. (n.p.: 1979), p. 12.

41. Research Libraries Group, Inc., *Selected Facts* (Stanford, Calif.: 1980), p. [8].

42. Michigan State University Library, *Staff Information Bulletin* 319 (1980): 2.

43. *The Role of the Library of Congress in the Evolving National Network* (Washington, D.C.: Library of Congress, 1978), p. 127.

44. *UTLAS: A Profile* (Toronto: University of Toronto Library Automation Systems, 1981), pp. 2-3.

45. "UTLAS: LCMS, a Promotional Brochure."

46. *The Role of the Library of Congress*, pp. 139-40.

47. Research Libraries Group, Inc., "News Release," dated March 26, 1979.

48. C. Lee Jones, "Linking Bibliographic Databases: A Discussion of the Battelle Technical Report." Draft No. 5, 9/24/80, pp. 5-6.

49. Ibid., p. 6.

50. Center for Research Libraries, *Handbook* (Chicago: Center for Research Libraries, 1981), p. 1.

51. Ibid., p. 139.

52. Center for Research Libraries, Program Committee, *Expanded Access to Journal Literature: General Program Design Statement* (Chicago: 1981), p. 2.

53. Center for Research Libraries, Press Release, dated April 13, 1981.

54. *ARL Newsletter* 106 (1981): 3.

55. Andrew Osborn, *Serial Publications: Their Place and Treatment in Libraries*, 3rd ed. (Chicago: American Library Association, 1980), pp. 349-50.

56. Council on Library Resources, *A National Periodicals Center: Technical Development Plan* (Washington, D.C.: 1978). The Plan's "Summary" is reprinted in *Serials Librarian* 3 (1979): 338-42. The quotation is from page xi of the *Technical Development Plan*.

57.   National Commission on Library and Information Science, *Annual Report, 1978/79* (Washington, D.C.: 1980), p. 22.

58.   Clara D. Brown and Lynn S. Smith, *Serials: Past, Present and Future* (Birmingham, Ala.: EBSCO Industries, 1980), p. 315.

59.   Public Law 96-374-Oct. 3, 1980: *An Act to Amend and Extend the Higher Education Act of 1965*, 94 Stat. 1387.

Annotated Bibliography

The Annotated Bibliography is divided into two parts: Working Tools, which are reference sources for serials department staff members; and Research Tools, which report studies made by other librarians and are secondary sources for serials librarians. Some entries in the Working Tools section have references to Eugene Sheehy's *Guide to Reference Books*, 9th edition (1976). Sheehy's full annotations supplement the brief ones in this Bibliography.

The author published a brief annotated bibliography on serials librarianship in *Title Varies*, vol. 4, no. 4, 5 and 6 (1977). Several of the annotations in this Bibliography are drawn from those in *Title Varies*.

WORKING TOOLS

I. General

1. Andriot, John L., ed. *Guide to U.S. Government Publications*. 1978-79 ed. McLean, Va.: Documents Index, 1979. 3 v.

This update of Andriot's *Guide to U.S. Government Serials and Periodicals* is arranged by issuing agency and is useful for the identification and bibliographic details of federal documents.

2. *Ayer Directory of Publications*. 1-   1869-   . Philadelphia: N. W. Ayer. (ISSN: 0145-1642)

An annual listing of newspapers and magazines published in the United States, its territories, Canada and a few other places. Arrangement is geographic with information about each state, province and city. A title must be published at least four times annually to be included. Data given include advertising rates, circulation and political slant. There are a title index and several classified lists, among them foreign language publications and college publications.

3. *British Union-Catalogue of Periodicals: A Record of the Periodicals of the World, from the Seventeenth Century to the Present Day, in British Libraries.* London: Butterworths Scientific Publications, 1955-58, and *Supplement to 1960*, 1962.

The British equivalent to the *Union List of Serials*, this work has differences which make it a good source for verification of titles. Earliest form of title is used, variant spellings are amalgamated and there are many cross references. See Sheehy AS 146.

4. *British Union-Catalogue of Periodicals, Incorporating World List of Scientific Periodicals.* 1964-80. London: Butterworths. (ISSN: 0007-1919)

The British equivalent to *New Serial Titles*, this work, published quarterly and cumulated annually, contains serials not listed in *NST*. British rules for entry make this a valuable source for verification of titles. See Sheehy AD 147.

5. *Catalogo dei Periodici Italiani 1981*, a cura di Roberto Maini. Milano: Editrice Bibliografica, 1981.

This is an Italian "Ulrich's," even to being distributed by Bowker. Each entry lists most of the following: editor, address, frequency, price, ISSN, beginning date. The scope of the catalog is serials currently published in Italy. This edition lists 7,873 serials in title, subject and editor lists. This much needed work should be revised annually.

6. *Directory of Speakers for Serials Workshops*, compiled by the Regional Serials Workshops Committee, Serials Section, Resources and Technical Services Division, American Library Association. Chicago: Resources and Technical Services Division, American Library Association, 1980.

Can be used for many purposes. Each entry includes specific aspect of serials work of concern to the person listed. Business addresses and telephone numbers are 1979 data. Subject, geographic and type-of-library indexes.

7. Gregory, Winifred. *American Newspapers, 1821-1936; A Union List of Files Available in the United States and Canada.* New York: H. W. Wilson Company, 1937.

Geographically arranged compilation of all American newspapers which were located in libraries, with the holding library listed. Since these newspapers were in their original form, it is likely that many of them no longer exist, unless they were filmed. Holdings listed may be complete runs or as little as one issue. There is a project to update this union list.

8. *Half a Century of Soviet Serials, 1917-1967.* Washington, D.C.: Reference Department, Library of Congress, 1968. 2 v.

A bibliography and union list containing 29,000 entries and 28,000 cross references. It includes works in Oriental languages.

9. *International Directory of Little Magazines and Small Presses.* 1-   1965-
   El Cerito, Calif.: L. V. Fulton.

This annual contains in one alphabetical list detailed information about both little magazines and small presses (titles are in bold face type). Subject and regional indexes. The length of entry varies perhaps because little is known about some titles, but in general both editorial and subscription information appear, along with comments of the editor and/or publisher.

10. *Irregular Serials and Annuals.* 1-   1967-   . New York: R. R. Bowker
    Company. (ISSN: 0000-0043)

A companion volume to *Ulrich's International Periodicals Directory*, this work covers serials published less frequently than twice a year, or irregularly. It is kept up to date by *Ulrich's Quarterly.*

11. *Library of Congress Information Bulletin.* 1-   1942-   . Washington,
    D.C.: Library of Congress. (ISSN: 0041-7904)

Published weekly, *LCIB* keeps one up to date on happenings in librarianship, especially those involving the Library of Congress. Brief articles cover cataloging, ISDS, CONSER and various meetings. Includes annual reports of LC divisions.

12. *Library of Congress Subject Headings.* 9th ed. Washington, D.C.: Subject Cataloging Division, Library of Congress, 1980.

Accepted as authoritative by the library community in the United States, these headings are indispensable for cataloging and public service. Updated by quarterly cumulative microfiche or paper issues.

13. *MLA Directory of Periodicals: A Guide to Journals and Series in Languages and Literatures.* 1st-   ed., 1978/79-   . New York: Modern Language Association of America.

This directory is a companion volume to the *MLA International Bibliography* and contains subscription and editorial information on all titles in the MLA's "Master List." Also included are manuscript submission information and MLA abbreviations. The directory is to be published every two years.

14. *Monthly Catalog of United States Government Publications.* 1895-   .
    Washington, D.C.: Government Printing Office. (ISSN: 0362-6830)

A monthly listing of all publications issued by the various branches of the government, this work is arranged by issuing agency and contains a title index. Periodicals are listed annually, but because of the serial nature of the majority of federal publications, the entire catalog is of value to serial librarians. See Sheehy AG 25-26.

15. *Monthly Checklist of State Publications.* 1-   1910-   . Washington,
    D.C.: Government Printing Office. (ISSN: 0027-0288)

Arranged alphabetically by state name, this bibliography lists state and territorial publications which the Library of Congress has received. Periodicals are listed semiannually in June and December, but the high percentage of state documents which appear in series make the entire contents relevant to serials work.

16. *National Union Catalog.* 1953- . Washington, D.C.: Library of Congress. (ISSN: 0028-0348)

Because of the authority of Library of Congress cataloging, this work constitutes the best manual tool for cataloging, verification and public service. Serials are included in the same alphabetical arrangement as monographs. After 1980 serials are not listed in *NUC.* For a full discussion and history of the *NUC* in all its editions, including its predecessors, see Sheehy AA 92-99.

17. *New Serial Titles: A Union List of Serials Commencing Publication after December 31, 1949.* 1953- . Washington, D.C.: Library of Congress. (ISSN: 0028-6680)

Monthly, with quarterly, annual and larger cumulations, this is the successor to the *Union List of Serials.* See Sheehy AE 134.

18. *New Serial Titles, 1950-1970 Cumulative.* New York: R. R. Bowker Company, 1973. 4 v.

This twenty-one year computerized cumulation of serials beginning publication after 1949 was, in addition to being a timesaver, the original listing of ISSN.

19. *Newspapers in Microform, 1948-1972.* Washington, D.C.: Library of Congress, 1973.

Published in two volumes, *Foreign* and *United States*, this union list is kept up to date by annual supplements. It is arranged geographically and gives owner of microform edition and specific information about the type of microform. Commercial and library publishers are listed, as well as libraries holding circulating copies. The years in the title refer only to the date libraries and publishers reported data to the Library of Congress; they do not reflect the years of the newspapers.

20. Orne, Jerrold. *The Language of the Foreign Book Trade.* 3rd ed. Chicago: American Library Association, 1976.

Arranged by language, this dictionary includes terms used in the book trade, in foreign booksellers' catalogs, and on title pages of serials. Three new languages were added in this edition, giving a total of fifteen.

21. Osborn, Andrew D. *Serial Publications: Their Place and Treatment in Libraries.* 3rd ed. Chicago: American Library Association, 1980.

In the third edition of his classic work on traditional serials librarianship Osborn has retained the historical perspective of developments and trends during the earlier decades of the century. He has brought his scholarly and comprehensive treatment up to the present, including automation, cooperation and reprography. There are extensive quotations from works published thirty and more years ago, as well as from more recent sources. This is a reference book to be kept at one's desk and consulted often.

22. Pitkin, Gary M. *Serials Automation in the United States: A Bibliographic History*. Metuchen, N.J.: Scarecrow Press, 1976.
An annotated chronological bibliography of the one hundred one articles on serial automation listed in *Library Literature* between 1951 and 1974. There are indexes by author and serial function.

23. *RTSD Newsletter*. 1- 1976- . Chicago: Resources and Technical Services Division, American Library Association. (ISSN: 0360-5906)
With its recent change to printed format, the *RTSD Newsletter* gives both items of current interest and brief articles of interest to members of the sections of the division: Cataloging and Classification, Preservation, Reproduction, Resources and Serials.

24. *Serials in the British Library*. June 1981- . London: British Library.
This quarterly succeeds the *British Union-Catalogue of Periodicals* as a listing of newly acquired titles and a limited union list. An annual cumulation will be available on microfiche.

25. *Sources of serials: International Serials Publishers and their Titles, with Copyright and Copy Availability Information*. 2nd ed. New York: R. R. Bowker Company, 1981. (ISSN: 0000-0523)
Arranged geographically, with 65,000 publishers (and addresses) listed alphabetically within each country. Title listings include frequency and ISSN. Alphabetical index of publishers. Useful in verification of orders, public service, claiming, and a variety of other serial functions. Publication at present is irregular; to be effective this work must be updated often.

26. *Standard Periodical Directory*. 7th ed. New York: Oxbridge Publishing Company, 1980. (ISSN: 0085-6630)
Arranged by subject with a title index, *SPD*'s scope is United States and Canadian "publications with a regular frequency of at least once every two years," and it includes some newspapers. It is valuable for small-circulation, ephemeral and processed publications. Some entries are annotated and advertising rates are given.

27. *State Publications Index*. 1975- , pub. 1978- . Englewood, Col.: Information Handling Services. (ISSN: 0197-5668)
Formerly *Checklist of State Publications*, this index to hard-to-identify material is arranged alphabetically by state and then by issuing agency. Subject index and keyword agency index. Data for the checklist come from several sources, including the Center for Research Libraries, *Monthly Catalog of State Publications* and lists from individual states.

28. *Ulrich's International Periodicals Directory*. 1- 1932- . New York: R. R. Bowker Company. (ISSN: 0000-0175)
This annual list of journals which are published at least twice a year is arranged by subject, with a title index and liberal cross references. Special features include

a list of new periodicals and a list of cessations since the previous edition. In addition to subscription information for each title, entries give ISSN and tell where a serial is indexed. Updated by *Ulrich's Quarterly*.

29. *Ulrich's Quarterly*. 1- Spring 1977- . New York: R. R. Bowker Company. (ISSN: 0000-0507)

Updates both *Ulrich's International Periodicals Directory* and *Irregular Serials and Annuals*, and has an index which cumulates to the end of a volume.

30. *Union List of Serials in Libraries of the United States and Canada*. 3rd ed. New York: H. W. Wilson Company, 1965. 5 v.

Still the best source for verification of serials beginning publication before 1950, with the authority of the Library of Congress cataloging. See Sheehy AD 133.

31. Vesenyi, Paul E. *An Introduction to Periodical Bibliography*. Ann Arbor: Pierian Press, 1974.

Two-thirds of this work is a selected, annotated list of periodical bibliographies including indexes, abstract journals, union lists, directories, etc. Emphasis is on humanities and social sciences. The first third of the book defines "periodicals," discusses periodical bibliographies from the seventeenth century on and reviews the American and British efforts at standardization.

32. *World List of Scientific Periodicals, Published in the Years 1900-1960*. 4th ed., edited by Peter Brown and George Burder Stratton. Washington: Butterworths, 1963-65. 3 v. Annual Supplements to 1970.

Contains over 60,000 twentieth-century titles in the natural sciences and is continued in *British Union-Catalogue of Periodicals, Incorporating World List of Scientific Periodicals*. See Sheehy EA 63.

33. *World of Learning*. 1- 1947- . London: Europa Publications, Ltd. (ISSN: 0084-2117)

In a geographical arrangement, *World of Learning* lists for each country: universities and colleges, learned societies, research institutes, libraries and archives, and museums and art galleries. It is good for addresses and verification of titles published by these institutions.

34. Yannarella, Philip A., and Aluri, Rao. *U.S. Government Scientific & Technical Periodicals*. Metuchen, N.J.: Scarecrow Press, 1976.

Two hundred sixty-six titles appear in the main part of this guide. The authors give bibliographic and availability data and annotate each entry. The history of a periodical is traced through title, agency and frequency changes. There is an unannotated section of bibliographies and lists of publications, and indexes by Depository Item Number, Superintendent of Documents number, Agency and Title/Subject.

II. Collection Development

35. *Annuaire de la Presse et de la Publicité.* 1- 1880- . Paris. (ISSN: 0066-2585)

A directory of French and some foreign newspapers and journals in a classified and geographical arrangement with several indexes, including alphabetical lists of French and foreign newspapers and periodicals.

36. *Assistant Librarian.* 1- 1898- . London: Library Association, Association of Assistant Librarians. (ISSN: 0004-5152)

This monthly journal occasionally contains a column entitled "Magazines," which is similar to Bill Katz's "Magazines" column in *Library Journal.*

37. Baer, Eleanora A., comp. *Titles in Series: A Handbook for Librarians and Students.* 3rd ed. Metuchen, N.J.: Scarecrow Press, Inc., 1978. 4 v.

Lists by name of series the author, title and publication data of individual volumes within monographic series. It is international in scope and contains series (including variant titles) and author/title indexes. The third edition includes "69,657 titles published in America and foreign countries to January 1975."

38. *Benn's Press Directory.* 1- 1846- . London: Benn Brothers, Ltd. (ISSN: 0141-1772)

Formerly *Newspaper Press Directory* (1946-1976), this is an annual guide to world newspapers and periodicals which supplements *Willing's Press Guide.* It is perhaps most valuable for the listing of newspapers and periodicals worldwide, by country, although it often gives only the title and frequency. Many titles listed in this British publication do not appear in *Willing's.*

39. *Booklist.* 1- 1905- . Chicago: American Library Association. (ISSN: 0006-7385)

A semi-monthly publication, *Booklist* reviews continuations and annuals of reference value in its "Reference and Subscription Books Reviews." No periodicals are included.

40. *Books in Series in the United States: Original, Reprinted, In-Print, and Out-of-Print Books, Published or Distributed in the U.S. in Popular, Scholarly, and Professional Series.* 3rd ed. New York: R. R. Bowker Company, 1980. (ISSN: 0000-0515)

This vast work is arranged by series, with author and title indexes and a subject index to series. Its editors used as sources of information Library of Congress *NUC* and MARC files, and various Bowker serial publication files: *Books in Print, American Book Publishing Record,* and *Irregular Serials and Annuals.* Unlike the first edition, a title does not have to be in print to be included. Even though nearly 200,000 titles published between 1950 and 1980 are listed and the work has expanded to three volumes, coverage is not complete. Bowker promises to continue to fill in gaps retrospectively in future editions.

41. Brown, Norman B., and Phillips, Jane. "Price Indexes for 19—, U.S. Periodicals and Serial Services." *Library Journal*, annually in July or August.

Published each year since 1960, this study uses index numbers based on the average 1967-1969 (and also now 1977-1979) price and gives, by subject, average price for each succeeding year. The number of titles in each category for each year is listed. The study is sponsored by the Library Materials Price Index Committee of the Resources Section of ALA/RTSD. To be included a title must be published more than twice a year.

42. *Choice.* 1- 1964- . Middletown, Conn.: American Library Association, Association of College and Research Libraries. (ISSN: 0009-4978).

A monthly column, "Periodicals for College Libraries," is compiled by Evan Farber and his staff at Earlham College Library. This listing supplements Farber's *Classified List of Periodicals for the College Library*. Titles included, all recommended, must have been published for several years; newer journals are mentioned briefly, and designated "worth consideration," but it is too early for "firm recommendation."

43. Farber, Evan Ira. *Classified List of Periodicals for the College Library.* 5th ed. Westwood, Mass.: F. W. Faxon Company, 1972.

Includes titles that began before 1969. Farber waits several years to evaluate new titles. Entries list title, beginning date, frequency, place of publication, and cost. Annotations give editorial responsibility, scope, special features, where indexed and LC card number. There is liberal use of cross references to related subjects and a title index. It is updated by the author's column in *Choice*.

44. Katz, William A., and Richards, Berry G. *Magazines for Libraries: For the General Reader, and School, Junior College, College, University, and Public Libraries.* 3rd ed. New York: R. R. Bowker Company, 1978.

A selection tool arranged by subject, for 6,000 basic, recommended titles noted in *Ulrich's*. Besides subscription and circulation data there is an annotation for each title, which may vary from two sentences to more than half a column. The audience level is specified, and microform and reprint availability noted.

45. *Library Association Record.* 1- 1899- . London: Library Association. (ISSN: 0024-2195)

Since March 1976, there has been a monthly column entitled "Vol. 1, No. 1" which contains brief, evaluative reviews of first issues of periodicals. Titles selected are both library-related and non-library-related. Data given in the reviews vary, but usually include publisher, frequency, ISSN and price. The scope is international. One complaint: this column is not listed in the index and is not always a part of the reviews section, which is indexed.

46. *Library Journal.* 1- 1876- . New York: R. R. Bowker Company. (ISSN: 0000-0027)

Each issue contains a column edited and often written by Bill Katz, which reviews new and fairly-new periodicals. It is an excellent source for identifying little magazines, but coverage of all types of new periodicals of interest to librarians is representative. Sometimes the entire column has a theme and may be written by a contributor.

47. Marshall, Joan K., comp. *Serials for Libraries: An Annotated Guide to Continuations, Annuals, Yearbooks, Almanacs, Transactions, Proceedings, Directories, Services.* New York: Neal/Schuman Publishers; Santa Barbara: ABC-Clio, Inc., 1979.

Two thousand serials selected by librarian subject experts appear in this work. The arrangement is by broad subject and is accessed through subject and author/title indexes. A useful feature is "When to Buy What," with lists by both title and month. Complements *Magazines for Libraries* as *Irregular Serials and Annuals* does *Ulrich's*.

48. Merriman, J.B. "Comparative Index to Periodical Prices." *Library Association Record*, August issue each year.

This study, sponsored by B. H. Blackwell, monitors the pattern of periodical prices for titles published worldwide. No definition of "periodical" is given. Data are sorted according to general and specific subject, and are further divided according to price. Index numbers are based on 1970 prices and data go back only one year. The sample is about half the size of that used by *Library Journal*.

49. *New Magazine Review*, 1-   November/December 1978-   . North Las Vegas, Nev.: New Magazine Review Publishing Company.

A bimonthly periodical containing about forty signed reviews of 100 to 300 words, usually of recommended titles. Wide variety in scope and format of periodicals included. Better for public and college than research libraries.

50. *Publishers' Trade List Annual.* 1873-   . New York: R. R. Bowker Company. (ISSN: 0079-7855)

Issued annually, *PTLA* is a multi-volume collection of American publishers' catalogs. Most include journals and monographic series. The contents are best accessed through *Books in Print* and *Subject Guide to Books in Print* if publisher is not known.

51. *Repertorio Analitico della Stampa Italiana.* 6th ed. Milano: Messaggerie Italiane, 1969.

Italian periodicals are described in a classified list; then there is an alphabetical list giving Italian and foreign subscription rates. Recently-ceased titles are also included. The objective of this directory is "to assist booksellers in their research efforts," but to do that it needs to be published annually; instead, it appears to have been discontinued.

52. *Reprints in Print: Serials.* 2nd ed. Dobbs Ferry, N.Y.: Oceana Publications, Inc., 1970.

Periodicals and monographic series are listed in one alphabet under title, author of monograph, series, and subject. It is international in scope and gives reprint publisher and price. The catalog needs badly to be brought up to date, but there are no plans to do so.

53. *Serials Review.* 1-   1975-   . Ann Arbor: Pierian Press. (ISSN: 0098-7913)

Each issue contains a feature review and several regular columns which pertain to serials: Tools of the Trade, Cumulative Indexes, Government Documents, etc. Reviews are signed and usually are several hundred words in length. Serial Review Index cites reviews to periodicals from a wide variety of sources. This is the pioneer attempt to create a bibliographic control for reviews of serials, and it appears to be succeeding. Recent issues have interpreted "review" differently and include articles on serials management.

54. *Stamm: Leitfaden für Presse und Werbung.* 1-   1947-   . Essen: Stamm Verlag GmbH (ISSN: 0075-8728)

An annual directory of German and major foreign newspapers and periodicals, with advertising information. There are alphabetical lists of titles, with East and West Germany separated, and a classified list, according to city of publication. Varied press information appears in other sections of the work.

55. *Top of the News.* 1-   1946-   . Chicago: American Library Association, Division of Libraries for Children and Young People. (ISSN: 0040-9286)

Each quarterly issue contains a review section entitled "Added Entries." Periodicals are frequently included among the titles reviewed. Some reviews are signed, some not; some are evaluative, some not.

56. *Willing's Press Guide.* 1-   1874-   . London: Willing. (ISSN: 0000-0213)

An annual directory of newspapers, periodicals, and annuals published in the United Kingdom, with growing lists for European countries, the United States, and the United Nations. A title list by country, a classified index, and other sections give added information about British newspapers.

III. Acquisitions

57. Allardyce, Alex. *Letters for the International Exchange of Publications: A Guide to Their Composition in English, French, German, Russian and Spanish.* München: Verlag Dokumentation K. G. Saur, 1978. (IFLA Publication. 13)

Divided into five sections according to language, this work is described as an "assembly kit" for the compilation of business letters in languages other than one's own. Construction of the book is such that one can easily locate the equivalent of any statement listed in his or her own language, in any of the others.

58. American Library Association. Resources and Technical Services Division. Acquisitions Section. Bookdealer-Library Relations Committee. *Guidelines for Publishers, Agents and Librarians in Handling Library Orders for Serials and Periodicals.* Chicago: 1974.

A "guide for librarians, agents and publishers in their efforts to provide good serial service to the ultimate consumer, the reader." Divided into three sections, one for each group, the booklet states what each should be able to expect from the other.

59. Brown, Clara D., and Smith, Lynn S. *Serials: Past, Present and Future.* 2nd (revised) ed. Birmingham, Ala.: EBSCO Industries, Inc., 1980.

An expanded edition of Brown's manual-format work on serial acquisitions, much of which was—and is—based on the system at Louisiana State University Library at the time the author was head of serials there. This edition also covers cataloging and other current issues in serials librarianship, and there is much information and advice which will benefit any serials librarian.

60. Buckeye, Nancy Melin. *International Subscription Agents.* 4th ed. Chicago: American Library Association, 1978.

Based on data collected from serials and acquisitions librarians in the United States and from questionnaires returned by agents. Arrangement is alphabetical by "significant element" of the agent's name, with cross references and a geographical index. Entries include countries covered, types of materials, services available, library response, and special notes. American subscription agents are listed for the first time in this edition.

61. *EBSCO Bulletin of Serials Changes.* 1-   1975-   . Birmingham, Ala.: EBSCO Industries, Inc. (ISSN: 0360-0637)

A bimonthly classified list of "changes" in serials: suspensions, mergers, delivery problems, new titles, etc. *EBOSC* has an alphabetical title index which cumulates throughout the volume. Unlike *Serials Updating Service, EBOSC* solicits publisher information monthly.

62. EBSCO Subscription Services. *Librarians' Handbook* 1-   1970/ 1971-   . Birmingham, Ala.: EBSCO Industries, Inc. (ISSN: 0093-1888)

An annual appearing in late summer, this catalog lists over 95,000 titles supplied EBSCO's customers. In addition to price, frequency and country of origin, there is often detailed information about availability and publisher conditions for subscribers.

63. F. W. Faxon Company, Inc. *Faxon Librarians' Guide.* 1931-   . Westwood, Mass.: F. W. Faxon Company, Inc. (ISSN: 0146-2660)

Published annually in the spring, this is a listing of serial titles for which Faxon supplies three or more orders and is supplemented by an optional microfiche of all other titles handled. Data given include price, frequency, current volume, Library of Congress class and where the title is indexed.

64. *Monographic Series.* 1-   1974-   . Washington, D.C.: Library of Congress. (ISSN: 0093-0571)

Issued quarterly and cumulated annually, it is arranged alphabetically by series entry and reproduces Library of Congress cards under each series. The criterion for inclusion is that the series appear on the LC card.

65. *Publishers' International Directory.* 1st-   ed., 1964-   . München: Verlag Dokumentation K. G. Saur. (ISSN: 0074-9877)

This often-updated work is an international listing by country (German form of name) of publishers' addresses, telephone numbers and specialties.

66. *Serials Updating Service.* 1-   1974-   . Westwood, Mass.: F. W. Faxon Company, Inc. (ISSN: 0093-2310)

Published monthly and distributed free of charge to Faxon's customers, *SUS* lists in one alphabet dated information from publishers about changes and irregularities in their serial titles. Quarterly and annual cumulations may be purchased.

IV. Cataloging

67. American Library Association. *A.L.A. Cataloging Rules for Author and Title Entries,* prepared by the Division of Cataloging and Classification of the American Library Association. Second ed., edited by Clara Beetle. Chicago: American Library Association, 1949.

An expansion and revision of the 1908 rules, this code was used until the introduction of the *Anglo-American Cataloging Rules* in 1967.

68. *Anglo-American Cataloging Rules,* prepared by the American Library Association, the Library of Congress, the Library Association and the Canadian Library Association. North American edition, with supplement of Additions and Changes. Chicago: American Library Association, 1970.

The cataloging code which was used from the time it replaced the *A.L.A. Cataloging Rules* in 1967, until the implementation of its second edition in 1981. Also published in England as "British Text," with substantial differences from the North American edition.

69. *Anglo-American Cataloguing Rules.* 2nd ed.; prepared by the American Library Association, the British Library, the Canadian Committee on Cataloguing, the Library Association, the Library of Congress, edited by Michael Gorman and Paul W. Winkler. Chicago: American Library Association; Ottawa: Canadian Library Association, 1978.

"Firmly based" on the 1967 first edition, this code was implemented in English-speaking countries in 1981. It is an attempt to amalgamate the two editions of *AACR* 1 and to incorporate changes of rules since the publication of the first edition.

70. *Dewey Decimal Classification and Relative Index,* devised by Melvil Dewey. 19th ed. Lake Placid Club, N.Y.: Forest Press, 1979.

Dewey is used by most public and smaller academic libraries and by some larger libraries. Its disadvantage is that it is not as easily expandable as the Library of Congress Classification, but its mnemonic factor assists browsing. There is also an abridged edition for use by small libraries.

71. Hagler, Ronald. *Where's That Rule? A Cross-Index of the Two Editions of the Anglo-American Cataloguing Rules.* Ottawa: Canadian Library Association, 1979.

Tables match *AACR* 1 rules against corresponding *AACR* 2 rules and vice versa. Differences are explained and commentaries given.

72. Library of Congress. *Library of Congress Classification.* Washington, D.C.: 1899- .

This multi-volume classification scheme is continuously undergoing revision. It is used by the majority of American academic and research libraries both because it is the system used by LC and because it is more easily expandable than the alternatives.

73. Library of Congress. Processing Services. *Cataloging Service Bulletin.* 1- Summer 1978- . Washington, D.C. (ISSN: 0160-8029)

This quarterly publication contains all rule interpretations from the Library of Congress, news about the implementation of *AACR* 2, LC's options, and the like.

74. Schley, Ruth, and Davies, Jane B. *Serials Notes Compiled from Library of Congress Cards Issued 1947—April 1951.* New York: Columbia University Libraries, 1952.

This mimeographed booklet contains examples of the wording of cataloging notes. It is based upon the old rules, but is still useful.

75. *Sears List of Subject Headings.* 11th ed., edited by Barbara M. Westby. New York: H. W. Wilson Company, 1977.

For use in smaller libraries, Sears follows the Library of Congress headings, but makes some modification.

V. *Preservation and Binding*

76. *The Abbey Newsletter.* 1- August 1975- . New Carrolton, Md.: The Abbey Newsletter.

A bimonthly publication covering current events in the various aspects of preservation of materials, with brief articles on specific preservation topics.

77. American Library Association. Library Technology Project. *Development of Performance Standards for Binding Used in Libraries. Phase II.* Chicago: 1966 (LTP Publications. 10)

Phase II of this study lists provisional minimum standards for library binding. Also included is a history of this joint project of the ALA/RTSD Bookbinding Committee and the Special Libraries Association.

78. American Library Association. Library Technology Project. *Development of Performance Standards for Library Binding. Phase I.* Chicago: 1961. (LTP Publications. 2)

Phase I of this study identifies the binding needs of various types of libraries.

79. Library Binding Institute. *Library Binding Handbook.* Boston: Library Binding Institute, 1963.

This pamphlet includes the 1963 standard and gives guidelines to librarians for use in decisions about binding.

80. Library Binding Institute. *Standard for Library Binding.* 6th ed., rev. Boston: Library Binding Institute, 1975.

Combines the revised terms of the 1933 Minimum Specifications for Class A Library Binding and the Standards for Reinforced (Pre-Library Bound) New Books, of 1939. It includes definitions and historical notes.

81. Library of Congress. Administrative Department. Office of the Assistant Director for Preservation. *Preservation Leaflets.* 1-   1975-
Washington, D.C.: Library of Congress.

A series of concise leaflets intended to provide the librarian, archivist or other individual basic information on the various aspects of preservation. Each is prepared in response to requests for information.

82. Tauber, Maurice F., ed. *Library Binding Manual: A Handbook of Useful Procedures for the Maintenance of Library Volumes.* 3rd ed. Boston: Library Binding Institute, 1971.

Tauber directs this thorough study of library binding history, concerns and procedures toward library science students and library staff involved in binding. He discusses binding in the context of preservation of library materials.

VI. Public Service

83. Alkire, Leland G., Jr., ed. *Periodical Title Abbreviations: By Abbreviation.* 3rd ed., Covering Periodical Title Abbreviations in Science,

the Social Sciences, the Humanities, Law, Medicine, Religion, Library Science, Engineering, Education, Business, Art, and Many Other Fields. Volume 1. Detroit: Gale Research Company, 1981.
This alphabetical list of 35,000 abbreviations and their full titles was compiled from 96 indexes, abstracts, bibliographies and databases (but not *Chemical Abstracts*). Subject coverage is more balanced than in the first two editions, because of the addition of *BIOSIS*. Two additional volumes are projected: volume 2 will be arranged by title and volume 3 will be "New Periodical Title Abbreviations," two inter-edition supplements.

84.   American Chemical Society. Chemical Abstracts Service. *Chemical Abstracts Service Source Index, 1907-1979*. Columbus, Ohio: 1980.
This cumulation includes titles from *Chemical Abstracts, Biological Abstracts, Engineering Index* and the Institute for Scientific Information database. It is useful for verification and abbreviations and as a union list. Arrangement is letter-by-letter, according to ISO abbreviation, and entries include CODEN, publication history, address and holdings of major libraries. *CASSI* is updated by quarterly supplements (ISSN: 0001-0634).

85.   *Database: The Magazine of Database Reference and Review*. 1-   September 1978-   . Weston, Conn.: Online, Inc. (ISSN: 0162-4105)
A quarterly publication, *Database* provides news, instruction and practical information about the various databases available through online bibliographic systems.

86.   Harzfeld, Lois A. *Periodical Indexes in the Social Sciences and Humanities: A Subject Guide*. Metuchen, N.J.: Scarecrow Press, 1978.
A list of selected current periodical indexes arranged by forty-eight rather broad subjects with a title/name index. The description of each index gives bibliographic data, scope, arrangement and publication schedule. There are cross references.

87.   *Lathrop Report on Newspaper Indexes: An Illustrated Guide to Published and Unpublished Newspaper Indexes in the United States & Canada*, compiled and edited by Norman M. Lathrop and Mary Lou Lathrop. Wooster, Ohio: Norman Lathrop Enterprises, 1979-   .
In loose-leaf format, this work contains a core collection of entries for newspaper indexes and will have annual updates. Arrangement is by compiling organization, and details provided include scope, availability, size, style and format. Examples of entries are included.

88.   Marconi, Joseph V. *Indexed Periodicals*. Ann Arbor: Pierian Press, 1976.
Contains 11,000 periodical titles from thirty-three periodical indexes, covering the years 1802-1973. The list is alphabetical by journal title and gives in three columns the name of the index, volumes of the index carrying the title, and dates of the journal indexed. There are history notes for each entry.

89.   Milner, Anita Cheek. *Newspaper Indexes: A Location and Subject Guide for Researchers.* Metuchen, N.J.: Scarecrow Press, 1977.

Arranged geographically by state, county and town, this directory lists in three columns the newspaper, its dates and location symbol for index. The section titled "Repository Locations" gives further information about the indexes, such as scope, availability, and reproduction costs.

90.   *Online: The Magazine of Online Information Systems.* 1-   1977-   . Weston, Conn.: Online, Inc. (ISSN: 0146-5422)

This quarterly gives news, instruction and practical information concerning the online bibliographic systems.

91.   *Online Review: The International Journal of Online & Teletext Information Systems.* 1-   1977-   . New York: Learned Information. (ISSN: 0309-314X)

More technical and scholarly than *Online* and *Database*, this quarterly journal gives news and book reviews, as well as articles, about online bibliographic systems.

92.   Owen, Dolores B. and Hanchey, Marguerite M. *Abstracts and Indexes in Science and Technology.* Metuchen, N.J.: Scarecrow Press, 1974.

Arranged in eleven broad subject groups with a title index, this work gives the following information for titles included: arrangement, coverage, guidance in using the work, indexes and other details.

93.   *Serial Sources for the BIOSIS Data Base.* 1978-   . Philadelphia: BioSciences Information Service. (ISSN: 0162-2048)

Formerly *BIOSIS: List of Serials* (ISSN: 0067-8937), this is an annual list of titles covered by *Biological Abstracts*, and is used for verification and abbreviations.

VII.   Networking and Library Cooperation

94.   American National Standards Institute. *American National Standard for Periodicals: Format and Arrangement.* New York: 1977. (Z39.1.1977)

Recommends the use of a "bibliographic strip" across the bottom of the cover of journals, which would contain the abbreviated title, volume number, issue number, pagination, date of publication and place of publication. The first ANSI Z39 standard ever adopted, it is now in its third edition.

95.   American National Standards Institute. *American National Standard for the Abbreviation of Titles of Periodicals.* New York: 1974. (Z39.5.1969 [R1974])

Provides the means for abbreviating periodicals as they would appear, among other places, in the "bibliographic strip." It is being revised again.

96. American National Standards Institute. *American National Standard: International Standard Serial Numbering.* New York: 1979. (Z39.9.1979)

A revised version of the standard which recommended and explained the use of "a concise, unique, and unambiguous code for serial publications"—the International Standard Serial Number.

97. *American Standard for Periodical Title Abbreviations: Quarterly Supplement to the Revised and Enlarged Word Abbreviation List.* Columbus, Ohio: National Clearinghouse for Periodical Title Word Abbreviations, 1967-73.

This group of lists supplements *American National Standard for the Abbreviation of Titles of Periodicals.* At the end of 1973 the responsibility for updating was transferred to the International Serials Data Program in Paris, which publishes revised standards and updates.

98. British Standards Institution. *Recommendations for the Abbreviations of Titles of Periodicals.* London: British Standards Institution, 1967.

The British counterpart to the ANSI standard, listing British abbreviations.

99. Bruns, Phyllis A. *MARC Serials Editing Guide.* 2nd CONSER edition. Washington, D.C.: Library of Congress, 1978.

Intended for use by CONSER participants, this guide, kept up to date by monthly supplements, directs those editing serial records for inputting into the OCLC system.

100. *CONSER: Conversion of Serials.* 1-   October 1978-   . Columbus, Ohio: OCLC, Inc. (ISSN: 0163-8610)

News of CONSER, statistics, and background reports on CONSER and other cooperative serials projects.

101. International Federation of Library Associations. Joint Working Group on the International Standard Bibliographic Description for Serials. *ISBD(S): International Standard Bibliographic Description for Serials.* London: IFLA Committee on Cataloguing, 1974.

The original publication of specifications for description and identification of printed serials. The document introduced the concept of "distinctive title." It was revised and reissued in 1977.

102. International Federation of Library Associations. Joint Working Group on the International Standard Bibliographic Description for Serials. *ISBD(S): International Standard Bibliographic Description for Serials.* 1st standard edition. London: IFLA International Office for Universal Bibliographic Control, 1977.

A revision of the preliminary edition of *ISBD(S)*, this edition of the standard benefits from the comments of cataloging agencies throughout the world and the developments in the revision of *AACR*. A primary goal of *ISBD(S)* is to further international cooperation in serials cataloging.

103. *International List of Periodical Title Word Abbreviations*. 1977- . Paris: Centre International d'Enregistrement des Publications en Serie.
Published by the ISDS International Center in agreement with the International Standards Organization, these lists contain all new abbreviations used by ISDS centers and others. There is a 1971-1976 cumulation.

104. *ISDS Bulletin*. 1- 1974- . Paris: Centre International d'Enregistrement des Publications en Serie. (ISSN: 0300-3000)
The bimonthly microfiche *ISDS Bulletin* supplements and updates the *ISDS Register*. There are cumulating ISSN and title indexes.

105. *ISDS Register*. 1977- . Paris: Centre International d'Enregistrement des Publications en Serie.
An annual microfiche publication, this contains the full International Serials Data System record for most titles in the ISDS machine readable file: ISSN, key title and abbreviated key title, variant and linking titles and publication details. There are ISSN and title indexes. The *ISDS Register* is updated by the *ISDS Bulletin*.

106. National Serials Data Program. *ISSN-Key Title Register*. Washington, D.C.: Library of Congress, 1977.
"An aid to libraries, abstracting and indexing services, subscription agencies, publishers and other members of the information community," the *ISSN-Key Title Register* lists NSDP assignments of ISSN through February 1975. Part I is an ISSN Register, by number, and Part II is an index, by title. Part I includes the full bibliographic description of the work.

107. OCLC, Inc. *Serials Control: Training Manual*. Columbus, Ohio: OCLC, Inc., 1979.
A step-by-step workbook for use by terminal operators who will create and update local data records.

108. Ohio College Library Center. *Serials Control Subsystem: Users Manual*. Columbus Ohio: 1975.
To be used by personnel authorized to work with the Serials Control Subsystem, this manual gives step-by-step procedures for each capability. It contains examples and definitions.

109. *Voice of Z39: News About Library, Information Science and Publishing Standards*. 1- 1979- . Washington, D.C.: American National Standards Committee Z39. (ISSN: 0163-626X)
This quarterly publication, which was preceded by *News About Z39* (ISSN: 0028-8942), reports the activities of this committee, as well as available standards and work in progress by the subcommittees.

110. Wyandotte-ASTM Punched Card Project. *Coden for Periodical Titles: An Aid for the Storage and Retrieval of Information and to Communication Involving Journal References.* Philadelphia: American Society for Testing and Materials, 1963.

A description and explanation of a scheme to provide serials with a mistake-proof permanent code for positive bibliographic identification. Widely accepted on a voluntary basis by the scientific community, it is largely superseded now by the more universal mandatory ISSN system.

RESEARCH TOOLS

I. General

111. *A.L.A. Yearbook.* 1- 1976- . Chicago: American Library Association.

Each year the *A.L.A. Yearbook* contains an annual review article of about four double-column pages on serials. William H. Huff has written all five of the articles to appear to date.

112. Asser, Paul Nijhoff. "Some Trends in Journal Subscriptions." *Scholarly Publishing* 10 (1979): 279-86.

Questionnaires to scientific journal publishers showed a trend toward a decreasing number of subscriptions and higher prices. Another survey attempted to identify causes of issues being lost in the mail. Among publishers' reasons were postal service, strikes, misdirection of mail within a large company or university, and poor wrapping.

113. Atkinson, Hugh C. "The Future of the Scholarly Journal." In: *Management Problems in Serials Work.* (Westport, Conn.: Greenwood Press, 1974), pp. 115-20.

Because of the rising costs of producing and storing little-used journals, Atkinson predicts a system of regional depositories holding microform copies of scholarly articles to be reproduced and sold inexpensively upon demand. His plan is an early version of the proposed National Periodicals Center.

114. Bernhardt, Frances Simonsen. *Introduction to Library Technical Services.* New York: H. W. Wilson Company, 1979.

One chapter, "Serials: A Challenge to Libraries" (pp. 265-85) covers all technical service and some public service aspects of serials work. Treatment is general and designed "specifically as a textbook for a course in technical services in a two-year library/media technology program." Especially good for small academic and public library perspective.

115. Bluh, Pamela, and Haines, Virginia C. "The Exchange of Publica-

tions: An Alternative to Acquisitions." In: *The Serials Collection.*
(Ann Arbor, Mich.: Pierian Press, 1982), pp. 151-57.

After a review of the history of library exchanges at the international level, the
authors encourage libraries to limit their exchange programs to material needed
by the library in order to reduce the expense of this means of acquiring serials.

116. Bluh, Pamela. "Serials Control: Is There a Need for Change?"
Serials Librarian 6 (Fall 1981): 17-23.

Libraries contemplating a change in the organization of serial functions need to
consider the implications of this action for staff and patrons and involve these
two groups in their planning.

117. Bourne, Ross, ed. *Serials Librarianship.* London: Library Association, 1980.

Divided into three parts—Processes and Operations, Libraries, and Wider Issues—
this work presents twenty brief essays covering all aspects of the topic. Part 2
contains chapters on various types of libraries and Part 3, as well as Part 2, looks
toward the future. The British perspective provides an opportunity for librarians to broaden their knowledge of serials treatment and of the British Library,
which figures heavily in the text. At the same time familiar American resources
are discussed.

118. Cargill, Jennifer. "Serials: Separate or Merged?" In: *The Serials
Collection.* (Ann Arbor, Mich.: Pierian Press, 1982), pp. 15-22.

The case for merging serial and monographic acquisition of library materials
into a single administrative department, utilizing cross-training of employees.

119. Collver, Mitsuko. "Organization of Serials Work for Manual and
Automated Systems." *Library Resources and Technical Services* 24
(1980): 307-16.

A strong case for the integrated serials department, based on James D. Thompson's principle of "reciprocal interdependence."

120. Collver, Mitsuko. "The Role of the Central Serials Unit in an
Automated Library." In: *The Serials Collection.* (Ann Arbor, Mich.:
Pierian Press, 1982), pp. 23-33.

A strong case for the grouping of reciprocally interdependent serial functions in
a central serial unit. Automation brings decentralized output of data, but requires centralized input.

121. Davinson, Donald. *The Periodicals Collection.* Rev. and enl. ed. London: Andre Deutsch, 1978. (Grafton books on library and information science)

Particularly strong in collection development, acquisitions and public service,
this work is written from the British perspective. However, many references and

examples are American, enabling the reader to compare and acquire a broader knowledge of the field. Extensive references are at the end of each chapter.

122. Dyal, Donald H. "A Survey of Serials Management in Texas." *Texas Libraries* 38 (1976): 164-72.
Forty-six Texas libraries responded to a questionnaire concerning serial functions (but not cataloging), and Dyal discusses the trends identified by the survey.

123. *Economics of Serials Management; Proceedings of the 2nd Blackwell's Periodicals Conference.* Loughborough: Serials Group, n.d.
Edited by David P. Woolworth, the book reproduces seven papers presented on various aspects of the topic, along with the subsequent discussion by participants.

124. Edgar, Neal L. "Some Thoughts in Response to Lanier and Anderson." *Serials Librarian* 6 (Fall 1981): 95-98.
A critique of "Dispelling the Serials Mystique" and a defense of unique procedures required for serials control.

125. Ervin, Linda. "Managing and Building a Newspaper Collection." In: *The Serials Collection.* (Ann Arbor, Mich.: Pierian Press, 1982), pp. 91-101.
Newspapers are serials with unique problems for libraries—identification, retention and access, in particular. Ervin advises on all these aspects in one of the few articles on managing newspapers in the library.

126. Foster, Allan, and Parker, Lynn. "Physical Forms and Storage." In: *Periodicals Administration in Libraries.* (London: Clive Bingley; Hamden, Conn.: Linnett Books, 1978), pp. 78-115.
Looks at alternative formats to the traditional journal, discusses binding considerations and alternatives, and touches on periodical shelving arrangements.

127. Fry, Bernard M., and White, Herbert S. *Publishers and Libraries: A Study of Scholarly and Research Journals.* Lexington, Mass.: Heath, 1976.
Using data collected between 1969 and 1973, the authors examine the economics of the interaction between journal publishers and libraries and seek to identify the separate and interdependent problems of each. The work presents conclusions and recommendations aimed at possible solutions, or processes for stabilizing the present deteriorating situation and the consequent drift toward a general crisis in journal communication. (Introduction)

128. Gable, J. Harris. "The New Serials Department." *Library Journal* 60 (1935): 867-71.
Lynn Smith's favorite article on serials management; read it on a rainy day.

129. Gorman, Michael, and Burger, Robert H. "Serial Control in a Developed Machine System." *Serials Librarian* 5 (Fall 1980): 13-26.

The authors propose a "complex network of simple records" as a solution to serial cataloging and access problems existing in MARC.

130. Grenfell, David. *Periodicals and Serials: Their Treatment in Special Libraries*. 2nd ed. London: Aslib, 1965.

The author concentrates on acquisitions and public service in this practical treatment of serials work.

131. Harvey, Joan M. "Types of Periodical." In: *Periodicals Administration in Libraries*. (London: Clive Bingley; Hamden, Conn.: Linnett Books, 1978), pp. 7-24.

Defines and discusses the various types of primary and secondary journals available in both paper and machine-readable format.

132. Hepfer, William. "Serials Organization in Academic Libraries: Is There a Best Way?" In: *The Serials Collection*. (Ann Arbor, Mich.: Pierian Press, 1982), pp. 1-8.

Hepfer urges openmindedness and flexibility in determining the best administrative organization for a library to process serials. He stresses that careful planning is the prerequisite for successful reorganization.

133. Hines, Theodore C., Winkel, Lois, and Collins, Rosann. "Microcomputers and the Serials Librarian." *Serials Librarian* 4 (1980): 275-79.

The authors describe their use of microcomputers and suggest serial-related uses for this equipment.

134. Kilton, Tom D. "National Bibliographies—Their Treatment of Periodicals and Monographic Series." *Serials Librarian* 2 (1978): 351-70.

Kilton examined twenty-four major national bibliographies to ascertain what information each provided on periodicals and series. His findings are listed in a useful set of charts.

135. Komorous, Hana. "Union Catalogue of Newspapers in British Columbia Libraries." *Serials Librarian* 3 (1979): 255-88.

A comprehensive report on this cooperative project, giving its history, objectives and future plans, and also including a detailed analysis of the coding format.

136. Kuhns, Kathleen. "Serials Librarians and their Discontents: or, What do Serials Librarians Want?" *Serials Librarian* 1 (1976/77): 173-81.

The author asks for good business practices by publishers, vendors and librarians, for communication and respect, and for continuing education to keep serials librarians informed on current issues in their field.

137. Lanier, Don, and Anderson, Glenn. "Dispelling the Serials Mystique." *Serials Librarian* 5 (Summer 1981): 15-17.
Serials are not "mystical" and do not require unique treatment. The authors take aim at J. Harris Gable, Clara Brown, Peter Gellatly and even *Title Varies*.

138. Lea, P. W. "Alternative Methods of Journal Publishing." *Aslib Proceedings* 31 (1979): 33-39.
Brief discussion of recent developments in synoptic journals, electronic journals, text processing and microforms.

139. *Library Resources and Technical Services*. 1-   1957- . Chicago: American Library Association, Resources and Technical Services Division. (ISSN: 0024-2527)
The quarterly official publication of ALA's Resources and Technical Services Division, *LRTS* contains, in addition to articles on the technical services aspects of serials work, an annual review of serials librarianship, listing publications and discussing new developments. Serials also are a part of the annual reviews of cataloging, preservation, resources and reprographics.

140. *Library Scene*. 1-   1972- . Newton Highlands, Mass.: Library Binding Institute. (ISSN: 0090-8746)
This quarterly emphasizes, but is not restricted to, articles about binding and preservation of library materials.

141. Lupton, David Walker. "Tracking the ISSN." *Serials Librarian* 4 (1979): 187-98.
Lupton surveyed the use of ISSN by publishers before the USPS requirement and found only twenty-five per cent use. The location on the piece and style of printing the number varied considerably.

142. McKinley, Margaret. "A Pragmatic Approach to Serials Data Conversion." *Serials Review* 7 (January/March 1981): 85-91.
A significant article emphasizing planning, communication and flexibility in designing and completing a conversion project.

143. McKinley, Margaret M. "Serials Departments: Doomed to Extinction?" *Serials Librarian* 5 (Winter 1980): 15-24.
Responding to an apparent trend toward decentralization of serial functions, McKinley points out that informal communication systems exist now and will continue to exist among serial specialists, even though they may cross organizational lines.

144. McKinley, Margaret. "Serials Staffing Guidelines for the 80's." In: *The Serials Collection*. (Ann Arbor, Mich.: Pierian Press, 1982), pp. 35-52.
The successful serials manager selects, trains, develops and respects staff mem-

bers. When the change to automation of serial functions comes, it is those who are familiar with serial processing and service who should be involved with planning and implementation of the system.

145. *Management Problems in Serials Work*, edited by Peter Spyers-Duran and Daniel Gore. Westport, Conn.: Greenwood Press, 1974.

This volume contains papers presented at the Conference on Management Problems in Serials Work, at Florida Atlantic University in 1973. Topics range from a detailed discussion of the F. W. Faxon Company's claim procedure to a prediction of the death of the scholarly journal in its present form. Each paper is listed in this Bibliography.

146. Melin, Nancy Jean. "Automating the Serials Manager: New Directions, New Opportunities." In: *Serials Management in an Automated Age.* (Westport, Conn.: Meckler Publishing, 1982), pp. 81-88.

The effective serial manager in an age of automation acts as informer and clearinghouse, as coordinator and as preparer, in order to make the decisions required by the changing technology and patron needs.

147. Melin, Nancy Jean. "Serials in the '80s: A Report from the Field." *Serials Review* 7 (July/September 1981): 79-82.

A survey of the status of serials in libraries, a look at trends and concerns, and an indication of what serials librarians need from subscription agents.

148. Muller, Robert H., Spahn, Theodore Jurgen, and Spahn, Janet M. *From Radical Left to Extreme Right: A Bibliography of Current Periodicals of Protest, Controversy, Advocacy, or Dissent, with Dispassionate Content-Summaries to Guide Librarians and Other Educators through the Polemic Fringe.* 2nd ed., rev. and enl. Ann Arbor: Campus Publishers, 1970-1976. [Vol. 2-3 have imprint: Metuchen, N.J.: Scarecrow Press, Inc.]

Intended as a selection tool for nonestablishment periodicals, this valiant effort at bibliographic control has wider application. A special feature is the journal editors' feedback to annotations of their publications.

149. National Enquiry into Scholarly Communication. *Scholarly Communication: The Report of the National Enquiry.* Baltimore: Johns Hopkins University Press, 1979.

This is a comprehensive survey of the entire scholarly communications network, emphasizing the humanities. Chapter 2 covers serials, and it includes discussions of the use and readership of scholarly journals, authors' and editors' assessments of the state of serial publishing, the financial problems and pressures of publishers and the impact on libraries, and journal substitutes and supplements. This is a very important and timely work that deserves a wide audience.

150. Pan, Elizabeth. *New York State Library Automated Serials Control System*. Albany: State Education Department, 1974.

This report describes a batch system which includes a wide range of serial functions: bibliographic control, check-in, claiming, binding and holdings update, invoice control, subscription renewal and management statistics.

151. Paul, Huibert. "Serials: Chaos and Standardization." *Library Resources and Technical Services* 14 (1970): 19-30.

The author advocates consistency of title and standardization of numbering, format, etc., in publication practices, as means of reducing libraries' serial processing costs. He proposes federal government assistance in enforcing *USA Standard for Periodicals: Format and Arrangement*.

152. Paul, Huibert. "The Serials Librarian and the Journals Publisher." *Scholarly Publishing* 3 (1972): 175-83.

The serials librarian/assistant editor of *PNLA Quarterly* writes about changes in acquisition and fulfillment procedures which would benefit both librarians and publishers, and he writes from both points of view.

153. Peregoy, Marjorie. "ALA Serials Scene, Summer 1976." *Title Varies* 3 (1976): 29+.

Peregoy reports news, developments and trends of interest to serials librarians from the ALA Centennial Conference. She covers particularly CONSER, education and cataloging.

154. *Periodicals Administration in Libraries: A Collection of Essays*, edited by Paul Mayes. London: Clive Bingley; Hamden, Conn.: Linnet Books, 1978.

The seven essays included are by British librarians and are directed toward "librarians [who] move into periodicals posts having had very little prior contact with 'periodicals'." Each essay is listed individually in this Bibliography.

155. Peterson, Theodore. "The Bright, Bleak Future of American Magazines." In: *Serial Publications in Large Libraries*. (Urbana: University of Illinois, Graduate Library School, 1970), pp. 1-10.

Are American magazines in trouble? Peterson reviews the evidence, then predicts that those which can adapt to their readers' and advertisers' needs will survive.

156. Pong, Alfred. "The Serials Department." *Australian Academic and Research Libraries* 12 (1981): 191-98.

Reviews recent literature on organization of serial functions and reports that a survey reveals a variety of administrative patterns in Australian libraries.

157. Potter, William Gray. "Form or Function? An Analysis of the Se-

rials Department in the Modern Academic Library." *Serials Librarian* 6 (Fall 1981): 85-94.

Potter traces the rise and decline of separate serials departments using the University of Illinois Library as an example. He advocates division of technical processes by function and foresees the time when all processing will be done by clerical staff, freeing the librarian to engage in a broad spectrum of service activities.

158. *Serials Management in an Automated Age: Proceedings of the First Annual Serials Conference, October 30-31, 1981, Arlington, Va.,* edited by Nancy Jean Melin. Westport, Conn.: Meckler Publishing, 1982.

Sponsored by *Microform Review,* this conference offered papers on all aspects of serials automation. Each paper is listed separately in this Bibliography.

159. Pulsifer, Josephine S. "The Special Problems of Serials." *Library Trends* 25 (1977): 685-702.

In the area of bibliographic control, the special problems of serials center around identification.

160. Randall, Michael H. "Popular Serials." In: *The Serials Collection.* (Ann Arbor, Mich.: Pierian Press, 1982), pp. 83-89.

The case for making available in libraries magazines for recreational reading, as well as for research. Randall covers selection, acquisition, cataloging, housing and retention.

161. Rom, Cristine C. "Little Magazines in Special Collections and Rare Book Departments." In: *The Serials Collection.* (Ann Arbor, Mich.: Pierian Press, 1982), pp. 127-49.

Collecting and making accessible little magazines poses special problems for the library. Rom believes this function belongs in a special collection unit and lists sources for their identification and control.

162. Saxe, Minna C. "The Central Serial Record at New York Public Library: An Analysis and a Survey." In: *The Serials Collection.* (Ann Arbor, Mich.: Pierian Press, 1982), pp. 67-77.

Methodology for an inventory of NYPL's serial records to be used for information and planning.

163. Schloman, Barbara Frick, and Ahl, Ruth E. "Retention Periods for Journals in a Small Academic Library." *Special Libraries* 70 (1979): 377-83.

The results of a questionnaire to users of Purdue's Biochemistry Library led to policy decisions concerning storage, weeding, cancellation and class of binding.

164. *Serial Publications in Large Libraries*, edited by Walter C. Allen. Urbana: University of Illinois, Graduate School of Library Science, 1970. (Allerton Park Institute. 16)

Allen has collected papers from the Allerton Park Institute on all phases of serials librarianship in a large library, including document serials work. Each paper is cited individually in this Bibliography.

165. *The Serials Collection: Organization and Administration*, edited by Nancy Jean Melin. Ann Arbor, Mich.: Pierian Press, 1982. (Current Issues in Serials Management. 1)

A group of essays ranging from those presenting different ways of organizing the library's serials functions to others covering work with specific types of serials. Each chapter is listed separately in this Bibliography.

166. *Serials Librarian.* 1-   Fall 1976-   . New York: Haworth Press. (ISSN: 0361-526X)

This relatively new quarterly journal covers all aspects of serials work in scholarly, theoretical articles, as well as in more practical contributions. There are occasional reviews of books related to serials work and a regular section of news reports. Edited by Peter Gellatly; Gary Pitkin edits "Serials News."

167. *Serials Management and Microforms: A Reader*, edited by Patricia M. Walsh. Westport, Conn.: Microform Review, Inc., 1979. (*Microform Review* Series in Library Micrographics Management. 4)

A collection of pro-microform articles reprinted in a single text. Broad topics covered are: the user, economics, applications and impact upon journal format. Newspapers are excluded. The editor introduces each section and lists further articles relevant to the topics.

168. *Serials; National Trends—Local Implications: Papers*, ed. by Marjorie Peregoy and Hal Hall. College Station, Tex.: Texas A & M University Library, 1976.

Three papers presented at a serials workshop: National and International Developments Affecting Serials, by Paul J. Fasana; Data-Bind Computerized Binding Slips, by Iris Jeffress; and Conferences, Symposia, Proceedings—A Research Headache, by Rita Estok.

169. Sheehy, Eugene P. *Guide to Reference Books.* 9th edition. Chicago: American Library Association, 1976.

A standard tool which includes serially-published reference works and sources for serials reference. It is updated by supplements between editions. Formerly edited by Constance M. Winchell.

170. Stine, Diane. "Serials Department Staffing Patterns in Medium-Sized Research Libraries." *Serials Review* 7 (July/September 1981): 83-87.

Application of Weber's and Collver's principles to a group of ARL libraries points up the variety of staffing patterns existing.

171. Taylor, David C. "The Serials Librarian as Activist." *Drexel Library Quarterly* 11 (July 1975): 3-10.

The time for librarians to try to influence the producers of serials is before, not after, publication. Combined efforts to educate publishers to librarians' need can succeed.

172. *Title Varies*. 1-   December 1973-   . Chapel Hill, N.C. (ISSN: 0092-6108)

Title Varies is a bimonthly newsletter which is the voice of "Librarians United to Fight Costly, Silly, Unnecessary Serial Title Changes (LUTFCSUSTC)." It discusses, usually in a humorous way, the frustrations caused serials librarians and patrons by title changes and other quirks of serials, but also tries to have one informational article in each issue. There are reviews of monographs and periodicals related to serials work and a list of recent title changes, one of which is awarded "Worst Title Change of the Year."

173. Tjarks, Alicia V. "Coping with Latin American Serials." *Serials Librarian* 3 (1979): 407-15.

Tjarks discusses problems related to bibliographic control and acquisition of Latin American serials and points out some recent political and economic developments which seriously hamper the regular flow of Latin American publications.

174. Weber, Benita M. "Education of Serials Librarians: A Survey." *Drexel Library Quarterly* 11 (July 1975): 72-81.

Serials librarians express lack of relevant library school education for their work and their need for continuing education. Weber recommends that the ALA Serials Section work for alleviation of these problems through library schools and library organizations.

175. Weber, Benita M., and Bearman, Toni Carbo. "Current Issues in Serials Librarianship." *Drexel Library Quarterly* 11 (July 1975).

Contains nine articles which identify and discuss: bibliographic control, choice of entry, NSDP, CONSER, cost of serials, activism and education. Each article is cited separately in this Bibliography.

176. Weber, Hans H. "Serials Administration." *Serials Librarian* 4 (1979): 143-65.

Weber discusses various aspects of the administration of an integrated serials department, including organization, personnel, communication, budgeting and statistics.

177. White, Herbert S. "The Economic Interaction of Scholarly Journal Publishing and Libraries During the Present Period of Cost

Increases and Budget Reductions: Implications for Serials Librarians." *Serials Librarian* 1 (1977): 221-30.
Using 1969-73 data from over four hundred libraries, White documents the problem of maintaining serial obligations with decreasing funds and discusses some ways libraries attempt to meet the problem. The only long-term solution he accepts is government supported resource sharing.

178. Wright, Geraldine Murphy. "Current Trends in Periodical Collections." *College and Research Libraries* 38 (1977): 234-40.
Investigates collection development, acquisitions, use of microforms, shelving, circulation and security of periodicals in medium-sized academic libraries.

179. Zink, Steven D. "Government Publications as Serials." In: *The Serials Collection*. (Ann Arbor, Mich.: Pierian Press, 1982), pp 115-26.
Government serials differ from other serials in bibliographic control, selection, acquisition, maintenance and use. Zink discusses published sources and specific practices to make this class of publication accessible.

II. Collection Development

180. Almagro, Bertha R. "The Qualitative/Quantitative Control of Collection Development." *Technicalities* 2 (February, 1982): 10-12.
A health sciences library uses vendor subject printouts to control spending and maintain balance in its serials collection.

181. Baughman, James C. "Toward a Structural Approach to Collection Development." *College and Research Libraries* 38 (1977): 241-48.
Collection development is the result of collection planning plus collection implementation plus collection evaluation.

182. Bélanger, Charles H., and Lavallée, Lise. "Towards a Periodical and Monograph Price Index," *College and Research Libraries* 42 (1981): 416-24.
A ten-year study at Université de Montréal reveals 1) a shift in funds from books to periodicals, with a decrease in number of titles in both groups; 2) higher prices for foreign titles than domestic; and 3) higher journal prices paid than those advertised.

183. Black, George W., Jr., "Statistical Determination of Bound Volume Journal Holdings in a Science Library," *Serials Librarian* 5 (Winter 1980): 31-39.
Methodology and discussion of a sampling technique designed to project the total number of bound serial volumes in a collection, with breakdown by classification, country of origin and other qualities.

184. Bolgiano, Christina E., and King, Mary Kathryn. "Profiling a Periodicals Collection." *College and Research Libraries* 39 (1978): 99-104.

Librarians at James Madison University learned more about their collection through examining data on currently received periodicals supporting the academic programs. They also analyzed interlibrary loan periodical transactions and journal citations in masters theses. The profile that resulted is used in evaluating the collection.

185. Borkowski, Casimir, and Macleod, Murdo J. "The Implications of Some Recent Studies of Library Use." *Scholarly Publishing* 11 (1979): 3-24.

This analysis of the Allen Kent Study at the University of Pittsburgh states that the report is biased and flawed and, therefore, should not be accepted.

186. Bourne, Charles P., and Gregor, Dorothy. "Planning Serials Cancellations and Cooperative Collection Development in the Health Sciences: Methodology and Background Information." *Bulletin of the Medical Library Association* 63 (1975): 366-77.

Using a study at Berkeley as a test, this article reviews various cancellation techniques.

187. Bower, C. A. "Patterns of Use of the Serial Literature at the BLLD." *BLL Review* 4 (1976): 31-36.

Analysis of a sample of requests revealed that 80% of the demand was supplied by 5% of titles in the collection. Most requested titles were in science and technology, published recently, and published in North America or the United Kingdom.

188. Bradford, S. C. "Sources of Information on Specific Subjects." *Collection Management* 1 (1976/77): 95-103.

This article, reprinted from the *British Journal of Enginering* (1934), describes the investigation that led to the "Bradford Distribution."

189. Brennan, M. M. "Periodical Cancellations: What Happened at Hull." *BLL Review* 5 (1977): 67-73.

"Faculty working parties" participated in the identification of titles to be cancelled. This means of evaluating the journal collection appears to have been as successful as the use of more sophisticated methods would have been.

190. Brittain, J. Michael, and Line, Maurice B. "Sources of Citations and References for Analysis Purposes: A Comparative Assessment." *Journal of Documentation* 29 (1973): 72-80.

Lists and evaluates five sources of citations and references: abstracting and indexing journals, national and other general bibliographies, subject bibliographies, primary publications, and review journals.

191. Broadus, Robert N. "Evaluation of Academic Library Collections: A Survey of Recent Literature." *Library Acquisitions: Practice and Theory* 1 (1977): 149-55.
Reviews and assesses leading methods for evaluating the strengths of college and university library collections.

192. Broude, Jeffrey. "Journal Deselection in an Academic Environment: A Comparison of Faculty and Librarian Choices." *Serials Librarian* 3 (1978): 147-66.
A deselection model based on librarian and faculty nominations for serial cancellation showed little overlap among titles. Nevertheless, use of such a model makes the cancellation process less subjective than otherwise.

193. Budd, John. "Little Magazines and Academic Libraries." *Journal of Academic Librarianship* 7 (1981): 152-55.
Justification for the collecting of little magazines by academic libraries.

194. Campbell, Steven. "Approaching Serial Cancellations at Western Washington State College." *Serials Librarian* 1 (1976/77): 153-59.
The article first examines an economic situation which led to a plan for reducing serial renewal costs, then evaluates the actual review process.

195. Clasquin, Frank F. "Financial Management of Serials and Journals through Subject 'Core' Lists." *Serials Librarian* 2 (1978): 287-97.
A proposal for the construction of core lists of periodicals, to be used as collection development tools. From this proposal came an ALA/RTSD Serials Section ad hoc committee.

196. Clasquin, Frank F. "The 1978-80 Faxon Periodical Prices Update." *Serials Librarian* 5 (Spring 1981): 81-90.
Study based on "authority groups of titles" in 36 subjects, drawn from Faxon files and weighted by the number of Faxon orders.

197. Clasquin, Frank F. "Serials: Costs and Budget Projections." *Drexel Library Quarterly* 11 (July 1975): 64-71.
Data from the F. W. Faxon Company illustrate the retrospective price comparison method of budget planning.

198. Clasquin, Frank F., and Cohen, Jackson B. "Biochemistry and Molecular Biology Journal Prices." *Serials Librarian* 4 (1980): 381-92.
A strong plea for government subsidy for academic libraries' purchase of scientific journals.

199. Clasquin, Frank F., and Cohen, Jackson B. "Physics and Chemistry Journal Prices in 1977-1978." *Serials Librarian* 3 (1979): 381-86.

This follow-up to an earlier article covering 1973-1976 prices documents inflation predictions in that study and urges federal aid to alleviate the acquisitions crisis in academic science libraries.

200. Clasquin, Frank F., and Cohen, Jackson B. "Prices of Physics and Chemistry Journals." *Science* 197 (1977): 432-38.
A survey of prices from 1967 to 1976 shows that cost is reducing accessibility of the literature of chemistry and physics to patrons of academic science libraries.

201. *Collection Management: A Quarterly Journal Devoted to the Management of Library Collections.* Vol. 1, no. 3/4- 1976/77- . New York: Haworth Press. (ISSN: 0146-2679)
Originally named *De-Acquisitions Librarian*, this journal is particularly concerned with ways of dealing with the problems facing today's libraries in the area of collection management.

202. Comer, Cynthia. "List-Checking as a Method for Evaluating Library Collections." *Collection Building* 3, no. 3 (1981): 26-34.
A basic review of the methodologies, advantages, disadvantages, and usefulness of list-checking as a means of evaluating book and serial collections.

203. Cooper, Marianne. "Criteria for Weeding of Collections." *Library Resources and Technical Services* 12 (1968): 339-51.
This review article expounds both theory and practice. Criteria for weeding and storage must be determined by institutional goals.

204. *De-Acquisitions Librarian.* 1, 1976. New York: Haworth Press.
Published in newsletter format, this title became *Collection Management* (ISSN: 0146-2679).

205. De Gennaro, Richard. "Escalating Journal Prices: Time to Fight Back." *American Libraries* 8 (1977): 69-74.
Research library materials budgets should no longer subsidize scholarly publishing. Librarians must resist escalating prices and increase their collection development skills.

206. Dhawan, S. M., Phull, S. K., and Jain, S. P. "Selection of Scientific Journals: A Model." *Journal of Documentation* 36 (1980): 24-32.
Examines and evaluates existing techniques for selecting journals and proposes a standard selection procedure based on indexing, citation and use.

207. Durey, Peter. "Weeding Serials Subscriptions in a University Library." *Collection Management* 1 (1976/77): 91-94.
A New Zealand library employed both a use study and faculty evaluation of subject lists to determine which titles could be cancelled.

208. Ellingson, Celia S., and Hedstrom, Lori A. "Using Online Databases as a Tool for Collection Development." (BRS Brief Paper, no. 15) Mimeographed. Scotia, N.Y.: Bibliographic Retrieval Services, 1981.

Discusses a special collection development service offered by BRS whereby all the citations produced through database searches are captured, tabulated, and reported by means of ranked serials lists on a semiannual and annual basis. Shows how such a service can be used in evaluating a social sciences serial collection.

209. Ervin, Linda. "Managing and Building a Collection of Russian and Soviet Newspapers." *Serials Review* 7 (October/December 1981): 69-73.

An overview of current Soviet newspapers and translation services, with a brief history of the Russian and Soviet press.

210. Feller, Siegfried. "Developing the Serial Collection." In: *Collection Development in Libraries: A Treatise*. (Greenwich, Conn.: JAI Press, 1980), pp. 497-523.

An organized, broad treatment of serial collection development from selection to discard. Although not comprehensive and extremely basic, this is one of the few treatments of serial collection development.

211. Feller, Siegfried. "Library Serial Cancellectomies at the University of Massachusetts, Amherst." *Serials Librarian* 1 (1976/77): 140-52.

The author describes and evaluates a 1974/1975 computer assisted serials review project which was designed to slow the increase in serial renewal costs by cancelling lowest priority titles.

212. Ferguson, Chris D. "Taming the Serials Budget." *Technicalities* 1 (July 1981): 7-8, 13.

Reviews currently used means for controlling serial expenditures, but emphasizes the necessity of adapting any model to the local situation.

213. Fitzgibbons, Shirley A. "Citation Analysis in the Social Sciences." In: *Collection Development in Libraries: A Treatise*. (Greenwich, Conn.: JAI Press, 1980), pp. 291-344.

This is a survey of citation studies in the social sciences, emphasizing their implications for collection development in large research and special libraries. The first part is a general discussion of citation analysis and the main characteristics it reveals about the literature of the social sciences. The second part summarizes the results of citation studies in seven major disciplines with complete bibliographies appended.

214. Flynn, Roger R. "The University of Pittsburgh Study of Journal Usage: A Summary Report." *Serials Librarian* 4 (1979): 25-33.

A two-year study of journal use in science departmental libraries indicated: 1) a small number of titles accounts for the greatest percentage of use; and 2) most use is of recent volumes. Flynn shows how data from the study may be used to aid in acquisitions, cancellation and storage decisions.

215. Fowler, Jane E. "Managing Periodicals by Committee." *Journal of Academic Librarianship* 2 (1976): 230-34.

The formation of an advisory committee for serials selection enabled Bates College to bring faculty and students into the process of collection development and also increased these groups' library support.

216. Fry, Bernard M., and White, Herbert S. "Impact of Economic Pressures on American Libraries and their Decisions Concerning Scholarly and Research Journal Acquisition and Retention." *Library Acquisitions: Practice and Theory* 3 (1979): 153-237.

The authors report on the continuation of their earlier study. This update covers 1975-76 and adds a section on foreign periodicals. Results indicate that American librarians have yet to accept the reality of economic pressures.

217. Garfield, Eugene. "Citation Analysis as a Tool in Journal Evaluation." *Science* 178 (1972): 471-79.

A classic on citation analysis, this article describes the journal citation information drawn from the *Science Citation Index* database and discusses its applications.

218. Goehlert, Robert. "Journal Use per Monetary Unit: A Reanalysis of Use Data." *Library Acquisitions: Practice and Theory* 3 (1979): 91-98.

Goehlert describes an experimental study of political science journals which ranks the journals by cost per use, cost per user and cost per page. While these data are valid criteria for collection evaluation, they cannot stand alone.

219. Goehlert, Robert. "Periodical Use in an Academic Library: A Study of Economists and Political Scientists." *Special Libraries* 69 (1978): 51-60.

The data for this detailed analysis of journal use came from a document delivery service for the two faculties. These data are used in another Goehlert article, concentrating on one aspect of the current cost problem.

220. Gordon, Michael D. "Citation Ranking versus Subjective Evaluation in the Determination of Journal Hierarchies in the Social Sciences." *Journal of the American Society for Information Science* 33 (1982): 55-57.

Gordon found a strong association between sociologists' ranked evaluation of professional journals and the "Journal Citation Reports" of *SSCI*.

221. Gore, Daniel. "Sawing off the Horns of a Dilemma: Or, How to Cut Subscription Lists and Expand Access to Journal Literature." In: *Management Problems in Serials Work.* (Westport, Conn.: Greenwood Press, 1974), pp. 104-14.

Gore urges cooperative sharing of periodical resources at the college library level in preference to increasing the number of subscriptions.

222. Griffiths, Suzanne N. "Journal Purchase and Cancellation: A Brief Look at the Problem in Five British Academic Libraries." *Serials Librarian* 3 (1978): 167-70.

These libraries are meeting the economic problem in various ways with varying degrees of success. One has a detailed cancellation procedure, three have not yet faced the problem, and one is cancelling and not ordering new titles.

223. Heroux, Marlene, and Fleishauer, Carol. "Cancellation Decisions: Evaluating Standing Orders." *Library Resources and Technical Services* 22 (1978): 368-79.

This paper describes a methodology for a comprehensive, primarily objective system for the review of nonperiodical serial standing orders. The authors use a point system to rate titles according to support of university programs, interlibrary loan availability, language, price, frequency, access by indexing tools, and circulation.

224. Holland, Maurita Peterson. "Serial Cuts vs. Public Service: A Formula." *College and Research Libraries* 37 (1976): 543-48.

The effect on public service of reduction of the serials budget can be measured by Holland's formula, based on access time.

225. Johnson, Carol A., and Trueswell, Richard W. "The Weighted Criteria Statistic Score: An Approach to Journal Selection." *College and Research Libraries* 39 (1978): 287-92.

A user survey in a special library identified a group of journals to be considered for cancellation.

226. Jones, C. Lee. "A Cooperative Serial Acquisition Program: Thoughts on a Response to Mounting Fiscal Pressures." *Bulletin of the Medical Library Association* 62 (1974): 120-23.

Jones proposes distributed commitment to serial resources, based on a regional union list. In his scheme each participating library would accept responsibility for purchasing and retaining an equitable share of unique titles and of commonly held titles.

227. Katz, William A. *Collection Development: the Selection of Materials for Libraries.* New York: Holt, Rinehart and Winston, 1980.

Chapter on Periodicals (pp. 178-200). Not useful for research libraries, but good for public and school libraries.

228. Katz, William A. *Magazine Selection: How to Build a Community-Oriented Collection*. New York: R. R. Bowker Company, 1971.

Directed toward small and medium-sized public libraries, this book examines the philosophy and mechanics of selecting magazines. It is somewhat dated and needs to be revised, but it is still useful.

229. Katz, William A. "Periodical Proliferation: Rejection and Selection." *Catholic Library World* 47 (1976): 376-79.

Katz discusses the librarian's responsibility to select conscientiously from the flood of periodical literature.

230. Katz, William A. "Serials Selection." In: *Serial Publications in Large Libraries*. (Urbana: University of Illinois, Graduate School of Library Science, 1970), pp. 11-28.

The author limits "serials" to his own specialty, magazines, and makes a case for library selection of those titles which meet the needs of youth and the nonintellectual.

231. Key, Jack D., Sholtz, Katherine J., and Roland, Charles G. "The Controlled Circulation Journal in Medicine: ℞ or Rogue?" *Serials Librarian* 4 (1979): 15-23.

While these journals are read, they appear to have little lasting value. The expense and effort required to publish them could, perhaps, be better used in primary journal communication.

232. King, Donald W., McDonald, Dennis D., and Roderer, Nancy K. *Scientific Journals in the United States: Their Production, Use, and Economics*. Stroudsburg, Pa.: Hutchinson Ross Publishing, 1981.

An authoritative and comprehensive study of the roles of authors, publishers, libraries, and readers in the world of scientific serials. Concentrates on the economics of journal publishing in the sciences (including social sciences), as well as the current and future role of the research periodical in the scholarly communication network. Chapter Five, devoted to libraries, concentrates on the economics of journal acquisition and on recent trends in serials collection development.

233. Kochtanek, Thomas R. "A Model for Serials Acquisitions." *Library Acquisitions: Practice and Theory* 4 (1980): 141-44.

Describes a health care center library's procedure for monitoring and purchasing current serials and producing an online bibliography of relevant articles.

234. Koenig, Michael E. D. "On-Line Serials Collection Analysis." *Journal of the American Society for Information Science* 30 (1979): 148-53.

Koenig proposes a design for an online serials collection analysis composed of citation data, serial record data, routing data, and user interface software.

235. Kohut, Joseph J. "Allocating the Book Budget: A Model." *College and Research Libraries* 35 (1974): 192-99.

Advocates balancing the purchase of serials versus the purchase of monographs on the basis of individual funding units.

236. Kraft, Donald H., and Polacsek, Richard A. "A Journal-Worth Measure for a Journal-Selection Decision Model." *Collection Management* 2 (1978): 129-39.

Develops a practical procedure for evaluating journal worth, including use, intrinsic value and relevant value, and availability elsewhere.

237. Kronenfeld, Michael B., and Thompson, James A. "The Impact of Inflation on Journal Costs." *Library Journal* 106 (1981): 714-17.

A study of United States periodical price increases and the Consumer Price Index confirms the belief that journal prices are increasing at a faster rate than overall American inflation.

238. Line, Maurice B. "The 'Half-Life' of Periodical Literature: Apparent and Real Obsolescence." *Journal of Documentation* 26 (1970): 46-52.

Line critiques use of the "half-life" measure and submits a model to determine "corrected half-life" of journals. The method may be used in collection evaluation.

239. Line, Maurice B. "The Influence of the Type of Sources Used on the Results of Citation Analysis." *Journal of Documentation* 35 (1979): 265-84.

Using the social sciences as an example, Line shows that the results of citation studies can vary greatly depending on source publications. Analysis of references not only shows significant variance between monograph and journal source publications, but also between high ranked and randomly selected journals. Line therefore concludes that citation studies based on a limited number and type of sources should be regarded with suspicion.

240. Line, Maurice B., and Sandison, A., "'Obsolescence' and Changes in the Use of Literature with Time." *Journal of Documentation* 30 (1974): 283-350.

Reviews the literature on this topic and lists areas in which further research is needed.

241. Line, Maurice B., and Sandison, Alexander. "Practical Interpretation of Citation and Library Use Studies." *College and Research Libraries* 36 (1975): 393-96.

Data in citation and use studies would be more useful if it were stated as uses per monetary unit, uses per unit of shelf space, uses per article, etc.

242. Line, Maurice B. "Rank Lists Based on Citations and Library Uses as Indicators of Journal Usage in Individual Libraries." *Collection Management* 2 (1978): 313-16.

Line supports his conviction that "no measure of journal use other than one derived from a local use study is of any significant practical value to libraries."

243. Lowell, Gerald R. "Periodical Prices 1979-1981 Update." *Serials Librarian* 5 (Spring 1981): 91-99.

Lowell continues the annual three-year study conducted by Clasquin until his retirement from Faxon.

244. McBride, Ruth B. "Foreign Language Serial Use by Social Science Faculty: A Survey." *Serials Librarian* 5 (Summer 1981): 25-32.

A University of Illinois study supports the hypothesis that faculty make little use of non-English language serials. Questionnaire responses provided data on faculty language skills and indicated a desire for translations of articles in specific languages.

245. McCain, Katherine W., and Bobick, James E. "Patterns of Journal Use in a Departmental Library: A Citation Analysis." *Journal of the American Society for Information Science* 32 (1981): 257-67.

A citation analysis of Temple University Biology Department faculty and student publications has influenced the Biology Library's collection maintenance and development decisions.

246. Mankin, Carole J., and Bastille, Jacqueline D. "An Analysis of the Differences between Density-of-Use Ranking and Raw-Use Ranking of Library Journal Use." *Journal of the American Society for Information Science* 32 (1981): 224-28.

Density of use value of journals, calculated by dividing raw use frequency by linear shelf space occupied by the title, produces a significantly different ranking of journals than raw use ranking, and it is a better basis for collection development decisions.

247. Manten, A. A. "Journal Prices: Why so Different?" *Journal of Technical Writing and Communications* 7 (1977): 325-31.

An explanation by a Pergamon senior editor of the factors which determine the price of a single commercial journal, as well as of the hidden subsidies of those journals published by societies.

248. Martyn, John. "The Growth of Journals—A Short Review." *Journal of Research Communication Studies* 1 (1979): 259-62.

Evaluates recent attempts to estimate the rate of growth of journal literature.

249.   Maxin, Jacqueline A. "Periodical Use and Collection Development."
       College and Research Libraries 40 (1979): 248-53.
In a sci-tech academic library, a record of periodical use has been built into a
collection development program.

250.   Maxin, Jacqueline A. "Weeding Journals with Informal Use Statis-
       tics." *De-Acquisitions Librarian* 1 (Summer 1976): 9-11.
Maxin describes the collection of journal use statistics at Clarkson Institute of
Technology and the application of these data in weeding and commercial bind-
ing decisions.

251.   Miller, Dick R., and Jensen, Joseph E. "Dual Pricing of Health
       Sciences Periodicals: A Survey." *Bulletin of the Medical Library Asso-
       ciation* 68 (1980): 336-47.
In 1978, 281 titles had an average 102.14% price differential between individual
and institutional rates. Both dual pricing and the average price differential
appear to be increasing. Although there are several valid reasons for this situation, "uncritical purchasing by libraries" may be a major factor.

252.   Morton, Donald J. "The Use of a Subscription Agent's Computer
       Facilities in Creating and Maintaining a Library's Subscription
       Profile." *Library Resources and Technical Services* 22 (1978): 386-89.
Describes the procedure used by a medical library to develop a subscription
profile tailored to its users.

253.   Myers, Judy. "A Subject Fund Accounting System for Serials."
       Serials Librarian 3 (1979): 373-80.
The University of Houston Library uses vendor supplied computer punch cards
to produce subject printouts of periodical renewal payments.

254.   Palmour, Vernon E., Bellassai, Marcia C., and Wiederkehr, Rob-
       ert R. V. *Costs of Owning, Borrowing, and Disposing of Periodical
       Publications*. Arlington, Va.: Public Research Institute, 1977.
This report develops a mathematical model for estimating when it is more cost
effective for a library to borrow a periodical than to subscribe, using formulas
that include costs that are both independent of and proportional to use. The
study concludes that the crossover point between subscribing and borrowing has
changed little during the past decade and continues to range between 6 and 7
uses per year in the typical case. Statistical and methodological appendices detail-
ing the cost/benefit models used are included.

255.   Perkins, David. "Periodical Weeding: Or, Weed it and Reap."
       California Librarian 38 (April 1977): 32-37.
After a general discussion of the pitfalls in weeding periodical collections—knowing

when and how much to weed—Perkins describes a two-step cancellation project at California State University, Northridge.

256. Presser, Carolynne. "Collection Management and Serials in a Changing Library Environment." *Serials Librarian* 6 (Fall 1981): 59-67.

Historical overview of the proliferation of serial titles and their escalating costs, with suggestions as to how academic libraries can accommodate these changes.

257. Reed, Jutta R. "Collection Development of Serials in Microform." *Microform Review* 9 (1980): 86-89.

Based on a paper presented at the Fourth Annual Library Microform Conference, the article focuses on effective collection development of serials in microform by setting up four sets of selection criteria.

258. Rice, Barbara A. "Science Periodicals Use Study." *Serials Librarian* 4 (1979): 35-47.

Rice's survey, made at SUNY-Albany, identified low-use titles for storage, cancellation or discard. The lack of a significantly positive correlation with Institute for Scientific Information data indicates that results of a study at one library may not be applicable at another.

259. Robertson, S. E. and Hensman, Sandy. "Journal Acquisition by Libraries: Scatter and Cost-Effectiveness." *Journal of Documentation* 31 (1975): 273-82.

The authors investigated alternative measures of cost effectiveness and concluded that there are better means than the Bradford Distribution, but that the results vary according to field.

260. Rodger, Elizabeth. "Pruning Periodical Subscriptions at Glasgow University Library." *Aslib Proceedings* 30 (1978): 145-53.

Describes and evaluates Glasgow's project that includes a use survey and assessment of current subscriptions by academic staff.

261. Rudolph, Janell, and Byunn, Kit. "Academic Library Newspaper Collections: Developing Policy." *College and Research Libraries* 43 (1982): 80-83.

Memphis State University librarians surveyed other southeastern libraries as to newspaper collection policies. Questionnaire responses and a few policies aided in the creation of a local policy.

262. Sandison, Alexander. "Densities of Use, and Absence of Obsolescence, in Physics Journals at MIT." *Journal of the American Society for Information Science* 25 (1974): 172-82.

Sandison maintains that raw frequency of journal use is misleading for use studies and citation analysis; data must be converted to allow for the number of available items.

263. Satariano, William A. "Journal Use in Sociology: Citation Analysis Versus Readership Patterns." *Library Quarterly* 48 (1978): 293-300.
A comparison of journals regularly read with a citation study indicates that not everything that is read is cited. Citation studies do not parallel readership.

264. Scales, Pauline A. "Citation Analyses as Indicators of the Use of Serials: A Comparison of Ranked Title Lists Produced by Citation Counting and from Use Data." *Journal of Documentation* 32 (1976): 17-25.
Journals are ranked by citation and by frequency of use, with little correlation.

265. Schwartz, Ruth. "A Periodicals Use Study." *Illinois Libraries* 60 (1978): 106-09.
A year-long study of periodicals use from the closed stacks of the library at Fairleigh Dickinson University showed that seventy-four per cent of the titles were used. Staff members identified a core list of 925 titles. Analysis of the data gave further information about use of the collection.

266. Seymour, Carol A. "Weeding the Collection: A Review of Research on Identifying Obsolete Stock. Part II: Serials." *Libri* 22 (1972): 183-89.
An excellent review article on weeding.

267. Shaw, W. M., Jr. "A Journal Resource Sharing Strategy." *Library Research* 1 (1979): 19-29.
Shaw's strategy requires that each library in a consortium identify journals that are not used, that a short-title union list identify duplication and nonuse, and that subscriptions meeting cancellation criteria be reviewed.

268. Shaw, W. M., Jr. "A Practical Journal Usage Technique." *College and Research Libraries* 39 (1978): 479-84.
Use of pressure sensitive labels on periodical volumes which must be reshelved is the basis for a use study at Case Western Reserve Library.

269. Singleton, Alan. "Journal Ranking and Selection: A Review in Physics." *Journal of Documentation* 32 (1976): 258-89.
A review of three main methods of ranking journals: citation analysis, use or user judgment and size (or productivity). Reinforces the necessity for the subjective role of the librarian and the patron.

270. Smith, Linda C. "Citation Analysis." *Library Trends* 30 (1981): 83-106.
Smith provides an extensive critique of citation analysis concentrating on the assumptions underlying this method and the problems which can exist with these sources of citation. This is followed by a description of the applications of citation analysis, both as a tool for librarians and as a means to analyze research activity. The article concludes with brief speculations about the future, including

whether the use of citation analysis will affect citation behavior and how citation analysis itself will be affected by electronic media.

271. Stenstrom, Patricia, and McBride, Ruth B. "Serial Use by Social Science Faculty: A Survey." *College and Research Libraries* 40 (1979): 426-31.

This study, done at the University of Illinois, Champaign/Urbana, indicates that social science faculty use library serials as a supplementary source of information, and search mainly for specific articles. It points out the need for more interaction between librarians and faculty as an aid to collection development.

272. Studdiford, Abigail. "Selection of Journal Titles for Cancellation in Academic Libraries." *New Jersey Libraries* 14 (November 1981): 9-11.

Serial evaluation and cancellation conducted during the 1970s serves as a basis for a new reduction in library serial collections, in the light of alternative means of access to traditional paper journals.

273. Swartz, Linda Jo. "Serials Cancellations and Reinstatements at the University of Illinois Library." *Serials Librarian* 2 (1977): 171-80.

Describes the procedure used in a massive cancellation program. When funds were available for new orders, few cancellations were reinstated. Despite certain damage to the collection and inconvenience to users, the experience enabled the library to gain better knowledge of and control over its serials collection.

274. "Systematic Serials Cancellation Planning for Library Consortia and Networks." *De-Acquisitions Librarian* 1 (Spring 1976): 11-13.

A description and evaluation of "Methodology and Background Information to Assist the Planning of Serials Cancellations and Cooperative Serials Collection in the Health Sciences," by Bourne and Gregor.

275. Taylor, Colin R. "A Practical Solution to Weeding University Library Periodicals Collections." *Collection Management* 1 (1976/77): 27-45.

An Australian university library used a reshelving survey to identify serials which could be placed in storage. Taylor's methodology includes the use of questionnaires placed in periodical volumes.

276. Thompson, James A., and Kronenfeld, Michael R. "The Effect of Inflation on the Cost of Journals on the Brandon List." *Bulletin of the Medical Library Association* 68 (1980): 47-52.

A core group of journals for the small hospital library increased in price over twenty years at a significantly higher rate than overall inflation.

277. Thorpe, Peter. "Inter-Library Loans Analysis for Journals Acquisition." *Aslib Proceedings* 31 (1979): 352-59.

In a new library where all retrospective journal use was through interlibrary loan, analysis of patrons' requests (together with a study of in-house use) indicated which periodical back files should be purchased and what adjustments should be made in the current subscription list.

278. Trueswell, Richard W., "Article Use and its Relationship to Individual User Satisfaction." *College and Research Libraries* 31 (1970): 239-45.

Trueswell points out the need to define terms carefully, since his work shows that there are important differences between satisfying a percentage of user circulation needs and satisfying a percentage of users. He concludes that librarians should consider individual users as well as overall use in terms of serial subscription decisions.

279. Trueswell, Richard W. "Some Behavioral Patterns of Library Users: The 80/20 Rule." *Wilson Library Bulletin* 43 (1969): 458-61.

Based on a study of the patterns of use and circulation in different types of institutions, Trueswell concludes that library collections share the characteristic of inventories in business and industry, that only 20 percent of the items represent 80 percent of the transactions. Given these similar patterns librarians can use the techniques developed to decide what to weed, to serve as a guide to multiple copy acquisitions, and even to determine the optimal size of a collection. Such a use pattern constitutes a powerful argument for creating substantial interlibrary loan networks for the less needed materials.

280. Turner, Stephen J. "Trueswell's Weeding Technique: The Facts." *College and Research Libraries* 41 (1980): 134-38.

The author reviews the controversy over Trueswell's technique to inform, clarify and correct misinterpretations.

281. Urquhart, John. "Relegation." In: *Periodicals Administration in Libraries.* (London: Clive Bingley; Hamden, Conn.: Linnet Books, 1978), pp. 116-26.

Suggested criteria for and costs of weeding the collection.

282. Waltner, Nellie L., King, Cyrus B., and Horner, William C. "Periodical Prices: A Comparison of Local and National Averages." *Library Acquisitions: Practice and Theory* 1 (1978): 237-41.

This study calculates average 1978 serial prices (by LC class) paid to two vendors. It then compares the findings with a study made by F. F. Clasquin.

283. Warner, Edward S. "Constituency Needs as Determinants of Library Collection and Service Configurations." *Drexel Library Quarterly* 13 (July 1977): 44-51.

This is an important methodological article discussing the relationship of collection and service configurations to demonstrated and perceived needs. It argues that insofar as possible library decisions should be based on scientifically observed objective data and only secondarily on perceptions. Warner further states that perceived needs should be determinant of collections and services only insofar as they are solicited on a systematic and ongoing basis.

284. Warner, Edward S., and Anker, Anita L. "Faculty Perceived Needs for Serial Titles: Measurement for Purposes of Collection Development and Management." *Serials Librarian* 4 (1980): 295-300.

In the absence of satisfactory evidence of demonstrated faculty need for specific serials, the staff of the University of North Dakota Library measured perceived need, a project which led to significant cancellation of titles and savings in serial costs.

285. Warner, Edward S. "The Impact of Interlibrary Access to Periodicals on Subscription Continuation/Cancellation Decision Making." *Journal of the American Society for Information Science* 32 (1981): 93-95.

This article discusses the impact of good interlibrary loan access on serials collection development, using the MINITEX system as the test case. Although faculty indicated that the library must subscribe to all titles rated essential, the existence of a network of proven effectiveness resulted in a widespread willingness to rely on interlibrary loan for noncore serials.

286. Warner, Edward S., and Anker, Anita L. "Utilizing Library Constituents' Perceived Needs in Allocating Journal Costs." *Journal of the American Society for Information Science* 30 (1979): 325-29.

Using an academic department expression of perceived need for journals, librarians at the University of North Dakota were able to consider the interdisciplinary nature of many titles in calculating the cost of library journal support to academic programs.

287. Wenger, Charles B., and Childress, Judith. "Journal Evaluation in a Large Research Library." *Journal of the American Society for Information Science* 28 (1977): 293-99.

Journals in two special libraries were evaluated on the basis of a use study, circulation and interlibrary loan records, a core list, local availability, questionnaires, subscription cost, and librarian and patron input.

288. White, Herbert S., and Fry, Bernard M. "Economic Interaction Between Special Libraries and Publishers of Scholarly and Research Journals: Results of an NSF Study." *Special Libraries* 68 (1977): 109-14.

This article concentrates on the impact of escalating journal prices on special libraries during the period 1969-73. The main conclusions are: in contrast to academic and public institutions, the budgets of special libraries have kept up with serials inflation generally and there have not been major shifts from the book line to cover serials; title cancellations, emphasizing duplicates and foreign language items, are climbing; and interlibrary loan is growing rapidly but has not yet adversely affected publishers of scholarly and research journals. The study also concludes that the rising subscription costs do not seem to represent excessive publisher profits—at least for the period studied.

289. White, Herbert S. "Factors in the Decision by Individuals and Libraries to Place or Cancel Subscriptions to Scholarly and Research Journals." *Library Quarterly* 50 (1980): 287-309.

White's article reports the results of a survey of the factors influencing individual and library subscription decisions. The survey found that a library's decision to add a title is largely a subjective and political one based on faculty requests, with objective data such as citation value or interlibrary loan borrowing typically not considered. On the other hand, cancellation decisions are typically made by libraries in response to financial pressures, with much less user participation. Finally, the article notes that subscription decisions are starting to be influenced by networks, consortia and cooperative collection development programs.

290. White, Herbert S., and Fry, Bernard M. "The Impact of Periodical Availability in Libraries on Individual and Library Subscription Placement and Cancellation: A Summary of Findings." *Library Acquisitions: Practice and Theory* 4 (1980): 163-68.

Brief summary of the results of a survey which is not described. Includes library and individual subscribers' reasons for purchasing and cancelling periodicals.

291. White, Herbert S. "Publishers, Libraries, and Costs of Journal Subscriptions in Times of Funding Retrenchment." *Library Quarterly* 46 (1976): 359-77.

White calls for new attitudes on the part of librarians, publishers and scholars, so current problems in journal cost will not accelerate. He predicts the need for federal subsidy of scholarly publishing.

292. Williams, Sally F. "Construction and Application of a Periodical Price Index." *Collection Management* 2 (1978): 329-43.

Williams describes the construction of Harvard's Widener Periodical Price Index for periodicals budget planning, and a technique for testing its relationship to published indexes. She found strong correlations, which indicate that the published indexes may be valid indicators of projected subscription costs.

293. Williamson, Marilyn L. "Serials Evaluation at the Georgia Institute of Technology." *Serials Librarian* 2 (1977): 181-92.

In this review project librarians examined current periodical titles and had their own ratings, as well as codes for such variables as country of origin and subject, entered into a subscription agency's database for future sorting and cancellation priority. Detailed procedures, criteria for evaluation and a checklist are included.

294. Windsor, Donald A. "Core Versus Field Journals: A Method for Weeding During Changes in Research Needs." *De-Acquisitions Librarian* 1 (Summer 1976): 1, 5-6.

When a program changes, those serials supporting it should be weeded, without pruning journals which support other disciplines.

295. Windsor, Donald A. "De-Acquisitioning Journals Using Productivity/Cost Rankings." *De-Acquisitions Librarian* 1 (Spring 1976): 1, 8-10.

Cancelling serial subscriptions according to Windsor's rank/cost factor enables a library to retain high coverage of major subject fields at the greatest saving.

296. Winkler, Karen J. "When It Comes to Journals, Is More Really Better?" *Chronicle of Higher Education* 24 (April 14, 1982): 21-22.

With an increasing number of journals (of varying quality) both librarians and faculty members need some means of evaluating individual titles. This article points out specific problems and mentions as possible aids citation analysis, use/user studies, and evaluative reviews.

297. Wittig, Glenn R. "Dual Pricing of Periodicals." *College and Research Libraries* 38 (1977): 412-18.

A study of different periodical prices for individuals and institutions reveals a widening trend in pricing, and an increasing influence on periodical budgets.

298. Wood, John B., and Coppel, Lynn M. "Drowning our Kittens: Deselection of Periodicals in Academic Libraries." *Serials Librarian* 3 (1979): 317-31.

A summary of the eleven presentations given at the California Library Association's "Seminar on Deselection of Periodicals in Academic Libraries" in December 1977.

299. Woodward, Anthony Michael. *Factors Affecting the Renewal of Periodical Subscriptions: A Study of Decision-Making in Libraries with Special Reference to Economics and Inter-Library Lending.* London: Aslib, 1978.

Based on a 1977 survey of two hundred fifty British libraries, Woodward's work gives substantial statistical data to back up his conclusions about the effects of financial problems on new orders, cancellations and renewal decisions. The interlibrary loan information was obtained from a brief questionnaire given to users of the British Library Lending Division.

300. Wootton, C. B. "The Growth of the Literature and its Implications for Library Storage: 2. Serials." *BLL Review* 4 (1976): 41-46.

Data on recent trends in cost and size of serials, based on BLLD most-used serials, are presented for cautious use in predicting short term future trends.

III. Technical Services

301. Brown, Clara D. "57 Ways of Keeping a Serials Librarian Happy." *Stechert-Hafner Book News* 23 (1969): 81-84; reprinted in *Serials Librarian* 1 (1976/77): 161-68.

The now-classic tale of frustrating things which happen—and are done—to serials and which keep the job of the serials librarian a lasting challenge.

302. Horny, Karen L. "NOTIS 3 (Northwestern On-Line Total Integrated System): Technical Services Applications." *Library Resources and Technical Services* 22 (1978): 361-67.

Horny describes Northwestern's locally-developed automated support system, with particular attention to technical services aspects. There is also some discussion of regional cooperative projects.

303. McGregor, James Wilson. "Serials Staffing in Academic Libraries." *Serials Librarian* 1 (1977): 259-72.

McGregor studied serials processing staff and procedures as they exist in nine large library systems. The results of the study and the interpretation of the data are a significant contribution to the literature of serials management.

304. Robertson, Howard W. "What Every Serials Publisher Should Know About Unnecessary Title Changes." *Serials Librarian* 3 (1979): 417-22.

Directed toward serial publishers, this article defines the magnitude of unnecessary serial title changes, then describes the title change procedure required at a medium-sized academic library. Finally, there is a list of facts for publishers, informing them of the implications to the library and its patrons of a title change.

305. Sadowski, Frank E., Jr. "Initially, We Need Some Definitions: The Problems of Initialisms in Periodical Titles." *Library Resources and Technical Services* 23 (1979): 365-73.

Sadowski sets forth the problems caused catalogers and patrons by initialisms and logos, then suggests definitions and rules which would ease the problems.

306. Silberstein, Stephen M. "Computerized Serial Processing System at the University of California, Berkeley." *Journal of Library Automation* 8 (1975): 299-311.

Silberstein discusses the continuing development of this serials management system and gives examples of the reports and other products available.

307. Taylor, David C. "Title Change: Who Is Responsible?" *Title Varies* 3 (1976): 14-15.

Documentation of the now-famous inadvertent title change of *Library Journal* to *LJ/Library Journal* and back to *Library Journal*.

308. Thompson, James. "Trial by Fury: Experiences in the Publication of a Microjournal." *Serials Librarian* 4 (1979): 209-14.

The editor of *Alternative Catalog Newsletter* defends his choice of microfiche format and presents possibilities for changes in format and distribution of the serial.

IV. Acquisitions

309. American Library Association. Resources and Technical Services Division. Serials Section. *Manually Maintained Serials Records: Report of the Ad Hoc Committee to Study Manually Maintained Serials Records.* Chicago: American Library Association, 1976. (ERIC Report: ED 125549)

A state-of-the-art presentation on the maintenance of serial records by manual methods in all types of libraries. The three-part document includes questionnaire responses, forms submitted by participating libraries and lengthy explanatory comments.

310. Begg, Karin. "LINX Serials Management System: View from a Test Library." *Serials Review* 7 (October/December 1981): 62-63.

A report on Boston University Library's test of LINX reveals favorable response and excitement about expanded future use of the system.

311. Bosseau, Don L. "The Computer in Serials Processing and Control." *Advances in Librarianship* 2 (1971): 103-64.

Bosseau's state-of-the-art report centers on the automated serials system at University of California-San Diego and discusses projections for the future and the place of standards.

312. Brynteson, Susan. "Serial Acquisitions." In: *Management Problems in Serials Work.* (Westport, Conn.: Greenwood Press, 1974), pp. 50-65.

A description of the methods employed by the University of Massachusetts Library to manage serial acquisitions in a period of expansion. Throughout there is an appeal for standardization, among library records and among regional and national libraries.

313. Brynteson, Susan. "Serial Acquisitions: Old Problems—New Costs." *Library Scene* 2 (1973): 4-6 + .

Brynteson discusses increasing costs of subscriptions and standing orders, expenses of duplicate records, value, and effectiveness of letters which seek explanation, make complaints and express protest.

314. Buckeye, Nancy. "Librarians and Vendors: the Fourth Edition

of *International Subscription Agents.*" *Serials Librarian* 2 (1978): 391-99.

The editor describes the planning and production of the guide and gives an indication of developing trends in subscription work, as revealed by responses to the questionnaire used to prepare the directory.

315. Carter, Harriet H. "Setting up an Exchange Operation in the Small Special Library." *Library Resources and Technical Services* 22 (1978): 380-85.

In response to budget cuts, a biomedical research library turned to two national exchange programs to fill gaps and expand its resources.

316. Cayless, C. F., and Merritt, C. G. "The Keeping Cost of Periodicals." *Australian Academic and Research Libraries* 8 (1977): 178-85.

Concerns a study made to calculate the hidden costs of acquiring and retaining a serial. The cost can then be considered with use studies to determine cost per use.

317. Chaney, Suzanne F. "*Ulrich's* References to Microform Availability." *RQ* 21 (1981): 70-71.

A survey showed that *Ulrich's* is sadly incomplete in this area. A better source for microform availability is *Guide to Microforms in Print*.

318. Clasquin, Frank F. "The Claim Enigma for Serials and Journals." In: *Management Problems in Serials Work*. (Westport, Conn.: Greenwood Press, 1974), pp. 66-88.

A statement of the responsibilities of the agent, publisher and library in fulfillment of serial orders leads to an explanation of Faxon's automated claiming system.

319. Clasquin, Frank F. "The Jobber's Side: Cost of Acquiring Periodicals." *RQ* 10 (1971): 328-30.

Explains the vendor's service charge, discussing agents' clearance margin and risk, and libraries' demand for service.

320. Clasquin, Frank F. "The Subscription Agency and Lower Serials Budgets." *Serials Librarian* 1 (1976): 39-43.

The agency's database is a resource which can be tapped by libraries for management data and mechanization of routine tasks, thus providing a better use of available funds.

321. Coplen, Ron. "Subscription Agents: To Use or Not to Use." *Special Libraries* 70 (1979): 519-26.

A hypothetical time/motion study is presented to assist librarians in calculating internal costs of processing serial invoices, so they can determine potential savings in dealing with a subscription agent. Coplen also gives librarian and agent responses to his questionnaire on the choice of vendor.

322. De Gennaro, Richard. "Wanted: A Minicomputer Serials Control System." *Library Journal* 102 (1977): 878-79.

It is time for the development of an online serials control system designed for its own minicomputer and sold as a separate system. In this way a key library function can be automated and be free to develop in its own way, independent of circulation and cataloging.

323. Eggleton, Richard. "The ALA Duplicates Exchange Union—A Study and Evaluation." *Library Resources and Technical Services* 19 (1975): 148-63.

Following a brief history of the DEU, Eggleton reports on a survey of members and suggests changes which he feels would lead to improvements in the program.

324. Evans, Calvin D. "An Experiment in Periodicals Claiming." *Stechert-Hafner Book News* 25 (1970): 26-27.

Evans' library had the same rate of success claiming directly from the publisher as through the subscription agent. This finding prompted a return to claiming through the agent. An added benefit of the study was increased efficiency in library claiming procedures.

325. Fayollat, James. "On-Line Serials Control System in a Large Biomedical Library: 1. Description of the System." *Journal of the American Society for Information Science* 23 (1972): 318-22.

326. Fayollat, James. "On-Line Serials Control System in a Large Biomedical Library: Part II. Evaluation of Retrieval Features." *Journal of the American Society for Information Science* 23 (1972): 353-58.

327. Fayollat, James. "On-Line Serials Control System in a Large Biomedical Library: Part III. Comparison of On-Line and Batch Operations and Cost Analysis." *Journal of the American Society for Information Science* 24 (1973): 80-86.

These three articles describe and evaluate the system developed at the UCLA Biomedical Library and used successfully since 1971.

328. Franz, Ted. "Automated Standing Order System, Blackwell North America." *Serials Review* 7 (January/March 1981): 63-66.

Describes the development, use and future of the system.

329. Gellatly, Peter. "Libraries and Subscription Agencies." *PNLA Quarterly* 31 (1966): 35-40.

Pros and cons of dealing with subscription agencies, with the emphasis on the latter. Practical no-nonsense article.

330. Gellatly, Peter. "The Serials Perplex: Acquiring Serials in Large Libraries." In: *Serial Publications in Large Libraries*. (Urbana: University of Illinois, Graduate School of Library Science, 1970), pp. 29-47.

A wide-ranging survey of considerations in acquiring and disposing of serials.

331. Greene, Philip E., III. "The Three-Way Responsibility: Dealer—Publisher—Library." In: *Management Problems in Serials Work*. (Westport, Conn.: Greenwood Press, 1974), pp. 89-103.

From the vendor's perspective, a discussion of problems involved in placing subscriptions and a plea for mutual cooperation and communication.

332. Greenfield, Stanley. "[The Librarian]. . .and the Subscription Agent." *Special Libraries* 63 (1972): 293, 298-304.

Explains what a subscription agent does and how librarians can help. Greenfield states what the library can expect from the agent and predicts what lies in the future.

333. Hamann, Edmund G. "Out-of-Print Periodicals: The United States Book Exchange as a Source of Supply." *Library Resources and Technical Services* 16 (1972): 19-25.

Defines and describes USBE services and holdings and comments on the exchange's underuse.

334. Hammer, Donald P. "Serial Publications in Large Libraries: Machine Applications." In: *Serial Publications in Large Libraries*. (Urbana: University of Illinois, Graduate School of Library Science, 1970), pp. 120-45.

Reviews various automated serial check-in systems (before the appearance of networks) and warns of pitfalls likely to be encountered by libraries attempting to automate.

335. Hentschke, Guilbert C., and Kehoe, Ellen. "Serial Acquisition as a Capital Budgeting Problem." *Journal of the American Society for Information Science* 31 (1980): 357-62.

By means of mathematical model, this article examines the expenses and benefits of three-year (over one-year) periodical subscriptions. Three-year subscriptions gave significant cost savings.

336. Huff, William H. "The Acquisition of Serial Publications." *Library Trends* 18 (1970): 294-317.

This survey of American libraries' serial acquisition practices is based on questionnaire responses of forty-nine ARL and smaller libraries. It discusses both regular purchase of serials and special acquisition programs.

337. Huff, William H. "Serial Subscription Agencies." *Library Trends* 24 (1976): 683-709.

Gives the history of subscription agents and relates recent changes in serial publications to changes in the vendors, their services and their charges.

338. Jackson, Isabel, ed. *Acquisition of Special Materials*. San Francisco: San Francisco Bay Region Chapter, Special Libraries Association, 1966.

The chapter by Mark H. Baer entitled "Serials and Out-of-Print Titles" is most directly related to serial acquisitions, but the chapters on government publications, technical reports and conferences and symposia are also useful. Extensive bibliography.

339. Katz, William A., and Gellatly, Peter. *Guide to Magazine and Serial Agents*. New York: R. R. Bowker Company, 1975.

Much more is covered in this book than the title indicates. The authors surveyed 1,245 libraries of all kinds and the major domestic and foreign agents. About forty per cent of the text is a section entitled: "Directories for Analyzing and Locating Serial Agents and Services." The first three-fifths of the book is a discussion of serial acquisitions work in general, with emphasis on the relationship between the library and subscription agent. Unlike many authors, Katz does not assume that all a library's orders will be placed through an agent—or that any of them will be. He gives both sides of the vendor question and goes into the responsibilities of each partner.

340. Kuntz, Harry. "Serials Agents: Selection and Evaluation." *Serials Librarian* 2 (1977): 139-50.

A full, balanced discussion of factors to consider in selecting a single or multiple subscription agents. The article includes a "Comparison and Evaluation Checklist."

341. Lazerow, Samuel. "Serial Records: A Mechanism for Control." In: *Serial Publications in Large Libraries*. (Urbana: University of Illinois, Graduate School of Library Science, 1970), pp. 108-19.

Lazerow discusses the evolution of LC's Serial Record Division, factors considered when organizational changes occurred, and problems created by this means of attempting to control a library's serial holdings.

342. *Library Acquisitions: Practice and Theory.* 1- 1977- . New York: Pergamon Press. (ISSN: 0364-6408)

Edited by Scott Bullard, this quarterly journal emphasizes the practical aspects of all phases of acquisitions work. The first issue received some unfavorable reviews, but later issues received a better response.

343. Loveridge, Eric. "Selection, Acquisition and Recording." In: *Periodicals Administration in Libraries.* (London: Clive Bingley; Hamden, Conn.: Linnet Books, 1978), pp. 40-77.

Criteria for collection development, sources for verification, data on check-in records and tips on claiming.

344. Lupton, David Walker. "The Duplicate Periodical Problem in the Academic Library." *Library Resources and Technical Services* 20 (1976): 167-70.

The author describes Colorado State University's procedures for verifying that "duplicates" actually are such and for processing them efficiently.

345. Lupton, David Walker. "A Funny Thing Happened on the Way to the Kardex." *Title Varies* 2 (1975): 25-26, 32-34.

Lupton shares his collection of publishers' anecdotes and excuses for their failure to supply what was due.

346. Lupton, David Walker. "Serials Subscription Payment Losses: An Analysis." *Library Acquisitions: Practice and Theory* 1 (1977): 3-6.

Lupton studied nineteen years of serial receipt and payment records and divided payment losses into ceases, claims, items not published and duplicate payments. Although losses were surprisingly low he urges care in authorizing and recording payments.

347. Maddox, Jane. "Serials Management at Otto Harrassowitz." *Serials Review* 7 (July/September 1981): 75-77.

Maddox describes computer applications to Harrassowitz' Continuations and Serials departments, stressing the individualized service available and manual controls used when needed.

348. Merubia, Sonia M. "The Acquisition of Serials at the Benson Latin American Collection." *Serials Librarian* 5 (Winter 1980): 41-48.

Practices discussed in this article can be applied by other libraries seeking to improve their success in acquiring Latin American serials. Includes list of selected dealers.

349. Montag, Tom. "Stalking the Little Magazine." *Serials Librarian* 1 (1977): 281-303.

Montag, editor and publisher of *Margins: A Review of Little Magazines and Small Press Books* (no longer published), presents his side in the struggle between librarians trying to obtain little magazines by using their normal acquisition procedures and the editor's efforts to present his message as best he can. The extensive annotated list of "Resources" is particularly useful.

350.   New, Doris E. "Serials Agency Conversion in an Academic Library." *Serials Librarian* 2 (1978): 277-85.

Describes the decision process, selection of an agent and implementation of the consolidation of 2,800 serial orders with a single vendor. University of California at Irvine experienced a minimum of disruption during this program because of planning, hard work and cooperation.

351.   New York Library Association. *Report on Survey of Subscription Agents Used by Libraries in New York State,* conducted by the Technical Committee in 1970. Woodside, N.Y.: 1971.

Includes a tabulation of library questionnaire responses and a breakdown by type of library, agent responses, and recommendation based on the survey.

352.   Nientimp, Judith A. "The Librarian . . . [and the Subscription Agent]." *Special Libraries* 63 (1972): 292, 294-97.

The librarian's side in the struggle between serials librarians and vendors. Nientimp raises several problem areas and proposes solutions.

353.   Osier, Donald V. "Serials Exchange—Minnesota Style." *Serials Librarian* 3 (1979): 423-27.

A statewide program using an existing network, MINITEX, and union list, MULS, enables libraries to fill serial gaps and recycle duplicates at little expense.

354.   Pan, Elizabeth. "Claiming—What and When." *Title Varies* 4 (1977): 5+.

Pan's article is based upon the excellent claiming section of her report describing the Automated Serials Control System of the New York State Library.

355.   Paul, Huibert. "Serials Processing: Manual Control vs. Automation." *Library Resources and Technical Services* 21 (1977): 345-53.

In defense of the manual serial check-in system, Paul shows how eight problem areas in serials control can be resolved manually, whereas shifting to an automated system because of these problems would be a mistake. A discussion-provoking article.

356.   Potter, William Gray, moderator. "Available Automated Check-In Systems: A Panel Discussion." In: *Serials Automation for Acquisition and Inventory Control.* (Chicago: American Library Association, 1981), pp. 77-99.

Representatives of EBSCO, Faxon, OCLC and PHILSOM discuss their online check-in systems available for purchase, including pricing, relationship to overall management system, local library applications and potential.

357. Riddick, John. "Manual vs. Automated Check-In: A Comparative Study of Two Academic Libraries." *Serials Review* 6 (October/December 1980): 49-51.

A time and cost comparison of Iowa State's manual check-in and Central Michigan's use of the OCLC Serials Control Subsystem.

358. Sineath, Timothy W. "Libraries and Library Subscription Agencies." *Library Scene* 1 (Summer 1972): 28-30.

Discusses the pros and cons of using a subscription agent and, briefly, the legal relationship between the library and the agent.

359. Smith, Katherine R. "Serials Agents/Serials Librarians." *Library Resources and Technical Services* 14 (1970): 5-18.

Discusses the traditional role of the agent in serial acquisitions and gives detailed advice in choosing an agent and evaluating the library's relationship with its vendor. Smith urges librarians, agents and publishers to communicate in an effort to attain standardization in their records.

360. Stevens, Jana K. and Swenson, Jennifer. "Coordinated System of Processing Gift or Exchange Serials at the University of Utah Library." *Library Acquisitions: Practice and Theory* 4 (1980): 157-62.

A description of the procedure used to originate and assimilate new gift and exchange serial orders into the technical processes. Examples of form letters and worksheets.

361. Stevens, Jana K., Kelley Jade G., and Irons, Richard G. "Cost-Effectiveness of Soviet Serial Exchanges." *Library Resources and Technical Services* 26 (1982): 151-55.

A study at Duke University Library indicates that Soviet serials may not be most efficiently acquired through exchange. The study raised questions about the economic practicality of library exchange programs.

362. Taylor, David C. "Notes Toward the History and State of the Art of Institutional Subscription Rates." *Title Varies* 1 (1974): 37 + .

In semi-outline form, Taylor traces the development of the institutional rate, explains why it happened and gives a few examples of apparent abuses by publishers.

363. Thyden, Wayne R. "Serials Publishing: A World of Variation." *Serials Librarian* 6 (Fall 1981): 69-76.

With more than 65,000 serial publishers, wide variation in policy and practice is inevitable. Thyden discusses types of serial publishers, fulfillment centers, cancellations, start/expiration date, payment, cessations, and new title mortality, all from the perspective of the library subscription agent.

364. Tuttle, Marcia, and Taylor, David C. "Claim Responses Without the Claims." *Title Varies* 3 (1976): 37 + .

This review article examines two vendor publications: Faxon's *Serials Updating Service* (and its quarterly and annual cumulations) and the *EBSCO Bulletin of Serials Changes*.

365. Wernstedt, Irene J. "Planning for the Automation of Serials Check-In." *Technicalities* 1 (May 1981): 3-4, 12.

Down to earth advice for serials librarians beginning the conversion from manual to automated check-in.

366. Wernstedt, Irene J. "Two Thousand Claims Later." *Serials Librarian* 4 (1980): 307-11.

A report on a project at Penn State University Library which was designed to make up for years of inadequate claiming. Wernstedt describes the procedure used and the means of dealing with problems caused by claim responses.

367. Willmering, William J. "On-Line Centralized Serials Control." *Serials Librarian* 1 (1977): 243-49.

Northwestern's online serials system encompasses all aspects of serial acquisitions and control. This article describes check-in and claiming in detail.

368. Wood, D. N. "Current Exchange of Serials at the British Library Lending Division." *Library Acquisitions: Practice and Theory* 3 (1979): 107-13.

An examination of problems and hidden expenses incurred in the international exchange of serial publications leads the author to conclude that such exchange programs are undesirable, but necessary.

369. Young, Roy. "Back Volume Miscellany." *Serials Review* 7 (April/June 1981): 67-68.

An experienced out-of-print bookdealer educates librarians, using his own experiences as examples.

370. *Your New Guide to USBE Services*. Washington, D.C.: Universal Serials and Book Exchange, Inc., 1979.

A promotional and informational booklet describing USBE's services and procedures.

V. Cataloging

371. "*AACR* 2: Background and Summary." *Library of Congress Information Bulletin* 37 (1978): 640-52.

A brief background sketch is followed by a discussion of rule deviations from previous cataloging rules.

372. "Alternative III, by University of Iowa Libraries Serials Staff..."
    Title Varies 2 (1975): 29+.
Iowa serials librarians respond to Joseph Howard's two alternatives for choice of main entry for serials by advocating the use of corporate entry for generic titles.

373. Byrum, John D., Jr., and Coe, D. Whitney, "*AACR* as Applied by Research Libraries for Serials Cataloging." *Library Resources and Technical Services* 23 (1979): 139-46.
Byrum and Coe present the results of a 1975 survey of the acceptance, application and assessment of *AACR* for serials. Responses revealed a wide degree of intentional variation from this standard.

374. Cannan, Judith Proctor, and Tucker, Ben R. "Serials Cataloging Under *AACR* 2." *RTSD Newsletter* 5 (1980): 19-21.
The authors provide cataloging for five titles according to *AACR* 2 and discuss questions arising from the use of the new code and its interpretation. Some LC rule interpretations for monographic cataloging are included and may be applied to serials, although the article is not to be considered policy.

375. Cannan, Judith Proctor. "Serials Cataloging Under *AACR* 2—Part 2." *RTSD Newsletter* 5 (1980): 29-32.
Cannan continues her earlier article by cataloging seven additional titles according to the new code.

376. Cannan, Judith Proctor. *Special Problems in Serials Cataloging*. Washington, D.C.: Processing Services, Library of Congress, 1979.
An overview of serials cataloging problems which were brought out in training programs at the Library of Congress. Cannan covers specific serial rules and gives illustrations of title pages with the corresponding LC cards, as well as insights into LC policy.

377. Carpenter, Michael. "No Special Rules for Entry of Serials." *Library Resources and Technical Services* 19 (1975): 327-32.
The abolition of specific rules for entry of serials and the use instead of rules for entry of monographs is Carpenter's suggestion for simplifying serials cataloging.

378. Carter, Ruth C. "Playing By the Rules: *AACR* 2 and Serials." In: *Serials Management in an Automated Age*. (Westport, Conn.: Meckler Publishing, 1982), pp. 11-29.
Advice for serials catalogers and other serials librarians who must integrate *AACR* 2 into existing serial records.

379. Cipolla, Wilma Reid. "*AACR* 2 and Serial Records." In: *The Serials Collection*. (Ann Arbor, Mich.: Pierian Press, 1982), pp. 53-66.
A discussion of the way *AACR* 2 affects the many library records controlling

serials, with questions about adapting records, concerning consistency of entry among single access point files.

380. Cole, Jim E. "*AACR* 6: Time for a Review." *Library Resources and Technical Services* 19 (1975): 314-26.
Cole proposes that *AACR* rule 6 be changed by adopting the British text of 6B and deleting 6C. These changes would simplify the cataloger's choice of entry for serials.

381. Cole, Jim E. "Unique Serial Title Entries." *Serials Review* 7 (October/December 1981): 75-77.
Why uniform titles were not needed under *AACR*, why they are required under *AACR* 2, and what further development of the concept is needed.

382. Decker, Jean S. "Catalog 'Closings' and Serials." *Journal of Academic Librarianship* 5 (1979): 261-65.
Decker raises many questions and gives a few answers about the effects on serial records of the implementation of *AACR* 2.

383. Edgar, Neal L. "CCRC Report: A Letter from Edgar." *Title Varies* 2 (1975): 23 + .
An optimistic report following the 1975 ALA Conference, assuring serials librarians that their concerns are being considered by the Committee.

384. Edgar, Neal L. "Catalog Code Revision Update." *Title Varies* 3 (1976): 31 + .
Edgar reports on deliberations of the Catalog Code Revision Committee which are of most interest to serials librarians: Rule 6, Chapter 7, *ISBD(S)*, organization of the Code and Rule 1.

385. Edgar, Neal L. "Impact of *AACR* 2 on Serials and Analysis." In: International Conference on *AACR* 2, Florida State University, 1979. *Making of a Code*. (Chicago: American Library Association, 1980), pp. 88-105.
A full discussion of serial-related changes in the new code, including background and the author's suggested alternatives. Comment on problems that remain to be solved or that will appear. A well-organized, informed presentation.

386. Edgar, Neal L. "Serials Entry—Quo Vadis?" *Title Varies* 3 (1976): 5 + .
A serials-oriented member of the Catalog Code Revision Committee expresses his own ideas on the problem of entry of serials.

387. Edgar, Neal L. "Some Implications of Code Revision for Serials Librarians." *Serials Librarian* 1 (1976/77): 125-34.
Edgar informs serials librarians of the changes to come with *AACR* 2.

388. Fasana, Paul. *"AACR, ISBD(S)* and ISSN: A Comment." *Library Resources and Technical Services* 19 (1975): 333-37.

A rebuttal to the proposal that *AACR* Rule 6 be replaced by the conventions for description of serials of *ISBD(S)*.

389. *Freezing Card Catalogs*. Washington, D.C.: Association of Research Libraries, 1978.

This work contains an introduction and three main papers: "Introduction—Closing the Card Catalog: A Survey of the Status of Planning in ARL Libraries," by Richard Dougherty; "Planning for the Catalogs: A Managerial Perspective," by Joseph Rosenthal; "Two Years with a Closed Catalog," by Robert H. Blackburn; "Implications for ARL Directors of Freezing the Library of Congress Catalogs," by H. William Axford.

390. Grosch, Audrey N. "Theory and Design of Serial Holding Statements in Computer-Based Serials Systems." *Serials Librarian* 1 (1977): 341-52.

Grosch illustrates and explains the University of Minnesota Library's scheme for giving the public issue-specific, natural-language serial holding statements, while at the same time preserving a high degree of automatic manipulation of data at the character level.

391. Hartman, Matt. "Serials Cataloging: UTLAS and the Machine Environment at the University of British Columbia." *Serials Review* 7 (January/March 1981): 93-95.

A candid article by a "good, career-oriented serials cataloger."

392. Hayes, Florence C. "Pre-AACR 2 Special Records: Cornell's Experience with a Closed Catalog." *Serials Review* 7 (April/June 1981): 85-86.

AACR 2 has implications for serials, with their tendency to change, that must be understood and adapted to.

393. Henderson, Kathryn Luther. "Serial Cataloging Revisited—A Long Search for a Little Theory and a Lot of Cooperation." In: *Serial Publications in Large Libraries*. (Urbana: University of Illinois, Graduate School of Library Science, 1970), pp. 48-89.

The author surveys, from the user's perspective, problems and trends in serials cataloging at the brink of the era of automation.

394. Hiatt, Robert M. *"AACR* 2: Implementation Plans." *Library of Congress Information Bulletin* 37 (1978): 710-12.

Outlines implementation plans for *AACR* 2 at the Library of Congress.

395. Hirshon, Arnold, Gleim, David, and Dowell, Arlene Taylor. "The Implementation of *AACR* 2: Some Questions." *RTSD Newsletter* 5 (1980): 57-59.

A brief but useful outline of questions raised in the implementation of *AACR* 2.

396. Howard, Joseph H. "Main Entry for Serials." *Drexel Library Quarterly* 11 (July 1975): 11-19; reprinted from *Library of Congress Information Bulletin* 33 (1974): A232-36.

Howard advocates title entry for serials (with a possible exception for generic terms), in an effort to attain clarity and standardization.

397. Hunter, Eric J. *Anglo-American Cataloging Rules 1967: An Introduction.* London: Clive Bingley; Hamden, Conn.: Linnet Books, 1972.

A programmed text on *AACR*, which is very helpful in understanding its principles and application.

398. Hunter, Eric J., and Fox, Nicholas J. *Examples Illustrating AACR 2: Anglo-American Cataloguing Rules, Second Edition.* London: Library Association, 1980.

Examples, primarily from British publications, illustrate not only title pages, but audiovisual materials, etc. The approach is by an index rather than chapter-by-chapter, rule-by-rule.

399. Kimzey, Ann C., and Smith, Roland. "An Automated Book Catalog for a Learning Resources Center Periodicals Collection." *Serials Librarian* 2 (1978): 405-10.

For patron access to an uncataloged college serial collection a computer generated book catalog was produced, giving access by title and subject. It is easily reproduced and widely distributed.

400. "LC/RTSD *AACR* 2 Institute: Report of the Washington, D.C. Institute." *RTSD Newsletter* 5 (1980): 37-48.

An update of previous articles and reports on LC's rule interpretations of *AACR* 2.

401. "Library of Congress Studying Options on *Anglo-American Cataloging Rules*, Second Edition." *Library of Congress Information Bulletin* 37 (1978): 90-92.

LC lets us know its thinking about choice of options to use when the new code is implemented.

402. McCallum, Sally Hart. "Some Implications of Desuperimposition." *Library Quarterly* 47 (1977): 111-27.
McCallum discusses how the Library of Congress and other libraries might handle desuperimposition.

403. Manning, Ralph W. *"Anglo-American Cataloguing Rules* [Review]." *Canadian Library Journal* 36 (1979): 381-82.
A non-American Review of *AACR* 2, pointing out differences from *AACR*.

404. Martinelli, James A. "Descriptive Cataloging of Serials: The National Library of Medicine versus the Library of Congress." *Bulletin of the Medical Library Association* 68 (1980): 40-46.
Compares the differences between the two libraries' cataloging and discusses the impact on cooperative online databases.

405. Maxwell, Margaret F. *Handbook for AACR 2: Explaining and Illustrating the Anglo-American Cataloguing Rules, Second Edition.* Chicago: American Library Association, 1980.
Intended for library school students and catalogers, this textbook both explains the rules and provides full cataloging entries to illustrate each rule. In many instances, a copy of the title page has been provided for further clarification of the rules. Maxwell's approach is chapter-by-chapter.

406. Peregoy, Marjorie. *"AACR* II and Serials Cataloging." *Serials Librarian* 3 (1978): 15-30.
Reviews the development of *AACR* 2 and *ISBD(S)*, points out changes in the cataloging of serials which will occur with the implementation of the new code, and generally does much to smooth what will be a difficult transition.

407. Peregoy, Marjorie. "Cataloging Varies." *Title Varies* 3 (1976): 39 + .
Not only do serial titles vary, rules for cataloging serials also vary. A report from the 1977 ALA Midwinter Meetings of the Serials Section's *AACR* Revision Study Committee.

408. *Planning for the Future of the Card Catalog.* Washington, D.C.: Association of Research Libraries, 1978. (SPEC Kit 46)
This kit is a package of documents from ARL libraries covering the various aspects of the question of what to do about the card catalog in the light of *AACR* 2 and advances in automation.

409. Potter, William Gray. "When Names Collide: Conflict in the Cata-

log and *AACR* 2." *Library Resources and Technical Services* 24 (1980): 3-16.

Planning for implementation of *AACR* 2, closing of catalogs, etc., is assisted by sampling the forms of personal author headings.

410.   Rather, Lucia J. "*AACR* 2 Options to be Followed by the Library of Congress: Chapters 1-2, 12, 21-26." *Library of Congress Information Bulletin* 37 (1978): 422-28.

Updates a previous *LCIB* article concerning option choices made by the Library of Congress. This discussion includes serial options.

411.   Roth, Dana Lincoln. "To Classify or Not to Classify. . . A Rejoinder." *Serials Librarian* 5 (Fall 1980): 83-85.

Science journals should not be classified, but arranged by title in broad subject groups near the standard indexes.

412.   Sauer, Mary E. "Automated Serials Control: Cataloging Considerations." *Journal of Library Automation* 9 (1976): 8-18.

Updates developments in *ISBD(S)*, ISDS/ISSN and choice of entry.

413.   Sauer, Mary E. "Key Title and Rules for Entry." *Library Resources and Technical Services* 19 (1975): 338-40.

Discusses the compatibility of *AACR* and *ISBD(S)* when one understands the latter's purpose—an internationally acceptable building block for national and other cataloging agencies.

414.   Shinebourne, J. A. "A Critique of *AACR*." *Libri* 29 (1979): 231-59.

A highly critical look at *AACR* 2 by a British library school professor.

415.   Simonton, Wesley. "An Introduction to *AACR* 2." *Library Resources and Technical Services* 23 (1979): 321-39.

A summary of changes in *AACR* 2, and a statement of options adopted by the Library of Congress.

416.   Simonton, Wesley. "Serial Cataloging Problems: Rules of Entry and Definition of Title." *Library Resources and Technical Services* 19 (1975): 294-300.

As an aid to *LRTS* readers, its editor prefaces a group of papers on serials cataloging with a summary of the arguments concerning rules of entry and the various definitions of "title" in ISDS, *ISBD* and *AACR*. He concludes with a survey of future activity in code revision and international agreement.

417.   Smith, Lynn S. *A Practical Approach to Serials Cataloging.* Greenwich, Conn.: JAI Press, Inc., 1978. (Foundations in Library and Information Science. 2)

In this first monograph devoted entirely to serials cataloging, Smith discusses every facet of this function, giving examples and illustrations. The topic is not treated in a vacuum, but is related to other aspects of serials work.

418.   Smith, Lynn S. "To Classify or Not to Classify. . ." *Serials Librarian* 2 (1978): 371-85.
A firm stand for classification of serial publications, so the entire library collection can be used comparatively, effectively and in depth.

419.   Soper, Mary Ellen. "Description and Entry of Serials in *AACR* 2." *Serials Librarian* 4 (1979): 167-76.
Discusses rules affecting serials in the new code and points out differences between it and *AACR*.

420.   Soper, Mary Ellen. "Entry of Serials." *Serials Librarian* 1 (1976): 23-37.
A survey of serial related developments leading to the implementation of *AACR* 2. It places the acronyms in perspective, so noncatalogers can make sense out of the code.

421.   Spalding, C. Sumner. "The Life and Death (?) of Corporate Authorship." *Library Resources and Technical Services* 24 (1980): 195-208.
Summarizes the history and philosophy of corporate authorship and theorizes that the concept is dead, because the framers of *AACR* 2 refused to treat serials as a unique case.

422.   Spalding, Helen H. "A Computer-Produced Serials Book Catalog with Automatically Generated Indexes." *Library Resources and Technical Services* 24 (1980): 352-60.
At Iowa State University Library a serials book catalog arranged by title and with multiple access points is the only public source of bibliographic information about serials. Spalding tells the history of its development.

423.   Stine, Diane. "The Cataloging of Serials in Microform under *AACR* II Rules." *Serials Librarian* 5 (Spring 1981): 19-23.
Use of *AACR* 2 instead of *AACR* for cataloging microforms makes the item more difficult for the patron to locate.

424.   Thompson, Jim. "Of *AACR* 2 and On-Line Catalogs." *RTSD Newsletter* 5 (1980): 59-60.
What the utilities and others involved with automated cataloging are doing about *AACR* 2.

425.   Tucker, Ben R. "Anglo-American Cataloging Rules - Second Edition." *Hennepin County Library Cataloging Bulletin* 36 (1978): 1-12.

Points out the major differences between *AACR* 2 and previous rules in a readable and succinct article, which uses many examples.

426. Turner, Ann. "*AACR* 2 and Serials." *Serials Librarian* 6 (Fall 1981): 27-39.

Discusses three groups of changes introduced by the new code: improvements over former codes, changes of a controversial nature, and cosmetic changes. The author's treatment is optimistic.

427. Turner, Ann. "The Effects of *AACR* 2 on Serials Cataloguing." *Serials Librarian* 4 (1979): 177-86.

There will be changes in the cataloging of serials when *AACR* 2 is implemented, but the author's study at the University of British Columbia indicates that most changes will be manageable.

428. Weintraub, D. Kathryn. "*AACR* 2: A Review Article." *Library Quarterly* 49 (1979): 435-43.

A general criticism of *AACR* 2, not specifically dealing with serials. Somewhat negative.

429. Wellisch, Hans H. "Freeze Not, Fear Not." *American Libraries* 11 (1980): 660-63.

A practical article on the integration of *AACR* 2 headings into existing catalogs.

VI. Preservation and Binding

430. Bailey, Martha J. "Selecting Titles for Binding." *Special Libraries* 64 (1973): 571-73.

Bailey describes a rating system used at Purdue to evaluate physics journals for binding when funds could not cover binding every title.

431. Banks, Paul N. "Some Problems in Book Conservation." *Library Resources and Technical Services* 12 (1968): 330-38.

There is need for a standard for an extra-cost binding for library materials of "permanent research value."

432. Boss, Richard W. "Putting the Horse Before the Cart." *Microform Review* 7 (1978): 78-80.

Before converting wholesale to microform, librarians would do well to consider user and staff attitudes and proceed carefully and careingly.

433. Coffman, R. J. "Microform Serials Collections: A Systems Analysis." *Serials Librarian* 1 (1976): 45-50.

Every institution should do a systems analysis before establishing policy concerning retention of journals in microformat.

434.   Dean, John F. "The In-House Processing of Paperbacks and Pamphlets." *Serials Review* 7 (October/December 1981): 81-85.
Johns Hopkins University Library found a means of binding paperback materials in-house that met the requirements of general applicability, low cost, capability of being rebound, nonspecialized equipment, strength and attractiveness.

435.   Farber, Evan Ira. "The Administration and Use of Microform Serials in College Libraries." *Microform Review* 7 (1978): 81-84.
College libraries, librarians and patrons have different needs for and attitudes toward microforms than university libraries and staff.

436.   Farrington, Jean Walter. "Adding Microforms to Academic Libraries: Developing a Journal Conversion Program." *Serials Librarian* 5 (Fall 1980): 79-82.
A conversion project should begin with a microform acquisition policy and a list of criteria for titles to be considered for conversion. Other relevant factors are discussed.

437.   Farrington, Jean Walter. "How to Select a Microfilm or Microfiche Reader: Some Practical Considerations." *Serials Librarian* 4 (1980): 291-94.
Farrington lists tools for determining what equipment is available, recommends *Library Technology Reports* for evaluation, and gives seven commonsense guidelines for the selection of mechanical readers.

438.   Feldman, Mrs. Herman A. "Get Better Service from Your Binder." *UNABASHED Librarian*, no. 21 (1976): 15-16.
This brief article lists very specific ways in which librarians can assist binders to give them good service.

439.   Finch, Curtis R., Copa, George A., and Magisos, Joel. "Impact of a Microfiche Research Journal." *Journal of Micrographics* 12 (1979): 213-18.
A survey of individual subscribers to an association journal distributed on microfiche resulted in generally positive response and several valid suggestions for improvement.

440.   Folcarelli, Ralph J., and Ferragamo, Ralph C. "Microform Publications: Hardware and Suppliers." *Library Trends* 24 (1976): 711-25.
Covers the current state of microform production and library use, lists micropublishers and sources of reviews of microform material and equipment, and looks at the future uses of microforms in libraries.

441.   Gabriel, Michael R., and Ladd, Dorothy P. *The Microform Revolu-

tion in Libraries. Greenwich, Conn.: JAI Press, 1980. (Foundations in Library and Information Science. 3)

Chapter 4, "Serials in Microform," covers the growth of library acquisition of this alternative method of retaining serials. Although the discussion is pro-microform, the authors consider disadvantages such as mechanical readers, maintenance, security and user (or librarian) resistance.

442.   Gabriel, Michael R. "Surging Serial Costs: The Microfiche Solution." *Library Journal* 99 (1974): 2450-53.

Retention of serials in microfiche is a solution to the increasing costs of binding, storing and replacing titles retained in the original paper format. Gabriel offers suggestions for overcoming user reluctance to microfiche.

443.   Gore, Daniel. "The Destruction of the Book by Oversewn Binding— And How to Prevent it." In: *Management Problems in Serials Work.* (Westport, Conn.: Greenwood Press, 1974), pp. 121-28.

After discussing the destructive qualities of the widely-used oversewn binding, Gore advocates the use of plastic rivet binding as a preservation and economic measure.

444.   Gray, Edward. "Subscriptions on Microfiche: A Progress Report." *Journal of Micrographics* 10 (1977): 169-72.

Gray predicts that microfiche journal publications will replace paper editions, because fiche is becoming cheaper and people are accepting it.

445.   Gray, Edward. "Subscriptions on Microfiche: An Irreversible Trend." *Journal of Micrographics* 8 (1975): 241-44.

An experiment with a simultaneous microfiche edition of *Tetrahedron Letters* indicates that this format may begin to replace paper editions of journals.

446.   Grochmal, Helen M. "Selection Criteria for Periodicals in Microform." *Serials Librarian* 5 (Spring 1981): 15-17.

Criteria for selecting microform over binding for retention of periodicals.

447.   "Guidelines for the Handling of Microforms in the Yale University Library." *Microform Review* 9 (1980): 11-20, 72-85.

Edited by Gay Walker and Merrily Taylor, these guidelines cover: 1) microform selection, acquisition, bibliographic control, physical handling and storage, and 2) relations with micropublishers. Included in the report are recommendations for solving current local problems associated with microforms.

448.   Hammer, Donald P. "HELP: The Automated Binding Records Control System." *Journal of Library Automation* 5 (1972): 137-45.

Describes the Heckman Bindery technique developed at the Purdue University Library and, by 1971, used by over seven hundred libraries.

449. Henderson, William T. "Binding—A Librarian's View." In: *Serial Publications in Large Libraries.* (Urbana: University of Illinois, Graduate School of Library Science, 1970), pp. 95-107.

There are two valid reasons for binding serials: preservation and convenience. Henderson's article covers each.

450. Joseph, Tony. "The Question of Microfilm." *New Library World* 79 (1978): 88-89.

A librarian steps into his other role as library user and gives his reasons for opposing the retention of newspapers on microfilm.

451. Kirsch, Kenneth C., and Rubenstein, Albert H. "Converting from Hard Copy to Microfilm: An Administrative Experiment." *Collection Management* 2 (1978): 279-302.

The conversion of *Chemical Abstracts* from hard copy to microfilm in an industrial research and development laboratory was not without its problems of user attitudes.

452. Laflin, Marjorie A. "Micropublishing Potential in Professional Journal Publications." *Journal of Micrographics* 10 (1977): 281-85.

Discusses the American Chemical Society's creative use of microfiche in the distribution of journal issues, supplementary material and articles related to the subscriber's area of interest.

453. Lakhanpal, S. K. *Library Binding Manual.* Rev. ed. Saskatoon: Serials Department, Murray Memorial Library, University of Saskatchewan, 1972.

This procedural manual covers commercial and in-house binding and contains illustrations of forms used in the author's library. The manual can be adapted to local library conditions.

454. Lanier, Don. "Binding—Is Standardized Standard?" *RTSD Newsletter* 5 (1980): 33-34.

In the wake of a swing from primarily Class A Library Binding to "Standardized" or non-Class A binding, the author advocates creation of a standard for the latter, so librarians will know what they may expect when they request that type of treatment.

455. *Library Binder.* 1-19, 1952-71. Boston: Library Binding Institute. (ISSN: 0024-2209)

Published by the LBI, an organization of binders "interested in the promotion and maintenance of highest standards in binding technique." Objectives were to educate librarians and promote binding standards. *Library Binder*, heavy on industry news, was superseded in 1972 by the more general and library-oriented *Library Scene.*

456. Lynden, Frederick C. "Replacement of Hard Copy by Microform."
   Microform Review 4 (1975): 15-24.

Discusses the factors each library must consider in contemplating a microform conversion project. The findings provide guidelines for the individual library.

457. Maxin, Jacqueline A. "Binding Selectively." *Special Libraries* 66 (1975):
   327-29.

The Clarkson College of Technology, faced with decreasing binding funds and a large binding backlog, made heavy use of temporary binding with Bro-Dart's Periodical Binding System, which was inexpensive and quick.

458. Niles, Ann. "Conversion of Serials from Paper to Microform."
   Microform Review 9 (1980): 90-95.

Niles pokes holes in the arguments commonly used to justify purchase of microform to replace hard copy: cost, space-saving, ease of handling, and permanence.

459. Orr, James. "Library Binding." In: *Serial Publications in Large Libraries*. (Urbana: University of Illinois, Graduate School of Library Science, 1970), pp. 90-94.

Issues and developing trends in library binding for large libraries from the commercial binder's point of view.

460. Peacock, P. G. "The Selection of Periodicals for Binding." *Aslib Proceedings* 33 (1981): 257-59.

Includes a decision table for selecting periodicals for binding, based on physical condition, frequency, degree of use, and value.

461. Peele, David. "Bind or Film: Factors in the Decision." *Library Resources and Technical Services* 8 (1964): 168-71.

Among the factors considered by Staten Island Community College were: likelihood of mutilation, nature of the material, physical condition and contents, user attitude toward microfilm, and cost.

462. Piternick, Anne B. "Effects of Binding Policy and Other Factors on the Availability of Journal Issues." *Bulletin of the Medical Library Association* 64 (1976): 284-92.

Because the immediate binding of medical periodicals takes them away from the library at the time of heaviest use, one library decided to hold high-use titles for two years before binding to make individual issues available longer.

463. Rebsamen, Werner. "Evaluation of Library Bindings." *Serials Review* 7 (April/June 1981): 89-94.

As a response to library problems with commercial binding, library binders and suppliers set up a Book Performance Book Testing Laboratory at the Rochester Institute of Technology. The laboratory's director justifies its existence and describes its equipment.

464. Reed, Jutta R. "Cost Comparison of Periodicals in Hard Copy and on Microform." *Microform Review* 5 (1976): 185-92.

Identifies sources of costs of retaining periodicals in both paper and microform. Reed compares the expenses and makes a convincing case for overall lower cost for microform.

465. Roberts, Matt T. "The Library Binder." *Library Trends* 24 (1976): 749-62.

Includes a section on selecting a library binder; describes the elements of a fair sample to send to several binders and details to evaluate when the sample is returned. Discusses binder services and trends in the library binding industry.

466. Roberts, Matt T. "Oversewing and the Problem of Book Preservation in the Research Library." *College and Research Libraries* 28 (1967): 17-24.

Describes the binding process, points out the disadvantages of oversewing and suggests preferable methods of binding which aid in the preservation of materials.

467. Roberts, Matt T. "The Role of the Librarian in the Binding Process." *Special Libraries* 62 (1971): 413-20; reprinted in *Library Scene* 2 (1973): 26-30.

A well-documented plea for the librarian to become more closely involved with binding decisions for the sake of preservation and public access.

468. Roughton, Karen G., and Roughton, Michael D. "Serials on Microfilm." *Serials Librarian* 5 (Summer 1981): 41-47.

The authors have examined reels of microfilmed serials and found frequent examples of shoddy production, which they discuss in a warning to librarians to examine microfilm before discarding original volumes.

469. Wilkinson, W. A., and Stock, Loretta A. "Machine-Assisted Serials Control: Bindery Preparation and Claims Control." *Special Libraries* 62 (1971): 529-34.

The library of Monsanto Company used a plastic card imprinted with binding information to produce bindery forms. This was the only record kept by the library or the binder.

VII. Public Service

470. Alkire, Leland G., Jr. "The Initial Problem." *Serials Librarian* 2 (1978): 401-04.

If periodical titles must be abbreviated, and they must, indexers and bibliographers are urged to follow existing standards and avoid the confusion resulting from "home-grown" abbreviations.

471. Baynham, Robert J., and Gallagher, Marian G. "Copyright: Colloquium Notes." *Serials Librarian* 1 (1976): 83-98.

Baynham defines and describes copyright and Gallagher summarizes the Williams and Wilkins case and the revised copyright law (at that time under consideration by the House).

472. Behles, Richard J. "Interplay—The Technical and Public Aspects of Serials." In: *The Serials Collection*. (Ann Arbor, Mich.: Pierian Press, 1982), pp. 9-14.

Serial processing staff members' expertise can be used, to the patron's benefit, in serial public service. Reference is left to the reference staff but interpretation of serial records is best done by serials personnel.

473. Bell, Winnie. "Serials—Implications of Costs and Copyright." *Arkansas Libraries* 33, no. 2 (1976): 17-21.

Cooperative ventures involving photocopy of journal articles threaten both authors and publishers. Librarians must work with these groups to secure copyright legislation which will benefit all parties.

474. Bopp, Richard E. "Periodicals for the Disabled: Their Importance as Information Sources." *Serials Librarian* 5 (Winter 1980): 61-70.

This bibliographic essay provides guidance to librarians seeking to serve disabled patrons.

475. Cargill, Jennifer. "Preparation of a Serials Holding List Using a Word Processor." In: *Union Lists: Issues and Answers*. (Ann Arbor, Mich.: Pierian Press, 1982), pp. 81-87.

A current periodicals list, formerly typed and printed every two years, is produced and updated on a word processor. The present method is more efficient and flexible than the manual one.

476. Cook, Colleen. "Serials Inventory: A Case Study." *Serials Librarian* 5 (Winter 1980): 25-30.

Methodology and evaluation of results of an inventory of 400,000 serial volumes at Texas A & M University Library.

477. Crawford, Walter C. "Building a Serials Key Word Index." *Journal of Library Automation* 9 (1976): 34-47.

Describes the University of California, Berkeley, project to improve access to serial titles, including techniques, problems, benefits and applications.

478. Clyke, Frank Kurt, and Wires, Catherine. "Periodicals for the Blind and Physically Handicapped." *Serials Librarian* 2 (1977): 49-65.

A description and brief history of the services of LC's Division for the Blind and Physically Handicapped and its network of libraries which provide public library services via Braille, recordings and cassettes to those who cannot use printed materials.

479. De Gennaro, Richard. "Copyright, Resource Sharing, and Hard Times: A View from the Field." *American Libraries* 8 (1977): 430-35.
Interpretation of statistics from the University of Pennsylvania and Cornell indicate that the new law will have little impact on library photocopying. De Gennaro also warns against unrealistic expectations from networking.

480. Devers, Charlotte M., Katz, Doris B., and Regan, Mary Margaret, eds. *Guide to Special Issues and Indexes of Periodicals*. 2nd ed. New York: Special Libraries Association, 1976.
Limited to American and Canadian "consumer, trade and technical periodicals," this work lists recurring topical issues, sections of issues, and indexes.

481. Farrington, Jean Walter. "Out of the Dungeon: Mainstreaming Microforms." *Serials Librarian* 5 (Summer 1981): 37-40.
In determining where microforms are to be housed in the library, consider 1) types of microforms owned, 2) type of library and sophistication of users, 3) library floor plan, and 4) local bibliographic control of microforms.

482. Feinman, Valerie Jackson. "Dilemmas and Consequences of Converting Periodical Holdings to Microformat." *Serials Librarian* 4 (1979): 77-84.
Adelphi was forced by space problems to convert some periodical backfiles to microform and store others off campus. After beginning a conversion project with little planning, the staff had to adapt to the situation and educate patrons. Their decisions proved to be correct for their situation.

483. Flacks, Lewis I. "Living in the Gap of Ambiguity: An Attorney's Advice to Librarians on the Copyright Law." *American Libraries* 8 (1977): 252-57.
Flacks, a U.S. Copyright Office attorney, answers in print nine often asked questions about the 1976 copyright law.

484. Fussler, Herman H., and Simon, Julian L. *Patterns in the Use of Books in Large Research Libraries*. Chicago: University of Chicago Press, 1969.
A classic use study which covers non-recorded as well as recorded use of serials and monographs.

485. Gillies, Thomas D. "Document Serials, Technical Reports, and the National Bibliography." In: *Serial Publications in Large Libraries*. (Urbana: University of Illinois, Graduate School of Library Science, 1970), pp. 146-60.

These special types of serials present special problems in bibliographic control. Gillies describes what is available and what is needed.

486. Golden, Gary A., Golden, Susan U., Lenzini, Rebecca T. "Patron Approaches to Serials: A User Study." *College and Research Libraries* 43 (1982): 22-30.

University of Illinois librarians studied patron use of a serials card catalog and analyzed the reasons for their success or failure.

487. Grochmal, Helen M. "The Serials Department's Responsibilities for Reference." *RQ* 20 (1981): 403-06.

Serials reference service is complex and requires careful and thorough training of staff members who assist and advise patrons.

488. Gouke, Mary Noel, and Murfin, Marjorie. "Periodical Mutilation: The Insidious Disease." *Library Journal* 105 (1980): 1795-97.

A follow-up study of university library mutilation indicates that a public relations program may reduce the destruction of journals.

489. Guy, Sue. "Use." In: *Periodicals Administration in Libraries.* (London: Clive Bingley; Hamden, Conn.: Linnet Books, 1978), pp. 127-35.

Discusses circulation, interlibrary loan, photocopy and ways of monitoring periodical use. Guy presents an array of choices in each category, so that a library can select or adapt.

490. Healey, James S., and Cox, Carolyn M. "Research and the *Reader's Guide*: An Investigation into the Research Use of Periodicals Indexed in the *Readers' Guide to Periodical Literature*." *Serials Librarian* 3 (1978): 179-90.

A study of citations in theses and dissertations supports the authors' hypothesis that "materials indexed in the *Readers' Guide* are of minimal research value five years after publication."

491. Hebert, Françoise. "Magazines for the Visually Handicapped in Canada." *Serials Librarian* 2 (1977): 151-53.

Canadian and other American magazines are available in Braille and cassettes through the private, nonprofit Canadian National Institute for the Blind, but there is still great need for international standards and coordination.

492. Hendrick, Clyde, and Murfin, Marjorie E. "Project Library Ripoff: A Study of Periodical Mutilation in a University Library." *College and Research Libraries* 35 (1974): 402-11.

Students answered questionnaires and journal mutilators were interviewed in this study to determine characteristics of mutilators and effective means of prevention. A publicity campaign and obvious penalty warning signs were felt to be effective.

493. Holley, Edward G. "Implementing the New Copyright Law." *Title Varies* 4 (1977): 7+.

The author advises librarians to follow the "rule of reason" in testing the 1976 copyright law.

494. Holley, Edward G. "A Librarian Looks at the New Copyright Law." *American Libraries* 8 (1977): 247-51.

History of copyright policies, a look at controversial sections of the new law, and examples pointing out vagueness and the need for compromise.

495. Hodowanec, George V. "Analysis of Variables which Help to Predict Book and Periodical Use." *Library Acquisitions: Practice and Theory* 4 (1980): 75-85.

The author uses multiple regression analysis in an attempt to identify variables which explain circulation use of library materials.

496. Kuhn, Joanne, and Slade, Alexander. "Standardizing Spine Information on Bound Serial Volumes." *Serials Librarian* 5 (Summer 1981): 59-65.

Librarians at the University of Waterloo developed standards for displaying numeric data on bound volumes in accordance with the title page and with cataloging rules. The standards are included as an appendix.

497. Kuhn, Warren B. "Service." In: *Serial Publications in Large Libraries.* (Urbana: University of Illinois, Graduate School of Library Science, 1970), pp. 175-90.

Kuhn urges user oriented means of housing and publicizing periodicals: current awareness service, subject alcoves, restriction of circulation and periodical reference stations.

498. Line, Maurice B., and Wood, D. N. "The Effect of a Large-Scale Photocopying Service on Journal Sales." *Journal of Documentation* 31 (1975): 234-45.

The authors find strong evidence from a study at the British Library Lending Division that large scale photocopying is not related to journal publishers' economic difficulties.

499. Martin, Murray S. "Promoting Microforms to Students and Faculty." *Microform Review* 8 (1979): 87-91.

Martin rejects the use of gimmicks to lure patrons into using microforms; instead he advocates promotion of this material as an alternative, not substitute, format, which has advantages and disadvantages.

500. Melin, Nancy Jean. "The Public Service Functions of Serials." *Serials Review* 6, no. 1 (1980): 39-44.

Melin discusses housing, circulation and reference as they pertain to serial publications.

501. Meyers, Hugh, Nathan, Peter E., and Kopel, Steven A. "Effects of a Token Reinforcement System on Journal Reshelving." *Serials Librarian* 4 (1979): 69-76; reprinted from: *Journal of Applied Behavior Analysis* 10 (1977): 213-18.

The program succeeded in changing the behavior of patrons at Rutgers University Library, easing a time consuming aspect of the circulation process.

502. Morehead, Joe. "Into the Hopper." Regular column in *Serials Librarian* 1:2-   1976/77-   .

Each of these columns about government document serials has a topic, such as the *Congressional Record*, treaty serials, presidential papers, etc., which is discussed at some length and with some irreverance.

503. Morehead, Joe. "A Status Report on the *Monthly Catalog* and *Serials Supplement*." *Serials Librarian* 4 (1979): 131-41.

Since July 1976 *Monthly Catalog* titles have been entered in the OCLC database, providing additional access points and *AACR* cataloging. Morehead discusses what one hopes are only temporary shortcomings in this reference source.

504. Murfin, Marjorie E. "The Myth of Accessibility: Frustration & Failure in Retrieving Periodicals." *Journal of Academic Librarianship* 6 (1980): 16-19.

A study at Ohio State University found that undergraduates located only fifty-five percent of *Readers' Guide* citations. Two-thirds of those not found were because of library operations failure, one-third because of user error.

505. Murfin, Marjorie E., and Hendrick, Clyde. "Ripoffs Tell Their Story: Interviews with Mutilators in a University Library." *Journal of Academic Librarianship* 1 (May 1975): 8-12.

Murfin and Hendrick reproduce and discuss three interviews with periodical mutilators at Kent State University Library.

506. Obler, Eli M. "Watch the Shells, Watch the Pea: Paying for Copyright Rights to Articles." *Serials Librarian* 4 (1979): 65-67.

The author believes that libraries may unknowingly pay fees to the Copyright Clearance Center for articles which are for purposes considered "fair use" under the United States Copyright Law.

507. O'Brien, Nancy Patricia. "Computerized Management of Microforms." In: *The Serials Collection*. (Ann Arbor, Mich.: Pierian Press, 1982), pp. 103-13.

Computer controlled retrieval systems are being used now in business and industry. O'Brien advocates their use to provide bibliographic control of and access to microform sets in libraries.

508. Pan, Elizabeth. "Journal Citation as a Predictor of Journal Usage in Libraries." *Collection Management* 2 (1978): 29-38.
Gives results of a study at Rutgers University Library which shows that citation analysis is a viable indicator of use.

509. Pascal, Naomi B. "Publisher to Librarian: Another Look at the New Copyright Law." *Serials Librarian* 3 (1978): 129-46.
The author, Editor in Chief, University of Washington Press, discusses some of the reasons for confusion over the new copyright law and some of the possible consequences, in terms of the operation of a nonprofit scholarly publisher.

510. Phillips, Linda L., and Raup, E. Ann. "Comparing Methods for Teaching Use of Periodical Indexes." *Journal of Academic Librarianship* 4 (1979): 420-23.
University of Tennessee reference librarians compared lecture and programmed methods of instructing students in the use of periodical indexes. They concluded that either is acceptable.

511. Sabowitz, Norman. "Computer Assistance in Arranging Serials." *Canadian Library Journal* 36 (1979): 211-13.
When two serial collections had to be merged without using temporary space, Sabowitz devised a computer program which produced the shelf location and label of each title (including space for growth) so that the collection could be moved randomly and efficiently.

512. Sleep, Esther L. "Periodical Vandalism: A Chronic Condition?" *Canadian Library Journal* 39 (1982): 39-42.
The installation of a tape security system appears to have neither eliminated nor greatly increased journal loss, and mutilation appears to have increased.

513. Steuben, John. "Interlibrary Loan of Photocopies of Articles Under the New Copyright Law." *Special Libraries* 70 (1979): 227-32.
A study applying CONTU guidelines to interlibrary loan records for periodicals in a large scientific library found little excess of the five-copy limit.

514 Stobaugh, Robert E., Weisgerber, David W., and Wigington, Ronald L. "Indexes and Abstracts—What Lies Ahead." In: *Serials Management in an Automated Age*. (Westport, Conn.: Meckler Publishing, 1982), pp. 53-72.
After a brief history of abstracting, a discussion of *Chemical Abstracts*: its current function, recent changes and possibilities for the future for *CA* and other abstracting services.

515. Swenck, Cynthia, and Robinson, Wendy. "A Comparison of the Guides to Abstracting and Indexing Services Provided by Katz, Chicorel, and Ulrich." *RQ* 17 (1978): 317-19.

An investigation of the accuracy of index and abstract journal information provided by these three standard reference tools showed that these publications are not reliable for this purpose.

516. Turner-Bishop, Aidan. "Promotion." In: *Periodicals Administration in Libraries*. (London: Clive Bingley; Hamden, Conn.: Linnet Books, 1978), pp. 136-49.

Suggests several ways to encourage the use of periodicals, among them display, indexes, book catalogs, current awareness services and publicity.

517. Velleman, Ruth A. "Library Service to the Disabled: An Annotated Bibliography of Journals and Newsletters." *Serials Librarian* 5 (Winter 1980): 49-60.

The titles listed are written for disabled persons and useful in assisting librarians to provide service to patrons who are disabled.

518. Veneziano, Velma. "Serials and the Online Catalog." In: *Serials Automation for Acquisition and Inventory Control*. (Chicago: American Library Association, 1981), pp. 100-19.

NOTIS, Northwestern Online Total Integrated System, has added a patron inquiry capability known as LUIS, Library User Information Service. This article discusses patron use of the NOTIS database and the planned enhancements designed to enable Northwestern to close its card catalog.

519. Vierra, Bobbie, and Trice, Tom. "Local Newspaper Indexing: A Public Library Reports its Experience." *Serials Librarian* 5 (Fall 1980): 87-92.

Guidelines and procedures discussed are useful to libraries considering a project of this type.

520. Waters, Richard L. "Telefacsimile: An Effective Document Transfer Tool?" *Serials Librarian* 4 (1979): 215-18.

In the belief that telefacsimile will become the predominant means of transfer of journal articles outside the library, the Dallas Public Library has initiated a second feasibility test.

521. Williams, Gordon, et al. *Library Cost Models: Owning Versus Borrowing Serial Publications*. Washington, D.C.: National Science Foundation, 1968.

For low-demand serials, the costs of borrowing can be less than the costs of owning, but this method of periodical access can succeed only with an improved system of borrowing or obtaining copies.

522. Woods, Bill M. "Bibliographic Control of Serial Publications." In: *Serial Publications in Large Libraries.* (Urbana: University of Illinois, Graduate School of Library Science, 1970), pp. 161-74.

From a science librarian's perspective, Woods surveys abstracting and indexing services and trends in the late 1960s.

523. Woodworth, D. P. "Bibliographical Control." In: *Periodicals Administration in Libraries.* (London, Clive Bingley; Hamden, Conn.: Linnet Books, 1978), pp. 25-39.

Woodworth surveys directories, union lists, vendor publications and automated services, from the British point of view.

524. Wyndham, Diana. "An Evaluation of References to Indexes and Abstracts in *Ulrich's* 17th Edition." *RQ* 20 (1980): 155-59.

A study of thirty-one journals reveals that *"Ulrich's* correctly listed only twenty-eight percent of the indexes/abstracts that were found to cover these journals."

525. Zesky, Russell H. "Newspapers on Microfilm: History as it Was Happening (and Indexes to Help You Find Your Way)." *Serials Librarian* 4 (1980): 393-99.

Describes the development of Bell & Howell's newspaper indexing project.

VIII. Networking and Library Cooperation

526. Allen, Arly H. "The National Periodicals Center: Will it be Ready by 1984?" *Journal of General Education* 31 (1980): 236-43.

A publisher's view of the *Report* of the National Enquiry into Scholarly Publishing and the *National Periodicals Center: Technical Development Plan.* Allen opposes the NPC on the grounds that the government will be in position to control the distribution of serials.

527. American National Standards Institute. *American National Standard Criteria for Price Indexes for Library Materials.* New York: American National Standards Institute, 1974. (ANSI Z39.20-1974)

Now being revised, this standard includes periodicals and serial services among the types of library materials for which price index criteria are given. The standard defines terms and presents a detailed method of compilation for each index.

528. Anable, Richard. "The Ad Hoc Discussion Group on Serials Data Bases: Its History, Current Position, and Future." *Journal of Library Automation* 6 (1973): 207-14.

Describes the group from which CONSER evolved and spells out objectives and plans for creating a cooperative serials database.

529. Anable, Richard. "CONSER: An Update." *Journal of Library Automation* 8 (1975): 26-30.

Answers to frequently asked questions about the CONSER project.

530. Anable, Richard. "CONSER: Bibliographic Considerations." *Library Resources and Technical Services* 19 (1975): 341-48.

Justifies compromises made for CONSER, by giving a concise history of serials cataloging and an overview of current questions and possible future directions of the project. This article is particularly well organized and well written.

531. Anderson, Sandy E., and Melby, Carol A. "Comparative Analysis of the Quality of OCLC Serials Cataloging Records, as a Function of Contributing CONSER Participant and Field as Utilized by Serials Catalogers at the University of Illinois." *Serials Librarian* 3 (1979): 363-71.

This study demonstrates statistically the extent to which serials cataloging copy generated from the OCLC database can be accepted without modification by the serials cataloging staff of the University of Illinois Library, and discusses the implications of the findings.

532. Avram, Henriette D., and Maruyama, Lenore S., eds. *Toward a National Library and Information Service Network: The Library Bibliographic Component.* Preliminary edition. Washington, D.C.: Library of Congress Network Advisory Group, 1977.

Gives background on existing networking activities and plans for the future network and its needs.

533. Bales, Kathleen. "The ANSI Standard for Summary Holdings Statements for Serials: The RLIN Implementation." *Serials Review* 6 (October/December 1980): 71-73.

Description of the standard and of RLIN's use of it, with a suggestion of improvements which could make the format more nearly acceptable for librarians.

534. Bartley, Linda K. "The International Standard Serial Number (ISSN) and its use by the United States Postal Service." *Unesco Journal of Information Science, Librarianship and Archives Administration* 2 (1980): 245-51.

The rationale and procedures used to implement the USPS requirement that ISSN be displayed on serials mailed at reduced rates. The project resulted in benefits to USPS, publishers and libraries.

535. Bernhardt, Børge. "A Union Catalogue of Serials in Scandinavian Libraries: The NOSP Project." *UNESCO Bulletin for Libraries* 30 (1976): 11-17.

Discusses plans for a union catalog of serials in Scandinavian libraries, including questions concerning conformity to international standards.

536. "Bibliographic Utilities and Networks," by Michael Moen, Virginia Shipler, Tina Kass, Jack Cain and Ray DeBuse. In: *Union Lists: Issues and Answers.* (Ann Arbor, Mich.: Pierian Press, 1982), pp. 37-41.
Representatives of Blackwell North America, OCLC, RLG/RLIN, UTLAS and WLN discuss their existing and planned serials control functions, emphasizing union listing.

537. Bosseau, Don L. "Case Study of the Computer Assisted Serials System at the University of California, San Diego." In: *Proceedings of the LARC Institute on Automated Serials Systems.* (Tempe, Ariz.: The LARC Association, 1973), pp. 77-118.
The evolution of one of the oldest automated serials systems.

538. Bradley, Isabel. "The International Serials Data System in 1978." *Canadian Library Journal* 35 (1978): 167-71.
The Chief of ISDS/Canada gives a concise and readable history of the system and its function, and discusses the purpose and use of the ISSN. Has a good description of the problems of using Bowker-assigned ISSN.

539. Bradley, Isabel. "International Standard Serial Numbers and the International Serials Data System." *Serials Librarian* 3 (1979): 243-53.
Bradley describes the background of ISDS and the place of ISDS/Canada in the emerging worldwide network, concentrating on registration procedures, uses and sources of ISSN, and key title problems.

540. Brewer, Karen, Pitkin, Gary, and Edgar, Neal. "A Method for Cooperative Serials Selection and Cancellation Through Consortium Activities." *Journal of Academic Librarianship* 4 (1978): 204-08.
Seven Ohio academic libraries joined in a successful resource sharing effort which resulted in savings from cancelled serial titles.

541. Brodie, Nancy. "National Developments in Serials." *Serials Librarian* 6 (Fall 1981): 49-57.
A mid-1980 report from a staff member at the National Library of Canada focuses on standards, sources of data, the national serials database, and hard copy products of the database.

542. Buckeye, Nancy Melin. "The OCLC Serials Subsystem: Implementation/Implications at Central Michigan University." *Serials Librarian* 3 (1978): 31-42.
Describes and evaluates the planning and procedures at each phase of implementation of the system. There is a statement of benefits to the library and a discussion of problems.

543. Cannan, Judith Proctor. "The Impact of International Standard-

ization on the Rules of Entry for Serials." *Library Resources and Technical Services* 19 (1975): 164-69.
Discusses provisions of *Guidelines for ISDS* and *ISBD(S)* which demand that changes be made in *AACR*.

544. Carroll, C. Edward. "Bibliographic Control of Microforms: Where Do We Go from Here?" *Microform Review* 7 (1978): 321-26.
Much research material is purchased by libraries in microformat, but it is not accessible to the user because it is not cataloged or adequately indexed. This is a plea for a cooperative solution to this expensive problem.

545. Carter, Ruth C. "Cataloging Decisions on Pre-*AACR* 2 Serial Records from a Union List Viewpoint." In: *Union Lists: Issues and Answers*. (Ann Arbor, Mich.: Pierian Press, 1982), pp. 77-80.
Participants in the Pennsylvania Union List of Serials were given a set of policy statements in advance to follow when *AACR* 2 was implemented. The project's adherence to national standards for both cataloging and holdings is a basic commitment.

546. Carter, Ruth C., and Bruntjen, Scott. "The Pennsylvania Union List of Serials: Initial Development." *Serials Librarian* 5 (Spring 1981): 57-64.
The statewide union list, developed according to national standards and online through OCLC, will be available on COM and will fill a need for equitable interlibrary loan service to the state.

547. Carter, Ruth C. "Steps Toward an On-Line Union List." *Journal of Library Automation* 11 (1978): 32-40.
Describes the Pittsburgh Regional Library Center Union List of Periodicals, its objectives and its relationship with OCLC.

548. Claridge, Aileen. "A National Serials Collection?" *New Zealand Libraries* 41 (1978): 118-20.
An appeal for movement towards a core collection of serials for New Zealand, to reduce the long delay in receiving loans or photocopies from overseas.

549. Clarke, Jack A. "The ACM Periodical Bank: A Retrospective View." *College and Research Libraries* 41 (1980): 503-09.
An evaluation of the ten-year cooperative program involving small midwestern academic libraries.

550. *A Comparative Evaluation of Alternative Systems for the Provision of Effective Access to Periodical Literature*; a report to the National Commission on Libraries and Information Science, by Arthur D. Little, Inc. Washington, D.C.: NCLIS, 1979.

The report hypothesizes three systems for periodicals access: System A, a non-intervention approach; System B, a central, subsidized National Periodicals Center; System C, a subsidized switching utility backed by a dedicated collection. The advantages and disadvantages of each system are presented, with several unresolved issues to be studied before a decision is made.

551. Connan, Shere. "Title II-C Serials Project." In: *Union Lists: Issues and Answers.* (Ann Arbor: Pierian Press, 1982), pp. 11-16.
Discusses the Stanford/UCLA/UC Berkeley program to create a merged database of serials, based on archive tapes. Connan stresses the need for open communication in the areas of procedures, sources, standards and software development.

552. Corey, James F. "OCLC and Serials Processing: A State of Transition at the University of Illinois." *Serials Librarian* 3 (1978): 57-67.
A thorough discussion of the use of OCLC for serials processing. Especially welcome is the reasoning which led to delaying a decision about using the serials check-in for this large library system.

553. Council on Library Resources. *A National Periodicals Center: Technical Development Plan.* Washington, D.C.: Council on Library Resources, Inc., 1978.
This plan was developed for the Library of Congress and proposes a means of improving access to periodical literature for libraries and their patrons. It includes a document delivery system, a way of working with publishers and the creation of a national library system. This study was a basis for discussions in Congress. Its bibliography lists reports of earlier efforts to increase periodical access.

554. Daniels, Mary Kay. "Automated Serials Control: National and International Considerations." *Journal of Library Automation* 8 (1975): 127-46.
A summary of the 1974 ISAD Institute, this article covers LC/MARC/CONSER, cataloging considerations, and international standards.

555. Davis, Carol C. "OCLC's Role in the CONSER Project." *Serials Review* 6 (October/December 1980): 75-77.
Describes correction of errors, elimination of duplicate records, interpretation of guidelines and other administrative services provided CONSER by OCLC.

556. Dodson, James T., and Miller, Laurence. "Soaring Journal Costs: A Cooperative Solution." *Library Journal* 105 (1980): 1793-95.
A Cooperative Journal Program enabled libraries of northern Texas institutions to reduce expensive duplication and add new subscriptions. The article describes the planning process.

557. Dunlap, Leslie W. "National and Regional Lending Libraries." In:

Management Problems in Serials Work. (Westport, Conn.: Greenwood Press, 1974), pp. 19-35.

In a paper written before the proposal for a National Periodicals Center, Dunlap discusses various ways for libraries to provide periodical articles required for their patrons' research.

558.   Durance, Cynthia J. "International Serials Cataloguing." *Serials Librarian* 3 (1979): 299-309.

Emphasizes the necessity for employing international standards for serials cataloging, so as to share efficiently the work of recording bibliographic data, particularly in the current period of great changes.

559.   Ellsworth, Dianne. "California Library Authority for Systems and Services." In: *Union Lists: Issues and Answers.* (Ann Arbor, Mich.: Pierian Press, 1982), pp. 17-22.

CLASS encountered numerous problems when it took over from the State Library production of the *California Union List of Periodicals*, serving the state's public libraries. Hard work and technology have resolved many of those problems, but there is still much to do to increase coordination and efficiency.

560.   Evans, Glyn T. "State of the Art Review." In: *Proceedings of the LARC Institute on Automated Serials Systems.* (Tempe, Ariz.: LARC Association, 1973), pp. 7-14.

An optimistic look at the future of serial automation.

561.   Falvey, Neil. "The PHILSOM Network: A Programmer/Analyst's View." In: *Procedings of the LARC Institute on Automated Serials Systems.* (Tempe, Ariz.: LARC Association, 1973), pp. 59-63.

A detailed trip from input to output.

562.   Fasana, Paul. "Serials Data Control: Current Problems and Prospects." *Journal of Library Automation* 9 (1976): 19-33.

Updates developments and identifies problems in standards, standards-setting projects, CONSER, and code revision activities.

563.   Fayollat, James E. "Online Serials Check-In at UCLA: A Design for the 1980's." In: *Serials Automation for Acquisition and Inventory Control.* (Chicago: American Library Association, 1981), pp. 20-39.

Using the UCLA Biomedical Library online serials system as a case study, Fayollat maintains that current technology is sufficiently developed to support automated check-in.

564.   Feagler, Virginia. "The PHILSOM Network: The Coordinator's Viewpoint." In: *Proceedings of the LARC Institute on Automated Serials Systems.* (Tempe, Ariz.: LARC Association, 1973), pp. 51-57.

An overview of the network and the coordinator's role as communicator.

565. Featheringham, T. R. "Paperless Publishing and Potential Institutional Change." *Scholarly Publishing* 13 (October 1981): 19-30.
Paperless publishing will come where it is efficient, and the development will have strong impact on libraries and librarians, as well as on the publishing industry. The author discusses the possibilities and the advantages.

566. Felter, Jacqueline. "Management Problems of the Network Manager." In: *Proceedings of the LARC Institute on Automated Serials Systems.* (Tempe, Ariz.: LARC Association, 1973), pp. 25-29.
Managing well money and people can ease the problems of the network manager.

567. Gallimore, Charles Reese, and Martin, Rebecca R. "Holder of Record: A Cooperative Health Sciences Journal System in a Hospital Library Network." *Bulletin of the Medical Library Association* 68 (1980): 271-73.
Cooperative acquisition and retention among VA hospital libraries depends upon one of the libraries accepting responsibility for maintaining every title in the union lists of serials.

568. Gates, Barbara A. *Serials Cataloging for the Ohio College Library Center System: A Manual.* Rev. ed. Richardson, Tex.: AMIGOS Bibliographic Council, 1976.
Now replaced by the CONSER manual, this work, developed as a training tool, contains in one document all the necessary information for cataloging serials in the OCLC system.

569. Gorman, Michael. "The Current State of Standardization in the Cataloging of Serials." *Library Resources and Technical Services* 19 (1975): 301-13.
Surveys current international standards in serials cataloging and raises questions which must be dealt with in the current search for standardization. Throughout the paper Gorman expresses the need for a recognition of the division between complete and not-complete publications.

570. Gorman, Michael. "The Future of Serials Control and its Administrative Implications for Libraries." In: *Serials Automation for Acquisition and Inventory Control.* (Chicago: American Library Association, 1981), pp. 120-33.
"Serials are an expensive and inefficient form of communication," and librarians must find a new and better way to communicate information.

571. Gray, Carolyn M., and Wetherbee, Louella V. "AMIGOS: The Growth of a Network." *Serials Librarian* 5 (Fall 1980): 59-63.
A brief history of the regional network and a look at its short term goals.

572. Groot, Elizabeth H. "Unique Identifiers for Serials: An Annotated, Comprehensive Bibliography." *Serials Librarian* 1 (1976): 51-75.
Groot has compiled an annotated bibliography documenting the development of four code systems for the unique identification of serials, and the struggle for supremacy between CODEN and ISSN.

573. Groot, Elizabeth H. "Unique Identifiers for Serials: 1977 Update." *Serials Librarian* 2 (1978): 247-55.
CODEN and ISSN are discussed from the user's point of view. The author no longer sees these systems as competing, but co-existing for the foreseeable future, with each making a contribution in the context of automation.

574. *Guidelines for the Coded Bibliographic Strip for Serial Publications.* (Paris: United Nations Educational, Scientific and Cultural Organization; International Council of Scientific Unions Abstracting Board; International Serials Data System, 1975).
A method for unique and concise identification of serials and serial articles. Related to ANSC Z39 *American National Standard for Periodicals: Format and Arrangement.*

575. Guillaume, Jeanne. "Computer Conferencing and the Development of an Electronic Journal." *Canadian Journal of Information Science* 5 (1980): 21-29.
Evaluates and analyzes the activities of the Electronic Information Exchange System and suggests steps to make such systems successful. EIES' failure to launch an electronic journal resulted from inadequate attention to the area of online group processes.

576. Gwinn, Nancy E. "A National Periodicals Center: Articulating the Dream." *Library Journal* 103 (1978): 2166-69.
Gwinn gives a practical description of the proposed NPC and illustrates her article with applications of the system.

577. Hartman, Anne-Marie. "The Implications of *AACR 2* on Serials Management and Union Listing." In: *Union Lists: Issues and Answers.* (Ann Arbor, Mich.: Pierian Press, 1982), pp. 71-75.
Questions on choice and form of entry are posed and discussed. Some have been resolved by individual union list personnel, but in general there are no uniformly satisfactory answers.

578. Hickey, Thomas. "The Journal of the Year 2000." *Wilson Library Bulletin* 56 (1981): 256-60; also in: *Serials Management in an Automated Age.* (Westport, Conn.: Meckler Publishing, 1982), pp. 3-10.
The paper journal will be supplanted by articles available primarily by means of electronic networks. Authors, readers and libraries will be pleased with the change, but publishers will be less so. The opening address at the First Annual Serials Conference.

579. Houghton, B., and Prosser, C. "Rationalization of Serial Holdings in Special Libraries." *ASLIB Proceedings* 26 (1974): 226-35.
The authors describe efforts to develop a procedural model based on use and cost, to enable special librarians to make optimum use of the British Lending Library.

580. Houghton, B., and Prosser, C. "A Survey of the Opinions of British Library Lending Division Users in Special Libraries on the Effects of Non-Immediate Access to Journals." *ASLIB Proceedings* 26 (1974): 354-66.
The results of a questionnaire survey of users of seven company libraries indicate that delay in receiving journal material is of less significance to users than librarians had supposed.

581. Humphreys, Betsy L. "Serials Control by Agents." In: *Serials Automation for Acquisition and Inventory Control.* (Chicago: American Library Association, 1981), pp. 57-76.
The National Library of Medicine employs subscription agents as contractors for such serial services as check-in, fiscal control, collection development control and union listing.

582. Ink, Gary. "Order from Chaos? Standardizing Serials." In: *Serials Management in an Automated Age.* (Westport, Conn.: Meckler Publishing, 1982), pp. 43-52.
Discusses what standards are, how they are developed and by whom, whether standards succeed, and what is still needed to standardize serials work.

583. *International Cataloguing.* 1- 1972- . Edinburgh: Longman Group Ltd. (ISSN: 0047-0635)
The quarterly bulletin of the IFLA International Office for Universal Bibliographic Control. It covers IFLA activities and national developments in bibliographic control and has articles on important cataloging questions.

584. International Conference on Cataloguing Principles, Paris, 1961. *Statement of Principles Adopted at the International Conference on Cataloguing Principles, Paris, October 1961.* Annotated ed., with commentary and examples by Eva Verona and others. London: IFLA Committee on Cataloguing, 1971.
Guidelines upon which national or international groups can base cataloging codes, the Paris Principles favor successive entry and corporate authorship (to some extent).

585. "ISDS Directors Hold Fifth Meeting." *Library of Congress Information Bulletin* 39 (1980): 46-48.
Reports matters discussed at the September 1979 meeting of directors of ISDS centers, including plans for revision of *ISDS Guidelines* and for a self appraisal.

586. Johnson, Millard. F., Jr. "A Design for a Mini-Computer Based Serials Control Network." *Special Libraries* 67 (1976): 386-90.

PHILSOM III is the topic of this article, which concerns the modification of the system used at Washington University School of Medicine Library, so that it can be expanded to a network of biomedical libraries.

587. Johnson, Millard F. Jr. "The PHILSOM Network: Maintenance and Design." In *Proceedings of the LARC Institute on Automated Serials Systems.* (Tempe, Ariz.: LARC Association, 1973), pp. 65-69.

A review of the concerns accommodated by PHILSOM's Research Associate in Machine Methods.

588. Kamens, Harry H. "OCLC's Serials Control Subsystem: A Case Study." *Serials Librarian* 3 (1978): 43-55.

Kent State University's objective in converting to OCLC online check-in was to provide better public service regarding serials; technical processing benefits are to come later. There is discussion of the way Kent State dealt with problems encountered in its conversion to the system.

589. Kamens, Harry. "Serials Control and OCLC." In: Allison, Anne Marie and Allan, Ann. *OCLC: A National Library Network.* (Short Hills, N.J.: Enslow Publishers, 1979), pp. 139-54.

An objective assessment of the OCLC Serials Control Subsystem's impact on the currently-manual serials department. Kamens notes the decisions that must be made before implementing the check-in.

590. Kilgour, Frederick. *The Impact of AACR 2 on the Economic Viability of Libraries.* Columbus, Ohio: OCLC, Inc., 1979.

In this mimeographed document Kilgour discusses OCLC's need to devise input standards. Also included is a paper by M. Gorman, as consultant for OCLC, entitled: "The Implications of *AACR* 2 and the End of Superimposition for OCLC; A Preliminary Report and Recommendations."

591. Kilton, Tom D. "OCLC and the Pre-Order Verification of New Serials." *Serials Librarian* 4 (1979): 61-64.

Kilton suggests OCLC modifications regarding subscription information which would increase the value of the database as a preorder searching tool.

592. Livingston, Lawrence G. "CONSER Inter-Relationships." *Drexel Library Quarterly* 11 (July 1975): 60-63; reprinted from *Library of Congress Information Bulletin* 34 (1975): A87-89.

Presents these interrelationships in diagram form with a keyed narrative explanation.

593. Livingston, Lawrence G. "The CONSER Project: Current Status and Plans." *Library of Congress Information Bulletin* 34 (1975): A38-42.

An update on activity concerning CONSER; points out the need for compromises to produce what is possible, based on standards for what is desired.

594. Lucht, Irma, and Stewart, Blair. "The ACM Periodical Bank and the British National Lending Library: Contrasts and Similarities." In: *Management Problems in Serials Work.* (Westport, Conn.: Greenwood Press, 1974), pp. 3-18.
The Periodical Bank of the Chicago-based Associated Colleges of the Midwest attempts to meet user needs, as does the British Lending Library, but different needs require different holdings and different procedures.

595. McKenzie, Mary A. "The New England Serials Service: Useful Component of a National System?" *Serials Librarian* 1 (1977): 251-58.
Sponsored by the New England Library Board, NESS acts as a nonprofit interlibrary loan agent for New England libraries of all types. This article covers the creation and development of NESS and considers the service within the context of the National Periodicals System.

596. Martin, Susan K. "The Quest for a National Bibliographic Network." *Library Journal* 103 (1978): 19-22.
Reviews the work of the Network Advisory Group and expresses reservations about the Group's work to date and serious omissions from its considerations.

597. Mayden, Priscilla. "The Problems of Entering a Computerized Serials Network; or, The Validity of Murphy's Law." In: *Proceedings of the LARC Institute on Automated Serials Systems.* (Tempe, Ariz.: LARC Association, 1973), pp. 43-49.
A comedy of errors, as the University of Utah Medical Library joins PHILSOM, cannot stop a successful conversion.

598. Maxin, Jacqueline A., and Chilson, Frances. "Cooperative Purchasing by a New York 3R's Council." *Serials Librarian* 2 (1978): 299-305.
Interlibrary loan requests were analyzed to select serials and bibliographic tools purchased with joint funds.

599. Miller, Susan L. "Inventory and Holdings Features of Serials Control." In: *Serials Automation for Acquisition and Inventory Control.* (Chicago: American Library Association, 1981), pp. 40-56.
Based on the Ohio State University Library Control System (LCS), Miller discusses problems involved in relating holdings statements, routing, binding and circulation of serials.

600. Morrison, Percy D., and May, Douglas R. "Cooperative Use of Serials in Australian Libraries." *Serials Librarian* 1 (1977): 231-41.
A geographically isolated but highly developed country must turn to means of

cooperation and centralization so as to make best overall use of the funds available for the purchase of serials. Bibliographic (union lists, cooperative collecting) and technical processing efforts are growing in Australia.

601. National Commission on Libraries and Information Science. Task Force on a National Periodicals System. *Effective Access to the Periodical Literature: A National Program.* Washington, D.C.: National Commission on Libraries and Information Science, 1977.

This document recommends that the Library of Congress be responsible for developing, managing and operating a national periodicals center. As a result of this, LC asked the Council on Library Resources to prepare a technical development plan, published in 1978 as *A National Periodicals Center.*

602. National Commission on Libraries and Information Science. Task Force on American National Standards Committee Z39, Activities and Future Directions. *American National Standards Committee Z39: Recommended Future Directions.* Washington, D.C.: NCLIS, 1978.

At a time of change for Z39, the task force reviewed its past work and governance and presented recommendations for its future which take into consideration developing technology, sponsorship and funding.

603. Neubauer, K. W. "The National Serial Data System in the Federal Republic of Germany." *Serials Review* 7 (January/March 1981): 73-80.

Discusses the national system's development, relations with regional systems, and future plans.

604. "Now, Add CONSER to Your Conversation." *American Libraries* 8 (1977): 21-27.

A group of brief articles by librarians involved in the project: I. A Brief Q & A Primer on CONSER; II. The Next Generation of CONSER, by Henriette D. Avram and Richard Anable; III. Mixed Feelings: Taking Part in CONSER, by Lois N. Upham; IV. Great Faith and a Few Big Questions: Notes from a Librarian Using the CONSER Data Base, by Minna C. Saxe.

605. Palmour, Vernon E., Bellassai, Marcia C., and Gray, Lucy M. *Access to Periodical Resources: A National Plan.* Rockville, Md.: Westat, Inc., 1974.

Published for the Association of Research Libraries, this study examines ways of increasing access to periodical literature through improvement of the interlibrary loan system and, possibly, creation of a national periodicals center.

606. Preston, Jenny. "Missouri Union List of Serial Publications." *Serials Librarian* 5 (Fall 1980): 65-77.

History, present status and future plans, including examples of entries and workforms.

607. Price, Joseph W. "International Cooperation in Serials: Progress and Prospects." *Drexel Library Quarterly* 11 (July 1975): 27-39.
Reviews current efforts to attain international standardization in the identification, description and control of serials.

608. *Proceedings of the LARC Institute on Automated Serials Systems*, edited by H. William Axford. Tempe, Ariz.: The LARC Association, 1973.
This collection of ten papers emphasizes serial automation, especially in medical libraries. Each paper is listed separately in this Bibliography.

609. Quintal, Cecile C. "SERLINE: On-Line Serials Bibliographic and Locator Retrieval System." In: *Proceedings of the LARC Institute on Automated Serials Systems*. (Tempe, Ariz.: LARC Association, 1973), pp. 31-42.
A technical description of this medical system.

610. Reid, J. E. Trent. "CANUC Serials Reporting and the Canadian MiniMARC Serials Holdings Format." *Serials Librarian* 3 (1979): 231-42.
After stating the need for standardization and definitions, Reid describes and illustrates the official Canadian approach to holdings statements.

611. Reimer, Diana. "The California State Universities and Colleges Union List of Periodicals." In: *Union Lists: Issues and Answers*. (Ann Arbor, Mich.: Pierian Press, 1982), pp. 23-27.
Procedures, governance and products of the combined automated finding tool for the state universities and colleges in California.

612. *Research Libraries in OCLC: A Quarterly*. 1-   1981-   . Dublin, Ohio: OCLC, Inc. (ISSN: 0273-2351)
Newsletter sponsored by OCLC's Research Library Advisory Group.

613. Rice, Patricia. "CONSER From the Inside." *Title Varies* 3 (1976): 13 +.
The rewards and frustrations of participating in this major serials cooperative project.

614. Riddick, John. "Serials Automation: Four Years Later." In: *The Serials Collection*. (Ann Arbor, Mich.: Pierian Press, 1982), pp. 79-82.
Central Michigan University Library staff and patrons are still pleased with the Serials Control Subsystem, but future acceptability depends upon certain enhancements: Sunday service, faster response time, a public service display screen and installation of claiming and binding components.

615. Robinson, Barbara M. "Cooperation and Competition among Li-

brary Networks." *Journal of the American Society for Information Science* 31 (1980): 413-24.
Although not specifically about serials, this article discusses OCLC, RLG/RLIN, UTLAS and WLN in relation to each other.

616. Robinson, Barbara M. "The Role of Special Libraries in the Emerging Library Network." *Special Libraries* 72 (1981): 8-17.
Discusses benefits to special libraries available through the national and regional networks and cooperatives.

617. Roughton, Michael. "OCLC Serials Records: Errors, Omissions, and Dependability." *Journal of Academic Librarianship* 5 (1980): 316-21.
The Serials Cataloging Section at Iowa State University Library studied a sample of 612 OCLC serial records in 1978. The results raise questions about the effectiveness of the online system as to currency and accuracy, because of policy decisions.

618. Sage, Charles R. "Utilization of the MARC II Format for Serials in an Inter-University Environment." In: Clinic on Library Applications of Data Processing. *Proceedings, 1973: Networking and Other Forms of Cooperation.* (Champaign: Graduate School of Library Science, University of Illinois, 1973), pp. 24-31.
Describes, illustrates and evaluates an experimental union list of three Iowa state university libraries' serials.

619. Salmon, Stephen R. *Library Automation Systems.* New York: Marcel Dekker, 1975. (Books in Library and Information Science. 15)
A thirty-three page chapter on "Serials Systems" covers early efforts to automate serials, the systems then in use, and the origins of CONSER.

620. Sauer, Mary. "National Serials Data Program." *Drexel Library Quarterly* 11 (July 1975): 40-48.
Surveys the history and functions of NSDP and its relationships to international and domestic organizations and projects. There is an explanation of the ISSN, including its uses and method of construction, and of the Bowker project.

621. Saxe, Minna C. "Going Online with Serials." In: *Serials Management in an Automated Age.* (Westport, Conn.: Meckler Publishing, 1982), pp. 31-42.
A state of the art report discussing several available automated serial systems and factors to consider in deciding whether to purchase one of these systems.

622. Schmidt, C. James. "Resource Sharing of Serials—Past, Present and Prospective: Old Wine in New Bottles or Substantial Change?"

In: *Serials Management in an Automated Age*. (Westport, Conn.: Meckler Publishing, 1982), pp. 73-80.

A realistic look at efforts to facilitate sharing of serial resources, especially the proposed National Periodicals Center, and at the requirements for success in the future.

623. Schmidt, Dean. "The PHILSOM Network: A User Library Viewpoint." In: *Proceedings of the LARC Institute on Automated Serials Systems*. (Tempe, Ariz.: LARC Association, 1973), pp. 71-75.

An early PHILSOM user's experience with and adaptation of the system.

624. Scott, Jack William, and Allison, Anne Marie. "United States Documents in an On-Line Union Catalog." *Serials Librarian* 1 (1977): 365-71.

In Fall 1974, in response to budget cuts, Kent State University Library began to add current U.S. document acquisitions to the OCLC database. A year later staff began to enter document serials, as preparation for entering the library's general serials collection. Manual files were closed, but not discarded.

625. *Serials Automation for Acquisition and Inventory Control*, edited by William Gray Potter and Arlene Farber Sirkin. Chicago: American Library Association, 1981.

Papers from the LITA Institute held in 1980. Each article is listed separately in this Bibliography.

626. "A Serials Discussion Group: Form of Entry." In: *Union Lists: Issues and Answers*. (Ann Arbor, Mich.: Pierian Press, 1982), pp. 53-60.

Union list editors discuss the problems of matching records of serials cataloged by different rules and for different audiences.

627. Schultz Baldwin, N. L. "BCUC and Serials...[ ]." *Serials Librarian* 6 (Fall 1981): 41-47.

Brief history and progress report of the British Columbia Union Catalogue's Serials Task Group, and suggestions for the resolution of the problems involved in adding serial holdings and processing.

628. Shaw, D. F. "Serials Control." *Aslib Proceedings* 34 (1982): 81-89.

Describes online serials control system at Oxford's Radcliffe Science Library.

629. Singleton, Alan. "The Electronic Journal and its Relatives." *Scholarly Publishing* 13 (1981): 3-18.

A review and analysis of the evolving electronic journal, focusing on the problems of access and economics. Discussion of "routes to the electronic journal," including mention of several European electronic document delivery projects.

630. Sleep, Esther L. "Whither the ISSN? A Practical Experience." *Canadian Library Journal* 34 (1977): 265-70.

Experiencing problems with conflicting ISSN, Sleep made a study of the numbers in Bowker directories and the 1950-1970 *New Serial Titles* cumulation. Her findings support her statement that one should use caution and rely only on ISDS publications for verification of ISSN.

631. Spalding, C. Sumner. *"ISBD(S)* and Title Main Entry for Serials." *Drexel Library Quarterly* 11 (July 1975): 20-26; reprinted from *Library of Congress Information Bulletin* 33 (1974): A229-32.

After reviewing recent international developments in cataloging, Spalding feels that there is need for entry under corporate body for some serials.

632. Taylor, Desmond. "The NAPCU Microforms Center: Proposal for a Northwest Regional Microforms and Storage Center." *PNLA Quarterly* 41 (Winter 1977): 4-12.

Recommends that an existing regional microforms center and a proposed last-copy center be combined to form a two-state service center.

633. Taylor, Desmond. "The Serials Microform Center: An Idea Whose Time Has Come?" *Serials Librarian* 4 (1979): 199-208.

Taylor presents a strong case for the regional microform resources center on the basis of cost, space and availability. He discusses current disadvantages which must be dealt with.

634. Thomas, Catherine M., and Subramanyam, K. "CONSER: An International Project." *Libri* 31 (1981): 238-42.

Reviews the creation, administration, problems and prospects of CONSER.

635. Tonkery, Dan. "Evolution of Automated Serials Control: Technical, Philosophical, and Political Issues." In: *Serials Automation for Acquisition and Inventory Control.* (Chicago: American Library Association, 1981), pp. 1-19.

The technology exists for serials automation. Library administrators must give this function higher priority, for the benefit of patrons.

636. Trezza, Alphonse F. "Toward a National Periodicals System." *Special Libraries* 68 (1977): 7-12.

A six-months' progress report on the Task Force on a National Periodicals Center of the National Commission on Libraries and Information Science.

637. Tyner, Sue. "UCULS and CONSER." In: *Union Lists: Issues and Answers.* (Ann Arbor, Mich.: Pierian Press, 1982). pp. 7-10.

In the late 1970s the University of California Division of Library Automation served two serial resource sharing roles: CONSER agent for the university system and compiler of the *University of California Union List of Serials*, a finding list for 28 campuses.

638. *Union Lists: Issues and Answers*, edited by Dianne Ellsworth. Ann Arbor, Mich.: Pierian Press, 1982. (Current Issues in Serials Management. 2)

Proceedings of a conference on union listing held in 1979. Emphasizes major California union listing projects and the automated utilities and networks supporting them. Each paper was updated in 1981. Each paper is listed separately in this Bibliography.

639. Upham, Lois N. "CONSER: Cooperative Conversion of Serials Project." *Library of Congress Information Bulletin* 33 (1974): A245-48.

Describes projected procedures to be used in building the CONSER database.

640. Upham, Lois N. "Minnesota Union List of Serials." *Serials Librarian* 3 (1979): 289-97.

Outlines the background, history and utilization of this MARC format serials database and union catalog, chosen to be one of the three start-up files for CONSER.

641. Van Houten, Stephen. "The PHILSOM Automated Serials Control System: An Introduction." *Serials Review* 7 (July/September 1981): 93-99.

Describes PHILSOM III, including illustrations of online and batch records and lists of products and online functions.

642. Vassallo, Paul. "The CONSER Project: An Analysis." *Drexel Library Quarterly* 11 (July 1975): 49-59.

Libraries, particularly the Library of Congress, must make a commitment to CONSER and build upon its serials file to develop the authoritative database which is needed.

643. Vassallo, Paul. "Introducing the National Serials Data Program." In: *Management Problems in Serials Work*. (Westport, Conn.: Greenwood Press, 1974) pp. 36-49.

A history of the program, discussion of its present activities and services, and a look toward the future.

644. Vassallo, Paul. "The National Serials Data Program." In: *Proceedings of the LARC Institute on Automated Serials Systems*. (Tempe, Ariz.: LARC Association, 1973), pp. 15-24.

A pre-CONSER report on the origins and mission of NSDP, and a discussion of its relationship to ISDS.

645. Velazquez, Harriet. "University of Toronto Library Automation Systems." *Online Review* 3 (1979): 253-64.

History and organization of UTLAS, with discussion of current services and plans for future developments.

646. Walbridge, Sharon. "Topical Report." *CONSER* 5 (October 1980): 1-5; reprinted in *Serials Review* 6 (July/September 1980): 109-12.

A discussion of the authentication of serial records by LC/NSDP and NLC/ISDS Canada, of the editing process by CONSER participants, and of the impact on American libraries.

647. Wittig, Glenn R. "CONSER (Co-Operative Conversion of Serials Project): Building an On-Line International Serials Data Base." *Unesco Bulletin for Libraries* 31 (1977): 305-10.

An early discussion and evaluation of CONSER, not entirely favorable. In 1977 the project had not yet had the significant impact on serials librarianship that it now has.

648. Wittorf, Robert. "ANSI Z39.42 and OCLC: OCLC's Implementation of the American National Standard Institute's Serial Holdings Statements at the Summary Level." *Serials Review* 6, (April/June 1980): 87-94.

Describes exactly how OCLC will follow the ANSI standard in its Serial Union Listing Capability.

649. Woods, Elaine. "Serials: The National Scene." In: *Union Lists: Issues and Answers*. (Ann Arbor, Mich.: Pierian Press, 1982), pp. 29-36.

Much effort has gone into standardizing the bibliographic identification of serials. Now there is urgent need for standards for location and holding statements. Woods reviews the work in progress and states her requirements for the ideal location and holdings notations.

Index to Bibliography

Index

315